易鹏 皮钧 / 主编

李玲飞 熊榆 / 副主编

"一带一路"节点国家态度研究：
下一个黄金时代

A Study on the Attitudes of Node Countries under the Belt and Road:
The Next Golden Era

（汉英对照）

中国青年出版社

图书在版编目（CIP）数据

一带一路节点国家态度研究：下一个黄金时代：汉英对照 / 易鹏，皮钧主编 . —北京：中国青年出版社，2017.6

ISBN 978-7-5153-4785-1

I.①一… II.①易…②皮… III.①"一带一路"—国际合作—研究—汉、英 IV.①F125

中国版本图书馆CIP数据核字（2017）第 134739 号

书　　名：一带一路节点国家态度研究：下一个黄金时代（汉英对照）
主　　编：易鹏　皮钧
副 主 编：李玲飞　熊榆
责任编辑：庄庸　陈静
特约编辑：张瑞霞
出版发行：中国青年出版社
社　　址：北京东四十二条 21 号
邮　　编：100708
网　　址：www.cyp.com.cn
门 市 部：(010) 57350370
印　　刷：北京盛通印刷股份有限公司
经　　销：新华书店
开　　本：710mm×1000mm　1/16
印　　张：21.75
字　　数：450 千字
版　　次：2018 年 11 月北京第 1 版
印　　次：2018 年 11 月北京第 1 次印刷
印　　数：0,001~5,000 册
定　　价：68.00 元（精装）

本图书如有印装质量问题，请凭购书发票与质检部联系调换。

联系电话：(010) 57350337

课题组作者简介

课题组组长

易鹏
盘古智库创始人、理事长、学术委员会委员，中国青年企业家协会指导委员会委员，中国生产力促进中心协会副理事长，阿里研究院学术委员会委员、中国经济体制改革研究会公共政策部研究员，多个地方政府的咨询委员会委员。

皮钧
中国青年出版总社社长。

课题组成员

刘友法
经济学博士、资深外交官。盘古智库高级研究员、盘古智库印度研究中心顾问，前中国驻孟买总领馆大使衔总领事。

朱锋
盘古智库学术委员会副主任委员、南京大学国际关系研究院院长、南京大学中国南海协同创新研究中心执行主任。

昝涛
盘古智库学术委员、盘古智库土耳其研究中心主任，北京大学历史学系副教授。

翟崑
盘古智库学术委员、北京大学国际关系学院教授。

熊榆

盘古智库学术委员、英国诺森比亚大学纽卡斯尔商学院终身讲席教授、英国科控集团董事，英国商务能源与产业战略部"中英创新合作专家组"核心成员。

许维鸿

盘古智库学术委员、中航证券首席经济学家、重庆金融学会副秘书长、央视特约财经评论员。

吕晶华

盘古智库学术委员会副秘书长，高级研究员。

李玲飞

盘古智库高级研究员、印度研究中心执行主任。

梁嘉敏

英国诺森比亚大学纽卡斯尔商学院博士，英国科控集团战略部研究员。

武海宝

南京大学国际关系研究院博士后。

常然

祖籍印度，生养于阿联酋迪拜，首届清华大学苏世民学者，硕士研究生，国际关系专业。2016 年毕业于美国密苏里大学。

An Brief Introuduction to the Authors

Head of the Research Group

Yi Peng

Founder and Chairman of the Pangoal Institution, member of its Academic Committee; member of the Steering Committee of China Youth Entrepreneurs Association; Vice Chairman of the China Association of Productivity Promotion Centers; member of Ali Research Institute Academic Committee; researcher of the Public Policy Department of the China Society of Economic Reform; member of the Consulting Committee of several local governments.

Pi Jun

President of China Youth Publishing Group.

Members of the Research Group

Liu Youfa

Doctor of Economics and Senior Diplomat. Previously serving as the Ambassadorial Consul General of the Consulate-General of the People's Republic of China in Mumbai, and currently working as the Senior Fellow of the Pangoal Institution & Adviser of the Center for Indian Studies, the Pangoal Institution.

Zhu Feng

Vice Chairman of Academic Committee of the Pangoal Institution, Professor & Dean of the Institute of International Relations, and Executive Director of China Center for Collaborative Studies of the South China Sea, Nanjing University.

Zan Tao

Academic Committee Member and Director of the Center for Turkey Studies, the Pangoal Institution, and Associate Professor of the History Department, Peking University.

Zhai Kun

Academic Committee Member of the Pangoal Institution, and Professor of the School of International Relations, Peking University.

Xiong Yu

Academic Committee Member of the Pangoal Institution, Chair Professor of Newcastle Business School, Northumbria University, Director of Cocoon Networks UK; Key member of Expert Committee on Cooperation Between China and Britain, Department for Business, Energy and Industrial Strategy.

Xu Weihong

Academic Committee Member, the Pangoal Institution; Chief Economist, AVIC Securities Co., Ltd.; Deputy Secretary-General, Chongqing Finance Institute; Special Finance Commentator of CCTV.

Lyv Jinghua

Senior Fellow, Deputy Secretary-General of Academic Committee, the Pangoal Institution.

Li Lingfei

Executive Director of the Center for Indian Studies and Senior Fellow, the Pangoal Institution.

Liang Jiamin

Research Fellow of Strategy Apartment, Cocoon Networks UK; and doctor of Newcastle Business School of Northumbria University.

Wu Haibao

Post-doctor of the School of International Studies, Nanjing University.

Anurag Ram Chandran

A Schwarzman Scholar at Tsinghua University, where he is studying for a Master's degree in International Relations. He is an Indian citizen, born and raised in Dubai, United Arab Emirates. In 2016, he graduated from University of Missouri.

目 录

Contents

前　言

由习近平主席倡导、我国政府全力推进的"一带一路"倡议已进入全面推进阶段，节点项目有序推进，早期收获项目开花结果。在世界经济增长乏力、贸易自由化处在十字路口的大背景之下，"一带一路"合作建设正成为推动贸易自由化的新动力，成为投资合作的新平台，成为产业合作的新载体，进而成为中国展示走和平发展道路的新纽带，成为中国为合作发展提供公共产品的大国担当，成为中国走向世界、融入世界的历史契机。

首届"一带一路"国际合作高峰论坛在北京召开之际，盘古智库秉持"天地人和、经世致用"的理念，组织力量跟踪国际社会对"一带一路"倡议的反应，研究部分节点国家参与合作建设的可能性、可行性，探讨相关国家参与合作建设与共同发展遇到的挑战，进而提出对策及思考。本期收入的研究成果集中体现了各研究中心的部分阶段性成果，研究深度和广度不一，谨供广大读者参考；相关论文存在错漏在所难免，敬请谅解。

盘古智库理事长

2017 年 6 月 12 日

Preface

The Belt and Road Initiative put forward by President Xi Jinping has been ushered into a full-swing development period, thanks to continuous promotion efforts of the Chinese government. Under the development background, many development projects are moving forward step by step. Those launched in the early period have yielded positive results. Despite of economic recessions and trade liberalization at a development crossroad, the Belt and Road Initiative is becoming a new driving force of trade liberalization, a new platform for investment cooperation, and a new carrier of industrial cooperation. Gradually, it even becomes a new bond for China to show its taking of the peaceful development path, a mission of China to provide public products for cooperation and development, and a historical opportunity for China to walk towards the world and get integrated into the world.

When the First Belt and Road Forum for International Cooperation was held in Beijing, the Pangoal Forum organized forces, by adhering to the concept of "Pursuing Harmony between Nature and Humankind, and Applying knowledge for Public Policy Solutions", to track response of the international community to the Belt and Road, study possibility and feasibility of some node countries to participate in construction cooperation, discuss challenges facing construction cooperation and joint development. Finally put forward countermeasures. The research findings collected in this book are a concentrated reflection of periodical research findings of different research depth and breadth. These findings are just for reference. Should there be any mistakes or omissions with relevant papers, we beg for your kind understanding and advise.

Yi Peng

Chairman of the Pangoal Institution

June 12, 2017

① 印度关于"一带一路"倡议立场成因及对策思考

刘友法

由习近平主席倡导、我国政府全力推进的"一带一路"倡议已进入全面推进阶段，节点项目有序推进，早期收获项目已经开花结果。然而，印度作为"一带一路"沿线最大的伙伴国家，迄今对倡议"半推半就"，拒绝参加"一带一路"国际合作高峰论坛，并与美国和日本合作构建亚非经济增长走廊，对冲中国倡议。然而，中印两国同为新兴发展中国家，互为搬不走的邻居，因而成为上述合作建设进程得以顺利推进的必备条件之一。新时期，如何创造条件争取印度有效参与合作建设，两国如何解决"战略思维错位"问题，如何透过双边和地区合作促进共同发展，如何通过合作发展消除相互战略猜疑，如何构建真正意义上的战略合作伙伴关系，如何探索发展中大国合作发展新模式，已成为考验两国领导人和政府战略智慧的重大课题。

印度关于"一带一路"立场之来龙去脉

六年前，中印两国政府先后换届，两国领导人随即开启了"个人外交"，开启了频繁的高层会晤进程，并决定携手推进战略合作伙伴关系。然而，在我国提出的"一带一路"倡议上，印度一方面积极参与亚投行建设，以期谋求中国市场、中国资本和中国技术。另一方面，又与上述倡议保持一定的距离，并不时采取"对冲"举措。究其原因是多方面的：

（一）**战略互信赤字有增无减**。中印两国于 2005 年建立了面向和平与繁荣的战略合作伙伴关系。2008 年国际金融危机导致世界经济发展进入"平台"状态，导致两国市场环境陡然恶化。在国际社会随后推进的危机救助和经济复苏进程中，中印两国"相互抱团取暖"，互助互救；两国在区域和国际治理领域共同语言愈益增多，双边经贸领域的合作关系有所推进，中印两国在传统及非传统安全领域具有广泛而共同的利益需求。中印两国都是"金砖国家"成员，两国在气候变化、粮食安全以及能源安全等领域面临共同的挑战，在维护地区和平与稳定、在推动建立新的国际经济秩序以及国际关系民主化等重大问题上有着共同的责任，在地区和全球治理进程方面有着共同的理念。然而，印度在战略层面依旧遵循"敌人之朋友必然是敌人"的理念，对我国与巴基斯坦、孟加拉等南亚国家及印度洋沿岸国家的任何经贸合作关系均保持高度警惕。经济上，印度一方面期盼通过双边和地区合作机制分享我国经济快速增长的"一杯羹"，同时又担心我国日益强大的经济辐射和传递能力冲击其自主发展模式，因而对中国资本和技术设置"隐形路障"。政治上，印度期盼成为联合国安理会常任理事国，最近又提出申请加入"核供应国俱乐部"。上述均是印度实施全球大国战略的头等要务，并期待中国予以理解和支持。我国坚持多边外交政策，依据相关多边条约的协定，迟迟未给予明确的支持。对此，印方颇多微词，进而在西藏问题上"搞小动作"，宣泄不满。安全上，印度各界迄今尚待摆脱冷战思维的桎梏，主观认定"一带一路"无异于"围堵"印度的又一个"珍珠项链"，随即提出"季节计划"进行对冲。

（二）**经贸关系深入发展面临"瓶颈"**。概而言之，中印同为人口大国，同为新兴经济体，同样具有日益增长的消费市场，同样具有扩大相互贸易的潜力。然而，进入 21 世纪以来，双边经贸关系发展开始面临一系列挑战。

第一，相互贸易能力"错配"问题。受国际风云格局变幻影响，中印建交以来经贸合作水平长期在低水平徘徊，但基本保持平衡，中方盈余有限。1993年印度实施改革开放以来，加强了对外贸易，并将中国作为发展外贸的主要对象，以期搭乘中国经济快速增长的"快车"。然而，中印两国经济结构不同。中国通过引进外资发展制造业，很快形成了强大的商品制造能力和外贸能力，进而跻身于全球制造大国行列。与此同时，印度经济以服务业为主导，在信息和软件产业领域走在发展中国家前列。其结果，印度市场开放后对价廉物美的中国商品形成了强大吸引力，但同期印度的服务产业对华贸易增长有限。上述货物与服务交换"错位"的后遗症很快显现出来。2006年，印度对华贸易开始出现赤字，由2005年的8亿美元顺差变为逆差41.2亿美元。2007年，印度对华贸易赤字上升到120亿美元。2016年，中印双边贸易在国际贸易下滑的大背景之下达到711亿美元，同时，印方逆差也达到了创纪录的560亿美元。有鉴于上述情况，贸易逆差始终成为双边关系发展的"路障"。由此可见，中印贸易失衡并非中国的"错"，而是双方对外贸易比较优势的差异和比较优势"错配"所致。

第二，"产业链错配"问题。众所周知，全球化的实质就是跨国公司在全球范围配置资源，在全球范围组织生产和销售，实现生产与经营利益最大化。中印两国先后实施改革开放战略，相继以本国产业优势加入跨国公司驱动的国际产业分工链条。其间，中国实施改革开放以来，总共吸引了将近2万亿美元的外国直接投资，目前有超过100万家外资企业在中国境内注册经营，因而使得中国成为"世界工厂"。与此同时，中国正成为对外直接投资大国，中国的企业主导的产业链正大踏步向国际市场延伸，因而正成为推动国际贸易的新动力。与之相对应，印度的产业优势主要集中在信息和服务领域，印度相关产业企业利用与发达国家的特殊关系和印度员工享有的"工作语言"英语优势，大量发展信息和软件产业，因而在服务贸易领域形成了比较优势。问题是，在国际层面，中印两国加入了不同的国际产业链，上述与贸易相关的"产业链"往往"鸡犬之声相闻，老死不相往来"。其结果，中国制造业发展所需软件主要从发达国家进口，而印度需求的工业制成品则从中国进口，长此以往必然导致贸易失衡。

第三，贸易能力"错配"问题。研究表明，经济全球化对传统的国家经济发展造成了两个非常突出的现象：一个就是跨国公司在全球范围配置资源和能源，在不同的国家进行生产与经营活动，导致全球范围内传统的商品生产、营销和消费发生分离。具体而言，任何一种商品可以在不同的国家完成不同部件的生产，最终在一个国家组装、包装，而后再从这个国家运销至世界各地。多年来，中国凭借地缘、劳动力和相关市场要素优势，通过改革开放加入国际产业链，继而成为全球40%以上的日用或耐用商品的生产国，使得"中国制造"流行于世界各地。需要指出的是，中国实际上仅仅是"世界制造和加工环节的工厂"。与此同时，印度迄今在已加入的国际产业链中也是处于"编程"环节。跨国公司上述自行组织的专利或品牌商品销售活动导致了第二个结果，导致国家之间传统的贸易流发生"转向"。具体到双边领域，印度有大量国民移居新加坡等国，上述印度族裔大多以中国和印度两端为市场，从事进出口贸易。依据传统的贸易理论，上述经由印度和香港等地输往中国市场的大量商品显然不再计入印度对华出口。这就是典型的"贸易转向"效应。与此同时，跨国公司在中国制造或加工的商品中，中国合作伙伴仅仅获得简单的劳务加工费和少量的税收，商品的最终利润大部分为跨国公司的终端营销商拿走。加之中国的对外贸易大部分由在华外国企业或外国进出口商把持，上述贸易利益大部分也被外国公司企业拿走。

第四，贸易政策"错配"问题。国际经验表明，双边贸易发展取决于伙伴之间的市场规模、消费能力和相互生产并提供商品进行交换的能力。中印两国分别是第一和第二人口大国，市场规模和消费能力都在迅速增长。从进出口结构上分析，印度对中国出口的商品主要是初级产品，其中矿产品和农产品占其对中国出口总额的一半以上。印度从中国进口的产品主要是机械制品，占印度从中国进口总额的将近一半，其余以此类推为化学制品、金属制品、纤维及纺织品。上述源于不同国家的商品进行交换，容易导致贸易失衡。进入本世纪以来，印度出于资源保护和制造业发展需要，相继停止了部分初级产品对华出口，更加剧了对华贸易逆差态势。新时期，信息产业领域本应成为最具潜力的合作领域。然而，受冷战思维和国家安全等因素驱使，印度对中国的"敌对情绪"和"安全防范心态"作祟，导致"中国威胁论"在印度各界蔓延，进而致使信息和服务产业合作迟迟不能提上两国政府议事日程。

第五，涉贸投资"错配"问题。从理论上讲，贸易和投资是推动双边经贸关系健康稳定发展的两大轮子。当两个国家的贸易关系发展到一定阶段，相互投资理应成为必由之路，两者相辅相成，缺一不可。冷战结束以来，中国和印度经济几乎同时经历了快速增长阶段，两国在不同产业领域均形成了一定的比较优势，通过相互投资带动产业合作理应成为推动经贸关系发展的新动力。但是，进入 21 世纪第二个 10 年以来，印度对华投资能力有限，同时对中国资本处处设限，结果导致两国相互投资呈现缓慢增长态势，总量在 20 亿美元左右。随着中国综合经济实力不断增长，中国对外投资开始走向世界各地，对外投资总量已接近 1 万亿美元，其中流向印度的不足 1%。这与我们两国的相互投资总量增长、两国市场潜力和双边关系发展正出现巨大的差异。

第六，贸易战略"错配"问题。中印都是人口大国，两国人口相加超过全球总人数的 1/3。随着两国经济不断增长，两国经济规模不断扩大，两国中产阶级的队伍正在大量扩张。有学者之所以将 21 世纪描绘为"亚洲的世纪"，主要原因之一就是亚洲拥有的无比巨大的消费潜力。研究表明，一个国家的消费能力和商品吸纳能力将直接决定相关国家的发展速度和发展前景。中印两国分别是第一和第七大经济体，各自具有比较优势，两国发展贸易具有诸多潜力。但是，一方或者另一方贸易政策改变，使得两国之间的商品无法正常流通。以中印贸易平衡问题为例，印度政府调整涉华贸易政策确实有可能暂时解决贸易失衡问题。但是，印度国民的消费能力在继续增长，因而需要从其他国家进口同样的商品，而进口的商品很可能还是"中国制造"，只是需要为同样的商品支付更多的贸易转口费用而已。因此，从长远看，政策调整不大可能解决印度的对外贸易逆差问题，而必须通过投资合作与产业合作这两个途径综合解决问题。

第七，统计数字"错配问题"。从技术上讲，贸易统计容易受人为因素干扰，一般而言贸易统计的误差率在 5%~10%。这是公开的秘密。总体而言，中国对印度出口的系大宗制造商品，批量出口，统计工作相对有案可稽。与之相对应，印度方面中小企业和进出口商参与对华出口居多，小额贸易统计疏漏的概率相对较高。加之中印双方对经由香港等第三地进入对方市场的贸易统计存在差异。因此，上述因素放大了中印贸易逆差规模。更为重要的是，印度服务贸易能力明显高于中国，而服务贸易却不包括在双边贸易之中。

（三）边界问题阴影"尾大难掉"。中印关系最大的历史症结是 1962 年发生的那场边界战争，中方称之为"中印边界自卫反击战"。1962 年 6 月 10 日至 11 日间，中国人民解放军与印度军队在藏南边境进行了一场军事较量，并在军事层面大获全胜，沉重地打击了当时国际上的反华逆流和中国西藏地区的分裂主义势力，维护了国家的领土完整和民族尊严。战争不是中方挑起的，责任也不在中方，为给印方以"改过自新"的机会，中国军队在战胜印军之后单方面将军队后撤到战前的双方实际控制线以北，但印方"得寸进尺"，立即全面占领藏南争议地区至今。

中印边界自卫反击战融军事、政治和外交斗争为一体，各种矛盾错综交织，其影响远远超出了军事领域。毛主席在不同场合曾经预言，这一仗至少可以保证中印边界 10 年稳定，但这场战争也一度导致两国关系跌近冰点。1979 年，中印重启两国边界谈判进程，并于 2003 年设立了边界问题特别代表会晤机制。2005 年，两国签署了《关于解决边界问题政治指导原则的协定》。此外，两国还先后签署了《关于保持边境地区和平与安宁协定》和《建立相互信任措施协定》，并建立了边境事务磋商和协调工作机制。2012 年 1 月，两国正式签署《关于建立中印边境事务磋商和协调工作机制的协定》，授权两国外交部门牵头推进边界磋商活动，并制定外交和军事官员协调与处理两国边境事宜的机制，旨在为谈判解决两国边界问题和促进两国关系发展创造条件。2013 年 4 月，李克强总理访印前夕，印方刻意挑起"帐篷对峙"事件，两国政府成功地化解了上述危机。同年 10 月，两国达成《中印两国政府边防合作协议》（BDCA），以避免战略误判，防止边界个案问题成为影响双边互利合作的干扰源。2014 年、2015 年和 2016 年，习近平主席和莫迪总理数度会晤，就上述问题进行政治决策，双方同意将边界问题"区隔"开来，集中精力推动其他领域关系发展。2017 年 2 月 22 日，中印举行战略对话。这是中印两国重要的对话与沟通渠道，旨在增进政治合作，扩大战略互信，促进战略伙伴关系。然而，印方依据惯性思维，依然坚持将边界问题与"一带一路"合作建设挂钩，导致相关合作计划难以实现。

（四）安全战略利益相互"踩脚"。 冷战结束以来，中印在改革开放进程中相互调整政策，促进政治关系"转圜"，推动经贸关系出现了快速发展，两国在多边领域利益汇合点不断增多，共同语言不断汇聚。尤其是在国际治理领域，中印两国协调政策，成为重大国际事务的参与者、决策者和推动者。然而，安全领域的合作始终成为双边关系的"短板"。印度自独立以来始终将印度洋和南亚国家视作其前庭后院，认为"印度洋是其生命线所系"。早在 1983 年，英迪拉·甘地提出了"印度版门罗主义"，表明印度要在南亚地区充当"管理人"角色。鉴此，印方对我国在印度洋周边地区的经济和商业存在统统视为安全威胁，对我国同该地区任何国家建立军事与安全合作关系统统视为对印度的"战略包围"，因而对我国上述任何政策举措均采取反制措施。印度主流舆论认为，中国作为北部邻邦，一旦发展壮大起来，"必然会从陆地南下进行扩张"，把"海上丝绸之路"与"陆上丝绸之路"相互连接起来，很可能成为中国"南下印度洋的战略工具"；中国与印度周边国家推进的经济、贸易与安全合作犹如一个个针对印度的"桥头堡"，并构成围堵印度的"安全项链"。正是基于上述战略考虑，印度认为，南亚及印度洋沿岸国家对海上丝绸之路发展倡议纷纷作出积极回应，是在对印度打"中国牌"，以便从中印双方之中谋取利益。2014 年下半年，我国潜艇编队停靠科伦坡港，更是挑动了印方敏感的神经，一时间关于"中国威胁论"的舆论在印度"沸腾"起来。作为回应，印度随即提出"季节计划"，摆出与我对垒的架势。与此同时，印度利用与斯里兰卡的特殊关系影响后者的大选，成功阻止对华友好的政府连任，进而导致我国在科伦坡港口工业园区建设一度生变。然而，南亚及印度洋周边各国政府工作的燃眉之急是发展问题，因而强烈期盼在市场、资本、技术和产业等领域获得外部拉力，并期盼从中国获得"公共产品"。显然，印度明知并不具备上述能力，但依旧提出"季节计划"，旨在吸引国际舆论注意力，谋求"外交对冲"效应。

（五）地缘战略利益相互"顶牛"。 回眸中印关系历史，印度在独立伊始继承了英国殖民当局的"远东战略遗产"。尼赫鲁政府制定和实施的国家安全战略将中国的西藏作为与中国战略博弈的"缓冲区"，因而在两国存在争议的边界问题上更是"咄咄逼人"，最终直接挑起边界战争。由于历史和地缘政治影响，整个冷战时期，印度与苏联构成"安全利益共同体"，同时中国则"以苏联划线"，以伙伴国家与苏联的关系亲疏来决定与对方的关系，上述两方面的因素综合作用，导致中印关系长期处于低水平发展状态。冷战结束以来，在两国领导人和政府的共同努力下，中印关系逐渐企稳向好，并于2005年建立了面向21世纪的战略合作伙伴关系。

然而，中印双方意识形态各异，战略利益不同，加之12.5万平方公里的领土争议，随着中国政治、经济和军事实力不断增强，并且与南亚其他国家的外交日渐增多，影响力不断提高，印度的"战略危机感"相应增强。为确保在南亚和印度洋地区的霸主地位，塑造地区安全主导力量的国际形象，印度把提高军事实力作为实现战略目标的主要手段，认为"外交必须以军事为后盾，军事必须以外交为补充，军事是外交上的一张王牌"。即使是在冷战后的今天，印度依然将大量国家预算用于国防，并将中国作为国防政策的重要考量因素。后金融危机时期，随着中国经济持续增长，美国和日本等发达国家加大了对中国的战略围堵。其间，印度作为上述国家地缘伙伴的筹码大大增加。尤其是莫迪政府上台以来，西方大国竞相向印度示好。与此同时，莫迪政府四下出击，谋求建立对华关系优势地位，绸缪同我国博弈的"牌"。与此同时，为实现其全球大国梦，莫迪政府制定和实施了全方位外交，积极调整与美欧发达国家的关系，谋划本国发展所需资金和技术；加快振兴制造业，带动经济实现跨越式发展；大规模扩充军备，以核武器为后盾确立世界核大国地位。在地区层面，印度依据不结盟政策，在印、美、俄、中四国关系上继续实施"战略自主"政策，表示不在美中之间"选边站"。然而，2015年1月美国总统奥巴马访印期间，两国发表《联合声明》指出："印度的'东向战略'与美国的'亚太再平衡战略'为印美两国以及其他亚太国家紧密合作、为加强相互地区关系提供了历史性机会。"2016年，特朗普执掌白宫后继承了奥巴马政府的对印政策，先于习近平主席与莫迪总理通电话，称"印度为美国最为友好的非盟国朋友"。鉴于印度上述"东向战略"与美国"亚太再平衡战略"利益汇合点增多，印度近期内已难有决心与我国"一带一路"全面对接。

（六）**克什米尔问题成为焦点**。半个多世纪以来，印巴关系长期处于剑拔弩张状态，双方在克什米尔地区时而兵戎相见。长期以来，克什米尔问题成为印度处理与邻国和其他国家关系的"重要考量因素"。然而，"一带一路"倡议框架之下的地区互联互通网络和我南下战略通道双双涉及印巴两国尚待解决的争议领土，涉及印度的"战略利益"，因而成为中印巴三国关系的"烫手山芋"，更成为区域合作发展乃至"一带一路"合作建设需要认真应对的外交和安全问题。

克什米尔是"查谟和克什米尔"地区的简称，位于印度、巴基斯坦、中国和阿富汗之间，面积约为 19 万平方公里。克什米尔问题是"分而治之"的殖民政策造成的。18 世纪中叶，南亚次大陆开始沦为英国的殖民地。二战结束后，南亚次大陆摆脱英国的殖民统治并获得独立。1947 年 6 月，英国最后一任驻印度总督蒙巴顿提出了把印度分为印度和巴基斯坦两个自治领的"蒙巴顿方案"。

根据"蒙巴顿方案"相关规定，印度教徒居多数的地区划归印度，穆斯林占多数的地区归属巴基斯坦。但对克什米尔的归属问题却规定由各王公土邦自己决定加入印度或巴基斯坦，或保持独立。当时，克什米尔地区 77% 的人口为穆斯林，他们倾向加入巴基斯坦；克什米尔土邦王是印度教徒，他先是既不想加入印度，也不愿加入巴基斯坦。因此，印巴分治时，克什米尔的归属问题未能得到解决。

印巴分治后不久，双方为争夺克什米尔主权于 1947 年 10 月在克什米尔地区发生大规模武装冲突，即第一次印巴战争。1947 年 12 月，印度将克什米尔问题提交联合国安理会。1948 年 8 月和 1949 年 1 月，联合国印巴委员会先后通过关于克什米尔停火和公民投票的决议，印巴均表示接受。1949 年 1 月双方正式停火，7 月划定了停火线。克什米尔分为印控区和巴控区，印巴分别在各自控制区内建立了地方政府。

1953 年 8 月，印巴两国总理会谈后发表联合公报宣布，克什米尔争端应通过克什米尔公民投票来解决。然而，1965 年 6 月，印巴围绕克什米尔问题爆发第二次战争。1971 年 12 月，在因东巴基斯坦脱离巴基斯坦而爆发的第三次印巴战争中，印度又占领了巴控克什米尔地区的部分土地。

1972 年 7 月，印巴签署《西姆拉协定》，双方同意在克什米尔地区尊重 1971

年双方停火后形成的实际控制线。为了解决克什米尔问题，印巴两国领导人和部长级官员数次举行会谈，但一直没能达成协议。1989 年后，双方在克什米尔地区不断交火，两国均蒙受巨大损失。

2003 年 11 月 23 日，巴基斯坦总理贾迈利宣布，巴军队将从穆斯林的重要节日开斋节（26 日）开始，在克什米尔印巴实际控制线的巴方一侧实现单方面停火。24 日，印度对这一建议表示欢迎，并于 25 日作出了积极回应。两国军方 25 日经磋商决定，自当天午夜起在克什米尔"国际边境"、"实际控制线"和"锡亚琴实际接触线"（印方称为"实际地面位置线"）一带实现停火。双方同意希望停火永久持续下去。2005 年 10 月 29 日上午至 10 月 30 日凌晨，经过长时间的谈判，巴印双方在伊斯兰堡达成协议，同意暂时开放克什米尔实控线 5 个检查站，以允许两国边民过境展开震后施救活动。

改革开放以来，我国调整了南亚政策，实施"保持中立、劝和促谈"立场，进而为中国与印、巴"双友好"南亚战略奠定了政治基础。然而，我国提出的"一带一路"倡议将巴基斯坦作为重要节点国家，并将"中巴经济走廊"打造为旗舰项目，携手构建连接我国喀什与巴基斯坦瓜达尔港的铁路、公路、油气管道和光缆的"四合一"交通运输和信息大通道。为此，我国已承诺投资 460 亿美元，而同期对印度的直接投资则"相形见绌"。更引发印度焦虑的是，"中巴经济走廊"相关工程行将穿越印巴克什米尔争议地区。对此，印方主观认定，中巴携手"侵犯了印方的核心利益"，因而不时提出抗议和交涉，进而在西藏问题上"做文章"，挑战我国的国家利益"红线"。

"一带一路"涉印项目建设对策思考

"一带一路"倡议推进的合作建设"开弓没有回头箭"。在南亚乃至更加广泛的地区，相关项目建设无法绕过印度。与此同时，随着中印两国不断发展壮大，两国经济疆界和利益疆界在南亚相互碰撞、相互激荡和相互融合在所难免。研究表明，成熟的国家关系必然伴之以复杂多变的矛盾和纠纷，这是国家关系发展之必然规律。中印关系亦然。进而言之，印度是我国实现民族复兴伟大梦想不可或缺的外部条件，是我国周边外交战略必须经营的重要伙伴关系，更是我国推进"一带一路"建设必须寻求的合作伙伴。有鉴于以上情况，上述合作建设进程必须获得后者的理解，必须争取后者的支持与合作，至少推动后者相向而行。

（一）积极寻求发展战略相互对接。放眼未来，中印两国全球和地区战略具有利益汇合点，两国关系利益汇聚远大于利益冲突，关键在于如何依据"不冲突、不对抗、互利共赢、携手前行"原则，坚持凝聚共识，汇聚利益，妥处分歧，共促发展。印度于 2014 年 9 月提出的"季节计划"涵盖南亚次大陆相关国家，进而从斯里兰卡向西延伸至伊朗等西亚国家，向东延伸至印度尼西亚等东南亚国家，向南延伸至东非地区相关国家。上述国家与"海上丝绸之路"沿线伙伴国家大多相互重叠。有鉴于上述情况，我国应通过对话与政策磋商增加相关战略的透明度，进而寻找"一带一路"倡议与"季节计划"的"利益汇合点"，避免上述计划相互"顶牛"。

其一，通过对话与谈判促进"一带一路"项下的互联互通规划与印度"十二五计划"基础设施发展计划对接起来，促进两国建设能力与建设需求有效对接。可考虑以印度现行铁路技术改造和高速公路建设为"突破口"，加快推进相关项目，让印方各界民众看到合作建设的"红利"，为其他领域的合作营造民意基础。鉴于印度目前修建高铁尚不具备经济与社会基础，且莫迪政府已将第一个项目交由日本公司建设，我方可静观其变，以便在总结日本经验和教训的基础上争取后续基础设施项目签订合同。鉴于印方对"一带一路"倡议的战略疑虑，可考虑将相关涉印项目"拆分开来"，主要通过双边途径加以实施，进而在合作建设中适应和遵循国际统一标准，并创造条件为"一带一路"周边基础设施网络经由东亚向南亚延伸提供对接窗口。

其二，以平衡双边贸易为"抓手"，推进双向投资合作进程。积极寻求信息产业领域的合作，促进中国硬件制造能力与印度的软件编制能力相互对接，扩大双边经贸合作基础，以期从根本上解决双边贸易失衡问题。

其三，以阿富汗重建为契机，充分发挥两国相关产业比较优势，在阿富汗国家重建领域加强合作，实现南南合作，发展"溢出效应"，彰显发展中大国的国际担当。

其四，积极探讨两国在环印度洋安全领域推进互利合作的途径，逐步增加项目和领域合作，增加政治互信与安全透明度。

其五，进而与印度及印度洋周边各国，合作挖掘"古丝绸之路"文化遗产，携手整理海上丝绸之路精神，使之成为世界文明的共同遗产，等等。

（二）积极寻求产业政策相互对接。 近年来，中印两国经济均呈现快速增长态势，两国经济互补性进一步增强，双方经贸合作势头趋强。据商务部统计，2008年以来，中国连续7年成为印度第一大贸易伙伴国。2008年，中印贸易额达433.8亿美元，印度成为中国的第八大贸易伙伴国。2016年两国贸易超过700亿美元，但印度在中国贸易中的位次却由七年前的第八位降至第十一位。国际经验表明，经济与贸易关系是国家关系的"稳定器"。新时期，中印两国政府应依据后金融危机时期世界经济发展新常态，加强政策协调，为双边贸易提供机制保障。中印两国国情不同，经济结构不同，发展阶段不同，产业比较优势不同，参与相互贸易的伙伴竞争力不同。因此，进一步发展双边贸易需要两国高层保持会晤和互访势头，就进一步推动双边贸易关系进行顶层设计和政治引导；需要相关政府部门定期会晤，落实两国领导人的共识，将高层政治决策转变为有案可稽的政策举措。充分利用我国与印度在多边机制中的良好合作关系，尽快开启双边自由贸易协定商签进程，为促进双边贸易和有效解决经贸纠纷提供法律保障。

（三）积极寻求经贸合作潜力相互对接。 以"一带一路"合作建设为载体，以加强双向投资合作为载体，促进经贸合作均衡增长。创造条件商签投资保护协定，为双边经贸合作提供法律和机制保障。目前，我方已是印度主要的贸易伙伴，但印方对华贸易逆差逐年拉大。这个问题已成为中印经贸关系无法绕过的"坎"。我方可通过双边途径推动中国企业对印度投资，以独资或合资形式生产与销售在印度市场适销对路的商品，并积极推动对第三方市场销售，间接纾缓印中贸易逆差。加快商签知识产权保护协定，为两国信息和技术合作提供法律保障，为中印开展三方合作提供政策引导。加强金融领域合作，印度在银行和金融监管方面经验丰富、传统优良。最新统计数据表明，在全球排名中，印度证券交易委员会在保护投资者领域名列第七位，位居金砖五国之首，甚至超过了美国、日本、法国、德国等许多发达国家。亚投行可望借鉴印度成功经验，进而服务双边和区域经济合作发展。

（四）积极寻求文化互鉴互学。以文化互鉴互学为抓手推进合作关系。文化产业是衡量世界各国发展阶段的重要领域，同样文化关系构成研判国家关系的"晴雨表"。印度文化历经 6000 余年风雨洗礼而光彩照人，古老的中华文化展示出东方魅力。历史上，佛教和印度教具有传承和发扬的关系，而"佛教缘"则构成海上丝绸之路沿线诸多国家共同的精神和文化遗产。正如莫迪总理在接待习近平主席访问之际所说，"中印两国是两个身体，一个大脑"。从这个意义上讲，文化领域合作可望构成两国携手推进"一带一路"建设的"最大公约数"。具体而言，应坚持将两国文化再创辉煌作为利益汇合点，加快落实两国领导人达成的文化合作政治共识，尽快商签两国合作研究协定，以"佛教缘"为纽带，考虑将涉印高铁和高速公路项目与印度重要历史文化古迹串联起来，着力推进两国文化资源对接，夯实推进合作建设所需人文和情感基础。

（五）积极寻求能源战略相互对接。以能源产业为载体促进产业合作。随着两国经济持续增长，中印在能源和资源领域对国际市场依存度均不断攀升。近年来，两国在"一带一路"沿线"找油"和"找气"时常不期而遇，事实上形成了竞合关系。未来，中印完全有可能在上述领域构建能源合作开发"利益共同体"，可考虑邀请印度参与连接中亚、南亚和西亚的能源资源运输网络建设，逐步深化在非洲国家的能源合作开发、合作加工，合作运输，合作维护管线安全，按比例分享油气，为各自经济发展奠定能源基础，以期缓解印巴敌对关系，推动南亚和平与稳定。以"中亚—西亚经济走廊"为载体，开辟动向延伸"窗口"，将中国与南亚国家的能源合作纳入其中，旨在以能源合作为载体，促进相互信任、相互支持，进而为其他领域合作奠定能源基础。

（六）积极寻求经济利益相互对接。妥善处理合作利益与道义的关系。中印作为两大邻国，在双边关系中出现这样那样的问题在所难免，关键在于"求同存异"，关键在于"着眼未来"。中印两国均致力于和平发展，均坚持走和平发展道路。中印两国没有必要，也没有可能互为对手；中印两国在政治领域共同立场日益增多，在经贸领域共同利益远远大于分歧，合作需求也远远大于竞争。关键在于把具体问题放在两国关系的适当位置，不能让具体分歧影响两国友好大局，不能让个案问题成为互利合作的障碍。进而言之，"一带一路"倡议的出发点是共同建设，携手推进互联互通网络；落脚点是共同发展和共同治理，携手促进相互贸易、相互投资与产业合作，创造条件实现经济一体化。其间，我国需要携手印度通过双边和区域合作适应国际通行的商业规范，确立南南合作规范，打造共同发展的战略平台。

中印两国均需要立足于传统文化和符合时代潮流的"义利观"，高举互惠互利、合作共赢的国际合作大旗，将"义利观"融入到共同建设与合作发展的全过程。政治上，在战略对话框架之下探讨相关涉印项目实施规划和实施细则，明确合作章程，划分各自权利与义务，促进两国优势产业、优势资源相互对接，加快各自发展，形成发展合力，为世界经济增长提供正能量。具体而言，相关涉印项目需要寻找与印方"向东看"和恢复"香料航道"战略的"利益汇合点"，强调互惠互利、合作共赢。在相关涉印项目建设进程中，应尊重印度的核心利益，打消印度对华战略疑虑。经济上，依法引导和鼓励本国企业守法经营，搞活与当地合作伙伴的商脉关系，尊重当地文化习俗，特别要处理好项目所在地寺庙搬迁和重建事宜；鼓励我国企业在印度投资兴业之际，依据相关法律承担相应的社会责任，打造与项目所在地的邦政府、当地政府和当地社团的"利益和责任纽带"，赢得有关各方支持与合作，共同维护项目建设与运营安全。

（七）积极探索人文合作新途径。毋庸置疑，"一带一路"倡议旨在推进发展、促进共同繁荣，最终改善伙伴国家民众的福祉。因此，相关涉印项目均应坚持以经济合作为基础，充分发挥各自产业与资源比较优势，优先推进交通基础设施、能源通道建设，促进双向贸易，培养贸易新的增长点，创新贸易方式，促进贸易平衡增长；大力拓展产业投资领域，加快投资便利化进程，鼓励两国企业合作参与印度政府倡导的经济带和重大城市互联互通网络建设。与此同时，以人文交流为支撑，扩大相互间留学生派遣规模，开展合作办学，弘扬和传承丝绸之路友好合作精神。考虑到印度反对我国在其境内建孔子学院，担心我国借以推行"文化扩张"，可考虑与印度就相互在对方设文化中心，合作推广太极和瑜伽等项目，相互推介两国优秀文化；探讨新闻媒体合作机制，携手开展世界遗产的联合保护工作；加强与印度旅游业合作；充分发挥政党、议会、传媒、智库、非政府组织等桥梁作用，夯实合作建设所需民意和社会基础。

（八）积极引导两国舆论。依据印度国情和民情制定和实施对印宣传合作机制，传递好中国声音，讲述好中国故事，为涉印项目建设提供正能量。毋庸置疑，在发展中国家中，印度新闻媒体堪称煽动"中国威胁论"的领头羊。有关政府部门应潜心研究印度新闻媒体相关法规，了解印度新闻媒体运作机制，建立和完善两国新闻舆论合作机制，加强官方及非官方媒体督导，把握好对印宣传尺度。用足用好对外宣传话语体系，准确阐释"一带一路"倡议的内涵，及时提供正面信息，主动引导舆论导向，强调"共商、共建、共享"原则，突出上述合作建设的互利性、开放性和包容性。

（九）着力搞活中印巴三角关系。巴基斯坦在我国周边安全大格局中占有极其重要的战略地位，并已成为"一带一路"建设的试验场和桥头堡。鉴于巴印两国关系及南亚政治经济态势，应通过双边战略对话机制解释我国构建南下经济与出海口的国情，有效纾缓印方的战略猜疑，进而通过区域和双边项目合作积极推动印巴两国摆脱现行惯性矛盾逻辑，探寻破解三国关系长期处于"你争我斗"、"连横合纵"的困境。鉴此，应充分利用"和平发展"这个三国关系最大的公约数，以中巴关系为主轴，全面推进两国全天候合作发展关系；以"中巴经济走廊"和"孟中印缅经济走廊"为载体，推动两国关系相向而行。在上述基础上，推动南亚各国，尤其是印巴两国参与区域互联互通项目建设，推动构建中印巴三国能源与资源合作开发利益共同体，合作规划、合作开发、合作加工和合作营销机制；以阿富汗重建为载体，构建三国安全合作利益共同体，推动构建中印巴安全信息合作机制，创造条件推进区域安全合作，建立三国合作反恐机制，推动印巴关系稳定发展；加强两国在地区反恐领域的合作，就马苏德·阿兹哈尔列入国际恐怖分子名单一事举行谈判，增进两国安全合作凝聚力。

（十）**着力解决战略互信赤字**。保持高层互访与会晤机制，就事关双边关系的重大事宜进行政治决策，就双边、地区和全球事宜进行战略规划；通过谈判就各自关注的重大事宜达成谅解，尊重并关照对方的核心利益，有效提升战略互信。充分发挥两国战略和经济对话机制，相互交流治国理政经验，协调相关产业政策，有序拓展合作的领域，探索解决经贸纠纷的有效途径。完善两国外交与战略对话机制，协调两国周边与地区政策，建立和拓展利益汇合点，形成区域政治、经济与安全合作利益共同体；继续发挥中俄印三国外长对话机制，促进相互贸易、投资和产业合作，促进经济协调发展。加强中印安全战略对话，增强两国战略透明度，建立两国重大军事和安全行动相互通报机制；创造条件构建中印在太平洋和印度洋安全合作机制，以良好的陆军合作为载体，拓展两国海军和安全部门合作；着力推进区域和国际治理合作进程，携手推进共同倡议，维护共同的发展利益，谋划共同的发展空间；就中巴经济走廊建设途经争议的克什米尔地区等问题举行对话，谋求印方谅解；有效推进两国学术界合作，以期合作研究两国关系历史渊源，挖掘和整理两国关系的历史与文化遗产，携手弘扬古丝绸之路精神，携手创造丝绸之路新辉煌。

1 Indian Stand on The Belt and Road Initiative and Policy Proposals

Liu Youfa

The Belt and Road Initiative, which has been put forward by President Xi Jinping and has been actively promoted by the Chinese government, has gone into full scale implementation, with key projects under orderly construction, and with early-harvest projects coming alone. However, India, as the largest partner country along the Belt and Road, has been hitherto "riding fences" in terms of participation in the above-said Initiative. It has refused to attend the Belt and Road Forum for International Cooperation in Beijing, and has teamed up with the US and Japan to launch the Asia-Africa Economic Growth Corridor, in an effort to hedge against the BRI. India and China are both emerging countries and are the inseparable neighbors to each other, which constitutes one of the preconditions for the smooth promotion of the BRI. Therefore, it will be a paramount subject to test the strategic wisdom of the leaders of both countries and governments on how to create conditions for India to fully engage in the joint construction, how to effectively resolve the issue of "misalignment of strategic thinking", how to promote common development via bilateral and regional cooperation, how to manage the mutual strategic suspicion via win-win cooperation, how to construct the real strategic partner relations, as well as on how to jointly explore the new cooperation modality of development between the two major developing countries.

Synopsis on the Reasons that Have Brought about the Policy Stand by India on the Belt and Road Initiative.

Six years ago, both China and India had the new governments and the leaders of the two countries soon started "personal diplomacy", and maintained frequent meetings at various bilateral and international occasions, during which the two leaders reached consensus on jointly prompting strategic partner relations. Nevertheless, India has hitherto adopted a "two-approach" policy toward the BRI. On the one hand, India outreached to China in becoming a founding member of the AIIB, in an effort to further explore the Chinese market, investment and manufacturing technologies. On the other hand, the former has kept distance with the latter, and adopted "hedging measures" from time to time. On the whole, various reasons have attributed to the above scenario.

(I) It is due to the growing deficit of mutual strategic trust. China and India established strategic partnership relations toward peace and prosperity in 2005, which have brought about closer cooperation at bilateral, regional and international levels. It is true that the two countries have the convergence of broad and common interests in both traditional and non-traditional security. Both countries are major developing economies, both members to the BRICS, are both faced with challenges in the field of the climate change, food security, and energy security, both shoulder the responsibility in maintaining regional peace and stability, and both share the common vision in regional and international governance. However, India has been adhering to the concept at strategic level that "friends of the enemy are natural enemies", and has thus kept a high vigilance on any Chinese economic and trade cooperation with countries such as Pakistan, Bangladesh, Myanmar, as well as other countries in South Asia or around the Indian Ocean. Consequently, India, at the economic front, has been eager to tap into the potentials of the rapid growth of the Chinese economy, and set up invisible "road blocks" on the entry of Chinese capital and technologies, against the fear that the growing Chinese economic radiation and transfer would "chip off" the modality of its modality of "independent development". At the political front, it has been the long cherished aspiration of India to become a permanent member of the Security Council of the United Nations and to join the nuclear suppliers club. India has regarded the above efforts as the paramount foreign policy in terms of its global strategy and has been counting on China for understanding and support. However, China has yet to give the "green light" on both issues either at bilateral level or multilateral level. Consequently, India has been complaining openly and has thus decided to "create some issues on Tibet" in order to show its dissatisfaction in the above regard. At the security front, India is still in bed with the redundant Cold War mindset, presume that the BRI is nothing but "a strategy of joint development sugar-coated by beautiful diplomatic versions" and constitutes no more than a new "pearl necklace" to contain India, which promoted India to offset the BRI with the "Project of Mausa".

(II) Economic and trade relations are faced with "bottlenecks". In short, China and India are the first and second most populous nation in the world, both are emerging nations, both demonstrating growing consumption market, and both have market growth potentials. However, since the 21st century, bilateral economic and trade relations are faced with series of challenges.

Firstly, it is the misalignment of trade capability. Due to the impact of the changing international situation, the bilateral economic and trade relations were lukewarm since the two countries established diplomatic relations, but maintained mostly a meager trade with a slight surplus on the Chinese side. However, since 1993, India started its own economic reform and opening up, which was aiming at fortifying foreign trade and regarding China as one main partner, in order to jump on the "wagon of the fast growth the Chinese economy". However, China and India have developed different economic structures. China has managed to build up the manufacture industries, elevated manufacturing capability as well as trade capabilities, and managed to join the rank of manufacturing nations. Meanwhile, India concentrated its national resources on information and service industries, joint the rank of information industry and software industry and become the leading nation among developing countries. Consequently, the cheap but quality goods from China has been popular at the Indian market, but the latter is still to export adequate service products to China, which resulted in the imbalance of the bilateral trade, growing from $800 million in 2005 to $4.12billion in 2006. And, the deficit inflated to $12 billion the next year. In 2016, the bilateral trade realized $71.1billion against the backdrop of the down-sliding global trade, which also brought the India-China trade deficit to an unprecedented $56 billion. Apparently, the trade deficit has long become an obstacle for the further growth of the bilateral relations. Based on the above analysis, China alone is not to blame for the growing trade imbalance.

Secondly, it is the misalignment of production chains. It is an open secret that the real nature of globalization is the fact that transnational corporations have been allocating factors of production around the world and carry out production and marketing of their patented products, in order to maximize expected commercial interests. Since China and India started economic reform and opening up strategies, the two countries have taken stock from their respective comparative advantages and joint the different global production chains, during which China has managed to attract the FDI totaled at more than $2 trillion. Currently, more than one million FDI related enterprises have registered and have been operating across the country, which have literally turned China into a "world factory". Meanwhile, China has also become a major overseas investing country, and Chinese enterprises have been extending their production chains into the international market in large scale, which have become the new force to power the global trade. In contrast, India has been dedicating its industrial endowments on information and service industries. The Indian enterprises have taken stock from the special relations that India enjoys with the developed nations as well as the comparative advantages in English, the global working language, promoted the rapid growth in information and service industries, and eventually established comparative advantages in service trade. The point is that, at the international level, China and India have joint different production chains, which are mostly not mutually complimentary in terms of bilateral trade. As a result, Manufacturing enterprises have to import the software products from developed countries, while India has to import manufacturing products from China, which has been providing fuel to the fire of trade imbalance.The above enterprises have been providing steam for China's economic development, and has transformed China into the largest trading nation and the second largest economy in the world. However, the ever growing trade surplus has also turned China into an easy target of the "anti-subsidiary" and "anti-dumping" investigation by trade partners including India.

Thirdly, it is the misalignment of trade capability. Research finds that economic globalization has produced two outstanding scenarios. One is that transnational corporations have been allocating resources at the global level, organizing productions and marketing of their end-products, which has led to the separation of commodity production, marketing and consumption around the world. To be specific, any product could be divided into various parts and be produced or manufactured in different countries any where in the world and be assembled and packaged in one country, and then be marketed in countries around the world. Over the years, China has taken stock from its Geo-position, relative cheap labor and huge market potential, managed to join the global production chains, build up the capacity to produce some 40% of the daily commodities and durable goods of the world, and managed to let "made-in-China" products to be popular around the world. Meanwhile, India has joint the global production chains with its software capability.

The above global chains have thus brought out the second scenario, which caused the "diversion" of the traditional trade flows between the countries. For example, India has large number of its citizens who are residing in Singapore and other countries or economies, who are specialized in indirect import and export trade between China and India. According to the traditional trade theory, the above transit trade from India to China would not be tallied as the Indian export to China, while direct trade has been mostly conducted by the Indian merchants. This is a typical case of "trade diversion".

Fourthly, it is the misalignment of trade policies. In accordance with the international experience, the development of the bilateral trade depends much on the market scale, the production capability as well as the capacity to provide each other with trad-able goods. China and India are the first and second most populous nation in the world, which are experiencing rapid expansion of consumption. From the perspective of structure of import and export, India exports mostly primary products to China, of which roughly half comes from the primary industries. Meanwhile, India imports mostly machinery products from China, contributing to about one half its annual total, and the rest are chemical products, metal ware, fibers and textile products, etc. Therefore, the above inter-industrial trade would easily cause the imbalance of the bilateral trade. Since the 21st century, the Indian government drastically cut down on the export of primary products to China, out of the consideration to protect natural resources and develop its manufacturing industries, which also added "fuel" to the burning trade deficit. Looking into the future, the cooperation in information industry could become one new area to promote the bilateral trade. However, the two countries are yet seriously to put the above cooperation on the agenda of the two governments, as India is still driven by the Cold War mentality, animosity toward and the security concern over China.

Fifthly, it is the misalignment of trade related investment. From the perspective of trade expansion, trade and investment are the "two wheels" for the healthy and stable bilateral economic and trade relations. When the trade relations reach to a certain level, expansion of mutual investment become the sure thing to further power the said relations forward, as the "two vehicles"are mutually complementary and inseparable to each other. Since the end of the Cold War, China and India both entered into the period of rapid economic growth and have evolved comparative advantages in different industries, which could have become the power-base for economic and trade cooperation via the two ways investment. However, since the second decade of the 21st century, the growth of mutual investment has been slow,with the total volume hovering around $20 billion. Meanwhile, Chinese capital has been outreaching to the world in large volumes, and has accumulated a total outbound flow of about $1 trillion, out of which India accounted for less than 1%. Apparently, the above scenario does not tally with the potential growth of the two-way investment, the growing market potentials as well as the prospects of the overall bilateral relations.

Sixthly, it is the misalignment of trade strategies. As mentioned above, China and India are the two most populous nations in the world, which collectively contribute to more than one third of the global population. As the two economies keep growing, the economic scales will expand accordingly, which are to result in the growing scale of the middle classes in the two countries, who are the main power for the global trade. The macadamia community has projected the 21st century to be the Asian Century, mainly based on the growing consumption on the Asian continent. Research finds that the consumption capability and its capacity to attract commodities are largely deciding the speed and the prospect of a nation in development. China and India are the second and seventh largest economy in the world, each has its own comparative advantages, and each has its own trade potentials. However, once one trade partner changes its trade policy, it would make it difficult for the bilateral trade to maintain the normal momentum. Take the China-India trade for example, the Indian government can readjust its China-related trade policy in order to address the bilateral trade imbalance by administrative measures for the time being. However, the actual consumption of the Indian people will continue to grow and will have to find other channels to import the same products,which are likely still the "made-in-China"products. The only difference is that the Indian customers have to pay more for the same products because of the "transit trade" factor. Therefore, in the long term, it is the industrial cooperation, rather than trade policy readjustment, will help address the issue of bilateral trade imbalance.

Last but not least, it is the misalignment of statistics. From the perspective of statistics, China has been exporting bulk manufactured goods which can be tallied accurately. Meanwhile, Indian exporters to China are mostly medium and small in scale and are mostly carrying out small scale exports to China which are easily missed in statistics by the Customs. In addition, China and India differ in the principle in the field of statistics in terms of transit trade via the third places such as Singapore and Hong Kong, which have helped to balloon up the Indian trade deficit with China. More importantly, India has comparative edge on China in the service trade, but it is not included in the statistics of the bilateral trade.

(III) The legacy of the border issue still at work on Indian side. The largest "historical crux" of the bilateral relations is still the border war in 1962. Between October and November 1962, the PLA launched the war of anti-aggression at the border at South Tibet between the two countries, and won the victory at the battle fields, maintained the security of its Southern border and dealt a heavy blow on the forces aiming at splitting Tibet from China. From the historical perspective, the war was not started by China and thus China was not to be held responsible for the war. However, in order to give the Indian side an opportunity to learn from the lesson, the Chinese troops withdrew to the northern side of the line of "actual control". However, the Indian troops took the advantage and occupied the disputed area of South Tibet until today.

The said border war was the end-result of military, political, security and diplomatic arm twisting between the two countries, which saw all the factors re-enforcing one another, producing impacts surpassing the pure military conflict. Chairman Mao Zedong gave comments on the war on several occasions and predicted that the war would bring peace at the border for at least 10 years. Unfortunately, it also brought the bilateral relations to the zero point at one time. In 1979, China and India restarted the negotiation on the border issue, and, for that matter, established the regular meeting mechanism of special representatives. In 2005, the two countries signed the "agreement on the political guidelines on the resolution of the border issue". In addition, the two governments also signed the "agreement on maintaining the peace and stability at the border area", the agreement on maintaining mutual trust, which allowed the two sides to establish a consultation and coordination mechanism on the border issues. In 2012, the two countries formally signed agreement in the above regard, which authorized the Ministry of Foreign Affairs of the two countries to lead the consultation on the border issues, drawing up regulations and procedures on the consultations and negotiations on the border issues among the officers and diplomats of the two countries, in order to facilitate conditions for the eventual resolution of the issue and for the development of the bilateral relations as a whole. In April, 2013, shortly before the scheduled visit by Premier Li Keqiang to India, the Indian side provoked the "tents confrontation" at the border area. However, the leaders of the two governments managed to avert the crisis. In October of the same year, the two governments signed the "agreement on border cooperation between the two governments"(BDCA), which is to prevent strategic misjudgment by either side and to prevent the border issues from becoming the "road blocks" for the bilateral relations of win-win cooperation. In 2014, 2015 and 2016 respectively, President Xi Jinping met with Prime Minister Modi on several occasions, during which they made political decisions on the border issue, and both leaders agreed to "compartmentalize" the thorny issue and concentrate on the cooperation in other areas. On February 22, 2017, China and India held the strategic dialogue, which also included the border issue. This has become an important channel of dialogue and communication which dedicates to the promotion of political cooperation and strategic trust, in order to cement the said strategic relations. However, the Indian side, in line with its consistent mindset, still insisted to link the border issue with possible Indian participation in the joint construction of the Belt and Road Initiative.

(IV) There are still conflicts of interests in security strategies. Ever since India realized its national independence, successive governments have regarded the Indian Ocean and the relevant countries in South Asia as its "front yard" or "rear yard", and "regarded the Indian Ocean as its life line." As early as in 1983, Indira Gandhi, the Prime Minister put forward the Indian version of "Monroe Doctrine," which stipulated that India would assume the responsibility of "manager" in South Asia. For that matter, India has always regarded any Chinese economic and commercial presence in the area as security to India, and regarded any military and economic cooperation between China and other countries in the region as the "encirclement on India". The main stream India media still has the view that, as the dominant neighbor, China would "exert south-ward expansion" once the country becomes strong and prosperous. And, as soon as the "new maritime silk road" manages to meet the "inland new silk road" in South Asia, the two roads would become the strategic tools for China to realize its strategy of "South-ward expansion". It is on the above assumption that India has regarded the positive responses to the BRI by the countries in South Asia and those around Indian Ocean as their "China cards" versus India. In the second half of 2014, the docking of the Chinese submarine fleet at the Colombo Port in Sri Lanka immediately sent the shocking waves to the sensitive political nerve of India, which promoted the rampant surge of "China threat." Consequently, India put forward the "Project of Mausa"as a tit-for-tat response. Meanwhile, India took stock from its special relations with Sri Lanka and succeeded in helping bring down the government friendly to China during the follow up general election, and made sure that the new government would put the harbor project on hold. However, the tall order of the countries in South Asia and around the Indian Ocean is the sustainable development which warrants the reliance on the Chinese market, capital, technologies and industrial transfers as well as the "public goods" that China could offer. Apparently, India was fully aware that it did not have those capabilities to satisfy their appetites, but still put forward the "Project of Mausa", in order to attract the attention of the international media and to reap the effects of "diplomatic hedging".

(V) There have been conflicting interests of the Geo-strategies. For long, India has regarded China as a competitor. It is true that China and India differ in ideology, strategic interests, and the two countries are still locked in the stalemate over the disputed border area of 125,000 square kilometers. For that matter, India has been on high alert as China moves forward fast in political, economic and military capabilities, carries out more and more interactions with other countries in South Asia and exerts more influence on its partners. Therefore, India has given paramount attention to the elevation of its military capability and regard it as the major tool to realize its national strategic goals, in order to ensure its dominating position in the region. It is still the view of India that "diplomacy must rest on the military might, and the former must subject to the latter, and the military capability is the "trump card" for diplomacy. For that matter, long since the end of the Cold War, India has been spending a large proportion of its annual budget on national defense and still regards China as the focal point for national defense policy. During the era of the post international financial crisis, as the Chinese economy keeps growing fast, countries headed by the United States have been intensifying their strategic encirclement on China, for which India found itself in a more favorable strategic position in terms of regional politics. For that matter, the developed countries have been courting collectively with India. Meanwhile, the Modi government has been outreaching in all directions, in an effort to gain an upper hand over China and "earning more chips" versus China. In order to realize its global strategy, the

Modi government has formulated and implemented an all round foreign policy, which dedicates to actively pursue relations with the developed countries in America, Europe and Asia, in order to attract the capital and technologies for its national development, to expedite industrial rejuvenation, realize the goal of leapfrog development, expand its military capability, and build up its global status as the nuclear power.

At the regional level, India still abides by the policy of "Non-alignment", and still carries out the policy of "strategic independence", in terms of the relations among India, the US, Russia and China, claiming not to take side with any other partner. However, in January 2015 when President Obama visited New Delhi, the two governments signed a joint communique, which stipulated that the "Indian Eastward Strategy" and the US "Pivotal to Asia" are to provide a historical opportunity for the two countries to step up closer cooperation with other countries in the Asia and Pacific, and provide steam for the regional cooperation. In 2016, President Trump basically inherited the Indian policy by the former administration and initiated telephone conversation with Prime Minister Modi ahead of President Xi Jinping, during which Trump called India as the best non-allied nation in the world. Based on the above analysis, India will find it hard to make the political decision to fully engage itself in the BRI.

(VI) Kashmir has remained a point for contention. For more than half a century, India and Pakistan have been standing face to face over the disputed area of Kashmir. For that matter, the two countries have been regarding the other side as the main competitor.

Kashmir is the short form of "Jammu and Kashmir", which is bordering with India, Pakistan, China and Afghanistan, and covers an area of some 190,000 square kilometers. The issue of Kashmir is the direct result of the policy of "divide and rule" by the British colonial power. In mid 18th century, the Indian Subcontinent became a colony of the British Empire. After WWII, India managed to win independence from the British colonial rule. In June, 1947, Mountbatten, the last British Governor to India drafted a master plan called "the Mountbatten Plan" to divide the Indian colony into two areas of administration and allow the latter to become two independent nations.

In accordance with the Mountbatten Plan, the areas where are mainly populated by the Hindus would belong to the future India, and where are mainly populated by the Muslims would belong to the future Pakistan. However, the British colonial masters made the decision that the future of Kashmir would be decided by the ruler of the native state to choose its future belonging or to remain independent. At that time, 77% of the local dwellers were Muslims, who preferred to join Pakistan. However, the king was Hindu who remained undecided at the initial stage, then shifting policy stands on whether to join Pakistan or India until the official separation of India and Pakistan, which resulted in the current status of Kashmir.

Soon after the separation, the two countries locked into the war in October of the same year over Kashmir, the first India-Pakistan War. In December 1947, the issue of Kashmir was put forward to the United Nations for arbitration. In August 1948 and January 1949 respectively, the United Nations passed the resolution to authorize the cease fire and authorize the referendum to decide the future of the territory, which were accepted by both India and Pakistan. Therefore, the cease fire came into force in January 1949, and cease fire line was drawn in July of the same year. According to the line, the area controlled by India would be under the administration of India, and that by Pakistan would under the jurisdiction of Pakistan, which allowed both sides to set up local authorities in the respective territories.

In August 1953, the prime ministers of India and Pakistan issued a joint communique after the consultation that the future of Kashmir would be decided by the local people in referendum. However, in June 1956, the two countries were locked into the second war over the same issue. In December 1971, the two countries were deep in the third war over the separation of East Pakistan from Pakistan, during which India sent the troops into part of the disputed area.

In July 1972, India and Pakistan signed the *"West Lamb Agreement"*, according to which both sides agreed to honor the cease fire line which was established in the 1971 agreement. In order to resolve the disputes, the leaders and ministers of the two countries held several talks but still failed to reach an agreement. Since 1989, the two countries encountered continuous armed conflicts over Kashmir, which brought huge damages to both sides.

On November 11, 2003, Mr.Jamal, the Pakistani Prime Minister announced that his government would withdrew the troops and would automatically stop fire on the Pakistani side of the line of actual control, effective on Balram (Id al Fitr). The next day, India welcome the above initiative and also adopted the reciprocal measures. Therefore, the military authorities of the two countries agreed after consultation the two Armies would stop fire starting from the midnight of the same day at the "international borderline" in Kashmir, the border line of actual control as well as at the Siachen actual contact line. The two sides also agreed to promote the permanent cease fire. On October 29, 2005, the two countries, after long negotiations, signed the Islamabad Agreement which warranted the opening of 5 check points along the line of actual control in Kashmir, allowing citizens to cross the line to carry out self-salvation after the earthquakes.

On the part of China, since late 1970s, the successive governments have readjusted the policy on South Asia and implemented the policy of "neutrality and peace promotion", which has provided the political foundation for China's strategy of friendly relations with both India and Pakistan. However, the BRI has enlisted Pakistan as one of the key countries, listed the China-Pakistan Economic Corridor as the flagship project, and jointly build the transportation and communication corridor which includes railways, highways, oil transportation pipelines, and optical cables. For that matter, Chinese government has committed a total investment of $46 billion while the proposed Chinese investment to India was only one third of the former. What is more, the CPEC is scheduled to cut across the disputed area of Kashmir where India and Pakistan are yet to seek agreement. Consequently, India subjectively assumed that China has joined hand with Pakistan to "infringe on the Indian core interests". In retaliation, India has lodged repeated protests and presentations.

Policy Thought on the BRI Projects Relating to India

Based on the above analysis, the Belt and Road Initiative has been moving forward in full swing, and the relevant trans-regional projects simply cannot bypass India. Meanwhile, as both China and India are on the fast track of growth, the economic frontiers of the two countries are bound to meet with each other which would naturally cause both contradictions and conversions. Looking into the future, India is an inseparable partner for China in terms of national rejuvenation, an indispensable condition as well as an important partner in successfully promoting the Belt and Road Initiative. Therefore, China has every reason to outreach to India and acquire the understanding of the latter, seek support and cooperation from the latter, or persuade the latter at least to go in parallel in regional cooperation in development.

(I) Actively promote strategic dialogues and seek the connectivity of strategies. Research finds that the "Project of Mausa" put forward by India in September 2014 covers countries on the subcontinent of South Asia, via Sri Lanka to extend westward to the countries in West Asia such as Iran,eastward to include countries in Southeast Asia such as Indonesia, southward to outreach to countries in East Africa, any of which are to converge with the potential partner countries of the maritime silk road. Therefore, China should carry effective bilateral dialogues and policy consultations with India, in order to promote the transparency of the BRI, promote the convergence of interests between the BRI and the Project of Mausa, avoiding possible confrontation between the two.

Firstly, the two sides should carry out dialogues and negotiations which would help promote the partnership between the regional connectivity networks under the BRI and the infrastructure scheme under the "12th Five Year Plan" by the Indian government, in order to promote the connectivity between China's building capacity and the demand by India in the same field. To start with, it is much desirable to start the cooperation in the areas of the technological renovation of the railways and highways across the country in India, expedite the process, in order to let people from all walks of life benefit from the "dividends" of joint construction, and pave the way for closer cooperation in other fields. As India has granted the first high speed railway project to Japan, China should wait for the next available opportunity to bid for specific contract, taking stock from the experience and lessons by Japanese company. As India is still harboring with strategic suspicion on the BRI, it is also desirable to detach India related projects from the BRI programs and carry them out via bilateral channels, observing the international standards, in order to facilitate compatible conditions for the BRI infrastructure networks to extend from Southeast Asia to South Asia and then move on to West Asia.

Secondly, further promote the bilateral economic and trade cooperation, in order to effectively address the imbalance of the bilateral trade. The two countries should actively pursue cooperation in the information industry which would provide the platform where the Chinese "hardware capabilities"could seek partnership with the Indian "software capabilities", in order to lay the foundation to expand bilateral economic and trade cooperation, and also to help address the issue of trade imbalance.

Thirdly, the two countries should take stock from the reconstruction of Afghanistan and give full play to the comparative advantages of the relevant industries of the two countries, which would bring out the "spill-over effects" of South-South cooperation and jointly display collective responsibility of emerging countries.

Fourthly, the two countries should join hands in identifying the areas of cooperation in regional security in and around the Indian Ocean as well as that in South China Sea, which would help promote cooperation in other areas and further promote political mutual trust and transparency of security policies.

Fifthly, the two countries should join hands with India as well as countries in and around the Indian Ocean, discover and preserve cultural legacies of the ancient maritime silk road, carry on and carry forward the new spirit of maritime silk road and facilitate conditions for it to be part of the common heritage of the global civilization.

(II) Strengthen policy dialogues and provide institutional support for the growth of the bilateral trade. China and India have different national situations, different economic structures, as well as the different industrial comparative advantages, which would jointly result in different capacity to participate in and to compete in the field of bilateral trade. Therefore, leaders of the two countries should take stock from the frequent visits and summits among leader of the two countries, during which they could make strategic decisions and provide political guidance on how to further promote the overall bilateral relations. The two governments should hold regular meetings, which would allow the relevant ministers to effectively implement the consensus of the two leaders, and transform the political decisions into concrete policy measures. The two countries should fully utilize the good working relations at the multilateral institutions, start negotiation on the long overdue bilateral free trade agreement, in order to provide legal framework for the bilateral trade promotion and effective resolution of the economic and trade disputes.

(III) Increase two-way investment and promote balanced economic and trade cooperation. The two countries should facilitate conditions to negotiate and sign the bilateral investment agreement, which would provide the legal and institutional support for closer cooperation in economy and trade. Currently, China has become the prime trade partner for India, but the latter is experiencing an ever growing trade deficit, which has become the "road block" that the two countries cannot pass-by. For that matter, China should encourage and support its national enterprises to increase investment in

India, produce and market appropriate products at the local market via joint adventure or sole capital, or jointly market the said products at the third markets around the world, which would help indirectly address the bilateral trade imbalance. The two governments should start negotiation and sign the agreement on protection of intellectual property rights,which would in turn provide legal protection for the information exchanges and technology cooperation, and provide policy guidance for the two countries to carry out trio-party cooperation with any other countries.

(IV) Promote mutual learning and adaptation and jointly promote cultural cooperation. Cultural industry is an important benchmark to judge the stages of development of a country, while the cultural relations constitute the "barometer" for the relations between or among countries. Indian culture is still shining with traditional characteristics after some 6,000 years over the history, while Chinese culture still carries the beauty of the oriental culture. Over the history, Buddhism was born from Hinduism but evolved into an independent religion, which became the spirit and cultural legacy among peoples in many countries along the maritime silk road. Prime Minister Modi said well when he was receiving the visiting President Xi Jinping that "India and China are the two bodies with one soul." Therefore, cooperation in culture could become the "greatest divisor" for the two countries to push forward the joint construction of the Belt and Road Initiative. To be specific, the two countries should regard it as the "convergence of interests" to rejuvenate the two cultures, and fortify the efforts to implement the political consensus in the said cooperation, negotiate and sign agreement on joint cooperation in research into the "Buddhist connectivity", endeavor to connect as many historical placed across India as possible via the joint construction of high-speed railway and highways, which would go a long way to promote the cultural connectivity between the two countries, and lay the solid human and cultural foundation for the joint construction.

(V)Promote industrial cooperation with energy industry as a platform. China and

India are faced with the spiral growth of dependency on the international market for energy and natural resources. Over the recent years, companies of the two countries have formed the actual partnership or become competitors on many occasions to look for opportunities to prospect and exploit oil and gas along the Belt and Road. Therefore, the two countries should have more reasons to form the partnership in the above area, which would be desirable to invite more Indian companies to join the construction of the transportation pipelines to connect Central Asia, South Asia and West Asia, deepen the existing cooperation in Africa in terms of joint exploitation, joint processing, joint transportation and joint management of the pipeline security, which would warrant the equal distribution of the dividends in proportion to the contribution by the stakeholders. This would certainly help to provide energy support for both countries in terms of economic development, and promote peace and stability in South Asia.

(VI) Effectively manage the relations between interests and moral obligations. The starting point of the BRI is the joint construction, in order to promote the mutual connectivity of infrastructure networks, while the foothold is to promote common development and coordinated governance, in order to provide steam for mutual trade, mutual investment and industrial cooperation, which would facilitate conditions for the regional integration. During the above historical period, China should join hands with India to promote the compatible international benchmarks via bilateral or multilateral cooperation, establish norms for South-South cooperation, and build up the platform for common development. Both countries should uphold the concept of moral and commercial profit, hold high the banner of "mutual benefit" and "win-win cooperation", and incorporate them into the practice of joint construction and common development. From the political perspective, the two countries should list the issue into the agenda of the bilateral strategic dialogue and establish the ways and means for India related joint projects, formulate regulations, ensure the fair rights and obligations, in order to promote the connectivity of the industries or resources with comparative advantages, expedite national development and harvest the benefit of the "spill-over effect", and provide "positive energy" for the growth of the world economy. To be more specific, future India-related projects should take into consideration of the interests under the Indian "Strategy to Look East" as well as those under the "Spice Voyages", in order to cement the spirit of "mutual benefit" and "win-win outcome", which would serve to soften the strategic suspicion of India on China. In the economic arena, Chinese government should educate and guide its national entrepreneurs to carry out business operations in line with the local laws and international practice, strive to build cordial relations with local partners, respect the local cultures and traditions, and carefully address the reallocation of the temples and their reconstructions. The government should educate and guide its national companies to carry out the corporate social responsibilities and establish the "interests and obligation bonds" with the local governments and social organizations, in order to win over their support and cooperation, which would in turn add steam for the maintenance of project construction and operation.

(VII) Search and establish new ways and means for human and cultural cooperation. There should be no doubt that the BRI is dedicating to the development promotion and common prosperity, which is eventually to improve the well beings of the peoples of the partner countries. For that matter, the India-related projects should regard economic cooperation as the foundation, give full play to the comparative advantages that both countries have, give priority to the joint construction in transportation, energy transportation pipelines, in order to promote the two-way trade, create new areas for trade growth, help to address the trade imbalance. Both countries should expand industrial cooperation, facilitate conditions for the two-way investment, and encourage enterprises of both countries to fully participate in the construction of economic belts and major connectivity networks in major cities. Meanwhile, both governments should attach importance to people-to-people exchanges, broaden scales of overseas students' programs and jointly establish colleges and universities, which would help to carry on and carry forward the cooperative spirit of the new silk road. Taking into account that India does not support the scheme to establish Confucius Institutes, suspecting that the scheme would result in "cultural expansion by the Chinese side", the two governments should allow each other to establish cultural centers which are to dedicate to promote Taiji and Yoga, and promote excellent cultures of the two countries. Explore possibilities of establishing cooperation mechanism of mass media between the two countries, join hands in preserving projects under the world heritage framework, step up cooperation in the tourist industry, and give full play to the function of "bridges" by the political parties, parliament, mass media, think tanks and the NGOs, in an effort to cement the foundation of public opinion and social foundation.

(VIII)Attach importance to education and guidance to mass media. The two countries should formulate the joint publicity mechanism in line with the national situation and public opinion in India,which would serve to present the real voice from China and present real Chinese stories, in order to provide "positive energy" for the construction of the India-related projects. There should be no denying that the Indian mass media is most outspoken in inciting "China threats" among developing countries. Relevant department of the government should dig deep into the relevant laws and regulations in India, do research into the current institution in the sector, and strive to establish institutional cooperation in the field of news and mass media, and strengthen supervision over the official and non-official mass media. China should take full advantage of publicity at the international arena, accurately explain the real essence of the BRI, provide the international community with "positive energy", take initiative in guiding the mass media, share light on the principles of "joint consultation, joint construction, and sharing", and stress the mutual benefit, openness and inclusiveness of the said joint construction.

(IX) Prudently handle the triangle relations among China, India and Pakistan. Pakistan is strategically located in the security structure of China's surrounding area, and has become the "experiment ground" as well as the "bridgehead" of the BRI. In accordance with the bilateral relations and political and economic situation in South Asia, China should conduct issue specific dialogues with India and explain China's absolute necessity to construct the South-bound seaport, in an effort to reduce Indian strategic suspicion, help India and Pakistan to get out of the vicious circle of "tit for tat" and construct the new ways for the trio-party relations to move out of the long standing stalemate of the disputes and conflicts. Therefore, China should fully utilize the "greatest divisor" of peaceful development among the three countries, promote all round cooperation among three countries. China should make full use of the platform of the China-Pakistan Economic Corridor" and the Economic Corridor of Bangladesh, China, India and Myanmar, which would help to push three pairs of bilateral relations to move forward in parallel. On top of that, China should persuade countries in South Asia, especially India and Pakistan to join the construction of the connectivity networks, facilitate conditions for the three countries to form the "interest community" in the field of energy and natural resources, via joint planning, joint development, joint processing and joint marketing. China should take stock from the reconstruction of Afghanistan, and form the interest's community of security cooperation, and contribute to the stable development of the bilateral relations between India and Pakistan.

(X) Attach importance on reducing deficit of political trust. China should maintain the momentum of high level visits and summits, which would allow leaders of the two countries to make political decision on major issues relating to the bilateral relations, and carry out strategic planning on bilateral, regional and global issues, contributing to elevating strategic mutual trust. China should give full play to the bilateral strategic and economic dialogues, exchange experience on national governance, coordinate industrial policies, expand areas of cooperation in an orderly manner, and search for effective ways and means to address the economic and trade disputes. China should improve the above said dialogue mechanisms, more effectively coordinate regional policies, establish and expand the convergence of interests, as well as the interests' community in the area of politics, economy and security. China should continue to give full play to the ministerial dialogue mechanism among China, Russia and India, in order to further promote mutual trade, mutual investment and industrial cooperation. China should join hands with India and promote regional and international cooperation in governance, put forward joint agendas, protect the common interests, and strive for the common international space for development. China should effectively deepen the bilateral academic cooperation, in order to jointly carry out researches on the historical connectivity, jointly discover and reconstruct the legacies of history and culture, jointly carry forward the spirit of the ancient silk road, and jointly create the new brilliance of the silk road.

2 韩国与"一带一路"倡议：在疑虑和参与中徘徊

朱锋　武海宝

自 2013 年底国家主席习近平提出"一带一路"的战略构想以来，我国政府于 2015 年 3 月 28 日在博鳌论坛上正式提出《推动共建丝绸之路经济带和 21 世纪海上丝绸之路的愿景与行动》的文件，希望有关各国秉持"和平合作、开放包容、互学互鉴、互利共赢"的理念，全方位推进务实合作，打造政治互信、经济融合、文化包容的"利益共同体"、"命运共同体"和"责任共同体"。在中国及有关各方的共同努力下，"一带一路"构想已经和正在得到越来越多国家的认可和支持。

2017 年 5 月举办的"一带一路"国际合作高峰论坛更是"一带一路"倡议提出以来的盛事。然而就在高峰论坛日益临近的这段时间，有一个国家则显得非常焦虑，因为作为亚投行创始成员国，韩国尚没有收到我国政府的正式邀请出席高峰论坛。韩国对中国的"一带一路"倡议有着怎样的认识和态度，韩国国内对"一带一路"倡议有哪些具体反应；在中韩关系上，中国政府应该如何切实处理好政治安全议题与经济议题之间的关系，韩国的看法值得关注。

韩国对"一带一路"的认知和态度

　　韩国关于"一带一路"的认知和态度呈现两极分化态势。自中国"一带一路"倡议提出以来，韩国国内大体出现以下两种声音和两种态度：一种是积极支持，另一种则是满腹犹疑，呈现两极分化态势。

（一）积极支持

　　新闻界、学术界以及政府工商部门、民间工商界人士一般都倾向于支持韩国积极对接中国的"一带一路"。这派观点认为，韩国现在的经济处于低迷状态，对接中国的"一带一路"倡议可能会使韩国经济有一个较为乐观的前景。他们看到"一带一路"与朴槿惠提出的"欧亚倡议"非常契合，认为如果两大倡议实现对接，将推动地区一体化进程，联通活跃的东亚经济圈和发达的欧洲经济圈，尤其可以把韩国与能源丰富的俄罗斯及欧洲和中亚的广阔消费市场紧密连接起来。[1]在助推中韩两国更加紧密地与世界经济融合发展的同时，激活欧亚大陆的经济增长潜力，并进一步影响和带动全球经济复苏。因此，他们积极支持更加紧密的对华经济互动，高度赞扬习近平主席提出的通过合作共赢的方式建设全球命运共同体的观点。在他们看来，中国通过"一带一路"计划试图构建的新型国际关系，即世界各国相互商议、共同建设、共享利益的秩序。不论社会主义国家还是资本主义国家，不论宗教信仰、价值观，所有国家都能相互合作[2]。同时，他们也对"一带一路"倡议实施最终取得成果充满信心。韩国《中央日报》把习近平的外交解读为"围棋外交"："一带一路战略构想是'三边通中央必胜'，即如果将亚洲、欧

---

　　[1]　［韩］Kim Hee-Jin：\"AIIB head 'optimistic' about Korea,\" *The Korea Joongang Daily*，September 10, 2015, p. 4。

　　[2]　［韩］刘尚哲：《习近平拟构建的国际新秩序》，《中央日报》，http://chinese.joins.com/gb/article. do?method=detail&art_id=134305&category=002005，2015 年 4 月 22 日。

洲和非洲三个大陆通过一带一路计划连接就一定会取胜的围棋打法。"①

（二）满腹疑虑

除了积极支持的声音外，韩国国内还有另外一种声音，即对中国"一带一路"持保留和疑虑态度。持这种态度的主要包括亲美人士以及一些国内智库机构。他们主要从政治上考虑问题，认为中国不可信任，"一带一路"的政治风险太高。在他们看来，"一带一路"虽然被描述为经济战略，但其中掺杂着中国的地缘政治意图。他们惧怕中国正在增长的地区优势，且担心"一带一路"最终变成排挤目前占主导地位的美国主导的安全战略的一个手段，使中国成为该地区唯——个有决定性影响的大国，进而侵蚀到包括韩国在内的亚洲邻国的经济和政治自主性。"对于那些向中国借钱用于建设的国家而言，如果项目进展不顺利，就有可能因为负债而被中国牵着鼻子走"，"'一带一路'并非单纯像中国所主张的那样是为了实现互惠互利，稍有差池便有可能会导致国家经济主权落入中国的手中。"② "韩国有可能再次被纳入中华秩序之中。在那种秩序下既没有公平正当的交易，也没有朝鲜弃核与韩半岛统一。"③ 同时，这些人对实施"一带一路"的可行性也抱有疑虑，认为其不可能成为一个改变亚洲和欧洲间经济和物流联系的计划。不过，值得一提的是，虽然他们持消极的看法，但是并没有彻底否定参与"一带一路"建设的可能性，只是强调要综合平衡经济上获得的收益和政治上所冒的风险。

总的来看，韩国国内尽管有两种不同声音，但是，随着中国政府推动"一带一路"战略的务实举措不断出台，亚投行和丝路基金的设立，周边外交攻势的加强，韩国对"一带一路"倡议的态度有逐渐向好的方面转变的趋势。即使是一些持消极看法的人士，他们也认为，"至少从目前看来，'一带一路'带来的中韩贸易壁

---

① ［韩］刘尚哲：《酷似围棋的习近平外交》，《中央日报》，http://chinese.joins.com/gb/article. do?method=detail&art_id=136059&category=002003，2015 年 6 月 3 日。

② ［韩］李吉星：《一带一路高铁驶不出中国》，《朝鲜日报》，http://cnnews.chosun.com/client/news/ viw.asp?cate=C01&mcate=M1002&nNewsNumb=20161046214&nidx=46215，2016 年 10 月 7 日。

③ ［韩］杨相勋：《在中国遇到的荒唐之事》，《朝鲜日报》，http://cnnews.chosun.com/client/news/ viw.asp?cate=C08&mcate=M1001&nNewsNumb=20160745562&nidx=45563，2016 年 7 月 29 日。

垒的削减、交通运输基础设施的合作都是值得欢迎的，而政治风险也是可控的。"①近期，《朝鲜日报》的一篇文章《中国"一带一路"打入希腊港口》就很能说明问题。该文指出，习近平最初提出"一带一路"时，很多人认为这不过是一种"政治性修辞"。中国媒体报道的"将44亿人口（全世界人口的63%）和21万亿美元经济圈（全世界的29%）连系在一起"，让人感觉不过是个梦。然而在中国国家主席习近平2013年9月首次提出"一带一路"战略后时隔2年零4个月，"一带一路"就打到了欧洲的眼皮底下。习近平每次出访海外时，都强调"一带一路"，中国当局已慢慢将自己的旗帜插在了海外据点港口上。中国进军的世界主要港口，已多达20多个。②这些充分说明，中国在推动"一带一路"上越是务实、越能给相关国家带来实实在在的利益，也就越容易得到包括韩国在内的多数国家的认可。

韩国矛盾性认知的原因分析

韩国对"一带一路"的矛盾性认知主要来源于其特殊的地缘政治和经济利益，其经济诉求高度依赖于中国，而政治和安全诉求高度依赖于美国是造成这种"精神分裂"的主要原因。

（一）经济上高度依赖中国

韩国是中国的重要邻国。中韩建交之初，双边贸易额约50亿美元，2014年，双边贸易额接近3000亿美元，比建交时增长约60倍。截至2015年6月，中国是韩国最大的贸易伙伴、最大海外投资对象国、最大出口市场、最大进口来源国、最大旅行目的地国、最大留学生来源国。中韩双边贸易额超过韩国对

---

① ［韩］Sukjoon Yoon："China's Belt and Road Initiative: The South Korean Perspective"，*China International Studies*，December 30, 2015, p. 4.

② ［韩］安勇炫、李伐沧:《中国一带一路打入希腊港口》,《朝鲜日报》, http://cnnews.chosun.com/client/news/viw.asp?cate=C01&mcate=M1002&nNewsNumb=20160143368&nidx=43369，2016年1月22日。

外贸易总额的 1/5，超过了韩美、韩欧贸易额的总和。

2015 年签署的中韩自贸协定为推动两国经济增长增添了新动力。据测算，中韩自贸协定能够拉动中国实际 GDP 增长 0.34 个百分点，拉动韩国实际 GDP 增长 0.97 个百分点。[①]中韩经济的这种高度依赖性使"一带一路"倡议在韩国有着深厚的"经济基础"。韩国政府以及国内民众对于这一点有着非常明确而清醒的认识。韩国在经济上高度依赖中国不是一个观点，而是一个事实。

时任中国外交部国际经济司副司长刘劲松曾拿"一带一路"的"陆海联运"为韩国朋友算过一笔账。他指出，长期以来，亚洲国家沿海地区比较发达，海运比较成熟，也确实便宜。但是近年来，随着中国高铁技术的成熟和高铁建设的蓬勃发展，欧亚大陆正掀起新一轮铁路建设的高潮，铁路运输的性价比正进一步优化。一个集装箱从东北亚的港口运至北欧，需要 35 天左右时间，花费两三千美元；现在如果用铁路运，只要 15 天时间，花费七八千美元。虽然运费还是高一些，但时间省了不少。而且从中国"渝新欧"等中欧班列运营的情况看，中外企业认为内陆地区的货物用铁路运输、陆海联运或多式联运的效益日益明显。中国各地已经创建了十多条中欧班列路线，它们是丝绸之路经济带的早期收获，给沿线国家带来了实实在在的利益。[②]

前面提到韩国的工商界积极支持对接"一带一路"倡议，其主要原因就在于他们从中尝到了与中国开展互利合作的甜头。比如，作为韩中两国共同开发的韩中 FTA 产业园区的新万金地区建设主要把"一带一路"视为该项目建设的主要机遇和依托。"只要新万金开发项目与中国的'一带一路'政策、中国的资本相结合，韩国和中国就能双赢。"[③]

另外，韩国近年来经济发展一直比较低迷，GDP 增速由 2011 年的 3.7% 大幅下

① 肖玮：《中韩自贸协定将拉动国内 GDP 0.3 个百分点》，新华网，http://news.xinhuanet.com/fortune/2015-06/03/c_127872850.htm，2015 年 6 月 3 日。

② 刘劲松：《"一带一路"对接韩国"欧亚倡议"，中韩如何利益共享？》，观察者网，http://www.guancha.cn/LiuJinsong/2015_07_22_327661_s.shtml，2015 年 7 月 22 日。

③ ［韩］金圣虎：《一带一路与新万金共同开创新机遇》，《朝鲜日报》，http://cnnews.chosun.com/client/news/viw.asp?cate=C01&mcate=M1001&nNewsNumb=20150640608&nidx=40609，2015 年 6 月 26 日。

滑至 2012 年的 2.3%，2013 年和 2014 年分别增至 2.9% 和 3.3%，但 2015 年至 2016 年，连续两年保持在 2.8% 的水平。[①]中国作为韩国最大的贸易伙伴，对韩国经济能否企稳回升具有绝对的影响力，这也使韩国对中国"一带一路"倡议更加倚重。

（二）政治和安全上高度依赖美国

尽管"一带一路"带来的利益诱人，但韩国依然不无戒心。这主要是因为，韩国在处理"一带一路"的对接问题上，不仅要考虑自身的利益以及中国的态度，还要同时考虑美国的态度。韩国在加入亚投行的拉锯战中表现出的犹疑不定，就充分体现了这一点。而这种矛盾心态是韩国所处的特殊地缘政治和经济状态所决定的。从经济上说，中国已成为韩国的第一大伙伴国；但安保上，韩国却严重依赖美国的军事力量。近期韩国不顾中国的强烈反对而坚持引进部署萨德可以看做韩国对于自身安全的隐忧和对美国安全依赖的集中表现。这种"双重户籍"的现象使韩国很难独立决定自己的政策，或者说韩国总是试图在平衡与中美两个大国的关系，希望在中美间尽量做到"左右逢源"，并在这个过程中争取最大的国家利益。韩国前外交部长尹炳世曾于 2015 年表达出这样一种观点：如果韩国能够通过现行外交策略来平衡中美这两个地区大国的影响力，韩国就应该能获得并享用自己的那份蛋糕。[②]而韩国的这种平衡术也确实发挥了一定作用。比如，它曾不顾美国反对而加入亚投行，同时也不顾中国反对引进部署萨德系统。

韩国对"一带一路"倡议的反应

韩国国内对于中国"一带一路"倡议的反应随着时间的推移，经历了一个从

---

① 王晨：《韩国央行：2016 年韩国 GDP 增速 2.8%，GNI 仍未突破 3 万美元》，环球网，http://finance.huanqiu.com/gjcx/2017-03/10389431.html?open_source=weibo_search，2017 年 3 月 28 日。

② ［韩］尹锡俊：《韩国积极参与"一带一路"，为何不怕美国生气》，澎湃新闻，http://www.thepaper.cn/newsDetail_forward_1338161，2015 年 6 月 4 日。

犹疑到理解、接受再到积极推进两国倡议对接合作的过程。这个过程大体分为以下几个阶段：

（一）欧亚倡议：韩国对中国"一带一路"战略的最初反应

韩国"欧亚合作倡议"是朴槿惠 2013 年 10 月提出的重要国际合作倡议和国家发展战略，该倡议以朝鲜半岛和俄罗斯远东地区为中心，主要合作对象是中国、中亚、俄罗斯、蒙古、土耳其，旨在通过与欧亚地区国家的经济合作，形成"团结的、创造性的、和平的大陆"，以实现欧亚地区的可持续繁荣与和平。欧亚倡议具体包含三个方案，即建设"丝绸之路快车"（从釜山出发，贯通朝鲜、俄罗斯、中国、中亚，直到欧洲），构建"欧亚能源网"，实现"欧亚经济统合"。韩国欧亚合作倡议的提出在时间上紧随习近平主席于 2013 年 9 月、10 月首次提出"一带一路"倡议之后，可以看做韩国对于中国"一带一路"倡议的最初反应。朴槿惠在 2015 年 6 月会见我国全国人大常委会委员长张德江时提及中国推进的"一带一路"构想，表示韩国政府正在推进的"欧亚倡议"与"一带一路"有很多共同点，希望两国携手合作，创造协同效应。[①]对于"欧亚倡议"与"一带一路"的关系，韩国对外经济政策研究院欧亚室室长李载荣曾解读道："欧亚倡议"和"一带一路"的契合点主要在中国的东北三省和俄罗斯，中方的财力资源、韩方的技术支持加上第三方国家的资源优势可以实现互惠共赢。[②]在朴槿惠提出欧亚倡议后，2013 年 11 月 29 日，韩国《中央日报》以"读者投稿"栏目（即评论）的方式，在题为《30 亿"丝绸之路经济圈"起步》的报道中，首次提及中国的"一带一路"："中国国家主席习近平 2013 年 9 月曾提议中国与中亚各国连接各国交通网，建成从太平洋直通波罗的海的大通道，这个所谓'构建 30 亿人口的丝绸之路经济圈'计划的核心，就是将中国与中亚的巨大市场连成一个单一经济合作体。"

---

① 韩联社：《朴槿惠会见中国全国人大常委会委员长张德江》，http://chinese.yonhapnews.co.kr/newpgm/9908000000.html?cid=ACK20150611003200881，2015 年 6 月 11 日。

② 刘劲松：《"一带一路"对接韩国"欧亚倡议"，中韩如何利益共享？》，观察者网，http://www.guancha.cn/LiuJinsong/2015_07_22_327661_s.shtml，2015 年 7 月 22 日。

随着 2014 年 7 月 3 日中国国家主席习近平对韩国的国事访问，"一带一路"在韩国的关注度进一步升温，韩国媒体开始对中国"一带一路"概念进行较为深入的介绍与解读，包括亲、诚、惠、容的理念和中国领导人的"一带一路"外交。韩国主流媒体《中央日报》甚至向政府建议，认为"有必要探索韩国的'欧亚计划'和中国的'新丝绸之路构想'之间的联系"，"如果两大构想能联系起来，那么中国将成为连接韩国与远东亚洲、中亚、中东、欧洲的桥梁，两国的竞争力也会得到进一步提高。"

（二）犹疑再三加入亚投行

2014 年 10 月 24 日，包括中国在内的 21 个国家代表汇聚北京，正式签署了《筹建亚洲基础设施投资银行备忘录》，由此，中国"一带一路"倡议的实践进入"亚投行时间"。针对加入亚投行的问题，韩国政府起初一直持保留态度，表现出较大的犹疑，这种犹疑的焦点主要在于考虑美国的态度和影响。在美国看来，亚投行的成立，是中国与美日欧的国际金融秩序主导权之争。而韩国与美国是军事同盟关系，因此，韩国不得不考虑美国的立场和态度。但是随着中国在博鳌亚洲论坛 2015 年年会上发起的外交攻势，韩国政府的态度有所变化。国内开始出现把经济考量与政治考量分开的论调："对于中国的新丝绸之路战略，要从经济角度而不是从政治角度来处理。只有这样才能营造加入的氛围。""新丝绸之路战略的核心地区中东和东南亚是韩国的第一、第二大建设市场。如果中国在该地区社会间接资本建设中投入巨额资金，对于韩国来说也是个机会。"[1]同时，韩国舆论也公开讨论中美两个大国在亚洲的角逐，认为习近平提出的"一带一路"与奥巴马提出的"亚洲网"相冲突，而韩国既是一带一路的后方，又是亚太再平衡的前方。[2]在这种讨论中，国内舆论开始明显倾向于务实的"国家利益"、"经济实用主义"等，

---

① ［韩］韩友德:《韩国要加入亚洲基础设施投资银行的理由：抓住"中国新丝绸之路战略"机会》,《中央日报》, http://chinese.joins.com/gb/article.do?method=detail&art_id=132009&category=002005, 2015 年 3 月 2 日。

② ［韩］蔡秉健:《习近平的"带"与奥巴马的"网"谁能覆盖亚洲？》,《中央日报》, http://chinese.joins.com/gb/article.do?method=detail&art_id=133308&category=002002, 2015 年 3 月 31 日。

认为韩国应该从务实的角度出发加入亚投行。最终，在英国的加入掀起亚投行参与的高潮后，韩国政府顺应大势，从两国关系的现状和未来发展考虑，在中国政府设定的申请成为亚投行创始会员国的最后期限来临之际，选择加入亚投行，将中韩关系提升到新高度。随后，国内还出现了对于美国干扰韩国加入亚投行的不满声音。《中央日报》援引美国前国务卿鲍威尔的文章称：亚投行是一个不错的构想，美国过于性急地对亚投行和加入亚投行的国家进行批判，这种批判应该停止。[①]随着韩国加入亚投行，韩国国内民众对于中国"一带一路"倡议的认识逐步深入。韩国国内媒体也加大了对中国"一带一路"倡议的宣介力度。《中央日报》社还组织实地采访组，分两组采访了中国连云港、郑州、兰州、乌鲁木齐、霍尔果斯，哈萨克斯坦的阿拉木图，吉尔吉斯斯坦的比什凯克，乌兹别克斯坦的塔什干，并推出了以《中国"一带一路"促进现状及对韩国产生的影响》为题的系列报道。

（三）中韩签订"一带一路"合作备忘录

2015 年 6 月，《中韩自由贸易协定》正式签署，为中韩在"一带一路"倡议与欧亚倡议实施的对接上奠定了坚实基础。10 月 31 日，在李克强总理和朴槿惠总统的见证下，双方签署了《关于在丝绸之路经济带和 21 世纪海上丝绸之路建设以及欧亚倡议方面开展合作的谅解备忘录》。两国领导人商定加强在制造业政策、设计领域研究、绿色工厂等领域的交流与合作，尤其是加快建立工业机器人领域的长期合作机制，推进韩国拥有的技术优势和中国的筹资能力相结合，携手进军第三国的基础设施建设和成套设备市场，积极推动韩国政府提出的"制造业创新 3.0"战略与中国政府提出的"中国制造 2025"挂钩，实现两国制造业转型升级。双方还商定将韩国的"欧亚倡议"与中国的"一带一路"战略联动，通过中国倡议建立的亚投行促进韩企进军海外。为此，两国决定研究共同设立基金提供资金支持的方案。在金融领域，两国商定在上海建立韩元对人民币直接交易市场，允许韩

---

① ［韩］金永熙：《鲍威尔：亚投行是一个好构想，美国批判过于性急》，《中央日报》，http://chinese.joins.com/gb/article.do?method=detail&art_id=134617&category=002002，2015 年 4 月 29 日。

国政府发行人民币债券。

（四）商议合作项目，构建对接平台

随着合作的深入，"一带一路"倡议与欧亚倡议的对接也逐步进入务实操作的层面。韩国副总理兼企划财政部长柳一镐在第 14 次韩中经济部长会议上表示，韩中两国应通过双赢合作实现"韩中梦"，并提出构建中国"一带一路"战略和韩国"亚欧倡议"对接平台，在重点推进"一带一路"战略的亚洲、非洲及基建、信息通信技术、能源、钢铁领域与中国展开联合调研，为开拓第三方市场加强信息交流，探索通过多边开发金融机构和进出口银行为企业提供金融支持，加快推进中国珲春和俄罗斯扎鲁比诺港开发试点项目。中方则提出以东北三省为重心对接两国倡议。两国还公布了参与共同开拓第三方市场试点项目的两国企业配对结果，并签署了关于创投合作的谅解备忘录。双方务实合作进一步深入。韩国企业也积极行动起来，今年 3 月，韩国大韩贸易投资振兴公社（KOTRA）组织的"机器人路演"登陆武汉和西安，并与当地 10 多家企业进行合作洽谈，推动韩国机器人企业大举进军中国市场。①

（五）未被邀请参加峰会表现焦虑

随着韩国亲信干政事件的发生，朴槿惠被弹劾，并被批捕入狱，新的总统大选正在如火如荼地进行中，韩国政局正在发生重大变化。但是，这些变化似乎并没有影响韩国对于"一带一路"倡议实施的热情。2017 年 3 月，韩国舆论对于未收到中国即将于 5 月举行的"一带一路"高峰论坛的正式邀请表现出一种失落和焦虑的情绪。《中央日报》3 月 4 日以醒目标题《中国举行"一带一路"论坛 韩国政府人士无一受邀》发布文章称，中国政府已经邀请全球 60 多个国家的领导人和部长级官员出席今年峰会，但韩国至今未曾接到任何邀请。连日本、澳大利亚等与中国存在矛盾或者与"一带一路"关系不大的国家，中国都向它们发出了经

① 韩联社：《韩"机器人路演"登陆武汉和西安》，http://chinese.yonhapnews.co.kr/newpgm/9908000000.html?cid=ACK20170313002400881，2017 年 3 月 13 日。

济部门部长级邀请函，甚至还正尝试邀请美国贸易代表办公室代表出席会议。然而，韩国政府不仅没有接到总统或总理邀请函，连部长级别的与会邀请也没有收到。该报道还称，韩国不止没有接到邀请函，中国甚至从未试探过韩国出席会议的意愿，只有国际交流财团和对外经济政策研究院的代表接到了参加智库下属委员会的邀请，也就是说从邀请规格来看，韩国沦为了规格最低的邀请对象。该报分析称，中国可能是因为部署萨德的问题而故意冷落韩国，同时也援引了东南亚国家某外交官的言论表达了一种忿忿不平的情绪："韩国作为与'一带一路'密不可分的亚洲基础设施投资银行理事会年会（6月举行）举办国，却被排除在会议的受邀对象之外，感觉有些过分了。"[1]据悉，时任韩国驻华大使金章洙已向中方商务、文化、旅游等相关部门申请面谈，但已过去几个月，却未得到任何答复。关于未被邀请参加高峰论坛一事，除"冷落韩国说"之外，韩国国内还有另外一种声音，即对韩国的外交政策进行反思。这种观点认为，不能将责任全部推给中国，因为韩国在努力解读中方战略意图、消除中国不必要的忧虑一事上存在疏漏。韩国某外交官员表示，2016年6月底时任总理黄教安访华，在会见中国国家主席习近平时曾称"未就萨德做出任何决定"，但在距此还不到10天后却突然宣布部署萨德。他认为，"我们不成熟的应对引发中国政府的不信任，这也是导致事情如此不顺利的重要原因之一。"[2]

（六）亚投行第二届年会表现积极

2017年6月16日，亚投行第二届年会在韩国济州岛开幕。在开幕式演讲中，新任总统文在寅对"一带一路"倡议给予了高度评价，称韩国是丝绸之路在远东这一端最东面的国家，非常明确地把韩国与中国的丝绸之路倡议连接起来。[3]而

---

① ［韩］芮荣俊：《中国举行一带一路论坛　韩国政府人士无一受邀》，《中央日报》，http://jciadmin.joins.com/gb/article.do?method=detail&art_id=163978，2016年3月4日。

② ［韩］芮荣俊：《韩媒：韩国外交不成熟　令萨德矛盾加剧》，《中央日报》，http://chinese.joins.com/gb/article.aspx?art_id=164028，2017年3月6日。

③ 王力为：《亚投行年会｜文在寅：半岛铁路重新连接　能更好搭建新丝绸之路》，财新网，http://international.caixin.com/2017-06-16/101102499.html，2017年6月16日。

对于"一带一路"倡议的重要组成部分——亚投行，文在寅也给予了很高的期望，认为亚投行在基建投资方面的追求，与韩国政府的追求一致，将会为韩国带来更多的就业机会和更好的经济前景。文在寅尤其提到朝鲜半岛铁路南北中断的现状，并希望朝鲜和韩国的铁路能够实现重新连接。据分析，文在寅此番发言向国际社会公开表明，韩朝铁路连接工作是亚投行推进的亚洲基础设施开发项目的重要组成部分，并致力于实现地区和平与稳定。[①]

总的来看，自"一带一路"倡议提出以来，韩国的反应是比较积极的，其对接步伐逐步从务虚走向了务实，其中在最后时刻加入亚投行和与中国签订自由贸易协定之事，是迈出实质性步伐的两大标志性事件。

政策建议

（一）加强"一带一路"的宣介力度

韩国在"一带一路"的认知上经历了一个由浅入深的过程，尤其是随着韩国本身加入亚投行，成为创始会员国，使韩国实际上卷入了"一带一路"的战略进程之中，积极对接"一带一路"是韩国的主流看法。但是，对于"一带一路"的发展模式、发展理念，也有部分政府官员、智库机构和民众仍然抱有消极和负面的看法。他们认为，中国崛起必然会对韩国等周边国家构成威胁；中国搞"一带一路"是为了挑战由美国主导的现有国际秩序，称霸亚洲、称霸世界；设立亚投行是为了独占利益、独霸话语权，担心亚投行的治理结构不透明、不符合多边治理模式，担心韩国利益因此受损，等等。韩国最初对参加亚投行表现犹豫迟疑，不能说和这种负面认知无关。韩国国防研究院首席研究员李相国曾表示，中国"一带一路"政策的追求目标有二：一个是经济发展，另一个是军事扩张。这些负面舆论充分说明，在韩国讲好"一带一路"的故事还有很多工作要做。

---

① 韩联社：《文在寅出席亚投行年会强调韩朝铁路相连重要性》，http://chinese.yonhapnews.co.kr/newpgm/9908000000.html?cid=ACK20170616003500881，2017 年 6 月 16 日。

（二）防止过度的"民族主义"

随着萨德部署引发的中韩政治矛盾以及由此带来的乐天事件发酵，中韩两国的民族主义思潮都有抬头。在韩国看来，他们面对中国这样一个发展中的大国，很是焦虑。韩国哲学家、著名思想家金容沃 2016 年在韩国媒体的一篇采访中道出了这种心态的内涵。在他看来，继孟子以来，中国是数千年来承袭王道的伟大和霸道的威严的帝国。但是，令人担心的不是中国的天下主义，而是在中国的复兴过程中表现出的过度的"中华民族主义"。[1]在很多韩国媒体和民众看来，中国人现在"大国病"很突出，"已经蔓延到连党的下属机构人员都敢肆意提及'大国'、'小国'"，他们在对待韩国时展现的是"傲慢和无礼"。"中国认为两国发生争执之后，小国让步是理所当然的。""中国人在南海问题上更加愤怒的原因也在于菲律宾是个小国。"随着萨德部署问题以及乐天事件在中国的发酵，韩国对于中国的敌视情绪在上升。一些在中国的韩国人的切身感受是中国人现在已经变得不愿意与韩国人见面，即使见面也会加上一句"周围都不让与韩国人见面"。在萨德问题上，他们不能理解中国对自身安全的关切，认为"韩国为了不死在朝鲜的核武器之下不得不部署萨德"，"萨德是为了防御朝核，而中国对朝核问题负有责任。"[2]朝鲜之所以还不崩溃，其中一个原因就是中国的保护。[3]种种迹象表明，中韩双方国内不断上升的民族主义思潮严重影响了中韩之间的"民心相通"，同时也对韩国对接"一带一路"造成负面影响。中国政府提出的"亲、诚、惠、容"以及"共商、共建、共享"等理念还需要进一步以实际举措落地，真正使韩国民众在认识上理解、在心理上接受中国"一带一路"的构想以及民族复兴的理想。

---

① ［韩］梼杌、金容沃：《中国或会成为比美国更宽厚的帝国》，http://china.hani.co.kr/arti/international/847.html，2016 年 4 月 26 日。

② ［韩］杨相勋：《在中国遇到的荒唐之事》，《朝鲜日报》，http://cnnews.chosun.com/client/news/viw.asp?cate=C08&mcate=M1001&nNewsNumb=20160745562&nidx=45563，2016 年 7 月 29 日。

③ 《总统候选人必须直视的北韩真面目》，《东亚日报》，http://chinese.donga.com/3/all/28/884696/1，2017 年 3 月 30 日。

（三）将政治与经济分开考虑

在由于萨德部署等政治问题带来的中韩关系紧张一时难以缓解的情况下，中国应谨慎地将政治问题与经济问题分开考虑，防止出现"政冷经热"的局面。前面提到，韩国的工商界对于中国的"一带一路"倡议抱有很大的兴趣和积极性，而且对接"一带一路"对于韩国振兴国内经济、以经济纽带稳定周边安全都具有重要的现实意义。韩国政府对此应该有深刻的认识。因此，在处理政治议题的同时，不排除经济上加大合作的可能。正如中国驻韩大使邱国洪所说的那样，中韩就像是夫妻关系，"即使夫妻之间有时吵得很厉害，甚至打碎了玻璃杯或碟子，但最终只能一起好好过日子，这是命运。"韩国经济副总理兼企划财政部长柳一镐也强调，中国是韩国最大的经济伙伴，韩国仍须扩大对华出口，部署萨德与否属于政治领域的问题，政治归政治，经济归经济。

（四）把握好朝鲜问题的定位

朝鲜在地域上是东北亚的核心地区国家，在政治上是实现东北亚地区和平与安全的关键国家，在经济上是实现各国互联互通的必经要道。没有朝鲜的参加，"一带一路"建设将不能实现周边合作圈的合围。但是，由于朝鲜接二连三的核试验已经造成地区局势动荡和中朝关系不协调，这给中国"一带一路"战略的实施带来了一定挑战。韩国在对接"一带一路"倡议的过程中，也非常明显地感到朝鲜问题的掣肘。它积极响应"一带一路"倡议，从经济上说，是希望借助中国对朝鲜的影响力、借助经济合作的力量来实现自身"向北看"、向欧亚市场拓展的目标；从政治上看，则是希望朝鲜半岛能够通过经济纽带的联系支撑地区的安全和稳定。因此，韩国式的"一带一路"战略中隐含着重要的经济实用主义和安全实用主义的内涵。其中，朝鲜问题是一个绕不开的问题。中国应在坚持朝鲜半岛无核化原则的同时，走出美日韩对朝压制政策形成的困境，将对朝工作的重点转移至扩大对朝鲜经济交流和合作，推动朝鲜摆脱在朝核问题上的恶性循环，使朝鲜在安全担忧度大幅下降的情况下以更平静和合作的心态对待难以解决的问题，进而推动朝鲜逐步融入东北亚区域合作的进程之中，这也许就是"一带一路"战略对缓解当前日趋紧张的东北亚局势可能做出的贡献。

2 Concerning and Anticipating: A Struggling Korea for The Belt and Road Initiative

Zhu Feng   Wu Hasbao

Translator: Li Yue[①]

The Belt and Road Initiative refers to the Silk Road Economic Belt and 21st Century Maritime Silk Road, a significant development strategy firstly proposed by Chinese President Xi Jinping in late 2013. During Boao forum for Asia 2015, on March 28th, the Chinese government officially issued Vision and Actions on Jointly Building Silk Road Economic Belt and 21st-Century Maritime Silk Road, in which the Chinese government advocates peace and cooperation, openness and inclusiveness, and mutual learning and benefit.

The Belt and Road Initiative is a way for win-win cooperation that promotes common development and prosperity amongst all the countries it spans. It is a road towards peace and friendship by enhancing mutual understanding and trust, and strengthening all-round exchanges. It promotes practical cooperation in all fields, and

---

① Li Yue, Executive Director of the Center for North-East Asia Studies, the Pangoal Institution.

works to build a community of shared interests, destiny and responsibility featuring mutual political trust, economic integration and cultural inclusiveness.

With the consistent joint efforts of China and related parties, the Belt and Road Initiative has gained increasing acknowledgement and support. The Belt and Road Summit in Beijing is the most notable event since the launching of the Initiative. The top leaders of 28 countries from Asia, Europe, Africa, and Latin America have confirmed their attendance, showing the serious recognition and support for both the Summit and the Initiative in relation to international society.

While the Republic of Korea, a founding member of the Asia Infrastructure Investment Bank, is anxiously waiting for the invitation to the Summit, let's take a comprehensive look at the attitude of Korea toward The Belt and Road Initiative.

Korea's perceptions and attitudes toward The Belt and Road Initiative

Ever since China's launching of The Belt and Road Initiative, two seemingly polarized views toward this grand strategy have emerged within Korea. While it has enjoyed warm hugs from some, it is facing deep doubts and suspicions from others with influence within the Republic of Korea.

1. Supporters and followers

Those inclined to accept and welcome the Initiative mainly come from the media, the academy, as well as the industrial and business departments and from both the public and private sectors. Considering the current economic downturn and depression, they take the Initiative as an economically optimistic outlook for Korea's future.

In the view of many, the Initiative matches well with the Eurasian Initiative proposed by former president Park Geun-hye in October 2013. The cooperation of the two grand Initiatives would promote the process of regional integration, bring together the active East Asian economic circle with the developed European one, and especially connect Korea with energy-rich Russia and the broad consuming markets of Europe and Central Asia. While the Sino-Korean strategical economic cooperation would propel both countries towards integration via global development, it could also activate the economic growth potential of the Eurasian continent and furthermore lead the recovery and development of the global economies.

For this reason, they strongly support the idea of closer economic interaction with China, speaking highly of President Xi's calling for a Global Community of Shared Destiny by way of win-win cooperation. China is trying to build a new type of international relations via The Belt and Road Initiative, developing a new order for the world, jointly built through consultation to meet the interests of all. Every country could find a way to cooperate no matter what their social systems, religions, or values happen to be. There is great optimism about the goals of The Belt and Road Initiative, which were coined by Korean JoongAng Ilbo as Weiqi Diplomacy. This is President Xi's foreign strategy, in which Asia, Europe, and Africa can be connected in a way that will promise the winning of the hinterland.

2. Skeptics and dissenters

There are also many people holding reservations toward the Chinese Initiative within Korea, who are labelled as pro-American and experts from some domestic think tanks. They judge the Initiative with a political view, coming to the conclusion that China is not trustworthy and the Initiative includes serious political risks. China's geopolitical strategy could be the true intention of this economic strategy. There are concerns regarding China's increasing regional advantages and influence with which China would slowly squeeze out US dominance, gradually change the security structure, and become the only decisive power in East Asia. With this newfound power, it could invade or erode the economic and political independence of both Korea other nearby countries.

These concerns are apparent on Korean media: "To those who borrow money from China for infrastructure, once the projects come into setbacks or failure, they would have to follow China, let by the nose","The Initiative is not just an offer of reciprocity and mutual benefit, there is also a risky possibility of losing economic sovereignty into the grasp of China", "Korea would be dragged into the Chinese Order again, under which there will be no fair and just deal, denuclearization of North Korea, or the unification of the Korean Peninsula". There are also doubts about whether the Initiative could change the long withstanding economic, logistical, and communications channels between Asia and Europe.

What's worth mentioning is that these negative attitudes don't indicate a complete denial of the possibilities for Korea's participation in The Belt and Road Initiative, pointing out the need to balance the economic benefits with political risks. China's continuous practical measures are adding pressure, along with the establishment of AIIB and Silk Road Funds, as well as the strengthening of neighborhood diplomacy. As we can see, Koreans are gradually reaching a common ground in favor of the Chinese Initiative. Some skeptics also admit that "So far the cooperation on reducing trade barriers and infrastructure of transportation within the Initiative are worth trying and welcomed. And the political risks are manageable."

A recent Chosun Ilbo Article titled "China's Belt and Road Initiative Leading into Greek Port" said, "When Xi proposed the concept of The Belt and Road, it was simply regarded as a political rhetoric. Newspaper readers just took it as an ambitious dream when China's medias reported the Initiative would link together the 4.4 billion people (63% of the world's population) and an economic circle of $21 trillion (29% of the world's GDP). However, just two years and four months later after Xi's Proposal in

September 2013, this Grand Strategy has already marched right onto the front of the eyes of Europe. Each time when Xi visits abroad, he must emphasize the importance of The Belt and Road Initiative. Chinese administration has raised their flags over more than 20 overseas stronghold ports one by one." All this provides strong evidence that the more practical the measurements and benefits China offers, the more recognition and acceptance it will receive from major countries including Korea.

Analysis on Korea's contradictory acknowledge

Korea's contradictory views toward China are rooted in its complicated national interests, which are composed of both geopolitics and economy. Both of these are heavily influenced by actions of the two powers of China and the US.

1. China: A dominant economic partner

China plays a very important role in the international trade of Korea. Ever since the establishment of diplomatic relations, Sino-Korean bilateral trade has enjoyed a sharp rise, from around $5 billion in 1992 to nearly $300 billion: a 60x increase by 2014. By June 2015, China had become the country's largest trade partner and goods market, the largest destination country of overseas investment and tourists, and the largest resource country of both imports and overseas students. The volume of Sino-Korean bilateral trade accounted for more than one fifth of Korea's total international trade, exceeding both Korean-American and Korean-European trade volumes.

The China ROK FTA, signed in 2015 has added new impetus to the economic growth of both counties. It is estimated that the FTA impacts GDP growth directly; 0.34 percent for China and 0.97 percent for Korea. The highly mutual interdependence of the Korea-China economy provides a solid economic foundation for The Belt and Road

Initiative within Korea. Both the government and mass population are fully aware that it is a concrete fact rather than an abstract concept that Korea deeply relies on China economically.

Mr. Liu Jinsong, then Deputy Director General of Department of International Economy of Ministry of Foreign Affairs, once made a bill concerning joint rail and water transportation within The Belt and Road Initiative for Korean friends. He pointed out that Asian countries had been taking advantage of cheap ocean shipping from their flourishing sea transportation industries along the coast for quite a long time. Now, a new railway construction boom all over the Asia-Europe continent has drawn the attention of the whole world. Railway transportation today is achieving optimal overall system cost thanks to the rapid development and advancement of the high-speed rail technology and infrastructure in China.

As an example, take Mr Liu, who transports a container from Northeast Asia to North Europe. It takes around 35 days and 2 to 3 thousand US dollars by shipping, while it would take only 15 days and 7 to 8 thousand US dollars by rail. The tremendous time saving are well worth the costs. With regular operation on Chongqing-Xinjiang-Europe rail lines, enterprises and firms from both China and foreign countries have noticed the increasingly significant benefits derived from the availability of joint transportation options including rail, shipping and multimodal transportation. Today, China has built about a dozen scheduled China-Central Europe rail lines. These are the early fruits of the Silk Road Economic Zone, and are providing practical benefits to the countries along them.

Supporters from Korean industrial and business circles, as mentioned above, welcome Korea cooperation with The Belt and Road Initiative, mainly because they had already benefitting from trade and business with China. The Saemangeum area program, a joint Sino-Korea FTA industrial park, takes the Initiative as a major advancement opportunity. "There would be surely a win-win situation for both Korea and China, as long as the Saemangeum project is combined with The Belt and Road Initiative, and the Chinese capital as well."

For years, Korea has been suffering a depressed economy, with its GDP growth stagnating at a relatively low level of 2.8%. China, as Korea's largest trading partner, has a dominant capability to help Korea obtain a stable and recovering economy, on which Korea will be able to rely on for the foreseeable future.

2. the US: A crucial security umbrella

Although The Belt and Road Initiative provides attractive profits, Korea remains cautious on its cooperation with the strategy. Korea calculates its gains and losses according to the attitudes of both China and the US. While China ranks as Korea's No. 1 international trading partner today, US military power has been acting as a crucial security umbrella against North Korea for around 60 years. When Korea wavered in determination to join the AIIB, its contradictory mind and thoughts toward the two powers were clear. Despite serious opposition from China, Korea moved forward with the deployment of THAAD. This is an expression of the country's deep concern for its national security, along with its reliance on the US for military defense.

It is very difficult for Korea to independently arrive at foreign policies under this dual status situation. In other words, Korea is always trying to balance its relationship with both China and the US, attempting to gain the most advantages from both sides. This train of thought could be explained by South Korea Foreign Minister Yun Byung-se's words in 2015; "Korea would be able to obtain and enjoy a piece of cake of its own, if we can balance the two regional powers' influences of both China and the US under the current foreign policies". Korea has been working efficiently on this balancing art so far, as evidenced by the decision of joining AIIB and deploying THAAD despite strong objections from either the US or China.

Korea's reactions and response toward BRI

Interior Reactions and response from Korea toward the Initiative had gone through a process of three major phases; from being suspicious and doubtful, to understanding and accepting, and finally actively welcoming and promoting it.

1.The Eurasia Initiative, an initial response to The Belt and Road Initiative

The Eurasia Initiative was first proposed by former President Park Geun-hye in October 2013, which was regarded as a national development strategy and also an important international cooperation initiative. The Korean government has drawn a grand map of a united, creative and peaceful Eurasian continent of sustainable prosperity and peace via regional economic cooperation. The Initiative takes China, countries of Central Asia, Russia, Mongolia, and Turkey as major partners, making a geopolitical circle with the Korean Peninsula and Far East Russia as the centered region. The Initiative is composed of three fundamental plans: Building Silk Road Express, from Busan to Europe, through countries of North Korea, Russia, China, Central Asia, constructing the Eurasia Energy Network, and realizing the Economic Union of Eurasia.

The Eurasia Initiative was presented right after the birth of The Belt and Road Initiative, many people took it as Korean initial response to the Chinese. When she met visiting Zhang Dejiang, Chairman of National People's Congress of China, in June 2015, Park Geun-hye delivered the hope of cooperation with China considering that the Initiatives of both countries had much in common. Mr. Lee Jae Yong, the Chief of Eurasia Office of Korea Foreign Economic Policy Institute, once offered his reading on the connection of the two Initiatives: "The fitting point of the Initiatives locates in the China's Northeastern provinces and Russia. Joint advantages of China's capital, Korea's technology, and natural resources of the third party will lead to a mutually beneficial win-win cooperation." Shortly after the proposal of Park Geun-hye's Eurasia Initiative, an article of Reader's Commentary in the Chosun Ilbo talked about The Belt and Road Initiative. This report, titled "A 'silk Route Economic Circle' with 3 Billion Population Starting" on November 19, 2013, delivered Korea's early words toward The Belt and Road Initiative of China, "Chinese President Xi Jinping had proposed a communication network between China and Central Asia September 2013, which was mapped as a grand passing channel from the Pacific right to the Baltic. The core meaning of this Economic Circle plan is to connect the giant markets of both China and Central Asia into a single cooperative economy."

Accompanied by the Chinese President Xi Jinping's State Visit to Korea July 3, 2014, The Belt and Road has gained further attention within Korea. Korean media provided various interpretations and introductions upon The Belt and Road concept, including the principle of amity, sincerity, mutual benefit and inclusiveness, as well as the Initiative Foreign policy of Chinese leadership. As a mainstream media outlet in Korea, the Chosun Ilbo even proposed suggestions to its government that "It is necessary to explore the connection between the Eurasia Initiative and The Belt and Road Initiative." and "Were the two grand Initiatives to be linked, China would become a connecting bridge between Far East Asia, Central Asia, Middle East, Europe and Korea, which would moreover promote the competitive powers for both countries."

2. Joining AIIB after repeatedly hesitation

On October 24, 2014, government representatives of 21 countries officially signed the Asia Infrastructure Investment Bank Memorandum, starting the practical clock of AIIB for The Belt and Road Initiative. The Korean government had been stuck in its reservations of joining AIIB from the very beginning, revealing its deep hesitation derived from concerns about the US, which considers the AIIB a threat to itself, Europe, and Japan as leading powers in international finance. Considering Korea's highly reliant relationship with the US, Korea cannot just ignore America's attitude and point of view.

Under the diplomatic "attack" from China at the Annual Meeting of Boao Asia Forum 2015, sophisticated changes had taken place within the Korean government. This includes the rising desire from the interior promoting the separate handling of issues concerning economy and politics, "Upon the matter of Chinese New Silk Road strategy, it would rather be handled as an economic issue than a political one, which is the only way to create an atmosphere of cooperation." "The Middle East and Southeast Asia, located in the core area of the New Silk Road strategy, rank first and second in constructing markets for Korea. If China is to pour huge amount of money through social indirect capital investment in this area, it would be a good opportunity for Korea, too."

Meanwhile, there has been a public discussion within Korea on the competition between the two powers of both China and the US in Asia, considering that The Belt and Road Initiative is to confront Obama's Asia Network. Korea plays double roles as the backing force of the China's Initiative and vanguard of the US Asia-Pacific Rebalancing. As the discussion deepened, public opinions gradually shifted to prefer practical national interests and Economic pragmatism, considering it is realistic for Korea to join AIIB. While witnessing Britain join AIIB of the international society, Korea definitely made the correct decision to join AIIB before the deadline set by China for founder members, recognizing the Sino-Korea current relationship and mega trend of future development, which promoted bilateral relations to a higher new level.

Moreover, there rose a dissatisfied voice within the country against the US disturbing Korea's joining of the AIIB. The Chosun Ilbo quoted an article of Colin Powell, former Secretary of State of the United States, saying that AIIB is not a bad vision. The US has rashly criticized both the bank and its members, and the criticism should be stopped. As Korea became a founding member of AIIB, its civil population is getting more aware of this Chinese Initiative, thanks to the Korean domestic media's popularization of the Initiative. Again, Chosun Ilbo, for example, sent two field interviewing groups to the key cities of both China and countries of Central Asia, and had presented Series Reports with the topic of "Current Advance of The Belt and Road Initiative and Effect on Korea".

3. Sino-Korea Memorandum of Cooperation on The Belt and Road Initiative

The official signing of the Sino-Korea Free Trade Agreement in June 2016, established a solid foundation for the fusion of The Belt and Road Initiative and The Eurasia Initiative. On October 31, the two governments signed Memorandum of Cooperation on The Belt and Road Initiative and The Eurasia Initiative under the witness of Premier Li Keqiang and then President Park Geun-hye. By signing the agreement, these two government leaders decided to strengthen bilateral exchange and cooperation in areas including manufacturing policy, designing research, and environment friendly plants. The long term cooperative agreement will speed many fields including industrial robots manufacture. The agreement promotes the fusion of Korean technology and Chinese Capital and the ability to jointly develop infrastructure and equipment markets for third parties. Both leaders agreed on the linkage of Korea's "New Manufacturing Creation 3.0" and "Made in China 2025", aiming at the transformation of manufacturing in both counties. The two governments also agreed to coordinate their strategies of Eurasia Initiative and The Belt and Road Initiative, providing more opportunities for Korean enterprises to go overseas via the China proposed AIIB. Under this plan, both countries also decided to begin investigating the possibility of a common fund for financial support. The two countries also came to an agreement on establishing a currency market in Shanghai for direct exchange between Won and RMB, and the permission for RMB bond issues by the Korean government.

4. Joint projects discussion and docking platforms establishment

Along with the deepening of bilateral cooperation between China and Korea, the fusion of the two grand Initiatives has ascended to a new stage of practical operation step by step. Mr. Yoo Il-ho, former Vice Premier and Chief Officer of Ministry of Strategy and Finance said at the 14th Korea-China Financial Minister Meeting, that Korea and China should realize the Nation Dreams of Both Korea and China by means of win-win cooperation. He also proposed to establish docking platforms for the two grand Initiatives, carrying out joint investigation into the field of infrastructure, communications technology, energy, and iron and steel in the major countries of Asia and Africa within The Belt and Road initiative. Both countries are to strengthen information exchange, and to explore means and ways to provide financial support to enterprises via multilateral financial agencies and import & export banks. He urged to accelerate such pilot projects as the development of seaports in Hunchun of China, and Sizhalubi Nobel of Russia.

At the same event, the Chinese counterpart proposed to start the bilateral cooperation from the development of the three Northeastern provinces of China. During the meeting, the two governments announced matching results of both countries findings from pilot projects regarding third party markets, and went on to sign the Memorandum on Cooperation of Development and Investment. These agreements indicated further practical cooperation between the two countries. Korean enterprises, such as KOTRA, have already taken steps towards cooperation by organizing exhibitions in Wuhan and Xi'an China and holding local business matching activities, to ambitiously develop Robotics markets in China.

5. Anxiety due to lack of invitation to the BRF Summit

There was also a story about the attendance of the BRF within the Korea right before the Summit. Dramatic political turbulence within Korea had bothered both the country and the world, highlighted the impeachment and arrest of former President Park Geun-hye, the fiercely ongoing election campaign, and anxiety stemming from not being invited to the BRF summit. Ever since the announcement of the May BRF Summit guest list by the Chinese government in early March 2017, there had been a public mood of desperation and anxiety within Korea.

An article strikingly titled as "China to host BRF, No Korea Official Invited" in Chosun Ilbo on March 4, said that Chinese government had sent invitations to top leaders or ministerial officials of more than 60 countries all over the world, including Japan, undergoing a hard time with the hosting country, and Australia, hardly related to The Initiative. China is even trying to invite representatives from Trade Representative Office of the US to be present at the Summit. On the contrary, not only had Korea not received an invitation for President or Premier, but not even for any ministerial official. The report also said that China had not even attempted to understand Korea's inclination toward the Summit. The only institutes that received invitations were International Exchange Consortium and Foreign Economic Policy Institute, whose representatives were invited to attend the Parallel Meeting of Think Tanks. That is, Korea as a country was put on the lowest level of attendants according to the invitation scale.

The article also suggested that Korea was intentionally slighted by China, mainly because of the deployment of THAAD. It also expressed the uneven emotion by quoting some diplomat from Southeast Asia saying that "As the hosting country of the Annual Meeting of AIIB Council in June, Korea was officially let out from the Summit. The response is a little extreme." It is said that Mr. Kim, Korea's Ambassador to China, had requested direct talks with related departments of trade and business, culture, and tourist, etc., but even after several months received no response.

Apart from feeling left-out, there is another voice calling for the rethinking of the Korean foreign policy. According to this point of view, Korea cannot push all the responsibility to the Chinese side, because there has been oversight from the government on the matter of understanding strategic intentions and diminishing unnecessary concerns of China. A diplomat said that "Then Premier Hwang Kyo-ahn told President Xi Jinping when he visited China at the end of last June that Korea had not made any decision upon THAAD, but the declaration of deployment of THAAD came up no less ten days after the meeting.", "Our immature [action] triggered distrust from the Chinese government, and this is one of the major reasons leading to all these unfavorable consequences."

Looking back from the day when The Belt and Road Initiative was presented, we could generally say that Korea has taken a relatively positive attitude toward it, although struggling in hesitating steps through the ideological to the practical. It is worth mentioning that joining AIIB at the last moment and signing Sino-Korea FTA mark two concrete measures Korea has recently taken. This may help us to understand why and how the Korea had been anxiously waiting for the invitation forward to the next one.

Policy Suggestion

1. Strengthening the Campaign of Propaganda

Korea has been involved in the strategic process of The Belt and Road with its joining and becoming a founding member of AIIB. Although there have been differing views toward the Belt and Road among Koreans, it is a mainstream concept that it is best for Korea to collaborate with China's strategy. There remain many negative views about the development and concept of The Belt and Road from officials, scholars, and civilians. Some argue that the rise of China will become a threat to neighboring countries like Korea, and that The Belt and Road strategy is meant to challenge the current international order led by the USA. Others say that China is seeking hegemony over Asia and even the world. Another claim is that the AIIB is meant to promote non-transparent or non-multilateral governance, damaging the national interests of Korea. Korea's initial hesitation toward AIIB was partially based on these negative points of view. Lee Xiangguo, Chief Researcher from Korea National Defense Institute, said that there were two major aims of The Belt and Road: economic growth and military expansion. All these negative public opinions illustrate that China still has a lot of work to do in framing the story of The Belt and Road in an agreeable way.

2. Avoiding over-nationalism

Both China and Korea have been hammered by rising nationalism due to Korea's decision for THAAD deployment and the Lotte incident which followed it. Korea's anxiousness toward the rising power of China is clear. In an interview on Korean media of famous thinker and philosopher King Wrong, it was said that China is a dignified empire of greatness and dominance with a history spanning thousands of years. However, it is the over-reacting Grand China Nationalism on the road to rejuvenation that worries neighboring countries most, not the traditional "Tian Xia" awareness. According to many Korean media personalities and civilians, China's power has 'gone to its head, with signs of "arrogance and rudeness" when dealing with Korea. China is also accused of treating Korea as below it, and hinting the idea that smaller countries should defer to larger ones during conflict. These ideas fail to explain why China is having so much issues regarding the South China Sea, even though the main regional challenger is the Philippines, a small country with much less power.

Korea is seeing an increasing feeling of hostility toward China with the development of THAAD, and the fermentation of Lotte incident. Some Koreans living in China are noticing that Chinese people are not willing to meet with them like before, or add with "not supposed to meet" even during a meeting. Koreans cannot understand the negative attitude of Chinese people toward Korean's legitimate security concerns regarding North Korea. Koreans believe that they must deploy THAAD against the threat of being eliminated by the North, and China has some responsibility for the nuclear issue of the North. Some even say that China is actively perpetuating the North Korean regime. All these unfavorable views caused by rising nationalism of both sides have seriously affected the people-to-people bonds, as well as Korea's co-operation with China's Belt and Road Initiative.

It is recommended that China should carry out more practical measures to help Korean civilians understand and accept the concepts behind the Initiative and the dream for the rejuvenation of China.

3. Respectively considering matters related to politics and economy

With the strained China-Korea relations wandering toward a cold economic situation due to the THAAD deployment, China should consider matters related to politics and economy. The industrial interests of Korea still hold desire and support for China's Initiative, because the Korean government is quite aware that this grand strategy has realistic benefits to the economic recovery of Korea and the security and stability of neighborhood. There is a high possibility for the Korean government to accelerate economic cooperation with China under the currently strong Sino-Korea political relationship. Just as Chinese Ambassador to Korea, Mr. Qiu Hongguo says, the Sino-Korea relationship is quite like a married couple, "even there is quarreling and arguing, sometime breaking glasses or dishes, they are doomed to get along with the days for the good." Mr. Yoo Il-ho, Korea's Vice Premier on Economy and Chief Financial Officer, emphasized that China is the largest economic partner, and Korea must increase exports to China…That the deployment of THAAD is a matter of politics, and let the economy do its job separately.

4. Handling the North Korea issue carefully

North Korea geographically locates at the core area of Northeast Asia, which is an important passage for the connection and communication of the neighborhood. For this reason, its stability is critical for the realization of peace and security in the region. The Grand Initiative would not achieve a full circle of communication for the nearby economies without the cooperation of North Korea. However, the continuous nuclear weapon tests have caused unease in the region and discomfort with China, as they have raised new challenges against the carrying out of the Initiative. Korea has clearly figured out the unfavorable effects during economic cooperation with China, which has two major intentions. Economically, Korea aims to explore Eurasian markets for its north-looking strategy, by means of economic cooperation and China's influence on North Korea. Politically, Korea hopes to realize the security and stability of the Peninsula via the connection and support of economic linkages among related parties. So, China's Initiative within Korea involves two purposes: economic pragmatism and security, both in which the issue of North Korea cannot be neglected.

Along with the sticking to the principle of a nuclear-free peninsula, there might be a second alternative for China. This is to explore a deeper economic exchange with North Korea. International sanctions by the US, Japan and Korea would lead to vicious spiral on the North Korea nuclear issue. Once the security concerns of North Korea are reduced, it might deal with the situation with an easy and cooperative attitude. It would be one of the contributions that Belt and Road Initiative could make for easing the intensive Northeast Asia situation, by gradually pushing North Korea into the development process of regional cooperation in Northeast Asia.

3 当代土耳其的发展愿景
——兼谈"一带一路"下的中土合作

昝涛

近年来，随着中国国家主席习近平提出"中国梦"以及"一带一路"战略构想和倡议，与此相关的国家也进入国人的关注与研究视野。这其中，土耳其受到了格外关注，不仅包括中东研究学者，也包括一些关注中国现实发展的人，他们因为对土耳其与中国之间一些特殊且敏感问题的兴趣，从而产生了对土耳其的知识需求。[①]在 21 世纪过去的十余年中，土耳其的发展引人注目，该国相继提出了三个层次雄心勃勃的"土耳其梦"（Türkiye hayal/Turkey dream）[②]：2023 年土耳其建国 100 周年时的计划（简称"2023 百年愿景"）、2053 年奥斯曼－突厥人征服伊斯坦布尔 600 周年时的展望（简称"2053 展望"）以及 2071 年塞尔柱－突厥人打

---

① 2015 年 3 月 17~18 日，经笔者联络，促成北京大学与印第安纳大学联合主办的"中国在中东：历史与现实"国际学术会议在北京大学举行，与会外国学者 30 多人，其中有关中土关系的那一场，发言人最多（共 7 人），引起了格外关注，探讨的问题也从文化、经济、军事、政治到极端主义等多个方面。

② "土耳其梦"是笔者所做的一个概括，这在土耳其并不是一个专有名词，土耳其人也极少使用"土耳其梦"（Türkiye hayal）来概括本文中涉及的那些愿景、展望和目标。倒是有一些英文的报道和分析会使用 Turkey Dream 这样的表达。在土耳其语境下，被讨论最多的是"2023 百年愿景"（2023 Vizyonu）。

败拜占庭帝国、开启安纳托利亚征服运动的曼齐克特战役胜利 1000 周年时的目标（简称"2071 千年目标"）。通过具体考释土耳其提出的这些发展规划、目标与愿景的过程，本文拟探讨土耳其提出这些宏大理想的时代背景，分析实现这些梦想的条件。最后，本文的落脚点在于从中土关系的角度看待土耳其这个国家的基本面，并探讨"一带一路"下中土合作的基础与前景。

"土耳其梦"的三个层次及其内涵

当下，土耳其领导人对该国未来发展充满期待，正如 2015 年 9 月 16 日土耳其媒体有关埃尔多安（Recep Tayyip Erdogan）在演讲中所言："我们真心地相信，土耳其的未来是光明的……当下我们生活在灰暗的日子里，但是，2023、2053 和 2071 愿景必将会实现。"[①]的确，以"2023 百年愿景"为核心的"土耳其梦"体现了该国一些具体的经济、社会、政治和外交等方面的发展目标。

（一）"2023 百年愿景"

土耳其的"2023 百年愿景"是在 2011 年最先提出的，并不断深化。2011 年 1 月 28 日，土耳其总理埃尔多安在《对人民讲话》（Ulusa Sesleni）的电视谈话节目中提出了正义与发展党（简称"正发党"）的 2023 愿景，具体内容："我们未来的 12 年中，国民收入至少再翻三番，希望在 2023 年能达到 2 万亿美元。12 年后，我们的人口预计将达到 8200 万。在这种情况下，我们将把人均国民收入提高到 25000 美元。此外，未来 12 年出口要再翻四番，达到 5000 亿美元，外贸总量达到 1 万亿美元。希望到 2023 年时，小学和中学入学率都达到 100%。在健康方面，我们现在已经达到了每 10 万人有 153 个医生，到 2023 年我们要提高到 210 个。在基础设施方面，过去 8 年中，我们修建了 13600 公里公路，这将很

---

① http://www.insanhaber.com/politika/erdogan-sikintili-gunler-yasiyoruz-ama-2023-2053-2071-vizyonlarihayata-gececek-58501,2016-1-11.

快达到 15000 公里，到 2023 年的时候，我们要再修 15000 公里。此外，我们还要铺 11000 公里新的铁路，南北高铁线路要完成。土耳其要成为世界十大空港之一。飞机、卫星要自己设计，并以本地技术生产。我们已经开始自主生产战舰、坦克、无人机，我们还有更多更大的计划。自己的防务卫星由土耳其的工程师设计，把卫星（Gokturk）发送到太空。我们计划通过建立航天工业区、船舶建造工业区，将土耳其打造成为连接三大陆的制造业和物流中心。总面积达 850 万公顷的净化水区域已经接近完工，希望到 2023 年就可以通水。在 2023 年建国 100 周年的时候，土耳其至少要建立三座核电站。根据我们的方案，现在每年 2850 万的游客到 2023 年时要增长到 5000 万，220 亿美元的旅游收入到 2023 年要达到 500 亿美元。一些区域工程（GAP、DAP、KOP）也将完工，我们举国上下要手牵手、肩并肩、心连心地把土耳其建成世界的粮仓和农业中心。"①

2012 年 9 月 30 日，正发党在第四次全国代表大会上正式发布了《正发党 2023 政治愿景》②（AK Parti 2023 Siyasi Vizyonu）。埃尔多安在演说中三次使用了"梦"（hayal）这个单词，声情并茂地表达了他对土耳其的未来充满坚定的信念。实际上，相较于前引埃尔多安的谈话内容，这次大会正式发布的《正发党 2023 政治愿景》这个党的文件对具体问题做了深化和细化，尤其对未来 11 年土耳其在政治、经济、民族、法律、文化、社会和外交等领域预期取得的成就均做了提纲挈领的阐释。

第一，在经济发展问题上，这份文件除了强调上文提及的 2011 年埃尔多安电视谈话节目中提到的诸项经济与社会发展指标以外，还提到"与通胀做斗争将继续是我们的优先考虑"，即鼓励国民创新、创业及努力工作。

第二，在民族问题上，正发党积极致力于通过强调文化自治、双语和多元主义来解决库尔德问题和国家统一问题。该文件明确表示反对军方监国体制。按照既有的方案，土耳其将推出一部"包容性的，而不是排他性的"新宪法，以取代 1980 年

---

① http://www.patronlardunyasi.com/haber/Basbakan-Erdogan-2023-hedeflerini-acikladi/98480，2016-01-15.

② 该文本可在正发党的官方网站上下载，本节出自该文本的内容，除特殊情况外，不再另加注释，see: 2016-01-15。

军人干政后颁行的宪法。此外，正发党力图重新界定土耳其民族的概念，赋予库尔德人以真正的少数民族地位，以及相应的文化自治权，并且将在公共服务中逐渐推行双语（土耳其语与库尔德语）。相对于土耳其长期僵化的民族政策来说，这个调整是革命性的，对于解决库尔德问题是积极的。由此可见，正发党的"2023愿景"很重视强调民主的宽容性，强调尊重和保护差异性与少数人的观点。正发党还承诺要扩大"仇恨罪"的概念，即包括所有的宗教性和种族性的言行。为了与库尔德工人党（PKK）的恐怖主义斗争，正发党提出了一个重要的民主方案，即"民族统一与繁荣进程"，正发党将其所贯彻的政策定位为：以人类为中心和基于自由的政治。正发党尤其强调多元主义作为国家统一的重要条件。以前的一些对少数族群的同化和歧视性政策已经被取消，埃尔多安还曾为历史上对库尔德人的迫害事件而道歉。①另外，正发党强调加大对东南部库尔德落后地区的投资、开发与援助。

第三，在对外关系方面，继续走多边主义的道路，既强调要加入欧盟，又坚持发展同伊斯兰—中东地区以及中亚的关系。在理念上，正发党坚信土耳其的伟大和强盛源自历史、文化与文明，要实现其历史使命，将土耳其变成能够塑造世界秩序的国家之一。正发党对土耳其的历史深度和文明版图持多维度和多方位的视角，强调从战略的纵深角度来重估土耳其的历史与地缘，继续肯定与邻国零问题的政策。②坚持土耳其加入欧盟的理想，同时强调要把"哥本哈根标准"定义为"安卡拉标准"，发誓要在2023年加入欧盟，成为完全会员国；强调与突厥语国家之间的合作；反对伊斯兰恐惧症；肯定所谓的"阿拉伯之春"。

第四，重新界定了世俗主义。在世俗主义的界定方面，正发党的"2023愿景"做了非常详细的说明，这代表的是正发党作为保守主义政党的一贯态度。实际上，正发党并不否定世俗主义，但是，在坚持政教分离的前提下，更加强调宗教信仰不受政治权力干预的自由，强调不同信仰的和谐共处。这是正发党重塑土耳其社

---

① 该文本可在正发党的官方网站上下载，本节出自该文本的内容，除特殊情况外，不再另加注释，see: 2016-01-15。

② 关于当代土耳其对外战略，参见拙文：《从历史角度看土耳其的多边主义战略》，载《阿拉伯世界研究》2015年第1期，第55~66页。

会的重要指南，因为：相对于凯末尔党人的以政治管控宗教的积极的世俗主义来说，强调宗教信仰自由则是一种消极的世俗主义，必将为宗教活动打开更大的空间。

自 2011 年埃尔多安提出"2023 百年愿景"以来，土耳其政界一直围绕"2023愿景"做文章，尤其是正发党领导人在国内外的多个场合不断提到"2023 百年愿景"，他们的态度大致可以概括为：表达信念，认识到困难，但从未放弃。2016 年 1 月中旬，土耳其总理阿赫迈特·达乌特奥卢（Ahmet Davutoglu）在伦敦面向 200多名投资人的演讲中再次坚定地重申了土耳其"2023 百年愿景"的经济目标。[1] 由此看来，"2023 百年愿景"可视为土耳其当下与未来一段时间该国重要的综合性国家发展战略。

（二）"2071 千年目标"

2071 千年目标是在 2012 年底由埃尔多安正式提出的，它不像"百年愿景"那样有一系列的具体计划和数据，可以说那是一种历史意识。实际上，在正发党第四次代表大会上，埃尔多安在论及正发党的历史定位时提到了 1071 年的那段历史，他认为正发党是"继承了 1000 年历史的积淀、经验、精神与灵感的政党"。这里所说的 1000 年指的就是 1071 年。埃尔多安说："距今大约 950 年前，在 1071 年 8 月 26 日，在曼齐克特②平原，苏丹阿斯兰骑在他的白马上对

---

① "Global investors invited to participate in Turkey's rise," in *Daily Sabah*, January. 19, 2016.

② 11 世纪初，拜占庭帝国在安纳托利亚的防御明显弱化。1068 年，罗曼努斯四世（Romanus IV Diogenes）成为拜占庭皇帝，他力图通过一系列军事行动结束突厥人的威胁。1071 年 3 月，罗曼努斯从君士坦丁堡出发去东部夺取曼齐克特和赫拉特的军镇，这个地方是从东部来的入侵者的主要路线。当时，阿斯兰正在叙利亚北部用兵。在得知拜占庭皇帝的行动之后，阿斯兰决定带兵打击罗曼努斯。当年 8 月，两军在曼齐克特遭遇，遂发生历史上最伟大的战役之一。结果是阿斯兰打败并俘虏了罗曼努斯，但阿斯兰当时的主要兴趣并不在安纳托利亚，而是埃及与叙利亚，所以他在要求了每年的纳贡以及提供军事帮助之后，就宣布了和平，并释放了罗曼努斯。不过，君士坦丁堡的官僚们在他返回首都之前就把罗曼努斯抛弃了。随后拜占庭发生了一系列内战，极大地便利了突厥人的入侵。Maribel Fierro, ed., *The New Cambridge History of Islam*, Vol. 2, Cambridge University Press, 2010, pp.302-303; Kate Fleet, ed., *The Cambridge History of Turkey*, Vol. I, Cambridge University Press, 2009, p.10.

将士们如是说：'啊！我的将领们！啊！我的士兵们！当所有穆斯林在讲经坛上为我们祈祷的时候，我想冲向敌人。要么实现目标取得胜利，要么成为烈士进入天国。我的士兵们！我已握紧马的缰绳，要像一个士兵一样战斗。如果我成了烈士，就让这白袍作我的裹尸布。弟兄们！要么随我一起战斗，要么离我而去，你们可以自由选择……神啊！我只信任你……我要为你而战……这样，带着信念、献身、荣耀与谦卑，苏丹阿斯兰参加了战斗，打开了持续千年的文明之门。'"①

从土耳其当下的官方历史叙事来说，1071 年确实是一个重要的起点，因为这是安纳托利亚突厥化和伊斯兰化的开端。②埃尔多安没有止于塞尔柱突厥人，而是将其描述为一个萌芽："这样的一个文明，在奥斯曼·加齐③手中时还只是小枝。那个小枝会长成矮树，那个矮树会长成参天大树，变成覆盖大地与海洋的、从高加索到阿尔卑斯、从两河流域到多瑙河的广阔领土的大树。请注意，在这棵大树的树荫下，塞尔柱、奥斯曼和共和国的土地上，没有流血，没有分裂，也没有分裂主义；没有暴政，没有压迫，也没有他者化；这里只有爱和友谊，这里相信知识的力量。正发党就是在这树枝上生长出来的。我们的道路，是苏丹阿斯兰的道路，是奥斯曼·加齐的道路，是征服者苏丹穆罕默德④的道路，是苏丹苏莱曼⑤的

---

① https://www.akparti.org.tr/site/haberler/basbakan-erdoganin-ak-parti-4.-olagan-buyuk-kongresi-konusmasinin-tam-metni/31771#1, 2016-01-15.

② 在凯末尔主政的时代，土耳其的历史叙事是超越 1071 年那段历史的，尤其是具有浪漫色彩的"土耳其史观"（Türk Tarih Tezi）坚决反对 1071 年突厥人才来到安纳托利亚的说法，它将突厥人迁徙的历史追溯到比这还早数千年，连小亚细亚历史上的赫梯人都被说成是突厥人。20 世纪 40 年代，土耳其放弃了上述史观，转而强调土耳其人对安纳托利亚历史上的多种文明的继承与发展。关于"土耳其史观"，参见拙著：《现代国家与民族建构——20 世纪前期土耳其民族主义研究》，三联书店，2011 年版。

③ 指奥斯曼一世（Osman I, 1258 ~ 1326），即奥斯曼帝国的开创者，其父亲为艾尔图鲁，属于乌古斯土库曼部落，是罗姆的塞尔柱突厥人的一个贵族。*A Portrait Album of the Ottoman Sultans*, Istanbul: Kaknus Publications, 2012, p.1.

④ 指穆罕默德二世（Mehmet II,1444 ~ 1446/1451 ~ 1481），是奥斯曼帝国第七任苏丹，他于 1453 年征服了君士坦丁堡，故被称为"征服者"（Fatih）。*A Portrait Album of the Ottoman Sultans*, p.7.

⑤ 指苏莱曼一世（Sulaiman I, 1520-1566），是奥斯曼帝国第十任苏丹，他被称为"大帝"和"立法者"。*A Portrait Album of the Ottoman Sultans*, p.10.

道路，是穆斯塔法·凯末尔①的道路，是阿德南·门德列斯②和图尔古特·厄扎尔③的道路。"④

通过回归历史，埃尔多安以浪漫主义的手法将过去美化，将征服的历史美化，尤其说没有压迫，没有流血，完全是罔顾史实。但通过这样一种叙事结构，埃尔多安将正发党置于土耳其的千年历史之中，置于一个从起源到当下的连绵不断的延续中，从塞尔柱到奥斯曼，从奥斯曼到共和国，在这千年一系的历史脉络中，正发党被抬到了历史的高度。应该说，这算是埃尔多安较早地将1071年作为象征纳入人们视野的一次讲话。

但是，"1071一代"（1071'in nesli）以及"2071目标"（2071 hedefi），是在正发党四大之后提出来的，所谓"2071目标"非常含糊和空洞，不像2023愿景那么具体，埃尔多安说到"2071目标"，只是笼统地说要达到"奥斯曼水平"（Osmanli derecesi）。2012年12月16日，埃尔多安在土耳其中部因保守而文明的城市科尼亚（Konya）发表演讲，指出了到2071年要实现的目标："希望从我们历史上的安纳托利亚运动开始到现在……到2071年，也就是第一千年的时候，真主保佑，那个时候的土耳其，将会达到塞尔柱人和奥斯曼人曾经达到的水平。当发达国家陷入严重的全球性金融危机的时候，我们土耳其还在继续稳步前进。我们是见不到2071年了。青年们！我是对你们说的，尤其是你们中的单身者，你们结婚吧。希望你们将养育1071一代。"埃尔多安鼓励年轻人为了一个"有活力的土耳其"而结婚，且每家至少生三个孩子。⑤埃尔多安提到的所谓古代帝国水平，无法得知用

---

① 即土耳其国父穆斯塔法·凯末尔·阿塔图尔克（Mustafa Kemal Atatürk，1881～1938）。

② 阿德南·门德列斯（Adnan Mendres），土耳其政治家。1950～1960年任总理，在1960年的军事政变中被推翻，后被判处绞刑。

③ 图尔古特·厄扎尔（Turgut Özal，1927～1993），土耳其政治家，曾担任土耳其总理（1983~1989）和第八任总统（1989～1993）。

④ "Bagbakan Erdoğan'in AK Parti 4. Olağan Büyük Kongresi konuğmasinin tam metni"，https://www.akparti.org.tr/site/haberler/basbakan-erdoganin-ak-parti-4-olagan-buyuk-kongresi-konusmasinin-tam-metni/31771#1，2016-01-15.

⑤ "2071 hedefi: Osmanli derecesi"，"Erdoğan: Gençler Evlenin, 1071 Neslini Sizler Yetiştireceksiniz"，2016-01-15.

什么来衡量。如果从历史的角度看，那时土耳其面积比较大，比周边的国家强盛。
埃尔多安说："我们将更加强大。"在同一天的议会演讲中，时任外交部长的达乌特
奥卢也说："到 2023 年，你们就会看到国家的崛起，到 2071 年的时候，你们将会
作为尊贵的公民生活在一个全球性的大国。"①

（三）"2053 展望"

较少被提及但也已经成为当下土耳其政治语言之一的是"2053 展望"。2013
年 5 月 7 日，埃尔多安在正发党的团体会议上向议员们讲话时提到了"2053 展
望"："我们在去年 9 月的大会上就宣布了 2071（千年）目标。就算我们看不到那
一天，为了今天出生的孩子们能够看到那一天，从现在开始我们也要准备了。伊
斯坦布尔在 1453 年被征服后的 600 周年，也就是 2053 年，我们也设定了正发党
的目标。如果没有苏莱曼，就没有艾尔图鲁·加齐②、奥斯曼·加齐。如果没有奥斯
曼·加齐在伊斯坦布尔被征服 150 年前的梦，也就没有征服者苏丹穆罕默德。一个
时代的门关了，一个新的时代不能开启。我们给今天的青年们灌输的是一种意识，
即成为一个一个的征服者，成为养育征服者们的父母。"③

从以上三者比较来看，土耳其的"2023 百年愿景"是很"实"的，它涉及该
国各方面要实现的具体目标。而"2071 千年目标"和"2053 展望"内容则非常的
笼统，后两者毋宁说主要是一种历史意识，属于大而无当的政治宣传，其背后所

① Quted from "Turkey Analysis: How Can Ankara's '2071' Vision See the Kurdish Issue?", http://
www.enduringamerica.com/home/2012/12/18/turkey-analysis-how-can-ankaras-2071-vision-see-the-kurdish.
html, 2016-01-15.

② 一般认为苏莱曼（Süleyman）、艾尔图鲁（Ertuğrul）分别是奥斯曼帝国创立者奥斯曼一世的
爷爷和父亲。关于他们的历史记载并不清晰。可以确定的是，到 1225 年的时候，随着蒙古人征服而
来的乌古斯部落的一支已经占据了凡湖附近的阿赫拉特地区，其领导者就是苏莱曼。艾尔图鲁可能是
苏莱曼的儿子抑或孙子，他的名字来自突厥语。几乎可以肯定的是，作为一个军事将领的艾尔图鲁所
占据的Bitinya 地区，要么是塞尔柱人册封的领地，要么就是他为了躲避蒙古人而来到这里。Jean-Paul
Roux, *Türklerin Tarihi: Pasifik'ten Akdeniz'e 2000 yil*, translated by Aykut Kazancigil & Lale Arslan-Özcan,
Kabalci Yayinevi, 2004, pp. 325-326.

③ http://www.radikal.com.tr/politika/erdogan-2053-vizyonu-ve-oy-oranlarini-acikladi-1132528, 2016-
01-15.

传递的信息和信念是：土耳其人过去曾经很强大，也一定可以复兴过去那种程度的强大，希望土耳其的发展能越来越好，现在的领导人不是目光短浅的人，他们不止是要为这一代人考虑，而且还要为子孙后代考虑，除了物质生活的持续改善，还鼓励土耳其人多生孩子，哺育未来一代。对于正发党的领导人来说，他们确实看不到2071年了，所以，在务虚的意义上提出所谓"千年目标"，旨在诉诸某种历史资源，借过去和未来而加强自身现在的吸引力与号召力。

"土耳其梦"提出的背景及其引发的相关争论

一个国家的领导人、政党或政府提出关于未来发展的计划或宏伟目标，较为常见。这既是一种政治宣示，也是一种发展思路。那么，正发党为何在其执政之初未提出如此宏大的计划，而是在执政近十年之时才提出来？围绕实现"土耳其梦"，该国国内又引发了哪些争议？

（一）"土耳其梦"提出的背景和原因

第一，正发党执政十年的经济成就是重要原因之一。土耳其在正发党执政的头十年中取得了空前的经济成就，成为经济实力最强的穆斯林国家。自20世纪80年代厄扎尔主政以来，土耳其积极融入全球化，实行出口导向的经济政策，经济实现了较快发展。2002年正发党上台连续执政以来，土耳其经济更是持续较快发展，尤其是2002～2007年，平均增速超过了6.8%，在世界舞台上表现卓越，土耳其在这几年迅速摆脱了本世纪初金融危机的影响，成为继"金砖国家"之后的新秀，成为"展望五国（VISTA）"、"灵猫六国"或"金钻十一国"成员。2008~2009年，受全球金融危机的影响，土耳其经济下滑，但很快突破困局，2010年和2011年该国经济增速达到了9%。[①]之后，土耳其经济增速放缓。根据世界银

---

① 笔者根据经合组织2015年9月数据整理，另参见土耳其统计协会网站：http://www.turkstat.gov.tr，2016-01-15。

行的统计，以美元现价计算，土耳其 2013 年的国内生产总值为 8221 亿美元，居世界第 17 位[①]，人均国民收入为 10971 美元[②]，2014 年，土耳其的国内生产总值总量按美元现价计算为 984 亿美元，排名第 18 位[③]，这个数据变化主要是受里拉贬值影响。世界银行预测土耳其 2016 年和 2017 年的增速分别为 3.9% 和 3.7%，而预估2015 年的经济增速则为 3.0%。[④]此外，正发党执政的前十年，跨国公司也愿意到土耳其投资，土耳其吸引外资超过了 1200 亿美元，在西亚地区数量最大。相对于陷入危机的欧洲和动荡的西亚北非地区而言，土耳其表现醒目。据此，土耳其一些乐观的观察家在 2013 年提出该国正面临提升高附加值技术产品的契机以及需进一步加大在该国不发达地区（东南部）在土地、资源和劳动力方面的开发。[⑤]

表 3-1　土耳其 2002~2014 年 GDP 增长水平[⑥]

2007	648753.606	101254.625	4.7
2008	742094.395	101921.73	0.7
2009	616703.325	97003.114	-4.8
2010	731608.367	105885.644	9.2
2011	773979.672	115174.724	8.8
2012	786282.517	117625.021	2.1
2013	823044.428	122556.461	4.2
2014	799001.454	126127.931	2.9

　　总而言之，土耳其提出雄心勃勃未来规划的时间点，恰恰是土耳其经济突飞猛进、高速发展的时候，反映的正是埃尔多安集团的信心。随着正发党连续赢得

---

　①　世界银行：《国内生产总值排名》，2016 年 1 月 15 日。

　②　世界银行网站：http://data.worldbank.org.cn/catalog，2016 年 1 月 15 日。

　③　本文成文时 2015 年的数据还不全，故采用 2014 年的数据，http://databank.worldbank.org/data/download/GDP.pdf，2016 年 1 月 15 日。

　④　http://www.worldbank.org/en/publication/global-economic-prospects/summary-table ,2016-01-15.

　⑤　"Turkey: A Landmark Decade Vision 2023"，http:// www.turkstat.gov.tr, 2016-01-15。

　⑥　The author built the chart according to OECD data in September 2015, Source: Turkey Statistics Associations, www.turkstat.gov.tr.

大选，它的自信心已经成为强大的政治意志。①值得注意的是，其中还有一个结构性的因素，即它有一个中东穆斯林世界的战略纵深，同时土耳其维持了与西方之间长期的特殊而紧密的关系。土耳其较好地利用了这种优势。尽管现在全球经济尚未走出危机的阴影，但若我们把眼光稍微放长，看看冷战结束以来的世界，全球化确实是让不同地区的民族或多或少都受益了，不用说金砖国家，阿拉伯世界和非洲都经历了一个加速发展的过程。随着土耳其的崛起，它必然也要寻求新的、与其实力相称的定位。

表 3-2　土耳其 2002~2014 年经济贸易数据变化 ②

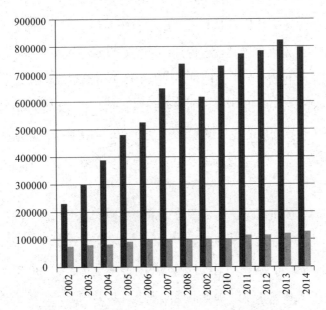

Left: GDP in current exchange rate of US Dollar (Unit: 100,000 US Dollar)

Right: GDP in fixed Lira rate of 1998 (Unit: 100,000 Lira)

---

① 福山曾指出，不管是什么政策或计划，关键还是要有强有力的体制和政治意志。[美]弗朗西斯·福山：《美国处在十字路口：民主、权力与新保守主义的遗产》，周琪译，中国社会科学出版社，2008 年版，第 107 页。

② The author built the chart according to OECD data in September 2015, Source: Turkey Statistics Associations, www.turkstat.gov.tr.

第二，土耳其的地缘优势在全球化时代日益突出。随着全球化的加深，尤其是全球经济重心的东移，新兴经济体国家的表现成为本世纪一道亮丽的风景线。在这个过程中，土耳其独特的地缘优势更加突出。以冷战的结束为背景，土耳其开始摆脱其"边疆国家"的地位，将自己定位成一个沟通东、西的"桥梁"国家和地处欧、亚、非三大洲之间的"中枢国家"，正发党执政之后就是将土耳其的地缘战略以"中枢国家"的认识定位为基础的。[①]

我们从正发党的官方网站上可以看到，"2023百年愿景"包含的很多具体项目与伊斯坦布尔有关，这主要是因其区位优势非常突出。伊斯坦布尔不仅交通便利，而且其地缘、经济和文明地位都有深厚的历史积淀。作为地区当之无愧的地缘、经济和文明中心，它同时也是去往中东、非洲和中亚的中转地。土耳其近年来的强势崛起，更是强化了其欧亚中枢的地位。正是在这个背景下，土耳其提出了建设国际航空中心的计划（如世界第一大机场伊斯坦布尔大机场计划）、跨越博斯普鲁斯海峡隧道的从北京到伦敦的丝绸之路计划、黑海和地中海贸易港口和路线的建设计划（包括海底隧道建设），以及将伊斯坦布尔建设成为新的金融中心[②]，等等，这都是基于土耳其本身的地缘优势，即它处于欧、亚、非三大陆之间，具有整合的条件。

第三，土耳其的帝国遗产与大国意识是其重要的心理基础与潜在因素。从历史来看，土耳其人曾是伟大的奥斯曼帝国（1299~1922年）的主人。作为世界上最后一个穆斯林帝国，它长期对欧洲构成明显优势与威胁。100年前，奥斯曼帝国崩溃，土耳其人在凯末尔的领导下建立了土耳其共和国，继承了帝国的部分遗产。帝国时代，土耳其人就参与欧洲事务，在帝国晚期又开启了效仿西方进行变革以求现代化的进程，这被土耳其共和国所延续。所以说，土耳其人不止是承载了帝国的失败和苦难，还延续了近300年的现代化理想，它一度还成为20世纪初一些其他国家的人的榜样。在20世纪60年代，土耳其就被西方学者认为是

---

① 参见拙文：《从历史角度看土耳其的多边主义战略》，载《阿拉伯世界研究》，2015年第1期，第54页。

② 同上。

继日本之后第二个实现了现代化的非西方国家。因此，土耳其的大国意识主要就是源于帝国遗产和成功的现代化。土耳其的帝国意识，并不能将其等同为帝国野心。历史既可能是一个负担，也可以是一种灵感之源，从凯末尔党人开始，土耳其人就善于利用历史为当下服务。土耳其的各种积极举动和战略目标与这样一种历史意识不无关系。在前述埃尔多安的讲话中，这种历史意识是非常明显的。

作为奥斯曼帝国的主人，土耳其人将帝国的伟大遗产及其记忆一并继承下来。土耳其人在凯末尔时代曾为了现代化和进步而排斥和否定帝国历史，在土耳其发展到一定阶段之后，又开始重新评价帝国，在 1999 年，土耳其还曾庆祝奥斯曼帝国建国 700 周年，这些都是其帝国意识的反映，将其说成是"新奥斯曼主义"的症候也不无道理。奥斯曼帝国的历史作为土耳其学生的必修课，对于塑造土耳其人的民族和历史意识具有重要的作用。这样的学习会强化关于帝国的知识，这是关于一个帝国兴起、征服、扩张、强盛与衰落的历史，它在领土范围上包括了今天的土耳其领土，还有叙利亚、伊拉克、黎巴嫩、巴勒斯坦、阿拉伯半岛、黑海以北、高加索的一部分、北非以及巴尔干等地区，它们都曾属于奥斯曼帝国的广阔领土。土耳其人的民族精神、历史意识和大国情怀就是通过这样的历史记忆被唤醒和塑造的，它自然地也会塑造土耳其人的国家观、历史观、未来观和世界观。正发党为土耳其人所设定的一系列目标，所反映的也正是这样的一种大国意识。

第四，它反映了土耳其历史发展到当前阶段的内在要求。正发党统治的时代，正是世界范围内新兴大国崛起的时代。在过去很长一段时间，土耳其坚持西方化，紧跟欧美，这是一种做学生的心态。随着土耳其自身的发展和自信心的增强，土耳其大国意识的觉醒使其要求一个更远大的、不一样的未来。这个未来不再是跟在西方屁股后面亦步亦趋，而是要克服凯末尔主义盛期的那种历史虚无主义，建立自己的主体性，对帝国和伊斯兰文明做重新的认可。对稳定秩序和繁荣未来的期许，使得土耳其人必须在当下提出适合其历史发展阶段的目标。

如果把眼光稍微放长远，就不难发现，正发党所继承与延续的是 20 世纪 80 年代末以来厄扎尔的遗产，土耳其领导人也主动承认过这一点，无论是前述埃尔多安在讲话中的历史重述，还是达乌特奥卢在阐述土耳其战略时的表述，都强调了对厄扎尔遗产的继承和发扬。厄扎尔所确定的是"伊斯兰+民主+技术现代性"。①厄扎尔的这个框架内涵了两种秩序：历史秩序与现实秩序。作为一个自我定位为中右的、保守民主的政党，正发党的政纲和展望并没有超出厄扎尔的框架。历史地看，厄扎尔的这个框架已经意味着对僵化的凯末尔主义的纠正。这是 20 世纪 80 年代以来土耳其在融入全球化过程中社会结构发生重大改变的结果，简单来说，这个改变就是以前被忽视、被压制和被边缘化的底层社会开始崛起，不仅仅是通过政治民主化，更重要的是通过经济上新中产阶层的崛起来实现的，他们开始挑战凯末尔主义国家精英对权力、资源、文化和意识形态的垄断，要重新确立土耳其的文明和文化的主体性。

重新界定世俗主义就是对凯末尔主义的一种超越。当前正发党的主张可以被标识为"埃尔多安主义"。②如果用历史秩序与现实秩序来定位当下的土耳其的话，历史秩序必然要包含两个层面：一是正发党的保守主义所代表的伊斯兰传统；二是以突厥认同和现代民族国家为基础的土耳其民族主义，它们提供的是精神和归属感。现实秩序指的是世俗主义、民主与技术现代性，这包含了物质和制度的维度，是对进步和发展的追求，但离开了历史秩序，单凭物质和制度的进步，土耳其人无法确立其主体性。正发党的定位和愿景正好为土耳其人提供了这两种秩序。

正发党统治的时代正赶上土耳其进入到下一个变革期。变革的重要表现就是要制定新宪法。土耳其近年来的以制宪为主要内容的政治辩论，是 20 世纪 80 年代以来土耳其政治变革尚未完成的表现。20 世纪 80 年以来的土耳其，一直使用军方所确立的宪法。这部宪法的一个重要作用，就是要把军方监国的地位予以巩固，并对土耳其的政党政治有所规训，尤其是要应对冷战时期土耳其出现的左倾化问题。显然，这早就是一部不合时宜的宪法了，其大部分内容都经历过修改，重新

---

① 具体可以参见拙文：《从历史角度看土耳其的多边主义战略》，载《阿拉伯世界研究》，2015 年第 1 期。

② 具体见拙文：《土耳其模式：历史与现实》，载《新疆师范大学学报》，2012 年 3 月。

制定一部宪法在土耳其是有普遍共识的，各政党已就此进行了多次协商。

综上，正发党提出的一系列发展目标和愿景，与冷战后土耳其经济与社会变迁的内在逻辑是耦合的。这是一个大变革的时代。从 20 世纪 80 年代的厄扎尔到现在的埃尔多安，土耳其现代历史已经进入到一个新阶段，如何重新定位国家、政治与文化，如何调整对外关系，都到了一个必须有所作为的关键时刻。在这个过程中，土耳其有一个"大国梦"。如达乌特奥卢所言，土耳其首先要成为一个地区性大国，要兼备软、硬两方面的实力，再进一步谋求全球性的大国的地位。

第五，领导人的个人因素也不容忽视。土耳其国内外现在基本都认可土耳其已经进入了"埃尔多安时代"。21 世纪过去的这些年，土耳其被深深地打上了埃尔多安的烙印。他是一个有显著领袖魅力（韦伯所谓"克里斯玛"）的人：穷苦出身，青年时代就加入伊斯兰主义政党；20 世纪 90 年代中期成为伊斯坦布尔市市长，政绩显赫；曾因伊斯兰主义政治言论而坐牢；2001 年与居尔一起创立正义与发展党，次年就问鼎土耳其最高权力，并掌控土耳其至今。埃尔多安是一个敢说敢做的人，讨好选民有独特的一套，打压政治对手毫不留情；他还是一个行事高调、好大喜功、经常口出狂言的人，但也因此深得一些铁杆"粉丝"的支持，他为土耳其人带来了生活上的实惠，也带来了自豪感和尊严。尤其是在 2007 年以后，正发党连续赢得大选胜利，使其自信心"爆棚"，他的政治野心也随之增长。当他感觉到自身权势受到威胁的时候，也越发想把权力集中到自己手里。2014 年 8 月，埃尔多安成为土耳其历史上第一个由民选产生的总统，成功地在土耳其复制了俄罗斯的"普京模式"。如果不出意外，埃尔多安可以连任干到 2024 年，正好是跨越了土耳其实现百年愿景的 2023 年。埃尔多安还希望能够使土耳其变为总统制，届时他将可以把更多权力集于自身，按照自己的意愿塑造土耳其。如果埃尔多安取得成功，他将比土耳其国父凯末尔主政的时间（1923~1938 年）还长，也将是凯末尔之后权势最大的土耳其领导人。①

从前述意义上说，"2023 百年愿景"既是正发党的愿景，也是土耳其的愿景，

① 昝涛、董雨：《埃尔多安、总统制与土耳其的未来》，载《澎湃新闻》，2015 年 12 月 26 日。

更是埃尔多安本人的愿景。这是埃尔多安对土耳其的承诺，是他对土耳其未来的某种历史性自觉。"2053 展望"和"2071 千年目标"反映的是埃尔多安利用历史资源和符号吸引眼球的政治营销策略，为了实现自己的政治野心以及按照自己的思路塑造土耳其，通过一系列的愿景和目标，设定话语和框架，激发起民众的热望，使土耳其人愿意追随他。

（二）围绕"土耳其梦"的争论

土耳其提出上述一系列发展战略畅想或规划后，在国内外引起了广泛的关注及不同的争议，体现在以下方面：既有赞美者，亦有批评、怀疑甚至嘲笑者。

第一种观点是赞扬埃尔多安和正发党。赞同者高度评价了埃尔多安和正发党提出的各项宏大目标，认为这些以未来为旨归的高远目标在土耳其历史上是不曾出现过的，对土耳其民族的发展、强盛和自信都将产生很大的促进作用，必将彪炳史册。赞同者对土耳其未来的畅想更加大胆：希望在 2053 年的时候，土耳其经济总量能进入世界前三；2071 年的时候，土耳其就能成为领导世界的首屈一指的强国。

持上述看法的以土耳其专栏作家穆斯塔法·余莱克利（Mustafa Yürekli）为代表。他首先阐述了土耳其发展愿景对正发党和埃尔多安的历史意义。2011 年 5 月 1 日，他在一篇文章中谈道："正发党的 2023 年全部目标，已经表达了使土耳其壮大的意志，它要给人类提供一个新的世界秩序，承诺带来和平、正义与美好。"穆斯塔法对埃尔多安的评价是："在埃尔多安当总理期间，土耳其开始崛起，要走自己的路（kendi yolunda yürüme），有意愿和意志让人听他的话，并打破了旧有的东西。埃尔多安的土耳其，努力做的是让伊斯兰世界获得希望、激情与团结。"他说，"正是因为有了埃尔多安，才使得土耳其在历史上首次有了关乎未来的计划，不管怎么说，这样的愿景和讨论都是好的。土耳其能走到今天，毫无疑问是埃尔多安的胜利。"穆斯塔法看重的是埃尔多安开启了土耳其人对未来的期许，并形成了全国性的讨论，大家都希望土耳其能成为真正发达的、强大的、有影响力的伟大国家。从这个意义上说，正发党与埃尔多安给了土耳其人信念、决心与意志。

其次，他对土耳其的各个愿景都表示肯定，尤其对中长期目标非常确信。他认为：土耳其仅有 2023 年目标是不够的，因为这还只是着眼于短期。"我们必须为 2071 年制定计划，使土耳其成为世界主导，成为世界的统治者。我们的大学、艺术家、作家，所有的知识分子，都有责任去助推土耳其的短、中、长期目标。这三个目标的确定是对国人的艰难考试，是诚实的考验，是忠诚的测试，是对祖国之爱的衡量。在这个层次上，埃尔多安在设定了'2023 目标'之后，如果也能够将 2053 和 2071 设为政治前景，就会在历史上占据非常特别的地位。"①

再次，他也对土耳其未来的目标提出了自己的畅想："土耳其在 2023 年必须要成为经济总量上世界前十名的国家。能够看到这样的意志与决心，我们民族就会很幸福。为什么不能在 2053 年将目标设定为成为世界前三名？30 年可以做很多事情……要自信，要有正确的计划，要有强大的民主意志以及艰苦的努力……在2071 年，或许可以实现伊斯兰的团结，土耳其在社会结构、经济以及政治方面将成为世界上首屈一指的国家，为什么不能成为领导世界的国家？2023 必然要激发2053，2053 也必然要带来 2071。"

穆斯塔法对正发党和埃尔多安的高度评价，对三个愿景的肯定和畅想反映的也正是土耳其经过十年发展后土耳其人日益上升的信心。

第二种观点是对"土耳其梦"的质疑和批评。有的人援引经济数据给埃尔多安和正发党"泼冷水"，认为那些愿景和目标不可能实现，纯粹只是"梦"而已；有的人提到土耳其国内面临的重大问题，比如：创新人才不足、能源严重依赖进口、库尔德分裂主义的挑战等；还有的人从狭隘民族主义的角度质疑正发党的新宪法设计，认为那实际上是屈从于库尔德工人党，是要分裂土耳其，包括埃尔多安喜欢使用的历史比附以及对征服历史的美化，都受到了批评。

具体而言，首先，批评者高度质疑土耳其经济与社会目标的可达性。在他们看来，过去十几年土耳其经济能够取得较大发展，主要是制造业对经济增长贡献

---

① 以上引文参见 Mustafa Yürekli："Erdogan in 2053 ve 2071 hedefi var mı？"，http://m.haber7.com/yazarDetay.php?id=739248，访问时间：2016 年 1 月 15 日。

大，靠的是人力资本。但是，如果土耳其不能发展到生产高附加值产品的工业阶段，它就会陷入"中等收入陷阱"①，不可能再保持高速增长。为此，土耳其必须投资于人力资本②。但批评者认为，土耳其的现实情况是在朝着相反的方向走——教育机构和有才能的人受到了压制。在这样的环境中，土耳其没有办法保持高速增长。这被认为是经济发展的普遍规律。③总之，正发党在设定"2023百年愿景"的时候，当时看是有可能实现的，但随时间的推移，已经越来越不可能了。④除了上述挑战，有的经济学家还指出，土耳其面临缺少能源的挑战，如何确保能源供应，对土耳其来说并不是一件轻松的事。另外，土耳其国内受库尔德问题的长期困扰，国内团结有待加强，尤其是需要整合落后的库尔德部落地区。⑤此外，按照较新的评估，土耳其的人类发展指数位列全球第83位，在男女平等方面做得不好，教育水平也偏低，土耳其的青年失业率过高，政府赤字攀升，经济泡沫化，这些都是土耳其实现其"2023百年愿景"的障碍。⑥

其次，批评之声还涉及正发党的民族政策。土耳其学者萨迪批评了正发党提

---

① 2006年，世界银行首次提出了"中等收入陷阱"（Middle Income Trap）的概念，指的是：一个国家在进入中等收入水平以后，往往会陷入经济停滞，在劳动力价格方面与低收入国家相比丧失了优势，而又无法在尖端技术研制方面与富裕国家竞争，因而很难成为高收入国家。

② 达乌特奥卢在2016年1月中旬的伦敦演讲中也指出，为了与经济低迷对抗，除了提高生产能力和强化资本市场，还必须增强劳动力市场的弹性，提升基本的和职业的技能，打造有质量的人力资本。"Global investors invited to participate in Turkey's rise" in *Daily Sabah*, Jan. 19, 2016.

③ 根据福山的综述，关于发展的思想大概经历过三个阶段：（1）在20世纪40年代，一个被广泛认可的信念是，相信通过大规模投资于基础设施建设，尤其是大型基建项目可以促进经济发展，与此相伴的就是公、私机构都在支持制定经济发展计划；（2）上述信念和做法在20世纪六七十年代就遭到了巨大的幻灭，随之出现的是强调促进人力资本的发展以及可持续性发展；（3）里根－撒切尔主义则强调自由市场和全球经济一体化。[美]弗朗西斯·福山：《美国处在十字路口：民主、权力与新保守主义的遗产》，周琪译，中国社会科学出版社，2008年版，第104~107页。

④ "Turkey's 2023 Goals: from Reality to Dream", http://mobile.todayszaman.com/anasayfa_turkeys-2023-goals-from-reality-to-dream_357254.html, see: 2016-01-15.

⑤ Turkey: A Landmark Decade Vision 2023, www.foreignaffairs.com/Turkey2013, see: 2016-01-05.

⑥ Jean-Pierre Lehmann, "Turkey's 2023 Economic Goal in Global Perspective", http://www.edam.org.tr/document/Lehmann-June%202011.pdf, see: 2015-12-22.

出的改革计划尤其是新宪法提议。①萨迪属于民族主义者，顽固地坚持土耳其旧的民族主义立场，批评正发党推动的多样化，认为实现多元化的土耳其会走向分裂，沦为"大库尔德斯坦"（Büyük Kürdistan）的应声虫。他在评论正发党的库尔德政策时称："今天，他们去找死刑犯、在监狱中的恐怖组织头子寻找解决方案，甚至要分裂我们的国家，从土耳其民族手中夺走它的主权，在这个条件下还要达成什么'协定'（mutabakat），我们深感忧虑。"这里，萨迪指的是正发党的"伊姆拉勒进程"。②这一进程对于土耳其来说至关重要，也是它解决长期困扰国家政治的库尔德问题的一个重要步骤。但从2015年下半年开始，土耳其国家与库尔德工人党再次陷入冲突，该进程实际上被搁浅了，土耳其目前几乎失去了对东南部地区的控制，当地再次陷入反恐泥潭，随着叙利亚局势失控，土耳其日益面临库尔德问题区域化和复杂化的局面。③萨迪还认为，"新的"宪法和前述少数民族政策是要清除土耳其民族的观念（Türk Milleti kavrami），这就等于是剥夺了土耳其人的主权；而以往的捍卫母语的条款被取消之后，司法也变成了是双语的，公共服务部门实行双语，对于土耳其民族主义者来说是不可接受的。公共服务中将有库尔德语翻译。为了使以本地语言所做之诉讼便于理解，公职部门将雇用翻译。而干部将被要求会多种语言。广播和教育也已经可以使用本地语言。④土耳其民族主义者认为，这些新的趋势将损害土耳其国家主权的完整，无异于分裂国家。

---

① Sadi Somuncuoglu: "2023 ve 2071 Vizyonu Ne Demek?", http://www.21yyte.org/tr/arastirma/milli-guvenlik-ve-dis-politika-arastirmalari-merkezi/2013/02/16/6881/2023-ve-2071-vizyonu-ne-demek, see: 2016-01-06.

② 从2012年11月起，土耳其政府重新启动了与库尔德工人党领袖厄贾兰的和平谈判，因为厄贾兰依然被关在伊姆拉勒监狱之中，因此该谈判被称为"伊姆拉勒进程"。

③ 当下正在酝酿的关于叙利亚问题的日内瓦和谈进程中，土耳其与俄罗斯、西方国家发生了分歧，原因是土政府将与库尔德工人党合作的叙利亚库尔德民主党联盟（PYD）及其支持的民兵组织"人民保护联盟"（YPG）视为恐怖组织，力主将其排除在和谈进程之外，但美国没有接受这个观点，还派总统特使与之接触，指出"人民保护联盟"与库尔德工人党有明显的不同。这是土耳其目前面临的库尔德问题区域化和日益复杂化的写照。CNN Türk, 2016年2月11日。

④ http://www.akparti.org.tr/upload/documents/akparti2023siyasivizyonuturkce.pdf, see: 2016-01-15.

再次，还有一种质疑的声音是针对埃尔多安多次引用历史上征服者并将他们美化，批评者认为，埃尔多安的美化不但不会成功，而且会将土耳其引入歧途。在西方学者看来，那些征服者都是侵略者，阿斯兰的目标是什叶派的、以埃及为根据地的法蒂玛王朝，曼齐克特也不是一个和平、繁荣与自由的国家形象，那里没有宽容、美德和善意；阿斯兰将脚踏在基督教王国的领导人罗曼努斯的脖子上以示侮辱，这个历史细节也不容忽视。埃尔多安的言论被视为某种奥斯曼帝国旧梦的复活，在地区外交层面上，这样的野心只会引发更多的疑虑和不安。甚至有评论者一直怀疑埃尔多安的伊斯兰主义倾向和野心，这样的一种伊斯兰主义的奥斯曼旧梦，会腐蚀凯末尔主义所确立的世俗政体，进而威胁到民主。批评者认为，埃尔多安的"2071千年目标"，带有宗教性和教派性暗示，很可能是针对什叶派的伊朗、基督教世界以及埃及。不过，当前的中东乱局已使土耳其的应对显得捉襟见肘，反对之声越来越多。埃尔多安无论诉诸奥斯曼主义还是伊斯兰团结，都很难改变中东地区与穆斯林世界分裂和动荡的局面，阿拉伯国家不会欢迎奥斯曼帝国的回归。[①]

上述从不同立场和角度提出来的赞成或质疑的意见各有其道理。任何一个愿景都是带着美好的愿望去畅想未来。土耳其的2023、2053和2071目标也是期望到将来的某个时候后人或后代的后代将生活得不一样，甚至全世界都能感到很幸福。这本身没有什么不好，尤其是能够为土耳其人带来实惠与希望，是值得肯定的。笔者已经指出，埃尔多安和正发党提出的各种愿景和目标植根于土耳其现代历史发展的内在逻辑，有其合理性与必要性，但也有很强的政治宣传色彩。不过，愿望是一回事，实际又是另外一回事。从经济数据和指标来看，土耳其到2023年实现其梦想几乎已是不可能的。据估计，土耳其唯有连续保持国内生产总值以10%的速度增长，才能在2023年达到世界前十。但是，从土耳其过去几年的数据来看，2011~2014年土耳其国内生产总值的平均增长率是4%；以过去的12年为单位，土耳其的年均增长率是5.8%，土耳其以这个速度发展到2023年，其国内生产总值会增长到1.3万亿

---

① "Erdogan's Grand Vision: Rise and Decline", http://www.world afffairs jounal.org, see: 2016-01-22。

美元。这样，"2023 百年愿景"中 2 万亿美元的目标就只是"做梦"而已。另外，如果达不到年增长率 10%，人均收入达到 25000 美元的目标也就实现不了。以当前的速度看，土耳其在 2023 年只能实现人均 15000 美元。土耳其的出口在 2003~2010 年期间的年均增长率是 17%，如果能够保持这个速度，则可以实现到 2023 年达到 5000 亿美元，但是，土耳其在 2011~2014 年均出口增长是 8.5%，显然是不够的。①因此，土耳其要实现其愿景和目标的希望确实越来越渺茫了。

正发党当前对此亦有清醒认识，正致力于通过改革和继续加大基础设施投资来扭转困局。②从新宪法尤其是民族政策的角度批评正发党的百年愿景，尤其是拒绝接受正发党政府与库尔德工人党的和解，不接受多元主义，只能说土耳其主流的民族主义还未受到根本的挑战。正发党的思路符合其一贯主张的以"更多的民主"解决库尔德问题的思路，如果不能推行下去，库尔德问题将困扰土耳其更长时间。关于土耳其的帝国情怀与大国梦，前文已有涉及，此处不再赘述。值得一提的是，批评者对埃尔多安伊斯兰主义倾向的担心，所谓埃尔多安和正发党威胁了世俗主义。在"2023 百年愿景"中正发党强调世俗主义是平等对待各宗教，不干涉宗教信仰的自由，这是从积极世俗主义向消极世俗主义的转变。仅以伊斯兰主义的视角观察埃尔多安和正发党，是非常片面与狭隘的，土民众对正发党的支持主要也不是因为其宗教主张。③此类批评更多的是源于某

---

① "Turkey's 2023 Goals: from Reality to Dream", http://mobile.todayszaman.com/anasayfa_turkeys-2023-goals-from-reality-to-dream_357254.html, see: 2016-01-15.

② 根据时任土耳其总理达乌特奥卢的介绍，土耳其现阶段的改革主要有三个部分：部门的转型（sectoral transformation）、结构性的大调整（structural-macro reforms）与欧盟（EU）进程；基础设施建设主要是"2023 愿景"提到的一系列投资计划，尤其是机场、港口和道路建设，目标在于将土耳其打造成一个物流中心。"Global investors invited to participate in Turkey's rise" in *Daily Sabah*, Jan. 19, 2016.

③ 从 2002 年正发党第一次赢得土耳其大选来分析，对当年选举影响最大的还是宗教因素，而不是愤怒和经济因素。正发党与世俗主义的共和人民党（CHP）的最重要区别就是对宗教的立场。正发党标榜的是要挑战对宗教自由的限制，比如头巾问题。根据学者的研究，对正发党的支持并不能完全说是出于宗教的原因。正发党算是温和化的伊斯兰主义，但这不是它获得支持的最主要原因，土耳其的选民区隔主要还不是世俗与宗教，而是关系到社会经济政策的左、右之分。AliÇarkoglu, Ersin Klaycioglu, Turkish Democracy Today,（I.B. Tauris, 2007），pp. 216-218.

种伊斯兰恐惧症。[①]

基于"土耳其梦"与"一带一路"倡议的中土合作

2013 年，中国提出了建设"一带一路"的倡议。这是中国对外开放的新思路，也提出了中国与不同国家进行新型合作的时代课题。土耳其是欧亚大陆上地理位置极重要的区域性大国[②]，对"一带一路"具有重要作用。2015 年 11 月，中国国家主席习近平在土耳其安塔利亚举行的二十国集团峰会前会见了土耳其总统埃尔多安，并强调中土两国应该加强战略沟通，对接发展战略，实现共同发展和共同繁荣。埃尔多安表示，土方愿积极参加"一带一路"框架下的合作，欢迎中国企业加大对土耳其基础设施等领域投资。中土签署了政府间共同推进"一带一路"建设谅解备忘录，为双方在"一带一路"框架内推进各领域合作提供重要政策支持。[③]可见，中、土两国已经明确要加强"一带一路"框架下的合作，尤其是习主席强调要实现两国发展战略的对接，这也是前文着重探讨土耳其发展战略（"土耳其梦"）的原因和意义。

（一）土耳其对"一带一路"的看法与观点

土方对中国的倡议非常关心，原因在于：一是中国在 2010 年已成为第二大

---

① 埃尔多安曾说："有的人提出，伊斯兰世界与西方世界的价值观之间存在尖锐的冲突。仿佛伊斯兰世界盲目地、狂热地并整体地要与西方敌对；也有人把伊斯兰教只是与恐怖主义等同，并昧着良心去制造一种全球性的伊斯兰恐惧症。不管是谁以什么名义，我们都坚决地反对这些做法。" R. Tayyip Erdogan, Küresel Baris Vizyonu, Istanbul: Medeniyetler Ittifaki Yayinlari, 2012, p.24.

② 近年来，中东地区出现剧变和动荡，土耳其在地区事务中也发挥着越来越重要而特殊的作用。"在很多方面，土耳其已经符合一个地区性大国的标准。" Sinan Ulgen, A Place in the Sun or Fifteen Minutes of Fame? Understanding Turkey's New Foreign Policy, Carnegie Papers, Carnegie Europe, Carnegie Endowment for International Peace, No. 1, Dec 2010, p. 5.

③ 《习近平会见土耳其总统，签署一带一路谅解备忘录》，http://www.cs.com.cn/xwzx/hg/201511/t20151115_4841281.html，2016 年 1 月 19 日。

世界经济体，具有世界性影响，土耳其不能忽略中国之存在；二是中国是安理会常任理事国之一，具有举足轻重的作用，对一些涉及土耳其国家利益的问题具有影响力；三是土耳其对中国贸易存在巨大逆差，一直在寻求可能的突破，也就是尽量弥补土耳其方面的贸易逆差，土方的基本考虑是吸引更多的中国投资，埃尔多安与习近平主席会见时也专门谈到了这一点；四是"一带一路"为土耳其实现"土耳其梦"提供了重要的机遇。亚洲基础设施投资银行和丝路基金的设立引起了土耳其方面的高度重视，土耳其已经成为亚投行的创始会员国。

那么，土耳其人对"一带一路"倡议的具体看法是什么呢？根据笔者近年来的调研，大致上可以归为以下几个方面：

第一，土耳其人认为，"一带一路"对土耳其有潜在的巨大利益。正发党很清楚，无论采用什么样的选举策略，都必须首先把经济搞好。目前，土耳其的经济出现了危机的前兆，里拉贬值很快，通胀较为严重，引起了正发党的忧虑，亟需进一步寻找新的经济机遇，"一带一路"的提出对土耳其意味着新的机遇。

第二，土耳其认为"丝绸之路"经济带是个好的理念。①土耳其自认是"丝绸之路"的传统通道，伊斯坦布尔是其终点，在土耳其境内有很多古代丝绸之路的遗迹，比如在土耳其前总统居尔的故乡开塞利，就有着长期的商贸传统，"丝绸之路"就是其新建博物馆的主打项目之一。土耳其与传统的"丝绸之路"有着密切的关系，渴望通过这样一个世界瞩目的历史理念的复兴，为当代土耳其的经济和文化繁荣寻找新的思路，并与中国的"一带一路"规划相结合。

第三，也有部分声音表达了对"一带一路"的担忧。土耳其与中国的经济结

---

① 早在 2008 年，土耳其联合阿塞拜疆、伊朗、格鲁吉亚、哈萨克斯坦以及吉尔吉斯斯坦发起了"丝绸之路倡议"，旨在扫除横亘于丝路沿线国家的贸易障碍。2009 年，土耳其总统居尔访华，在与国家主席胡锦涛会谈时表达"希望通过两国政府的共同努力，重新振兴古丝绸之路"。2012 年 2 月，时任国家副主席习近平访问土耳其，中土两国领导人都提到了复兴丝绸之路的设想。2012 年 4 月，土耳其时任总理埃尔多安访华时，就振兴古丝绸之路与中国领导人进行了讨论，提出希望双方共同推动铁路联通古丝绸之路的建设。参见唐志超：《中国与土耳其对接"一带一路"需注意五大风险》，http://www.mesi.shisu.edu.cn/0d/a4/c3711a69028/page.htm，访问时间：2016 年 1 月 25 日。

构有很大的相似性，两国之间的经济发展模式也是相似的。①土耳其也面临着向海外寻求市场和吸引投资的计划。中、土两国领导人在会晤期间多次提到要将中国提出的"丝绸之路经济带"与土耳其的"中间走廊"计划②相对接，将中国的倡议与土耳其的全方位发展计划相对接。土耳其将中亚视为自己的势力范围，因为那里的民族被土耳其人视为语言、宗教和文化上的"亲戚"，这是土耳其的"泛突厥主义"意识，表达为文化和政治上的倾向性。土耳其将高加索视为非常重要的势力范围，也有在阿塞拜疆与土耳其之间、格鲁吉亚与土耳其之间投资铁路的规划。也因此，部分土耳其人表达了对中国"丝绸之路经济带"的疑虑：中土之间是不是存在竞争关系。对于内陆欧亚地区（Central Eurasia），土耳其的战略主要还是立足于扩大市场份额，将自身打造成为这个地区丰富能源的转运通道国家，同时利用语言、宗教、种族、历史等方面的软实力扩大自己的影响。

第四，土耳其人认识到，丝绸之路经济带不只是一个经济规划，也是一个文化和安全方面的计划。"一带一路"的提出，除了与产能转移有关之外，也与中国西北边疆地区的安全形势有关系，因此，土耳其人比较多地关注新疆与丝绸之路经济带的关系。

从总体上看，土方对"一带一路"的反应普遍是积极的、有兴趣的。

（二）土耳其的独特优势与问题③

在了解了土耳其对"一带一路"的关切之后，从开展"一带一路"框架下中土合作及实现双方发展战略对接的角度来说，该如何看待土耳其的优势及潜在的问题呢？

在笔者看来，土耳其具有五方面优势。第一，在地缘格局方面，土耳其地处欧、亚、非三大陆结合部，北临俄罗斯，东临高加索、中亚、伊朗，西近欧洲，

---

① 中土经济结构相似，都比较依赖于劳动密集型产业，搞出口导向发展，两国在纺织品出口方面长期处于竞争关系；两国都渴望在中东和非洲地区扩大影响力。

② 土耳其近年来提出的"中间走廊"（Orta Koridor），是一个连接亚洲和欧洲的交通网络（ulaşim ağini），覆盖的范围是从土耳其、阿塞拜疆经里海（Hazar Denizi）一直到中亚和中国。

③ 这一节系笔者 2015 年 12 月 16 日在中国人民大学中土智库对话上的发言整理而成。

其南与东南是北非——阿拉伯地区，土耳其还扼守黑海通往地中海的海峡，拥有得天独厚的地缘优势，战略地位极为重要。这样一个独特的区位优势，使得土耳其成为沟通东西方经济与文化的桥梁。就像达乌特奥卢曾说过的，"土耳其的优势是可以同时讲两种文明的语言"。从推进"一带一路"的角度说，首先需要重视的就是土耳其的这种辐射广阔的区位优势。

第二，在经济上，土耳其虽然现在面临经济增速放缓的挑战，但回顾过去的十余年，土耳其在正发党的领导下，经济与社会发展都取得了长足进步，加入欧盟的进程仍然在继续推进。该国还是二十国集团的重要成员国，是很多伊斯兰国家的榜样。土耳其有 7700 万人口，且平均年龄在 30 岁左右，非常年轻，潜力很大。土耳其不是个能源丰富的国家，能取得今日之成就，说明它的经济发展模式和产业结构比主要依靠能源创收的国家要健康得多。

第三，政治上，土耳其是一个较为稳定的已经完成了政治转型的国家。建国92 年以来，土耳其长期实行西方化政策。1946 年土耳其进行了政治改革，向多党民主制过渡。在世界范围内的非西方国家中，从中东变局引发的动荡来看，土耳其的政治制度和体制是相对稳定和成熟的。从制度环境来说，土耳其的政治、经济、投资、社会福利、文化、媒体等方面都以欧洲为标准，虽并未完全达到，但长期的加入欧盟的进程已经且正在改变土耳其，使其变得更加规范，也更适合外国投资。达乌特奥卢也于 2016 年 1 月中旬在伦敦的演讲中特别强调要改善制度环境，使土耳其更适合投资，并强调了欧盟进程对土耳其的重要意义。[1]换个角度说，欧盟和北约都是土耳其的重要外部规定性。

第四，在文化与体制上，土耳其是个世俗国家，向来以国父凯末尔·阿塔图克确立的世俗体制而闻名。凯末尔主义的世俗体制是土耳其各方都尊重的底线，目前尚未受到根本性挑战。土耳其的国民素质较高，文化上很开放。"土耳其版本的伊斯兰"也更温和与包容。尽管在土耳其的民族叙事中，突厥是一个很重要的古老认同，甚至之前的鲜卑、匈奴也一并被认同了，但作为与奥斯曼帝国的兴起

---

[1]　"Global investors invited to participate in Turkey's rise," in *Daily Sabah*, January 19, 2016.

直接相关的突厥力量，他们是在 11 世纪的时候才登上近东历史舞台的。尤其是在 1258 年蒙古人攻破巴格达并残杀了阿巴斯王朝的哈里发之后，阿拉伯的伊斯兰帝国崩溃了，这时奥斯曼－突厥人是以伊斯兰帝国的继承者和复兴者面貌出现的，土耳其人成了伊斯兰的拯救者。[①]由于皈依伊斯兰较晚，还不断吸收古波斯、拜占庭、古希腊、罗马等多方面的历史文明遗产，而且主要通过"苏菲主义"[②]的修行方式皈依，土耳其的伊斯兰教呈现出相当不同的特色，简单来说就是更强调神秘主义的内敛传统，较少教条化的理解[③]；亦积极通过伊斯兰教发挥与扩大自身的影响力[④]。

第五，在教育方面，土耳其也拥有较发达的资源。土耳其的高等教育水平较高，大部分优秀高校已经实现了英文教学，努力与先进的西方模式和标准接轨。土耳其已经承认中国的高考成绩，在接收中国学生方面没有制度性障碍。在相关领域，中、土未来合作的空间很大。此外，土耳其的宗教教育也很先进与发达，其"去极端化"经验值得借鉴。

与此同时，土耳其当下也存在五个问题。第一，土耳其处于复杂的地区格局中。中东地区长期动荡，近年来，伊拉克、叙利亚形势恶化，土耳其作为邻国深受影响，包括"伊斯兰国"问题、库尔德问题、200 多万难民滞留土耳其的问题，以及因战机事件与俄罗斯关系恶化等问题。

第二，以埃尔多安为首的土耳其领导层在处理内外危机方面存在颇多争议。比如，正发党政府与居兰运动的关系、俄土战机事件、购买中国的红旗九导弹等。

---

① 诚如希提（Philip K. Hitti）所言，1258 年之后是蒙古人的"亲戚"——奥斯曼土耳其人——"恢复了伊斯兰教军事光荣，把伊斯兰教的旗帜胜利地竖立在广大的新地域"，奥斯曼土耳其人"是阿拉比亚宗教最后的捍卫者"。[美]菲利浦·希提：《阿拉伯通史》（上），马坚译，第 10 版，新世界出版社，2008 年，第 445 页。

② 在宗教现象学看来，苏菲主义属于一种宗教神秘主义，参见[意]马利亚苏塞·达瓦马尼：《宗教现象学》，高秉江译，人民出版社，2006 年，第 307~308 页。

③ 在凯末尔时代甚至出现了以发明出来的突厥世俗传统对抗伊斯兰认同的倾向。参见拙著：《现代国家与民族建构——20 世纪前期土耳其民族主义研究》，三联书店，2011 年，第 326~327 页。

④ 根据笔者 2015 年 2~3 月两次在土耳其的实地调研发现，不只是国家，更重要的是土耳其的民间宗教力量还以企业协会等非政府组织的形式在巴尔干、非洲和中亚等地区亦扮演了重要角色。

在处理这些问题方面的争议伤害了土耳其领导层的威望和"靠谱性"。埃尔多安力推总统制更是引发了批评者的担忧，认为他是在谋取更大的、不受约束的个人权力。甚至有土耳其评论家说，埃尔多安想要的根本就不是总统制，而是独裁①，或者当一个合法选举上台的"苏丹"。

第三，在经济上，土耳其已显出增长缓慢、动力不足，面临"中等收入陷阱"。土耳其人均国内生产总值已超 1 万美元，是中高收入国家。跨越"中等收入陷阱"的关键是产业升级、科技创新，需要大量人才，非短期政策可以奏效。

第四，土耳其的长期稳定受制于日益严重的教俗冲突。正发党有不容忽视的伊斯兰主义背景，自 2002 年上台以来，虽政绩显赫，但该党代表土耳其的保守主义势力，欲复兴伊斯兰，其包括取缔头巾立法在内的一系列"小动作"，已经引起世俗派的警觉，他们深恐土耳其的世俗化民主制度被侵蚀。近年来，土军方与正发党政府的关系、世俗派与保守派的关系、自由派与埃尔多安之间的关系，都越来越成为土耳其不稳定的诱因。

第五，土耳其长期面临极端民族主义的挑战。在 2015 年的两次选举中，"库尔德问题"一直是焦点。代表库尔德人的政党人民民主党（HDP）成功进入议会。"伊姆拉勒进程"已终止，对恐怖主义和库尔德分裂主义的担心引发了土耳其主体社会的民族主义反弹。针对库尔德工人党的反恐行动，包括对其在叙利亚北部基地的轰炸，迎合了这种民族情绪，提升了埃尔多安的支持率。②极端民族主义也不断出现在针对中国新疆问题的不理性言行上。

土耳其的上述优势和问题，是中国在推进"一带一路"过程中需要重视的。概言之，土耳其的优势使得对土合作和投资具有较大的吸引力；土耳其的问题又潜在地使这种合作存在一定的风险，尤其是地区局势和双边关系中的复杂和敏感问题，需要中国认真研究和理性对待。总之，土耳其的战略地位、综合实力以及在经济、政治和文化等方面跟中国的相关性，都不容轻视，中土关系在"一带一

---

① Ahmet Hakan, "Erdogan in istedigi sistem 'baskanlik sistemi' degil", http://sosyal.hurriyet.com.tr/yazar/ahmet-hakan_131/erdogan-in-istedigi-sistem-baskanlik-sistemi-deg_28095730, see: 2015-11-15.

② 参见拙文:《地区反恐需要稳定的土耳其》，载《环球时报》，2015 年 11 月 3 日。

路"框架下还存在很大的进步空间。

（三）中方在土耳其推进"一带一路"需注意的问题①

中国要与土耳其共同推进"一带一路"，我们除了需要了解土耳其对"一带一路"的态度、整体上把握土耳其的优势和问题，以及找准"土耳其梦"与"一带一路"战略倡议的对接点②之外，还需注意以下问题：

第一，中国与土耳其的关系确实涉及一些不容忽视的敏感问题。国内关于土耳其的知识生产的量和质都不够，难以满足外交、学术、思想和媒体等领域对有关土耳其的知识需求。③土耳其"骨子里"是一个支持、同情甚至主张"泛突厥主义"的国家——不是政治上的，就是文化上的。④中、土两国之间在"东突"问题上存在难解之结。⑤

第二，土耳其在中亚地区有软实力。亨廷顿曾说，土耳其是被布鲁塞尔拒绝，它又拒绝了麦加，它的命运将归于塔什干。无论是被布鲁塞尔拒绝，还是它拒绝

---

① 本节内容曾在笔者给盘古智库的研究报告《大选之际看土耳其——历史遗产、地缘政治及与中国的相关性》中论述过。参见"盘古智库"微信公众号或 http://toutiao.com/a4486026022/，访问时间：2015 年 12 月 12 日。

② 关于"一带一路"倡议下中、土具体的合作领域契合点，学界已有研究，本文不再赘述，详见王勇、[土耳其] 希望、罗洋：《"一带一路"倡议下的中国与土耳其的战略合作》，载《西亚非洲》2015 年第 6 期，第 70~86 页。

③ 这一点与民国时代就颇为不同。民国时代的国人，尤其是 20 世纪二三十年代，对土耳其具有相当程度的常识性认知。那个时候的中国政治和文化精英们，在文化上是言必称希腊的，在政治上则是言必称土耳其的。到了 40 年代，毛主席对土耳其有了一个资产阶级革命的定位之后，有关土耳其的认识在中华人民共和国就基本上没有突破伟大领袖的定位。60 年代初，门德列斯主政的土耳其被毛主席说成美帝国主义的走狗，是被谴责的。直到改革开放之后，中国人对土耳其的认识才从革命史观走向了现代史观，开始日益重视土耳其取得的各方面现代化成果对中国的可能的启示。见拙著：《现代国家与民族建构——20 世纪前期土耳其民族主义研究》，三联书店，2011 年，第 427~430 页；拙文：《六十年来的中国土耳其研究：回顾与展望》，载《西亚非洲》2010 年第 4 期，第 68~70 页。

④ 参见拙著：《现代国家与民族建构——20 世纪前期土耳其民族主义研究》，尤见"结论"部分。

⑤ 参见拙文：《土耳其与"东突"的"不解之缘"》，载《中国经济》2009 年第 83 期，第 116~121 页。Zan Tao, "An Alternative Partner to the West? Turkey's Growing Relations with China", in Niv Horesh, ed., Toward Well-oiled Relations? China's Presence in the Middle East Following the Arab Spring, Palgrave Macmillan, 2016, pp.19-29.

麦加，都是一个文明层面的判断。换言之，一个亲西方的、世俗的土耳其也是为"麦加"所拒绝的。说土耳其的命运在塔什干，是注意到土耳其与中亚之间特殊的种族、历史、语言和文化的联系。亨廷顿做这个判断时正是土耳其在冷战结束之初出现泛突厥主义复兴之际，厄扎尔本人曾积极支持泛突厥主义。只看意识形态是不够的，尽管土耳其像中国一样已经成为世界体系中的生产性民族，但土耳其的生产力不足以支撑中亚重新进入世界分工体系，中亚诸国对中国经济的依赖程度也远远高于对土耳其的依赖。故所谓土耳其的"塔什干命运"只能是文化或文明的，而不是硬实力的。亨廷顿的论说契合了土耳其三重身份中的一个——中亚。[①]事实上，土耳其在中亚的影响是通过推广其软实力实现的，种族、语言、文化和宗教等方面的联系被广泛地加以运用。在中亚国家 20 世纪 90 年代初独立后的一段时间里，土耳其的世俗民主政治和市场经济作为一种模式对中亚国家曾产生过一定的吸引力。虽然正发党政府宣称放弃了泛突厥主义或者"突厥语世界的统一"的政治诉求，但土耳其在中亚的文化影响力依然不可小觑。泛突厥主义已经从"领土统一主义"转变为合作性与文化性的诉求。土耳其通过不同层次的机制与中亚诸突厥语国家保持了特殊联系，值得中国重视和借鉴。

第三，中土关系要进一步发展，需探索一些新议题。在既有的国际组织和架构方面，中土都认识到加强合作以提高在其中权重的重要性，但目前还很难获得实质性突破（比如土耳其谋求提高其在联合国的地位，以及在国际货币基金组织等机构中与中方合作）。从另一方面来说，中、土作为新兴经济体以及地区性大国，都面临 21 世纪人类所共同面对的恐怖主义挑战。如何在这个领域中设置议题、加强合作，并将两国关系中的许多问题置于国际发展和全球治理的框架下加以认知，突破传统的民族国家间关系的认知框架，可能是两国关系获得突破的重要切入点。考虑到土耳其在突厥语世界的软实力，以及中国在其中所具有的相对更强的硬实力，中、土两国也确实有在"一带一路"框架下加强合作的必要性和可行性。这也是两国在这一背景下打造新型双边关系、实现发展战略对接

---

① 土耳其的三重身份分别是：迫切想融入的西方、魂牵梦萦的故乡中亚，以及历史征程中逐渐转变成为穆斯林世界（中东）的一部分。这三重身份之间有内在的张力。

的突破口。

结 论

　　土耳其有明显的地缘优势，但关键还是要把这种优势转化为实在的经济辐射力。如果土耳其能够恢复其经济发展的势头，克服"中等收入陷阱"，其在欧亚的中枢地位是有望确立和巩固的。对土耳其而言，未来影响最大的还是其内政问题。一方面，土耳其能否巧妙地摆好其在伊斯兰世界与西方之间的平衡关系；另一方面，土耳其国内的库尔德问题是其长期掣肘，短期内看不到解决的可能，但土耳其当前正在进行多方面的努力，若此问题处理得好，土耳其的稳定与发展将有进一步的保障。另外，中东地区长期动荡，土耳其所处的外部环境也是限制其发展的一个因素，保持中东地区长期的相对和平状态符合土耳其的切身利益。

　　中土关系尽管经历过个别的挫折期，但总体来看，是在向着好的、积极的方向快速发展。尤其是中国提出"一带一路"构想和倡议之后，双方的合作有了进一步提升的空间。我们把土耳其的发展目标概括为三个层次的"土耳其梦"，即"2023百年愿景"、"2053展望"、"2071千年目标"。这些宏大目标既涉及土耳其自身的建设与发展，也涉及周边。它是全方位的，不只是经济上需要吸引包括中国在内的大量投资，而且还在对外战略方面有其特殊关注和定位。对此，中国需要在客观认识土耳其的优势与问题的前提下，通过将"一带一路"战略与"土耳其梦"对接，实现双赢和共同繁荣。

3 "Turkey Dream" and the Sino-Turkish Relationship under BRI

Zan Tao

In recent years, with Chinese President Xi Jinping's proposing of the "China Dream" and the "Belt and Road Initiative", relevant countries have caused more and more attention of the Chinese people especially those who are doing research related to these issues. Among these, Turkey has a special position, for which the reason is that, Turkey's achievement of development is so remarkable in the past decade of the 21st century. The country proposed very ambitious development project to which the author of this paper would accordingly name them as "Türkiye hayal" (Turkey Dream) on three levels[①]: the vision for the 100th anniversary of Turkish Republic in 2023 (referred to as the "centennial political vision of 2023"), the outlook for the 600th anniversary in 2053 of the Ottoman Empire's conquest of Istanbul (referred to as the "sexcentenary

---

[①] The "Turkey Dream" is not a special term in Turkey, but instead, a summarization created by the author. The Turks also seldom use the word "Türkiye hayal" to refer to the visions, outlook,and goals mentioned in this article. Nevertheless, the English news and analysis will use a phrase like "Turkey's Dream". In Turkey, the focal point of the hottest discussion is the so-called "2023 Vizyonu".

outlook of 2053"), the goals for the 1000th anniversary in 2071 of the victory in Battle of Manzikert, in which Seljuk Turks defeated the Byzantine Empire and started the campaign to conquer Anatolia (referred to as the "millenarian objective of 2071"). Via specific analysis and interpretation over the process that Turkey proposes these development plans, goals and vision, this article will explore the context of these grand proposals, and analyze the conditions and possibilities to achieve the Turkey Dream. Finally, this article will focus on some fundamental aspects of Turkey as a country from the perspective of Sino-Turkish relationship, and it will also discuss the foundations and prospects of Sino-Turkish cooperation under framework of the "Belt and Road Initiative"[1].

Three Levels and Connotation of "Turkey Dream"

At present, Turkish leaders are still full of hope for the future of their country. The most popular expectation towards the future development of the country is the realization of specific development goals in such fields as the economy, society, politics, and diplomacy, referred to as the centennial political vision of 2023. When further analyzing remarks of Turkish leaders, we will find that they not only have in mind a centennial vision, but also the sexcentenary outlook of 2053 and the millenarian objective of 2071. For example, in a speech delivered by Recep Tayyip Erdogan, the Turkish president said that "We truly believe, the future of Turkey is bright…We are currently living in dark days, however, in 2023, 2053, and 2071, our visions will surely come true".

---

[1] Erdogan: Sıkıntılı Günler Yasıyoruz Ama 2023, 2053, 2071 Vizyonları Hayata Geçecek (2015: September 16). Retrieved May 1, 2016, from http://www. insanhaber.com/politika/erdogan-sikintili-gunler-yasiyoruz-ama-2023-2053-2071-vizyonlari-hayata-gececek-58501.

1.The "Centennial Political Vision of 2023"

Turkey's "2023 Vision" has become a lip-service in Turkish leaders' mouths in recent years. It was first proposed in January 2011, when Turkish Prime Minister Erdogan mentioned the "centennial political vision of 2023" of the Justice and Development Party (AKP) in a TV talk show of "Ulusa Seslenis"[1]. On September 30, 2012, the AKP officially released the "AKP 2023 Political Vision (AK Parti 2023 Siyasi Vizyonu)" at its 4th National Congress. [2] In terms of economic development goals, the AKP's centennial political vision of 2023 includes: the GDP volume of Turkey to rank among the Top 10 in the world; to steadily reduce inflation and keep interest rates at a single digit rate; export to grow to $500 billion; the national income per capita to reach $25,000; GDP to reach $2 trillion in 2023; to bring down unemployment rate to 5% and increase the employment rate by 50% compared to the current figure. In addition, this document also has some unique merits: 1) with regard to the ethnic problems, it encourages Turkey to actively solve the Kurdish problem and the problem of national unity by emphasizing cultural autonomy, bilingualism and pluralism; 2) in terms of external relations, it continues to take the path of multilateralism, not only stressing the need to join the European Union (EU), but also adhering to the development of relationship with the Islamic Middle East and Central Asia. While adhering to the accession of Turkey to the EU, it also stresses the need to define the "Copenhagen criteria" as the "Ankara criteria". It pledges to join the EU in 2023, and becomes a full member state; it emphasizes collaboration among the Turkic speaking countries and fight Islam ophobia; it speaks highly of the "Arab Spring"; 3) it redefines secularism. Under the premise of adhering to the separation of church and state, it has put more

---

[1] Basbakan Erdogan, 2023 Hedeflerini Açıkladı (2011: January 28). Retrieved May 1, 2016, from http://www.patronlardunyasi.com/haber/Basbakan-Erdogan- 2023-hedeflerini-acikladi/98480.

[2] The full text can be downloaded from AKP's official website.Contents quoted from it in this article will be foot noted unless there is a special case.See http://www.akparti.org.tr/upload/documents/akparti2023siyasivizyonuturkce.pdf.

emphasis on freedom of religion, which should not be affected by political power, and emphasizes the harmonious coexistence of different faiths.

Since 2011, AKP leaders have often mentioned their "2023 centennial political vision" on various occasions, during which their attitudes could be simply generalized as the following: they are eager to express their hope and faith for this vision; while realizing the difficulty that they may face in achieving their goals, they never gave it up. It is safe to say that "2023 centennial political vision" has become the most important general strategy for development of Turkey.

2. The Millenarian Objective of 2071

The millenarian objective of 2071 was first officially proposed by Erdogan at the end of 2012. Unlike the "2023 centennial political vision," the millenarian objective of 2071 is more likely a historical consciousness than a series of concrete plans and figures. At the 4th National Congress of AKP, Erdogan had already mentioned the year of 1071in history[1]. According to the official narrative of Turkey about the history, 1071 is indeed an important starting point. This is because it marked the origin of Turkification and Islamization of Anatolia[2]. The "Generation of 1071" (1071'in nesli) and "2071 Objective" (2071 hedefi) were proposed after the 4th National Congress of the AKP. The so-called "2071 Objective" is very vague and hollow, quite unlike the specific plan of the "2023 Vision". When Erdogan talked about the "2071 Objective", he just said in general terms that the country would return to the "Osman level"(Osmanli derecesi). In a speech delivered on December 16, 2012, Erdogan mentioned the goal to be realized by 2071, stating that, "By 2071, that is, the 1000th anniversary, God bless, at that time,

---

① "Bağbakan Erdoğan in AK Parti 4. Olağan Büyük Kongresi konuğmasının tam metni" , https://www.akparti.org.tr/site/haberler/basbakan-erdoganin-ak-parti-4.-olagan-buyuk-kongresi-konusmasinin-tam-metni/31771#1, 2016-1-15.

② Zan Tao, Modern State and Nation Building—A Study of Turkish Nationalism in the Early 20th Century, Joint Publishing Beijing, 2011.

Turkey will reach the level that Selcuk and Osman dynasties had ever reached. When the developed countries were caught in a serious global financial crisis, we Turkey still continue to advance ahead steadily. We can't live to 2071. But, young people! I am talking to you, and in particular to those of you who are still single. You please get married. I hope you will bring up a generation of 1071"[1].

3. The Sexcentenary Outlook of 2053

The sexcentenary outlook of 2053 is mentioned less frequently but it also has become part of the current political discourse in Turkey. On May 7, 2013, Erdogan mentioned the 2053 Outlook in the following way, "600 years after the conquest of Istanbul in 1453, that is, 2053, we also set the AKPs goal... "Without Osman Gazis dream of the conquering of Istanbul 150 years before the conquest, there will be no the Conqueror Sultan Mehmet, who opened a new era and terminated the old one. We are instilling a sense of consciousness to today's young people, that is, to become the parents of a generation of conquerors"[2].

In contrast, Turkey's centennial political vision of 2023 is more practical, which involves various objectives to be met; however, the sexcentenary outlook of 2053 and the millenarian objective of 2071 are very general and are part of impractical political propaganda.

---

① Bostan,Y.(2012:December 17).2071 Hedefi:Osmanli Derecesi.Retrieved May1, 2016, from http://www.sabah.com.tr/gundem/2012/12/17/2071-hedefi-osmanli-imparatorlugu-derecesi.

② Erdoğan "2053Vizyonu" VeOyOranlarınıAçıkladı(2013:May7).Retrieved May1, 2016, from http://www.radikal.com.tr/politika/erdogan-2053-vizyonu-ve-oy-oranlarini-acikladi-1132528/.

The Background of the "Turkey Dream" and Related Arguments about It

In this part, we will first discuss why the AKP has put forward such a series of grand goals at this point of time, and especially we will explain why it did not put forward such ambitious projects at the beginning of its rule. Then, we also analyze the disputes regarding the possibility of realization of the "Turkey dream".

1. The background and causes of the "Turkey dream"

a)The most important reason is the 10 years' economic success under AKPs rule.

Turkey has achieved unprecedented economic success in the first ten years under the AKP rule and has become the most powerful Muslim country economically. Rapid economic growth has made Turkey a beacon of the world economy and the whole nation's confidence has soared. A structural factor has contributed to this: setting the Middle East as a strategic region, while maintaining a long-term, special and close relationship with the West. Since the Özal administration in 1980s, Turkey has actively participated in globalization; with the implementation of export-oriented economic policy, the Turkish economy has grown rapidly. Since the AKP came to power in 2002, Turkey's economy has continued to develop rapidly (see Table 1 and Table 2). The time that Turkey proposed the Centennial vision and objectives of the millennium, is exactly the period that Turkish economy experienced leaps and bounds, and it reflects the confidence of the Erdogan's administration.

Table 3–1 Turkey's Economic Figures 2002-2014[①]

2007	648753.606	101254.625	4.7
2008	742094.395	101921.73	0.7
2009	616703.325	97003.114	-4.8
2010	731608.367	105885.644	9.2
2011	773979.672	115174.724	8.8
2012	786282.517	117625.021	2.1
2013	823044.428	122556.461	4.2
2014	799001.454	126127.931	2.9

Table 3–2 Changes in Turkey's Economic Figures 2002-2014[②]

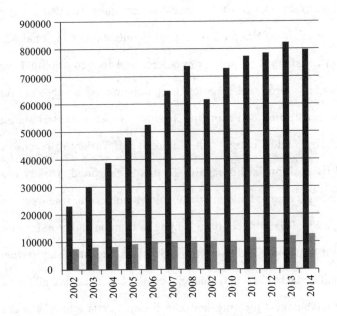

Left: GDP in current exchange rate of US Dollar (Unit: 100,000 US Dollar)

Right: GDP in fixed Lira rate of 1998 (Unit: 100,000 Lira)

---

① The author built the chart according to OECD data in September 2015, Source: Turkey Statistics Associations, www.turkstat.gov.tr.

② Ibid.

b)Turkey's geographical advantages have become increasingly prominent in the era of globalization.

With the development of globalization, especially the eastward shift of the global economic gravity, the performance of emerging economies has become a brilliant highlight in this century. In this process, Turkey's distinctive geopolitical advantage has been more prominent. In the background of the end of cold war, Turkey has begun to get rid of the status of "frontier state" and defined itself as a "bridge" country connecting west and east, and a "central" country locating between Europe, Asia and Africa. After AKP took office, it developed Turkey's geopolitical strategy on the basis of the recognition of "central" country.

We can see from AKP's official website that many detailed programs in "2023 Vizyonu" are relevant to Istanbul, owing to its outstanding regional advantage. The transportation in Istanbul is quite convenient, and its geographical, economic and civilized status has a profound historical accumulation. As an absolute regional center of geopolitics, civilization and economy, Istanbul is also a transfer station linking the Middle East, Africa and Central Asia. Rapid rise of Turkey in recent years has also strengthened its position in this regard. To this background, Turkey proposed many projects, including a plan to build international aviation center (the world largest airport, for example), a Silk Road Project from Beijing to London and crossing Bosporus Strait, a plan to build trade port and route through Black Sea and Mediterranean, and the ambition to build Istanbul as a new financial center, etc. These are all based on Turkey's geographical advantage—locating between Europe, Asia and Africa and having the condition of integration.

c)Turkey's imperial heritage and great power consciousness constitute an important psychological basis.

From history's perspective, Turks were the master of great Ottoman Empire (1299-1922). As the last Muslim Empire in world history, Turkey has long-term and evident supremacy over and threats towards Europe. One hundred years ago, the Ottoman Empire collapsed, Turks established the Turkish Republic under the leadership of Mustafa Kemal while inheriting some legacy of the empire. Turks participated in European affairs in the era of empire, and they also imitated western countries to pursue modernization in the late imperial period. These trends were all extended by the Turkish Republic. So, Turks not only inherited pain and failure from the empire, they also inherited 300-year dream of modernization, and it even became the model of some Oriental countries in the early 20th century. In 1960s, Turkey was recognized by western scholars as the second non-western country who has managed to have modernized itself after Japan. Therefore, the consciousness of being a great power among Turks comes from the legacy of Ottoman Empire and successful modernization in modern history. However, this consciousness does not equal to ambition. History can be a burden, but it can also be the source of inspiration. Turks have been good at using the narration of history to serve the present since Kemalist period. These kinds of positive actions and strategic goal are closely related to this historical awareness, which could be found quite evident in the speeches and discourse of Erdogan.

As the master of the Ottoman Empire, Turks inherited the Empire's grand legacy and memory together. In the age of Kemal Atatürk, Turks used to deny and reject the history of the Empire in order to facilitate the modernization of the nation. After it reached a certain level of development, Turkey started a process of re-evaluation of the Ottoman Empire; in 1999, Turkey even celebrated the 700th anniversary of the founding of the Ottoman Empire. These reflect its consciousness as an old empire, and it is not unreasonable to say that it is the symptom of "new Ottomanism". The history of the Ottoman Empire is a compulsory course for students in Turkey, which has an important role in shaping the Turkish national and historical consciousness. Such learning will enhance knowledge about the Empire—it is a history about the rise, conquests, expansion, prosperity and decline of an empire, which includes the territory of Turkey as well as Syria, Iraq, Lebanon, Palestine, the Arabian Peninsula, north of the Black Sea, part of the Caucasus, North Africa and the Balkans and other regions, which all belong to the vast territory of the Ottoman Empire. Turkish national spirit, historical consciousness and complex of being a great power were awakened and shaped through this historical memory. It naturally shapes the Turks' view of nation, view of history, view of the future and view of the world. A series of goals set by the AKP for the Turks are a reflection of the sense of a great power.

d)The inherent requirements of the historical development of Turkey at the current stage.

The era of the AKPs ruling corresponds to the period of the rise of emerging powers in the world. Expectations on the stability of the order and prosperity of the future make it necessary for today's Turks to present their goals in line with the country's historical development phase. At present, the proposals of the AKP can be depicted as the "Erdogan doctrine"[1]. From a historical perspective, a series of development goals and visions put forward by the AKP is in line with the internal logics of the economic and social changes in Turkey in the post-cold war era. From Turgut Özal in the 1980s to today's Mr. Erdogan, modern Turkish history has entered a new stage; it has come to a critical moment when something must be done to address the questions of how to identify the country, politics and culture and how to adjust its foreign relations accordingly. I would like to contend that it is in this historical context, that AKP put forward its ambitious vision and objectives.

e)The individual impact of Turkish leader cannot be ignored.

Turkey's various vision and goals are also closely associated with the ambitions Erdogan's. In 2007, Turkey, under the leadership of the AKP, amended the constitution. The new change indicated that in the future, the President would no longer be elected by

---

[1]　ZAN, T. (2012:March). "Turkey Mode: Past and Present", Journal of Xinjiang Normal University (Social Sciences), No.2.

the Grand National Assembly, but instead, would be elected directly by the people. In August 2014, Erdogan became the first democratically elected president in the history of Turkey. If no accident, Mr. Erdogan can be reelected and remain in power until 2024, just after the conclusion of Turkey's Centennial vision in 2023. Erdogan also wants to ensure that Turkey can implement the presidential system. If Erdogan succeeds, he will rule for a longer time than the Father of Turkey Mustafa Kemal Atatürk (1923-1938). He will also be the most powerful leader of Turkey after Atatürk[1].

In the foregoing sense, the Centennial Vision of 2023 is both a vision for the party and a vision for Turkey, and a vision for Erdogan himself. This is Erdogan's commitment to Turkey, a kind of historic self-consciousness about Turkey's future. "2053 Outlook" and "2071 Millenarian Objective" reflects Erdogan's political marketing strategy, in a way of eye-catching of using history resources. And in order to realize his political ambitions, shape Turkey in his own mentality, Erdogan was setting discourse framework, inspiring people's aspirations, making Turkish people be willing to follow him, through a series of vision and goals.

2. Disputes around the "Turkey Dream"

After Turkey proposed its centenary visions and the Millennium goals/prospects, it has caught wide attention and resulted in disputes both at home and abroad. It receives applauses, and at the same time, criticisms, doubts and even taunts.

On the one hand, there are people praising Erdogan and the AKP. One representative is the Turkish columnist Mustafa Yürekli. Early on May 1, 2011, in his article, Mustafa Yürekli illustrated the historical significance of the AKP and Erdogan. He also spoke highly of the centenary vision, "the AKP's goals in 2023 have expressed its determination to develop Turkey; it is going to provide human beings with a new

---

[1]   Zan, T. & Dong, Y. (2015: December 26). "Erdogan, Presidental System and the Future of Turkey", Retrieved May 1, 2016.from:http://www.thepaper.cn /newsDetail_forward_1413443.

world order, and promise to bring peace, justice, and goodness"[1].

On the other hand, there are also criticisms of the "Turkey dream" from different perspectives. Some people cite economic data to reprove Erdogan and the AKP, saying that the vision and objectives cannot be achieved, and are purely a "dream"; some people point out that Turkey is facing major problems, such as the lack of innovative talents, heavy dependence on imported energy, challenges from Kurdish separatism, etc.; there are also some people who question the party's new constitution design from a narrow perspective of nationalism, saying that it is actually succumbed to pressure from the PKK and aims at dividing Turkey. Even the historical analogy and beautification of the conquest in history that Erdogan loves to use are subject to criticism. These issues raised by critics are great obstacles to the realization of the dream of Turkey.

The above opinions from different positions and angles, no matter in favor or against the 2023 Vision, both make some sense. The vision and goals Erdogan and the AKP set forth are rooted in the inherent orbit of modern Turkish history. Not only it bears certain rationality and necessity, but also it is a political propaganda.

However, the wish is one thing, and the reality is another. According to economic data and index, it is almost impossible for Turkey to achieve its dream by 2023. It is estimated that Turkey will achieve top 10 in 2023 only if it maintains GDP growth of 10 percent. But from Turkey's data over the past few years, Turkey's GDP grew at an average rate of 4% in 2011-2014. For the past 12 years, Turkey has grown at an average annual rate of 5.8%, and Turkey's GDP will grow to $1.3 trillion by 2023. Thus, the $2 trillion goal of the 2023 centennial vision is just "dreaming". In addition, a target of $25,000 per capita would not be achieved if the growth rate was less than 10%. At current rates, Turkey can only achieve $15,000 per capita in 2023. The average annual growth of Turkish exports during 2003 ~ 2010 was 17%, if they can maintain this speed,

---

[1] Yürekli, M. "Erdogan'ın 2053 ve 2071 hedefi var mı?" Retrieved May 1, 2016, from http://www.haber7.com/yazarlar/mustafa-yurekli/739248-erdoganin-2053-ve-2071-hedefi-var-mi.

Turkey can reach $500 billion by 2023, however, The annual export growth of Turkey in 2011 ~ 2014 was 8.5%, obviously is not enough. As a result, hope for Turkey to achieve its vision and goals is indeed fading.

AKP is currently aware of this and is committed to changing the situation through reform and continuing investment in infrastructure. Criticizing AKP's Centennial Political Vision from the perspective of New constitution, especially the national policy, and refusing the reconciliation between the AKP government and the PKK, not accepting pluralism, which only show that Turkey's mainstream nationalism has not yet been fundamentally challenged. The AKP party's way of thinking is in line with its long-held idea of a "more democratic" solution to the Kurdish problem, and if it does not, the Kurdish problem will be set Turkey for much longer.

What is worth mentioning is that the critics are worried about the Islamist preference of Erdogan and the AKP, that is, Erdogan and AKP are threatening the Turkish legacy of secularism. In fact, to examine Erdogan and the AKP from the perspective of Islamism is very one-sided and narrow. Turkish peoples support for the AKP is not due mainly religious claims[1].

Cooperation between China and Turkey based on the "Turkey Dream" and the "Belt and Road Initiative"

Turkey is a regional power located in Eurasia with an extremely geopolitical position and thus plays an important role in the "Belt and Road Initiative". In November 2015, the G20 summit, which Chinese President Xi Jinping attended, was held in the

---

① Çarkoglu,A.&Klaycıoglu,E.(2007).Turkish DemocracyToday,I.B.Tauris.Erdogan:GençlerEvlenin,1 071NesliniSizlerYeti?tireceksiniz (2012:December.16).Retrieved May1, 2016, from http://www.haberler.com/ erdogan-gencler-evlenin-1071-neslini-sizler-4175698-haberi/.

Turkish city Antalya. President Xi stressed that the Chinese would "adhere to its deep integration into the global economy, carry out the 'Belt and Road initiative'...... and build a community of common interests"[1]. Before the summit, Xi met with Erdogan. Xi emphasized that both countries should strengthen strategic communication and build development strategies; the two sides should actively use platforms, such as the Silk Road Fund and the Asian Infrastructure Investment Bank (AIIB), and explore innovative cooperation channels and models, to achieve common development and common prosperity; Erdogan said that Turkey attached great importance to relations with China and was willing to work with China to deepen cooperation in various fields, and Turkey would actively participate in the cooperation under the "Belt and Road" framework, welcome Chinese companies to increase investment in infrastructure and other areas of Turkey. China and Turkey signed the "memorandum of understanding for the government to jointly promote the construction of the 'Belt and Road initiative'", which provided important policy support for both sides to promote cooperation in various fields in the Belt and Road Initiative framework[2].

Therefore, both countries have made it clear to strengthen cooperation under the framework of the "Belt and Road". In particular, President Xi emphasized the need to achieve buttressing the development strategies of the two countries, which is the reason why and significance of the article's focus on the development strategy of Turkey (the "Turkey dream"). On this basis, it is necessary for us to analyze Turkey's attitude and needs on China's "Belt and Road initiative" from the angle of China, in order to understand the basic condition of Turkey, and to research the possibility of "docking Turkey dream" and the "Belt and Road".

---

[1]   Xinhua, 2015: November 6.

[2]   Wei, J. & Li, B. (2015: November 15). "Xi Jinping Met with Turkish President and Signed Memorandum of Understanding on the Belt and Road Initiative", Retrieved May 1, 2016, from http://news.xinhuanet.com/finance/2015-11/15/c_128430116.htm.

1. Turkey's views and perspectives on the "Belt and Road"

On the whole, Turkey is generally positive about and interested in the "Belt and Road Initiative". However, Turkey also has serious concerns about China's initiative; this is because: Firstly, China has become the second largest economy in the world since 2010 and has strong influence of power in the world; Turkey cannot ignore the existence of China's rising power; secondly, China is a permanent member of the Security Council of UN; it plays a pivotal role and has influence on some of issues that relates to Turkey's national interests; Thirdly, there is a huge trade deficit in Turkey's trade with China. It has been seeking a possible breakthrough for long and is trying to make up for Turkey's trade deficit by attracting more investment from China. Erdogan also specifically talked about this when he met with President Xi Jinping; Fourthly, the Belt and Road initiative provides an important opportunity for Turkey to achieve the "Turkey dream". The Turkish side attaches great importance to the establishment of the Asian Infrastructure Investment Bank (AIIB) and the Silk Road Fund. Turkey is a founding member of the AIIB.

So, what are the Turks' specific views on the "Belt and Road initiative"? According to the research this author conducted in recent years, they can be roughly classified as the following aspects:

First, Turkey has a huge potential benefits in the "Belt and Road initiative". Turkey's current economy is experiencing some consequence of the economic crisis; the lira depreciates quickly, and inflation is serious, which has caused AKPs concern. Therefore, searching for new economic opportunities has become an urgent need. The "Belt and Road" means new opportunities for Turkey.

Second, the Silk Road Economic Zone is a good idea. Turkey is considered as a traditional channel of the Silk Road, in which Istanbul is the end; there are a lot of ancient Silk Road remnants in the territory of Turkey. Turkey has a close relationship with the traditional Silk Road. It desires and wishes to find new ideas for economic and cultural prosperity of contemporary Turkey by such a remarkable revival of historical philosophy, and docking with China's the "Belt and Road initiative".

Third, some have voiced concerns over "The Belt and Road Initiative". Turkeys economic structure has a great similarity with China's, and the economic development models of the two countries are similar.[1] Turkey has also elaborated a plan to find markets and attract investment from abroad. Leaders of China and Turkey mentioned several times during the meeting that they would connect the "Silk Road Economic Belt". Together with China, Turkey put forth the "Middle Corridor" plan[2], and connected the initiative to their all-round development plans. Turkey views Central Asia as part of its sphere of influence, and the Caucasus is regarded as a very important sphere of influence, therefore, some Turks expressed their doubts about China regarding the "Silk Road Economic Belt": Is not there competition between China and Turkey?

Fourth, the Turks realize that the Silk Road Economic Zone is not only an economic project, but also a cultural and security plan. Turks are more concerned about the relationship between Xinjiang and the "Silk Road Economic Belt".

In general, the attitude and reaction of Turkey towards The Belt and Road is positive and interested.

2.Turkey's unique advantages and problems

From the perspective of China-Turkey cooperation and docking of the development strategy of the two sides under the framework of the Belt and Road, Turkey has "five advantages" and "five problems".

---

[1] Turkey has a similar economic structure as China. They both rely on labor-intensive industries, focus on export-driven development, and the two sides have been in competition in the field of fabrics export for a long time. The two countries are both eager to expand influence in the Middle East and Africa.

[2] The Middle Corridor (Orta Koridor) put forward by Turkey in recent years is a communicational network (ulagım agını) connecting Asia and the Europe. It covers an area from Turkey and Azerbaijan to Central Asia and China via the Caspian Sea.

Turkey's five advantages

(1) In terms of geopolitical pattern, Turkey connects to parts of Europe, Asia, and Africa. It is in the south of Russia, west of the Caucasus, Central Asia, and Iran, and east of Europe. The Arab North Africa region is in its southern and southeastern flank. Turkey also controls the Strait connecting the Black Sea and the Mediterranean Sea; it has a strong geographical advantage, and its strategic position is very important. Such a unique geographical advantage makes Turkey a bridge for the communication of Eastern and Western economies and cultures. As Ahmet Davutoglu said, Turkey's advantage is the capability to speak languages of two civilizations. In terms of the promotion of the "Belt and Road", first of all, we need to pay attention to Turkey's geographical advantage.

(2) In the economy, although Turkey is now facing the challenges of economic slowdown, reviewing the past decade under the AKPs leadership, we found that Turkey has made great progress in economic and social development. It is still making progress in its application to membership to the EU and is an important member of the G20. Turkey has a population of 77 million, and the average age is 30 years old, which is very young and provides great potential. Turkey is not an energy abundant country. The fact that it can achieve today's success shows that its economic development model and industrial structure is healthier than countries relying on energy as their main income source.

(3) In politics, Turkey is a relatively stable state that has already completed the political transition to democracy. Ninety years since the founding of the Republic of Turkey, it has been implementing the westernized policy; in 1946, Turkey made political reforms to achieve a multiparty democracy. In terms of the system environment, Turkeys politics, economy, investment, social welfare, culture, media and other aspects are all based on European standards; although it has not fully met the European standard yet, the long-term join effort to join the EU has changed and is changing Turkey,

making it more standardized and more suitable for foreign investment. Mr. Davutoglu also emphasized improving the institutional environment in his London speech in mid-January of 2016, in order to make Turkey more suitable for investment. He also stressed the importance of Turkey's application to join the EU.

(4) With regard to the culture and system, Turkey is a secular state. The Kemalist doctrine of a secularist system is accepted by all parties in Turkey. It has not yet been subjected to fundamental challenges. In addition, Turkeys version of Islam is also more moderate and inclusive. Because Turks converted to Islam later than others, had been constantly absorbing many historical and cultural heritage of ancient Persian, Byzantine, ancient Greece-Rome, and converted to this belief mainly through the practice of Sufism, Turkey's Islam showed quite unique characteristics: in simple terms, it has more emphasis on introverted tradition of mysticism, and has less dogmatic understanding[1]; it also actively plays a role and expands its influence through Islam.[2]

(5) In education, Turkey also has relatively advanced resources. Turkey has a relatively high level of secondary education: most outstanding universities have carried out teaching in English; they try to catch up with advanced Western models and standards; Turkey has recognized China's college entrance examination scores, therefore there are no institutional barriers in admission of Chinese students. In related fields, there is a lot of space for future cooperation between China and Turkey. In addition, religious education in Turkey is also very advanced, and its "de-radicalization" experience is a good lesson to learn from.

---

① Zan, T. (2011). Modern State and Nation Building: A Study on Turkish Nationalism in the Early 20th Century, Beijing: SDX Joint Publishing Company, pp.326-327; In the era of Kemal Atatürk,there even was attendency to balance against Islam identity with the invented secular tradition of the Turks.

② From the field research in Turkey in February-March 2015,the author found that not just the state,but,more importantly,Turkish Folk Religious Force also played an important role in the form of business association and other non-governmental organizations (NGOs) in the Balkans, Africa and Central Asia.

Five problems of Turkey

(1) Turkey is part of a complex regional pattern. The Middle East region suffers from long-term instability. In recent years, the situation in Iraq and Syria have deteriorated. Turkey, as their neighbor, has been affected: such as the "Daesh" issue (ISIS), the Kurdish issue, that more than 2 million refugees stayed in Turkey, and the deterioration of relations with Russia because of fighter incident, etc.

(2) The practice of Turkish leadership led by Erdogan in the treatment of internal and external crises is very controversial. Examples include the relationship between the AKP government and the Gülen movement (the movement led by Fethullah Gülen, also known as cemaat or hizmet hareketi), aircraft incident between Russia and Turkey, and the purchase of HQ-9 Anti-aircraft Missiles System from China[1], and so on. The disputes in dealing with these issues have hurt the prestige and reliability of the Turkish leadership. The presidential system proposed by Erdogan also raised concerns among critics. They hold the view that Erdogan is seeking larger individual power which is not subject to constraints. Some Turkish critics even said that what Erdogan wants is not a presidential system, but an authoritarian one[2], or to become a "Sultan" through a legitimate election.

(3) In the economy, Turkey has shown a slow growth and a lack of growing force; it is facing the middle-income trap. Turkey's per capita GDP has exceeded $10,000; it is one of the middle and high income countries. The key to overcome the middle-income trap is the industrial upgrading and technological innovation, which needs a lot of

---

[1] Hu, L. (2015: November 18). Depth: There Is No Loss to China for Turkey Did Not Buy Chinese Red Flag 9, and Turkey Do Not Want to Play with China, Retrieved May 1, 2016 from http://mil.news. sina.com.cn/2015-11-18/1238844222.html; Turkey decided to manufacture military equipment in its own.It finally decided not to purchase the HQ-9Anti-aircraft missiles System from China with the excuse of "self-manufacturing".

[2] Hakan, A. (2015: February 1). Erdogan'in jstedigi Sistem "Bağkanlık Sistemi" Değil, Retrieved May 1, 2016 from http://sosyal.hurriyet.com.tr/yazar/.

talents and cannot be solved with a short-term policy.

(4) The long-term stability of Turkey is subject to the increasingly serious conflict between religious and secular forces. The AKP has an Islamist background, which cannot be ignored; since it came to power in 2002, although it has made prominent achievements, the AKP represents Turkey's conservative forces, and therefore wants to revive Islamic values. A series of "little tricks" by the AKP, including the lifting of the ban of heads carves legislation, have raised concerns among Turkey's secular factions. They are afraid that Turkey's secular democracy will be harmed. In recent years, relations between Turkish military and the AKP government, the relationship between secularists and conservative factions, and the relationship between the liberals and Erdogan, have become sources of instability in Turkey.

(5) Turkey is facing long-term challenges from extreme nationalism. In the two elections in 2015, the Kurdish issue was the hot topic. The HDP on behalf of the Kurdish people successfully took a seat in the Parliament. "The process of Imrali" has been terminated. The fear of terrorism and Kurdish separatism has resulted in the rise of nationalism within Turkish mainstream society. Antiterrorism operations against the PKK, including the bombing of the military base in northern Syria, had been catering to nationalist emotions, and eventually improved the poll in favor of Erdogan[1].

Extreme nationalism also led to irrational remarks and activities about China's Xinjiang issue. The "Anti-China" incident in July 2015 marks the sensitive issues between the two countries which have spread to the mass media, and have impacted relations between the two countries and people's emotions in different degrees. As a result, the image of Turkey in Chinese public opinion has also deteriorated. The normal development of bilateral relations between the two countries will inevitably be affected by public opinion and the negative impression and mood.

---

[1] Zan, Tao. (2015: November 3). Regional anti-terrorism needs a stable Turkey, *Global Times*.

The advantage that Turkey has the great attraction for China-Turkey cooperation and investment; indeed, the problems of Turkey potentially increase the risks for cooperation, especially the complex and sensitive issues in the regional situation and bilateral relations. China needs serious research on these and treat them rationally. In short, Turkey's strategic position, comprehensive strength and correlation with China in economic, political and cultural aspects, cannot be ignored; there is still great space for progress in bilateral relations under the "Belt and Road" framework.

3. Issues that China should pay attention to promoting the "Belt and Road" initiative in Turkey

To work with Turkey to promote the "Belt and Road" and dock it with the "Turkey dream", in addition to understanding the attitude of Turkey on the "Belt and Road", and the overall grasp of the advantages and problems of Turkey, China also need to pay attention to the following issues.

First of all, the relationship between China and Turkey does involve some sensitive issues which cannot be ignored. The quantity and quality of knowledge production regarding Turkey are not sufficient in China, and it is difficult to meet the demand of knowledge on Turkey in the fields of diplomacy, science, ideology and media. Since the 7/5 incident, Turkey's image in the eyes of the Chinese people took a turn for the worse[1]; that is, Chinese people believe Turkey "underneath" is a supporter and sympathizer, or even an advocate of "pan-Turkism" – either in politics or in culture[2]. The East Turkistan Islamic Organization is a barrier to the relationship between the two countries.

Secondly, Turkey has soft power in Central Asia. Huntington once said, Turkey

---

[1] Karaca, R. & Wang, L. (2015). Sino-Turkey Relations: Concept, Politics and Prospects, Istanbul: Gelisim University Press, pp. 227-250.

[2] Ibid.

was rejected by Brussels, and it refused Mecca; its fate will be attributed to Tashkent. He linked the fate of Turkey with Tashkent because he noticed the special connection between Turkey and Central Asia in race, history, language and culture. Huntington made this judgment at a moment when Pan-Turkism was rejuvenating soon after the end of the cold war. Özal himself used to actively support pan Turkism, but the output level of Turkey is not large enough to support Central Asia to re-enter the world system of division of labor; the dependence of Central Asian countries on China's economy is far higher than on Turkey's. Therefore, the so-called "Tashkent fate" of Turkey can only be a culture or civilization, rather than hard power. Huntington's argument fits one of Turkey's triple identities - Central Asia. In fact, Turkey's influence in Central Asia is widely used through the promotion of its soft power including race, language, culture and religion. During the period after the independence of the Central Asian countries in the early 1990s, the secular democratic politics and market economy of Turkey as a model had a certain attraction towards the Central Asian countries. Although the government is claiming to abandon the Pan-Turkism or "Turkic world of unity", the political demands, but Turkey's cultural influence in Central Asia is still not to be overlooked. Pan-Turkism has changed from "irredentism" to cooperative and cultural demands. Turkey has maintained a special connection with the Central Asian Turkic-speaking countries through different levels of mechanism, which is worthy of China's attention and reference.

Third, some new issues need to be explored to further develop China-Turkey relations. In the context of existing international organizations and structures, China and Turkey have recognized the need to strengthen cooperation to increase the importance of weighting among them, but it is still difficult to achieve substantive breakthroughs (for example, Turkey is seeking to improve its status in the United Nations, IMF and other institutions). On the other hand, China and Turkey, as emerging economies and regional powers, are facing with the challenges of terrorism which mankind in the 21st century are all confronting with. How can we set up subjects in this field, and strengthen cooperation and bilateral relations? Breaking through the traditional cognitive framework of national relations maybe an important breakthrough point. Considering Turkey's soft power in the Turkic world and the relatively strong hard power that China has, both China and Turkey do have the necessity and feasibility to strengthen cooperation in the framework of "the Belt and Road" initiative, and this is also the breakthrough point of creating a new type bilateral relations and realizing development strategy docking in this context.

Conclusion

Turkey has obvious geographical advantages, but the key is to turn this advantage into real economic reverberations. If Turkey could resume its economic development momentum and overcome the middle income trap, its central position in Europe and Asia is expected to be established and consolidated. Its internal problems will have the biggest impact on the future of Turkey. On the one hand, it is uncertain whether Turkey can skillfully and gracefully find a balance between the Islamic world and the West; on the other hand, Turkey's Kurdish problem is a long-term constraint which cannot be solved in the short term. But Turkey is currently making efforts in many aspects; if handled well, Turkey's stability and development will be further guaranteed. In addition, Turkey's external environment is also a factor that limits its development—the Middle East has been in turmoil for a long time. To maintain the long-term relative peace of the Middle East serves the vital interests of Turkey.

Although the bilateral relations between the two countries have experienced some setbacks, overall, they pursue rapid development in a good and positive direction. Especially after the initiative of the "Belt and Road", there is a wider space for further enhancement of the cooperation between the two countries. We summarize Turkey's development objectives as three levels of "Turkey Dream", namely the centennial political vision of 2023, sexcentenary outlook of 2053 and millenarian objective of 2071. These ambitious goals involve both the construction and development of Turkey, and the surrounding countries. It is global, based not only on an economic need to attract a large number of investments from foreign countries, including China, but also on a foreign strategy. In this regard, knowing about both the advantages and disadvantages of Turkey's objectively, China could accordingly dock the "Belt and Road initiative" and the "Turkey dream" to achieve win-win interests and common prosperity.

4 "一带一路"背景下中国与印尼的合作及其发展前景

翟崑

2013 年，中国国家主席习近平访问印尼期间，首次提出了共建"21 世纪海上丝绸之路"的倡议。印尼地处太平洋和印度洋、亚洲和大洋洲的交汇处，是"海上丝绸之路"的重要枢纽和战略支点。印尼以"全球海洋支点"构想为核心的海洋强国战略与我国"海上丝绸之路"倡议契合。五年来，在习近平主席和佐科总统的大力推动下，中印尼积极对接"21 世纪海上丝绸之路"倡议和"全球海洋支点"战略，全面深化各领域务实合作和友好交流，雅万高铁等一批重大标志性合作项目逐步落地，基础设施建设、产能、贸易、投资、金融、电子商务等领域互利合作不断推进，两国关系发展的新动能、新机遇不断涌现。根据北京大学"一带一路"五通指数研究课题组编撰的《2015 年"一带一路"沿线国家五通指数报告》研究，在沿线的 63 个国家中，印尼整体排名第五，位列合作"顺畅型国家"。[①]这表明中国与印尼两国在"一带一路"倡议各方面合作中均处于较高水平。然而，随着合作的广度与深度不断拓展，一系列深层次问题也日益凸显。双方如不对此予以应有重视并采取有效措施解决，势必在一定程度上对两国"一带一路"

---

① 北京大学"一带一路"五通指数研究课题组：《2015 年"一带一路"沿线国家五通指数报告》，经济日报出版社，2016 年，第 38 页。

倡议的推进与落实产生消极影响。本文着力通过总结中国与印尼在推动"一带一路"倡议方面取得的成果，分析其中存在的深层次问题及印尼方面的真实态度，据此提出相关对策建议。

进展与成果

进入 21 世纪以来，尤其是中国提出"一带一路"倡议后，中—印尼关系发展步入快车道，两国在经贸、政治领域的交流不断深化并取得显著成果。

（一）政治领域

两国高层互访频繁、机制构建完善、政治互信不断加深，合作成果丰硕。中国与印尼建立全面战略伙伴关系以来，双方政治互信不断加深，务实合作成果丰硕。两国关系持续深入发展符合两国人民的共同利益，也为地区和平稳定和世界发展繁荣作出了重要贡献。2013 年，习近平主席出访印尼期间提出建立"21 世纪海上丝绸之路"的倡议，彰显出中国对印尼的高度重视和印尼在"海上丝绸之路"中的重要支点作用。2014 年，印尼总统佐科·维多多（Joko Widodo）上任后，中—印尼两国交流与合作更加紧密。印尼建立"海洋强国"的宏大愿景与习近平主席"21 世纪海上丝绸之路"的提法高度契合，两国在全球海上支点和建设海上高速公路等合作领域达成诸多共识。中国和印尼共同推动新"海上丝绸之路"建设，对东南亚地区具有重要的引领、辐射和示范作用。印尼是中国提议建立的亚投行创始国之一，并积极寻求该行总部落户雅加达。中国和印尼在地区和多边层面拥有广泛的共同利益，在维护地区和平稳定、促进世界繁荣发展、全面推动南南合作、应对全球性议题方面具有重大共同利益，是重要合作伙伴。

中国提出"一带一路"倡议后，中国与印尼高层互访频繁。2014 年 10 月，习近平主席应约同印尼总统佐科通电话。2015 年，中国与印尼高层互动频繁：2 月，中央政法委书记孟建柱访问印尼；3月25日至28日，应国家主席习近平的邀请，印尼总统佐科对中国进行国事访问并出席博鳌亚洲论坛年会，两国共同发表关于加强两国全面战略伙伴关系的联合声明；4月，习近平主席赴印尼出席亚非领导人会议和万隆会议60周年纪念活动，两国共同发表《中华人民共和国与印度尼西亚共和国联合新闻公报》；7月，全国政协主席俞正声访问印尼；11月，习近平主席在出席二十国集团领导人峰会期间会见佐科。

2016年两国高层互动继续进行：3月，印尼副总统卡拉来华出席博鳌亚洲论坛年会；4月，印尼政治法律和安全统筹部长卢胡特访华，并与杨洁篪国务委员共同主持中—印尼副总理级对话第五次会议；5月，国务委员杨洁篪赴印尼与印尼经济统筹部长达尔敏共同主持中—印尼高层经济对话第二次会议；9月，习近平主席同印尼总统佐科在二十国集团杭州峰会期间举行会见。

两国建有副总理级的双边对话、高层经济对话、人文交流三大合作机制。两国还建有政府间双边合作联委会（外长牵头）、经贸合作联委会（商务部长牵头）、防务与安全磋商（副总长级）以及航天、农业、科技、国防工业等领域副部级合作机制。[1]双方除在首都互设使馆外，我国还在印尼泗水、棉兰、登巴萨设有总领馆，印尼在香港、广州、上海设有总领馆。

（二）经贸领域

21世纪以来，中—印尼经贸关系方兴未艾，合作的广度和深度不断扩大，雅万高铁项目持续推进。中国连续6年成为印尼最大贸易伙伴，双边贸易年均增速超过20%。印尼已成为中国对外投资的重要国家之一，2016年，中国在印尼由第十大投资来源国跃升为第三大投资来源国。2011年，中国与印尼的双边贸易额为491.5亿美元，超过新加坡成为印尼第一大进口来源国。[2]由于合作初期中国与

① 《中国同印度尼西亚的关系》，中华人民共和国外交部官网，2016年12月，http://wcm.fmprc.gov.cn/pub/chn/gxh/cgb/zcgmzysx/yz/1206_43/1206x1/t6115.htm.访问时间：2017年4月10日。

② 陈万灵、胡安琪、刘胜：《中国与印尼在"一带一路"中的战略合作》，选自《"一带一路"建设发展报告（2016）》，社会科学文献出版社，2016年，第92页。

印尼的贸易规模较小，印尼在双边贸易中处于顺差地位，但随着两国经贸合作的不断加深，印尼逐渐"转顺为逆"。2006年印尼对华贸易顺差为17亿美元；2007年为11亿美元；2008年印尼首次在两国贸易中出现逆差，随后逆差额持续扩大，2008年为36亿美元，2010年为48亿美元，2014年达130.18亿美元，2015年为143.65亿美元。[①]

"一带一路"项目在印尼推进后，两国经贸合作的广度和深度不断加深，越来越多的中国企业到印尼寻找发展机遇。印尼是东南亚国家中消费者最多的国家，拥有2.3亿人口，市场潜力巨大。目前，在印尼投资的中国企业已超过1000家，投资范围涵盖了能源、矿产、交通、通讯、电力、金融、农业等多个领域。在两国政府、企业的共同努力下，中—印尼经贸合作的潜力将进一步释放，两国友好交流更加密切。2016年G20峰会期间，印尼总统佐科走访了中国著名IT企业阿里巴巴，并邀请其董事局主席马云担任印尼的经济顾问，以助印尼国内800万中小企业于2020年实现电商化。[②]此外，百度、腾讯、阿里巴巴等IT行业巨头，Oppo、Vivo和华为等手机大户也在印尼落户，为中企投资印尼起到良好的带动和示范效应。

目前，两国经济合作最大项目雅加达—万隆的高速铁路项目（以下简称"雅万高铁项目"），项目伊始即受到两国政府的高度重视。2015年10月16日，经过两国各界的不懈努力，中国企业联合体（BUMN China）和印尼国企联合体（BUMN Indonesia）正式签署"雅万高铁项目"合作协议。双方组建了合资公司——印中高铁公司[③]，并由其负责"雅万高铁项目"的建设与运营。2016年1月22日，"雅万高铁项目"举行奠基仪式；3月16日，印中高铁公司正式与印尼交通部签署特许经营协议，这标志着雅万高铁的全面开工建设获得了重要法律保

---

① 罗海峰：《印尼与中国贸易现状及存在的问题分析》，《对外经贸》2016年第3期，第30页。

② 《马云接受印尼政府邀请，要做他们国家的电商顾问》，腾讯科技，2016年9月9日，http://tech.qq.com/a/ 20160909/056534.htm。

③ 《中国称高铁项目将"全部采用中国元素"》（Cina Sebut Proyek Kereta Cepat "Unsur Cina Sepenuhnya"），英国BBC广播公司印尼语网站（BBC Indonesia），2015年10月16日，http://www.bbc.com/indonesia/berita_indonesia/2015/10/151016_majalah_keretacepat_cina。访问时间：2017年4月10日。

障。[①]一周后，5 公里先导段正式全面开工。[②]直到当年 7 月，历经重重波折，"雅万高铁项目"最终获得了全线建设的许可证。2017 年 4 月 4 日，《雅万高铁工程总承包（EPC）合同》在雅加达签署，这标志着该铁路作为"一带一路"建设的一项早期重要成果进入全面实施阶段。

（三）人文领域

两国建立副总理级的人文交流机制后，在文化、教育、青年交流和旅游等方面发展迅速，2016 年中国首次成为印尼最大外国游客来源地。"国之交在于民相亲"，推进中国与印尼人文领域的交流合作，有利于塑造中国良好的国家形象，减少印尼对"一带一路"倡议及中国的顾虑，从而保障两国间关系的顺畅、健康发展。[③]因此，中国与印尼间的人文交流有着重要意义。

"一带一路"倡议推进后，中—印尼两国建立了副总理级的人文交流机制，这是中国与发展中国家建立的首个高级别的人文交流机制。[④]2015 年 5 月，国务院副总理刘延东访问印尼并主持召开了上述机制的首次会议。2016 年 8 月，印尼人类发展与文化统筹部长布安来华出席第九届中国—东盟教育周暨第二届中国—东盟教育部长圆桌会议开幕式，并同刘延东副总理共同主持中—印尼人文交流机制第二次会议。在此背景下，两国在人文交流中文化、教育和旅游等领域取得了众多重要成果。

文化领域，中—印尼在电影、电视、新闻、出版、图书馆、文艺表演等方面开展官方和民间交流与合作。比如，2014 年 11 月 11 日，中国驻印尼大使馆举办

---

① 《印尼雅万高铁项目获得印尼交通部特许经营权》，环球网，2016 年 3 月 17 日，http://world.huanqiu.com/hot/2016-03/8725134.html。访问时间：2017 年 4 月 10 日。

② 《印尼雅万高铁项目先导段全面开工》，中华人民共和国驻印度尼西亚共和国大使馆官网，2016 年 3 月 25 日，http://www.fmprc.gov.cn/ce/ceindo/chn/ztbd/ywgt710/t1351158.htm。访问时间：2017 年 4 月 10 日。

③ 韦宝毅：《关于中国与印尼人文交流的探讨》，广西大学中国—东盟研究院官网，2015 年 3 月 19 日，http://cari.gxu.edu.cn/info/1087/6393.htm。访问时间：2017 年 4 月 10 日。

④ 《郝平：中印尼人文交流机制具有里程碑意义》，新华网，2015 年 5 月 28 日，http://news.xinhuanet.com/world/2015-05/28/c_1115438348.htm。访问时间：2017 年 4 月 10 日。

的"2014年中国电影周"活动在印尼首都雅加达拉开帷幕，反响热烈。受国务院新闻办公室委托，五洲传播出版社于2014年启动《我们和你们》系列丛书，按照"一国一品"的概念，讲述中国和周边国家传统的和当前的友谊与合作。其中，中文版的《我们和你们：中国和印度尼西亚的故事》于2016年3月出版，该书的印尼语版也于2017年初顺利出版。

教育领域，中国与印尼的教育交流与合作蓬勃发展，主要集中在高等教育方面。两国高等院校的合作成为其主渠道，学生流动则成为合作的中心，在语言教学、互派留学生、合作办学、校长交流等方面均取得了长足的进步。目前国内现有15所大专院校开设印尼语专业，设立了6个印尼研究中心，2016年还成立了"中国—印尼高校智库联盟"，很多高校开设了对外汉语研修项目。据2011年中国教育部公布的数据，约有10957名印尼学生在华留学，在来华留学生人数最多的国家中排名第七。[①]

旅游领域，中国和印尼互为重要游客的来源国。中国与印尼联合开展旅游推介活动，促进旅游便利化，提高能力建设，鼓励扩大对旅游产业的投资。2013年两国签署《中国—印尼旅游合作谅解备忘录》。2014年印尼政府邀请成龙作为印尼的旅游大使，通过在杭州等6个中国城市推广"奇妙旅游计划"、在济南举行"印尼经贸旅游投资推介会"等举措吸引中国游客。2015年2月，印尼旅游部推出"郑和旅游线"计划，以吸引中国游客；同年初印尼鹰航航空公司已开通北京—巴厘岛的常规直飞航班，该航线每周3班，加上原有的从北京、上海、广州直飞雅加达的航班，印尼鹰航已开通4条直飞中国的航线。此外，印尼鹰航还将在旅游旺季开通直飞包机，开通自哈尔滨、重庆、成都、昆明、西安、沈阳、宁波直飞巴厘岛的7条包机航线。随着中国与印尼双边关系的不断升温，来印尼旅游的中国游客连年递增。据印尼中央统计局公布的数据显示，目前中国赴印尼旅游的人数已由2014年的95万人次跃升为2016年的142.9万人次，同比增长13.96%，中国已成为印尼

---

① 许利平等著：《中国与周边命运共同体：构建与路径》，社会科学文献出版社，2016年，第144页。

第一大旅游客源地。①印尼旅游部期望在 2017 年能吸引 200 万人次中国游客。

存在的问题

（一）政策沟通尚有提升空间

中—印尼间"一带一路"与"全球海洋支点"战略对接措施不具体，纳土纳群岛海域重叠成海洋合作的主要障碍。目前中—印尼两国在海洋合作方面存在"说多做少"现象，许多协议与承诺有待落地。两国领导人在许多会面中取得的共识和口头承诺，相关部门后续跟进效果不明显，合作项目的推进效率亟待提高。

战略对接过程中的政策沟通略显不足。一方面表现为现有机制尚未被充分利用。比如，中印尼海上合作委员会自 2012 年建立以来，仅举办过两届会议。中印尼海上合作技术委员会原计划每年举行一次会议，但 2014 年未举办。原定于 2015 年举行的第十次会议也未如期举行。②另一方面，参与定期沟通的涉海部门较少。除了国家海洋局和上述两个政府级别的委员会外，中方其他相关政府部门和非政府机构几乎没有与印尼建立有关海洋合作的常规机制。沟通机制的缺失或缺乏活力、参与部门有限，使双方的海洋战略无法实现无缝对接，海洋合作难以达到彼此的战略预期。施政效率低下主要表现为三个问题：尚未形成"一带一路"合作的中长期规划，项目推进缓慢，缺乏成果验收的标准。③

纳土纳群岛海域重叠影响双方的合作氛围。中国印尼双方的海洋合作无法回避南海问题引发的领土主权争端。虽然印尼表示自己并非南海主权声索国，但双方

---

① 《中国跃升为印尼最大旅游客源地》，中华人民共和国国家旅游局官网，2017 年 2 月 17 日，http://www.cnta. gov.cn/xxfb/jdxwnew2/201702/t20170217_815114.shtml。访问时间：2017 年 2 月 18 日。

② 《中国—印尼海上技术合作委员会第九次会议顺利召开》，外交部网站，2015 年 1 月 20 日，http://www.fmprc. gov.cn/web/gjhdq_676201/gj_676203/yz_676205/1206_677244/xgxw_677250/t1229707. shtml。访问时间：2017 年 2 月 9 日。

③ 薛松、许利平：《印尼"海洋强国战略"与对华海洋合作》，《国际问题研究》2016 年第 3 期，第 76 页。

却因纳土纳群岛附近海域与中国的传统海域重叠而屡屡发生冲突。同时，印尼作为东盟最大的经济体，其在南海问题上的立场和态度在一定程度上影响该问题协商进程。因此，印尼在南海问题上并非"利益无关方"，其与中国在纳土纳群岛海域问题上的争议是真实存在的。因此，印尼在南海问题上的立场并不中立，其对涉及争端的其他东盟国家情感上同情、行动上支持。同时，印尼内部对此问题的立场也并不统一[①]。渔业纠纷、南海问题等将使中国与印尼的关系发展面临压力测试。[②]

（二）设施联通面临诸多阻碍

印尼的征地问题突出，政府行政审批程序繁复，贪腐问题严重，政府的协调能力有限，用工问题突出。"征地难"已成为中国企业在海外投资的主要阻碍因素。中企在海外投资基础设施项目往往缺乏全面细致科学的可行性调研，忽视或低估征地难度。据 2015 年中国出口信用保险公司《"一带一路"国家基础设施行业专题研究报告》，"征地难"是制约中国投资印尼基础设施的第二大问题，仅次于行政许可。[③]报告指出，在实施《加速和扩大印尼经济发展的总体规划》（简称MP3EI）的第一年里，在项目进展低于预期的 59 个项目中，有 27 个项目因征地问题难以推进，约占总项目的 46%。"征地难"同样反映在中—印尼"一带一路"的合作中，其中最为突出的是雅万高铁，这也是印尼基础设施建设和投资建厂中的普遍问题。即使各方面证照齐全以后，截至 2017 年 2 月中旬，雅万高铁项目的加拉璜—普沃加达路段仍面临着征地问题，仅该路段可能还需 2 万亿盾的征地补偿款。[④]雅万高铁能否如期完工，令人担忧。

在中央和地方分权制的背景下，印尼行政审批程序尤为繁复，各级政府的协

① 潘玥：《试析中印尼在南海问题上的互动模型》，《东南亚南亚研究》，2017 年第 1 期，第 21 页。

② John Mcbeth, "Vigilance over South China Sea Incidents", Tempo, April 5, 2016, https://magz.tempo.co/konten/2016/04/05/KL/31497/Vigilance-over-South-China-Sea-Incidents/33/16, last accessed by December 21, 2016.

③ 单勇起、张宇：《"一带一路"之投资印度尼西亚：土地征用工作实践与探索》，《中国矿业》，2015 年第S1 期，第 51 页。

④ 《雅加达－万隆高铁工程仍因征地问题受阻》，《印华日报》，2017 年 2 月 17 日，A5 版。

同和协调能力有限，程序性贪腐问题肆虐。中企项目在印尼落地会出现项目已由国家层面商定，但具体执行的政府部门或地方政府拖而不办、办而不畅的情况。导致期间消耗企业大量的沟通和时间成本，造成了经济损失。虽然印尼中央政府试图努力提高工作效率，但地方政府行政改革很难跟上，尤其是在批复土地收购许可、矿产开采许可等事务上效率极低。在地方分权制度下，县与县之间的物产所有权划界纠纷也增加了投资风险。各部门间缺乏沟通，互相扯皮，行政管理能力低下，政府政策延续性差，政府形象大大受损。

用工问题突出在印尼多次引起广泛争议，出现了许多针对中国和佐科的谣言，并可能引发社会冲突，严重影响"一带一路"相关项目的推进。印尼技术工人较少，工作和生活节奏较慢，民众时间观念淡薄，工作效率低下，导致工程进展缓慢。于是中企雇佣非法的中国劳工，以加快工程进度。然而在印尼劳工部、移民局的搜查中，员工被捕并被媒体曝光，印尼全国哗然，中国形象受损。此举又引起印尼社会的不满，认为中国企业没有社会责任感，违反合同，未能为当地创造足够的工作机会，侵犯了其就业权，使得印尼劳工部不得不一再收紧中国工人的工作签条件。中国式的工作速度与印尼的工作节奏不匹配，印尼缺少熟练的技术工人与中国技术工人难以获得工作签，成为用工问题中的两组重要矛盾。

（三）贸易通而不畅

中—印尼间贸易通而不畅现象普遍，印尼国内部分优惠政策无法落地，商业证照手续繁复，营商环境亟需大力治理。比如，根据《中国—东盟全面经济合作框架协议》《中国—东盟全面经济合作框架协议货物贸易协议》和《中国—东盟全面经济合作框架协议投资协议》等文件，中国和印尼逐步削减货物贸易的关税水平。据悉，2010年初建成"中国—东盟自由贸易区"后，中国和印尼90%以上的进出口产品实现了零关税[①]，即中国的货物出口至印尼，如果办理了中国—东盟自

[①] 《印度尼西亚对外国投资合作的法规和政策（2014年版）》，南博网，2015年7月15日，http://www.caexpo.com/news/asean/yinni/zcfx_yinni/fghj/2015/07/15/3648299.html。访问时间：2017年2月16日。

贸区"原产地证"（又称"格式E"，或"Form E"），出口货品可获得一定的关税减免优惠。然而，在实际操作中，中国货物出口至印尼，在办理了"原产地证"后，并不是每次都能获得关税减免；即使同样的货物，同样的"原产地证"，如果遇上不同的海关官员，给出的通关结果都可能不同。出口商往往因为证书受查而无法顺利享受普惠制或自贸区关税优惠，也可能因此导致货物受阻口岸，产生"仓储费"，从而蒙受一定程度的经济损失。由此说明，印尼海关缺乏协同和统一，缺乏业务知识的学习与培训，对于此类关税减免证照的认可度较低，主观性强，缺乏对海关官员的监管。

商业证照手续繁复，印尼一直把简化投资许可作为改善商业环境的重要举措。世界经济论坛的《2014~2015年全球竞争力报告》指出，印尼政府官僚程序效率低，是继贪腐、融资困难和通货膨胀之后制约印尼经济发展的最大障碍。[1]在2015年世界银行发布的《世界营商报告》中，印尼排名第114位，在开设企业、办理施工许可、纳税和执行合同等4个关键项目上的排名分别是第155、153、160、170位。[2]据印尼中央投资统筹机构公布的数据，2014年印尼实际吸引外国直接投资额285.3亿美元，同比增长13.5%，但与2013年增长了22.4%相比，增速明显减弱。主要原因是印尼投资许可证申请程序繁杂，阻碍了投资项目实施，至2014年底，共有约330亿美元的投资项目受阻。因此，政策与审批问题将是佐科政府在经济发展中必须扫清的首要障碍。

针对上述问题，2015年印尼政府正式启动全国投资许可"一站式综合服务平台"（PTST），批准公司成立和核发执照，以协助投资者获得服务救济、财政便利和投资咨询。[3]根据标准操作程序（SOP），完成整个程序要超过3年（1125天）。

---

① 《引资提速，印尼推一站式服务》，中国日报网，2015年2月11日，http://www.chinadaily.com.
cn/hqcj/gjcj/ 2015-02-11/content_13217690.html。访问时间：2017年2月17日。

② 许培源、陈乘风：《印尼与"海上丝绸之路"建设》，《亚太经济》2015年第5期，第24页。

③ 《"一带一路"沿线国家法律风险防范指引》系列丛书编委会著：《"一带一路"沿线国家法律风险防范指引（印度尼西亚）》，经济科学出版社，2015年，第51页。

在新体系下，全部程序设计时间缩短了 80%。①然而，不少中企反映，虽然"一站式综合服务平台"的设想很理想，但施行起来存在许多执行的问题。投资审批程序依然复杂，规章与细则非常烦琐拖沓，行政效率低下，部门掣肘多、协同少，程序性腐败多，打击了投资者的积极性。为了加快审批速度，不少企业不得不选择中介服务，支付高昂的中介费用，甚至在证照办理过程中缴纳"加急费"和"好处费"，无形中助长了贪污腐败的歪风邪气，增加了企业的运营成本。

（四）资金融通存有一定风险

投资印尼，我国企业和金融机构面临成本高、收益低、风险大等不利因素。印尼的经济基础薄弱，偿还货款和贷款的能力较低，违约的可能性较高，基础设施项目本身存在工期长、成本高、回本周期长的特点，这也增加了我国金融机构在印尼推进项目的风险，尤其是亚投行。另外，印尼政府对当地银行不提供政府担保，一旦印尼商业银行资本流动性降低、不良贷款增多，则极有可能产生资金链断裂等问题，并进一步导致挤兑风险。其中，流动性风险问题突出。由于对外资的高度依赖，印尼的流动性很容易受到国际流动性的变化而敏感波动。当前，全球流动性趋紧，印尼通过干预来维护外汇稳定，维护投资者信心。印尼政府通过货币贬值来提振国内出口，刺激国内经济。因此，印尼盾贬值的风险相对而言较为明显。②

此外，汇率风险也值得重视。目前，中国企业在印尼开展项目合作时，合同价款通常由美元和部分当地货币即印尼盾构成，由于美元的疲软和印尼盾的不稳定，使中国企业面临较大的汇率风险。一方面，由于长期以来与美元挂钩的固定汇率、中国经济高速增长，以及贸易顺差过大带来的升值压力等原因，人民币自2005 年汇率改革以来，总体处于升值的过程中。另一方面，由于受经济危机的影

---

① 潘玥、姜柯柯：《印度尼西亚基本国情及投资风险评估》，摘自《东盟十国基本国情及投资风险评估》，中国社会科学出版社，2016 年，第 251 页。

② 《印尼政府采取措施应对货币剧烈贬值》，中华人民共和国驻印度尼西亚共和国大使馆经济商务参赞处，2014 年 12 月 17 日，http://id.mofcom.gov.cn/article/ziranziyuan/huiyuan/201412/20141200839082.shtml。访问时间：2016 年 4 月 26 日。

响，加之印尼政局不稳定，近年来印尼盾不断贬值。1997 年发生的亚洲金融危机中，印尼盾贬值 200%。2008 年美国次贷危机引发的全球性经济萧条，使印尼盾再次大幅贬值。2015 年 7 月的通胀率也高达 7.6%。而印尼盾对美元汇率却不断下跌，在实际的兑换中，从 2015 年 11 月的 1:13400，跌至 2016 年 1 月的 1:14000，跌幅达 4.29%。[①]

（五）民心相通仍需加强

印尼社会对"一带一路"认识水平较低，误解颇多，"中国威胁论"或"新殖民主义"有一定市场。这突出表现在印尼媒体对该倡议的相关新闻报道上。2017 年初，中宣部委托道琼斯旗下 Factiva 全球新闻及公司数据库，对"一带一路"沿线十几个国家的新闻报道进行关键词抓取[②]，从中分析各国媒体对"一带一路"倡议的态度。所抓取和筛选的印尼语新闻约 56 条、俄语新闻为 900 多条、阿拉伯语新闻为 500 多条。当然，多个国家使用俄语或阿拉伯语报道新闻，但相比之下，印尼语新闻的绝对值还是较少。这反映了两个问题：第一，相比起使用俄语和阿拉伯语的国家，印尼对"一带一路"倡议的关注总体较少；第二，由于是使用"一带一路"、"丝绸之路经济带"、"21 世纪海上丝绸之路"和"丝路经济"等关键词进行抓取，很有可能并非印尼媒体对"一带一路"倡议不关注，而是它们并不能准确或相对完整地写出这几个名称，这说明印尼媒体对"一带一路"倡议认知不足，也反映了我国相关部门在此方面的对外宣传力度不足，方式和渠道有待丰富和优化。

"中国威胁论"或"新殖民主义"在印尼社会有一定的市场。根据 2016 年一项针对印尼对"中国文化印象调查"的数据，受访者对中国及中国文化的总体印象有待提高。其中，"中国不断发展"得分最高，其次是"中国有创新力"和"中国富强"，而"中国可靠可信"则得分最低。调查结果还显示，日本是印尼人最喜

---

① 潘玥：《佐科维执政初期印尼华人社会状况初探》，《东南亚研究》，2016 年第 3 期，第 78 页。

② 非对象国媒体用对象国语言，对"一带一路"倡议的报道并不在考察范围之内，如 BBC Indonesia、CNN Indonesia 和中国国际广播电台等。

欢的国家。①这说明，相比起日本，印尼民众对中国的好感度有待提高。

企业更多使用中国员工、中国员工素质欠佳造成许多问题。"一带一路"倡议落地与推进后，印尼爆发了多次关于中国劳工的争议。比如中国企业常常为了早日完工而带去数千名中国工人，无论是管理层、初级工人，还是技术工人，并没有为印尼当地创造足够的就业机会。另外，部分中国工人缺少必要的海外务工培训，文化程度较低，既不会印尼语，也不会英语，在印尼生活和工作的过程中，往往由于"无知"而对本地人的生活和宗教习惯不够尊重；素质欠佳，在公众场合大声喧哗，插队加塞等，往往使得当地民众对中国和中国人的印象大打折扣。这严重损害中国及其企业的国际形象，影响两国在"一带一路"倡议中的合作。

印尼学界成为反对声音的主要来源，相当一部分专家学者对"一带一路"倡议的定位和内涵存在一定程度的误读和偏见。②由于专家学者被普遍认为是印尼研究中国问题的权威，因此，他们在民众中拥有一定的话语权和较高的说服力，这使得从国家层面上讲，"一带一路"倡议在印尼不仅缺乏较坚实的民意基础，还缺乏智力支持。比如他们将"一带一路"倡议等同于美国的"马歇尔计划"，认为其实质是解决中国国内产能过剩和失业人口过多的问题。甚至有激进的伊斯兰报刊把中国对印尼的投资行为称为"新殖民主义"（Penjajahan Baru）或"中国式经济霸权"。③

① 许静、韩晓梅：《品牌国家策略与提升中国文化国际影响力——基于印尼"中国文化印象调查"的分析》，《外交评论》（外交学院学报），2016年第3期，第57~59页。

② 米拉、施雪琴：《印尼对中国"一带一路"倡议的认知和反应述评》，《南洋问题研究》2016年第4期，第83页。

③ "Bebaskan Indonesia Dari Penjajahan dan Perbudakan Cina?", *Voice of Islam*, 1 Mei 2015, http://www.voa-islam.id/read/opini/2015/05/01/36684/bebaskan-indonesia-dari-penjajahan-dan-perbudakan-cina/#sthash.VWvISedR.dpbs.See: 2015-04-15.

对策与建议

（一）国家层面

1. 两国应加强顶层设计和沟通交流，和平协商解决纳土纳群岛海域重叠问题。

两国应继续积极推动高层互访与交流，形成良性互动格局。中国应积极邀请印尼领导人参加中国主办的各种活动，进一步夯实双方的政治共识，加强顶层设计。2016 年，"亚投行"的运作、"丝路基金"的建立、人民币的国际化、基础设施互联互通等，都是中国推动"21 世纪海上丝绸之路"的重要举措。[①] 推动中—印尼人文交流高层磋商机制第二次会议、中—印尼副总理级对话机制第五次会议、中—印尼高层经济对话第二次会议等成功举行，在政治互信、经贸投资、人文交流三大领域做好谋划，扩展合作空间。[②] 两国应加快商议并签订关于落实中—印尼全面战略伙伴关系的行动计划，细化两国各领域合作的路线图。稳步推进两国已签订的双边与多边协议，加强海上合作、中国—东盟海上合作，要确保"一带一路"与东盟共同体整体规划相契合、相补充。

中国和印尼的政党、经济部门、海洋部门、地方政府官员、智库等要真诚、平等沟通。一方面，中国要全面介绍"一带一路"的背景、定位、目的、内涵和行动计划，印尼要进一步提出自身的关切和期待，两国就此沟通，消除疑虑，营造政治互信的良好氛围；另一方面，中国和印尼要主动设计和细化具体合作意向和实际措施，在照顾双方需求和舒适度的基础上，制定细化、具有可操作性的执行方案、路线图和时间表，将两国领导人的共识落到实处。

在与印尼处理纳土纳群岛的专属经济区与中国的传统海域重叠问题上，中国的"一带一路"战略迎合了印尼当下以经济发展为重点的外交政策，这将有利于

---

① 李皖南、王亚琴：《从雅万高铁看中国印尼战略对接》，《亚太经济》，2016 年第 4 期，第 21 页。

② 郭仁萧：《中国"海上丝绸之路"倡议与印尼"全球海洋支点"战略对接的基础与挑战》，外交学院 2016 年硕士论文，第 29 页。

避免纳土纳群岛问题扩大化，有利于中—印尼双方解决纳土纳海域的重叠问题。在总统佐科的领导下，比起自负地维护领土主权，印尼更重视本国的商业利益、外国直接投资和未来的基础设施援助项目。①印尼官方把纳土纳群岛海域争端定位为渔业问题，称其为经济上的"海上资源之争"，而非政治上的"领土主权纠纷"，旨在淡化事件的政治意味。如果没有外部势力的介入，通过中—印尼两国的交涉与协商，将更有可能、更为容易地解决纳土纳专属经济区与中国传统海域重叠问题。综上，双边关系处于空前"蜜月期"②的中—印尼两国都倾向于采取和平而温和的方式去协商与解决问题，付诸武力的可能性极低，双方极有可能将纳土纳问题控制在"斗而不破"的范围内。然而，美国、日本、澳大利亚等外部势力的介入，并鼓吹"中国威胁论"，将在一定程度上影响解决该问题的进程，进而影响地区的和平与稳定。

2. 中国应重视对外宣传工作，理清基本概念，消除疑虑与猜忌。

推进"一带一路"倡议，还需消除印尼各个方面，尤其是政府和智库层面对"一带一路"倡议的疑虑和偏见。只有消除他们的不安和猜疑，中—印尼才能集中力量推进该倡议的落地与合作，实现中—印尼两国的繁荣共建。

消除印尼疑虑的一个重要途径，就是中国的文化、教育与宣传部门应注重在印尼民众，尤其是原住民群体中，树立真实积极的中国形象。另一个重要途径就是媒体。首先，中国媒体应改变原有充满"战略化"的话语体系。新加坡学者郑永年认为，国内有些研究和话语经常把经济活动战略化，用"战略"甚至是"军事战略"的概念来描述中国的对外经贸策略，用"西南战略大通道"、"桥头堡"、

---

① [印尼]皮埃尔·马蒂纳斯：《对中国熟视无睹：印尼的南中国海政策》，《东南亚问题研究》，2016 年 6 月 20 日，http://mp.weixin.qq.com/s?__biz=MjM5MTc0NzI2Nw==&mid=2650305021&idx=4&sn=f7b84705a069a84c6388b896b34dcfcc&scene=1&srcid=0621yAesfwqykAkG3zzBCg4b#wechat_redirect。访问时间：2016 年 9 月 8 日。

② [印尼]利尼·乌达米（Rini Utami）：《中印尼关系：从苏加诺到佐科》（Hubungan Indonesia-Tiongkok: dari Soekarno hingga Jokowi），安塔拉新闻网（Antara News），2015 年 4 月 13 日，http://www.antaranews.com/ berita/490460/hubungan-indonesia-tiongkok-dari- soekarno-hingga-jokowi。访问时间：2015 年 4 月 15 日。

"西进"等概念，给地方政府或者企业的贸易投资行为人为地添上战略色彩。如东盟国家对"桥头堡"也很警觉，认为这个概念包含过多的军事因素。[①]

此外，中国官方媒体应定期与印尼当地的媒体保持良好沟通。只有民心所向，获得更多民众的支持和认可，"一带一路"倡议才能顺利推进。另一方面，沟通是相互的，中国媒体也要在国内做好这方面工作。中国媒体普遍习惯从《雅加达时报》(*Jakarta Post*)、美国有线电视新闻网、路透社、法国新闻社等外媒采编国外新闻，这些新闻来源以英语为主，并不能如实反映情况。中方媒体有必要掌握一定的话语权和主动权，在印尼设立相应的新闻媒体站、开设社交媒体平台，与外交部设立联动机制，及时对印尼社会中针对中国的不实言论进行批驳，努力打破"先传谣再辟谣"的传统新闻模式。中国媒体应加强媒体建设，尝试引进熟练掌握印尼语的采编人员，采访国内知名的印尼专家学者，减少直接转引西方媒体的报道。

加大与印尼智库、高校间的机制化联系，通过建立联合研究交流计划和"一带一路"研究基金等形式，引导双方学者加强在共同议题上的研究，从而为本国的政府决策提供智力支持。

3. 中国应积极开展公共外交，促进人文交流与沟通，增进与印尼社会的理解和信任。

公共外交在外交舞台上发挥作用日益凸显。通过相互沟通与交流，实现政策理念、思想、文化和价值观的传递和认知，增进彼此的理解与认识。公共外交是中国与周边国家达成共识、构建共同价值的重要桥梁。[②]中国政府应重新审视与研究制定对印尼的公共外交政策，以开放包容的态度，继续在全方位推动人文交流，深入开展文化、旅游、科教、地方合作等友好交往的同时，抓住机遇，充分发挥各个交流渠道的功能，增进中国与印尼的相互了解、友谊和感情。

---

① 郑永年：《不宜把丝绸之路的话语"战略化"》，光明网，2014 年 10 月 20 日，http://theory.gmw.cn/2014-10/20/content_13587011.htm。访问时间：2015 年 4 月 15 日。

② 许利平等著：《中国与周边命运共同体：构建与路径》，社会科学文献出版社，2016 年，第50 页。

中国与东南亚地区国家之间文化艺术交流的活跃程度仅次于东北亚,文化产业贸易规模虽然与东北亚地区相差很大,但也形成了一定的规模。①文化交流应逐渐从"政府推动"转向"民间自发"。政府无须过多地策划文化交流活动。文化流动具有自发性,但政府仍然需要设立监督机制和引导性政策,以引导民间的文化艺术交流朝着健康的方向发展。文化艺术交流应该以丰富民众文化生活、促进文化艺术发展,通过文化艺术交流增进中—印尼两国的相互了解为目的。文化艺术交流与国家间的政治合作、经济合作确实存在相互促进的作用,但是文化艺术交流本身不应承担政治任务,不应带有过于浓重的商业气息,同时还要提防民族主义的膨胀。

4. 印尼应意识到需着力解决国内的深层问题,比如中央与地方的协同性问题、政策法律的连续性问题、贪腐问题、劳动立法和执法的问题、征地法律和实施的问题等。

对于印尼内部的政治、法律和制度性问题,建议印尼应提高中央与地方政府的协同能力,加强各政府部门间的沟通与配合,简化投资审批程序,着力于打击贪污腐败问题,营造良好的投资环境。也应看到,腐败问题并不能在朝夕解决,打击贪腐问题需要长时间的努力。政府在严厉打击贪污、官商勾结行为的同时,还应该出台一些积极的措施,鼓励官员主动施政,提高政府的效能,让反贪与经济发展、政府效能走上良性协调的发展轨道。另外,征地问题已成制约印尼吸引外资的巨大障碍。因此,有必要对现有的土地法律和制度进行必要的改革,明确土地权属问题(尤其是共有地),制定高效公平的征地流程,有利于加快印尼的基础设施建设与大幅推动经济的发展。当地劳动部门既要加强对中国工人工作签的审批工作,打击持商务签、无证打工等非法行为;另一方面,建议与当地高校和企业合作,培训和培养大量印尼技术工人,以改善现有的用工问题。

---

① 许利平等著:《中国与周边命运共同体:构建与路径》,社会科学文献出版社,2016年,第132页。

（二）企业层面

1.中国企业应从观念上建立起对印尼投资环境的正确认识，做好长远布局。

中企在投资印尼前，应建立评估、投保、退出、本土化和多元化机制，根据印尼市场的实际情况制定投资策略，避免一哄而上和主观臆测，规避风险，提高投资回报率。中资企业在印尼投资已有一定规模，各类协会商会林立，应尽可能利用现有的资源。如初来乍到就贸然行事，必会吃亏，但若做好长远规划，真正融入印尼，将会得到较高的投资回报。

另外，还要树立本地化经营观念。不少中资企业抱着投机的心态来到印尼，没有本地化经营的理念，经营过程仍然以中国为主，比如某些产品在印尼出售后，出现质量问题，售后服务还要客户找中国生产企业，这样的做法适得其反，非但投机不成，反而在印尼投资很可能会失败。中资企业应该充分利用印尼本地资源，将企业文化、人力资源、产品、品牌等一系列环节在印尼实现本地化，这样才能促进企业健康发展。

2.中方企业具备一定的资金实力和风险承受能力是投资印尼项目不可或缺的必要条件。

印尼市场上中国投资最热门的应属能源矿业类和基建设施类项目，这两类项目都具有项目周期较长、证照手续繁多的特点，尤其矿产资源项目在印尼新矿业法出台后要求原矿石必须在本地建厂经过加工后方允许出口，更是加大了投资的难度。既然是长久战，又得逐级获批，再加上贪腐现象严重，其中的资金成本和风险性不言而喻。同时，也应该看到印尼政府高度重视并着力打击贪腐问题，民主政治也在不断完善。因此，从长远来看，贪腐问题必将得到显著的改善。但从短期来看，贪腐现象普遍，中方企业在与地方政府打交道时，给予"小费"、"好处费"、"介绍费"等非常规费用，无疑增加了企业的运营成本，降低了企业的办事效率。因此，企业在与地方官员接触时，要更加谨慎，遇到索要贿赂的情况，应保留证据，必要时考虑向商会、上级主管部门、肃贪委员会和财务稽查局（BPK）揭发举报。

避免存款损失风险。中国企业在印尼开展项目时，应尽量将存款存于中国银行/工商银行的印尼分行。在当地银行存放的资金，应只保留小额，以供日常支付使用。

对于原产地证等东盟退证查询问题，企业在积极利用原产地证书、享受关税减免优惠时，应关注以下几点：一是对出口印尼的货物，清关发票应与证书的出口商保持一致；二是对出口印尼的货物，各商业单据和证书上的商品名称描述应做到一致；三是经香港、澳门转运的货物，无论提单是否显示，应尽早在当地有关部门办理"未再加工证明"加签事宜；四是对于货物通关时发生的证书受质疑等问题，建议企业积极联系检验检疫原产地业务部门寻求帮助及时解决。[①]

3. 中国企业应重视合法用工问题，优化人力资源结构。

在中企对外投资时，既要按照协议，为当地创造一定比例的就业机会，对于准备在印尼长期投资发展的中资企业来说，应该注重包括印尼员工在内的人力资源培训，为企业发展储备人才。同时，又要给到国外参与项目的中国员工办理好真实有效的工作签证，并做好基础的海外培训工作，包括基本的语言培训和对象国国情介绍。中方企业是中国"走出去"战略的实际执行者，中国员工是中国国际形象的外在表现，也是中国文明和礼仪的使者。力求中国员工在海外参与工程项目时，掌握基本的交流沟通技能，尊重印尼民众的宗教信仰和社会风俗习惯。

另外，应与地方政府的劳动部门合作，与所雇用的本地员工签订正式有效的劳动合同，规定好双方的权利义务，并对本地员工进行职业技能和岗前培训。如果任何一方出现违约行为，都将按劳动合同行事，合理合法地保护中企和当地员工的合法权益。

合作前景

中印两国在"一带一路"倡议合作中拥有广泛合作空间和发展前景，尤其在

---

① 《输东盟货物应正确运用原产地证规则避免退证查询》，江苏新闻网，2016年10月24日，http://www.js.chinanews.com/75/2016/1024/21338.html。访问时间：2017年2月16日。

印尼基础设施建设方面。印尼国内经济仍处于快速增长阶段，基础设施建设领域具有很大需求，是中国在东南亚地区开展承包工程业务最大的潜在市场。根据印尼《2015~2019 年中期建设发展规划》，未来 5 年印尼将建设 2650 公里公路、1000公里高速公路、3258 公里铁路、24 个大型港口、60 个轮渡码头、15 个现代化机场、14 个工业园区、49 个水库、33 个水电站，并为约 100 万公顷农田建立灌溉系统。由于国家预算有限，政府将鼓励国企和国内外私营企业参与，并可通过公私合营（PPP）模式开展合作。①可以预期，若以上项目能够顺利进行，印尼的基础设施水平将会明显改善。可喜的是，中国与印尼在互联互通、基础设施合作领域已经取得一定成绩，印尼泗马大桥、加蒂格迪大坝、塔杨桥等一批工程项目顺利完工，建立了良好口碑。印尼制定的《印尼 2015~2019 年中期建设发展规划》和《印尼 2015~2019 年使用外国贷款项目清单》，把公路、铁路、桥梁、港口、码头等列为基础设施重点项目，预计总投资 6000 亿美元。中国和印尼应将此类项目列入双方重点合作经贸清单。中国有能力、有意愿支持印尼政府发展基建，可参与港口、电站、公路、铁路、机场、桥梁等项目承包建设和投资运营，并提供规划和设计等支持。中国公司已经在参与印尼东部 30 多个码头的新建或改扩建项目，帮助印尼提升海上互联互通水平。雅加达丹戎不碌港设计规划和改建、扩建工程，巴淡—民丹跨海大桥建设，都为中国支持印尼"海上高速公路"建设提供了良好的投资合作机会。

随着近年来中印尼两国关系和经贸关系的持续发展，特别是中国向印尼提供 28 亿美元优惠出口买方信贷和有关项目的落定，双方在承包工程在内的基础设施领域合作面临着难得的发展机遇。中方企业在海外投资时，需调整经营理念，在"惠己"的基础上兼顾"利人"，一定能抓住世纪机遇创造双赢。相信在未来 5~10年内，印尼的基础设施建设在中资企业参与建设下将得到较大的提升。

---

① 《未来 5 年印尼基础设施建设需约 4245 亿美元资金》，中华人民共和国驻印度尼西亚共和国大使馆经济商务参赞处，2015 年 6 月 11 日，http://id.mofcom.gov.cn/article/ziranziyuan/jians/201506/20150601009653.shtml。访问时间：2016 年 4 月 26 日。

4 Current Status and Prospect of Sino-Indonesian Cooperation under the Background of The Belt and Road

Zhai Kun

During his visit to Indonesia in 2013, President Xi Jinping proposed the initiative to co-build "21st Century Maritime Silk Road". Located at the intersection between Pacific and the Indian Ocean as well as between Asian and Oceania, Indonesia is a critical pivot and strategic fulcrum of "Maritime Silk Road". Indonesia's maritime power strategy, which is centered on the vision of "Global Maritime Axis", is consistent with the "Maritime Silk Road" initiative. For five years, China and Indonesia have been actively communicating their "21st Century Maritime Silk Road" initiative and "Global Maritime Axis" strategy and deepening practical cooperation and friendly exchanges. A lot of major cooperative projects, such as Jakarta-Bandung High-speed Railway Project, have been finalized. Cooperation of mutual benefit in fields such as infrastructure construction, trade, investment, finance, e-business, etc, is making constant progress. According to 2015 Report on Five Connectivity Indexes of Countries along the Belt and Road compiled by the research team of Peking University on Five Connectivity

Indexes of countries along the Belt and Road, Indonesia ranks the fifth among all 63 countries along the Belt and Road. This shows that the cooperation between China and Indonesia in fields of the Belt and Road Initiative is on a relatively high level. However, with the broadening and deepening of cooperation between the two countries, a series of problems have begun to surface. If the two parties do not pay enough attention to those problems or take measures to solve them, they will have negative influence on the implementation of the two countries on the Belt and Road Initiative. The present report will summarize the achievements of China and Indonesia in implementing the Belt and Road Initiative, analyze the underlying problems and the real altitudes of Indonesia, and propose some recommendations.

Progresses and Achievements

Since we entered into the 21st century, especially since the China proposed the Belt and Road Initiative, Sino-Indonesian relations have embarked on a fast track. The two countries have conducted sustained communications in fields such as trade, economy and political exchanges, and have made outstanding achievements.

1. Political field

High-level visits between the two countries are frequent, political mutual trust is deepening, and cooperation between the two countries is fruitful. Since the establishment of comprehensive strategic partnership between China and Indonesia, political mutual trust has been deepening, and practical cooperation has been fruitful. Sustained development of Sino-Indonesian relations is not only to the interest of the people of the two countries, but also has made outstanding contributions to regional stability and world peace. The initiative proposed by President Xi Jinping to co-build

"21st Century Maritime Silk Road" during his visit to Indonesia in 2013 is a sign that China highly values Indonesia and that Indonesia plays a critical role in "Maritime Silk Road". Since Indonesian President Joko Widodo took office in 2014, the exchanges and cooperation between the two countries have become closer. The grand vision of Indonesia to build a "maritime power" highly corresponds to the "21st Century Maritime Silk Road" initiative proposed by Chinese President Xi Jinping. China and Indonesia are making joint efforts to construct the "Maritime Silk Road". This will have a positive influence on the Southeast Asian region. Indonesia is a founding nation of the Asian Infrastructure Investment Bank (herein after referred to as AIIB) initiated by China, and it once proposed that the headquarters of AIIB be located in Jakarta. China and Indonesia have common interests in both regional issues and multilateral issues such as enhancement of world peace and prosperity, improvement of South-South cooperation, etc.

After China proposed the Belt and Road Initiative, there have been frequent high-level visits between China and Indonesia. In October 2014, President Xi Jinping talked to Indonesian President Joko Widodo over telephone. In 2015, there were more high-level visits between the two countries. In February, Meng Jinzhu, Secretary of the Political and Judiciary Commission under the Central Committee of the Communist Party of China, visited Indonesia. From March 25 to 28, at the invitation of Chinese President Xi Jinping, Indonesian President Joko Widodo paid a state visit to China and attended the Boao Forum for Asia Annual Conference. The two countries released a joint statement on strengthening comprehensive strategic partnership relations. In April, President Xi Jinping attended the Asian-African Leaders Conference and the 60th Anniversary of Bandung Conference. The two countries released Joint Press Communiqué of People's Republic of China and Republic of Indonesia. In July, Yu Zhengsheng, Chairman of the Chinese People's Political Consultative Conference, visited Indonesia. In November, President Xi Jinping met with Joko during G20 Summit.

In 2016, high-level visits between the two countries continued. In March, Indonesian Vice President Kalla came to China and attended Boao Forum for Asia Annual Conference. In May, State Councilor Yang Jiechi went to Indonesia and served as one of the two chairmen of the second conference of Sino-Indonesian high-level economic dialogue. In September, President Xi Jinping met with Indonesian President Joko during G20 Summit in Hangzhou.

The two countries have established three cooperative mechanisms, namely, deputy-prime ministerial bilateral dialogue, high-level economic dialogue and cultural communications. They have also established deputy-ministerial level cooperative mechanisms in fields such as space, agriculture, science and technology, national defense, etc. Besides embassies in Beijing and Jakarta, China has set up several consulate generals in Indonesia, and Indonesia has set up several consulate generals in Hongkong, Guangzhou and Shanghai.

2. Economic and trade field

Since 21 century, the economic and trade relations between China and Indonesia has just been unfolding, the breadth and depth of the economic and trade cooperation has continued improving, Jakarta-Bandung High-speed Railway Project has continued promotion. China has become the biggest trade partners of Indonesia in the last six years, the annual average growth rate of the bilateral trade has been more than 20%. Indonesia has become one of the most important external investment countries of China, in 2016 China has jumped to the 3rd source of foreign investment in Indonesia from the 10th. In 2011, the bilateral trade between the two countries reached $49.15 billion, China has exceeded Singapore as the largest source country of import in Indonesia. Indonesia had a surplus position at the beginning of cooperation with China due to a small trade scale, but with the deepening of the economic and trade cooperation, Indonesia was gradually turning surplus into unfavorable balance. Indonesia's trade surplus with China in 2006 was $1.7 billion; $1.1 billion in 2007; Indonesia had a deficit in the bilateral trade in 2008 for the first time, and the deficit gap kept widening, with $3.6 billion from 2008, to $4.8 billion in 2010, $13.018 billion in 2014, $14.365 billion in 2015.

Since the Belt and Road Project implemented in Indonesia, the breadth and depth of the economic and trade cooperation between the China and Indonesia has continued improving, and more and more Chinese enterprises have begun to go to Indonesia for development opportunities. With a population of 230 million, Indonesia is the Southeast Asian country with the largest number of consumers and it has great market potential. Currently, there are more than 1000 Chinese enterprises investing in Indonesia, and their investments cover areas such as energy, mining industry, transportation, communication, power, finance and agriculture, etc. With the joint effort of governments and enterprises of the two countries, the potential of Sino-Indonesian trade and economic cooperation will be further released, and the friendly communications between the two countries are becoming closer and closer. During G20 Summit in 2016, Indonesian President Joko visited the famous Chinese IT enterprise Alibaba, and invited Ma Yun, the president of Alibaba, to be the economic advisor of Indonesia. Joko hoped that Ma Yun could help 8 million small and medium-sized enterprises in Indonesia to get E-commercialized by 2020. What's more, IT giants such as Baidu, Tencent, Alibaba, etc, and mobile phone manufacturers such as Oppo, Vivo and Huawei, have settled down in Indonesia, which has set a good example for Chinese enterprises in Indonesia.

At present, the largest cooperation project between China and Indonesia is the Jakarta-Bandung High-speed Railway Project. This project has been highly valued since its inception. On October 16, 2015, BUMN China and BUMN Indonesia formally signed Jakarta-Bandung High-speed Railway Project Cooperation Agreement. The two parties established a joint venture corporation, namely, PT Kereta Cepat Indonesia China (KCIC). It is responsible for the construction and operation of Jakarta-Bandung

High-speed Railway Project. On January 22, 2016, the ground breaking ceremony of Jakarta-Bandung High-speed Railway Project was held. On March 16, 2016, PT Kereta Cepat Indonesia China formally signed a franchise agreement with the Transportation Ministry of Indonesia, which meant that the overall construction of Jakarta-Bandung High-speed Railway Project obtained critical legal assurance. One week later, a five-kilometer-long pilot railway went under construction. In July, 2017, Jakarta-Bandung High-speed Railway Project finally got the license for overall construction. On April 4, 2017, the Engineering Procurement Construction Contract of Jakarta-Bandung High-speed Railway Project was signed in Jakarta, which was a sign that this project went into full implementation phase.

3. Human field

The two countries have established a deputy prime ministerial level human communication mechanism. The exchanges in culture, education, youth communication and tourism developed very fast. In 2016, China became the largest foreign tourist source of Indonesia for the first time. Development of communication and cooperation between China and Indonesia in these fields is beneficial to the shaping of a good image for China and will reduce the worries of Indonesia about the Belt and Road Initiative as well as about China, therefore ensuring smooth and healthy development of the relations between the two countries. In short, the human communications between the two countries are of great significance.

After the Belt and Road Initiative was implemented, China and Indonesia established a deputy prime ministerial level human communication mechanism, a first of its kind for China. In May 2015, Deputy Prime Minister Liu Yandong visited Indonesia and chaired the first meeting of this mechanism. In August 2016, Bouan, the minister of Indonesia's Human Development and Cultural Ministry came to China and attended the ninth Sino-ASEAN Education Week and the opening ceremony of the second

Sino-ASEAN Education Minister Roundtable Conference. Bouan also co-chaired the second meeting of Sino-Indonesian Human Communication Mechanism. Under this background, the two countries have made great achievements in fields such as culture, education, tourism, etc.

In the field of culture, China and Indonesia have conducted official and non-official communications and cooperation in film, television, publishing industry, art shows, etc.

In the field of education, China and Indonesia have made prosperous progresser, which are mainly in higher education. The cooperation between universities of the two countries is the main channel, and student communications are the core of the cooperation. The two countries have made great progress in language teaching, visiting students, etc. Currently, 15 Chinese universities and colleges have set up in Indonesia. There are six Indonesian research centers in China. In 2016, China set up "China-Indonesia University and Think Tank Union". According to data published by Chinese Education Ministry in 2011, about 10957 Indonesian students came to learn in China, and Indonesia ranked the seventh in terms of number of visiting students to China.

In the field of tourism, China and Indonesia are important tourist sources to each other. China and Indonesia jointly conduct tourism advancement activities in order to enhance tourism convenience, improve capacity building and encourage enlargement of investment in tourism. In 2013, the two countries signed China-Indonesia Memo random of Understanding in Tourism Cooperation. In 2014, Indonesia invited Jack Chen to be the Tourism Ambassador of Indonesia. In February, 2015, Indonesia's Ministry of Tourism released "Zheng He Tourist Path" Plan to attract Chinese tourists. Garuda Indonesia initiated regular non-stop flight course between Beijing and Bali Island. Combined with the existing non-stop flight courses between Jakarta to Beijing, Shanghai and Guangzhou, Garuda Indonesia had four non-stop flight courses to China. Besides, Garuda Indonesia will also initiate non-stop charts in peaking tourism seasons. It will initiate seven non-stop charts between Bali Island and Harbin, Chongqing,

Chengdu, Kunming, Xi'an, Shenyang and Ningbo. With the warming bilateral relations between China and Indonesia, Chinese tourists to Indonesia keep increasing year by year. According to data released by Central Statistic Bureau of Indonesia, in 2016, the number of Chinese tourists to Indonesia was 1.429 million, a 13.96% growth than that of 2015, which was 0.95 million. China has become the largest tourist source of Indonesia. Indonesia's Ministry of Tourism expects that in 2017 about two million Chinese tourists would go to Indonesia.

Problems

1. Policy coordination: there is room for policy coordination.

The two countries lack integration strategies between the Belt and Road Initiative of China and the "Global Maritime Axis" Strategy of Indonesia. Natuna Islands are the main obstacle to maritime cooperation between the two countries. Currently, China and Indonesia have the problem of "more words, less actions" in terms of maritime cooperation. Many agreements and commitments are yet to be implemented. Those common agreements and oral commitments reached upon by leaders are not well implemented by relevant agencies. The efficiency of project advancement is to be improved.

Policy coordinations are not sufficient strategic integration. On the one hand, existing mechanisms should be fully utilized. For instant, there were only 2 conferences held since China-Indonesia Maritime Cooperation Committee was set up in 2012. An academic meeting was planned to hold once a year by China-Indonesia Maritime Cooperation Committee of Technique, but it was not held in 2014. The scheduled 10th meeting in 2015 was not held neither. On the other hand, maritime agencies regularly participating in policy communications is not enough. Besides China's State Oceanic

Administration and above-mentioned two government-level committees, there is hardly any regular mechanisms about maritime cooperation between Indonesia and Chinese relevant government sectors and non-governmental organizations. The lack of communication mechanism or of vitality, the limited participating sectors, are making it very difficult for mutual maritime strategy to seamlessly integrate, and it is very difficult to reach the expectations. Low administration efficiency mainly shows up three problems: the medium and long term plan is not yet formed in The Belt and Road cooperation; project promoting is very slow; lack of acceptance standard.

Overlapping sea waters around the Natuna Islands have a negative influence on the atmosphere of cooperation. Sovereignty disputes arising from South China Sea issues are unavoidable in Sino-Indonesian maritime cooperation. Although Indonesia declares that it is not a sovereignty claimant in South China Sea, the two parties have frequent confrontations due to the fact that sea waters around the Natuna Islands and traditional Chinese waters overlap. Meanwhile, as the largest economy of ASEAN, Indonesia's stance and attitude toward the South China Sea disputes will exert some influence on the negotiation process.

2. Facility connectivity faces many obstacles.

Land acquisition is another critical problem in Indonesia. The administrative review and approval process is very complicated, and corruption is very serious. The coordinating ability of the government is limited. Difficulties in land acquisition have become a main hindrance to Chinese overseas investments. The investments of Chinese enterprises in overseas infrastructure projects often lack comprehensive and scientific feasibility surveys, and those enterprises often neglect or underestimate difficulties in land acquisition. Difficulty in land acquisition is the second most serious hindrance to Chinese investments for Indonesian infrastructure companies. The most serious hindrance is administrative approval. The report notes that in the first year of implementing Indonesia "MP3EI", among the 59 projects whose progress were lower than expectation, there were 27 projects hard to promote because of the "land acquisition problem". This problem was also reflected in the Sino-Indonesia cooperation on The Belt and Road, especially in Jakarta-Bandung High-speed Railway Project, constituting the general problem for Indonesian infrastructure building and investment of building a factory. It is worrying whether the Jakarta-Bandung High-speed Railway can be completed on time.

In a country where the central government and local governments are divided, the administrative review and approval process in Indonesia is very complicated. The coordinating abilities of all levels of governments are limited, and procedural corruptions are very common in Indonesia. There exists a situation that enforcement divisions or local governments are just hanging up and not implementing it really, although the projects are already decided to do by national policy circles. So it inevitably costs a lot of time for chinese companies to communicate and causes economic losses. Although Indonesian central government tries to improve working efficiency, administrative reform of local governments is hard to keep pace with it, especially in approving of land acquisition licence and mineral exploitation licence. Under the decentralization system, delimitation disputes of property ownership among counties is also enhancing investment risks. Lack of communication among sectors, low administration efficiency, poor continuity of government policies, the image of Indonesian government is damaged more or less.

Labor force is another critical problem that causes widespread disputes in Indonesia. There are many rumors about China and Joko. Those rumors may lead to social instabilities and seriously affect the implementation of relevant projects of the Belt and Road. Indonesian skilled workers are not so many, the pace of life and work there is quite slow, leading to slow progress of projects. Therefore, Chinese companies hire illegal Chinese workers in order to quicken the pace of projects. However, this move was exposed by media and caused dissatisfaction of the Indonesian society because they thought Chinese companies had no sense of social responsibility, violated terms of contract, could not create enough job opportunities, so they had to tighten up the work visa conditions for Chinese workers. Chinese style of work pace is not matching Indonesian one, lack of skilled workers in Indonesia but Chinese workers hard to get visas, are two sets of contradiction in labor force problem.

3. Unimpeded trade: Trade is unimpeded but it is not smooth.

Trade between China and Indonesia is not smooth, which is a common phenomenon. Many preference policies cannot be implemented in Indonesia. The procedures to apply for business certificates are very complicated and the business environment of Indonesia need improving. It is reported that after the establishment of "ASEAN-China Free Trade Area" (ACFTA) at the beginning of 2010, tariffs on more than 90% goods were cut to zero between China and Indonesia, that is, all exports which have certificates of origin of ACFTA (Also known as "format E", or "Form E") can get tariff exemptions. However, in real cases, exporters cannot get exemptions every time even they hold certificates, and the same goods with the same certificate may have different clearance results since the customs officers are different. Exporters will not enjoy the Generalized System of Preferences (GSP) or FTA tariff exemption, or endure storage costs since the export goods are blocked at the port. This shows that the Indonesian customs lack of synergy and unity, lack of training of business knowledge, lack of recognition of tariff exemption license, and lack of supervision of customs officials.

Indonesia continues to view simplification of foreign investment license as one of the measures to improve its business environment. It was pointed out by *Global Competitiveness Report* of WEF that low efficiency in bureaucratic procedures is the biggest barrier following corruption, financing difficulty, inflation, which restricts the economic development of Indonesia. The 2015 *Doing Business* report published by the World Bank ranked Indonesia No. 114 in total, No. 155, No. 153, No. 160, No.170 respectively in the four key items such as setting up business, applying for Construction Work Permit, taxation and carrying out a contract. According to the data published recently by Indonesia Central Investment Coordination Agency, in 2014 Indonesia attracted FDI $28.53 billion, with year-on-year growth of 13.5%, but comparing to 22.4% in 2013, the growth was apparently slow down. The main reason is Indonesian application procedures of investment licence is very complicated and miscellaneous, deterring investment projects from implementing. Until the end of the year of 2014, the investment projects costing about $33 billion were blocked. Therefore, approving policy problem will be the vital handicap that Joko government should overcome in the economic development.

In response to the above-mentioned problems, Indonesian government formally initiated "One-stop Comprehensive Service Platform" of nationwide investment approval in 2015. This measure was to approve set-up of companies and issue certificates. Investors could obtain service assistance, finance convenience and investment consultancy. According to the Standard of Operation Procedure (SOP), it takes over 3 years (1125 days) to get the whole procedure finished. Under the new system, it reduces by 80%. However, many Chinese companies reflected that "One-stop Comprehensive Service Platform was quite ideal, but not fitting in implement. The procedure of investment approving is still complicated, the regulations are still very cumbersome, the administration efficiency is quite low, and the procedural corruption is serious, which discourage investors badly. Many Chinese companies have to choose mediation service to quicken the approving process in the price of high mediation fee, even offering an extra charge for a quick service, imperceptibly facilitating corruption and adding the operation costs of enterprises.

4. Financial Circulation faces some risks.

Chinese enterprises and financial organizations investing in Indonesia face many adverse factors such as high cost, low income and high risks. The economic infrastructures of Indonesia are weak; the abilities to pay for loans are weak, and the probability of breaching is high. What's more, infrastructure investment projects have the features of long duration, high cost and long repaying cycle. All these factors increase the risks of Chinese financial organizations in investing in Indonesia, especially AIIB. In addition, the Indonesian government does not provide government guarantees to local banks. Bad debt will increase and funding chains will break down once capital flows are reduced, further lead to run-off risks. Among them, the liquidity risk problem is highlighted. Due to the high degree of dependence on foreign investment, Indonesia's liquidity is susceptible to fluctuations in international liquidity and sensitive fluctuations. At present, the global liquidity is lower, Indonesia has to maintain foreign exchange rates stability and investor's confidence through interventions, also boost domestic export and stimulate the domestic economy through currency devaluation, may lead to the depreciation of the Indonesian Rupiah.

Besides, risks of exchange rate are also worth our attention. At present, Chinese enterprises which participate in local project cooperation usually use US dollar or Indonesian Rupiah as payment currencies. They may face higher risk due to the weak dollar and the instability of the Indonesian Rupiah. On the one hand, since the exchange rate reform in 2005, RMB is in the process of appreciation due to the fixed currency policy pegged to the US dollar, rapid economic growth, and the trade surplus. On the other hand, the Indonesian Rupiah has been devalued in recent years because the impact of the economic crisis and the unstable political situation. The Rupiah depreciated about 200% during the Asian financial crisis, and a big devaluation in global economic recession triggered by US subprime mortgage crisis. In July 2015, the inflation rate of Indonesia was 7.6% , at the same time the exchange rate was still declining. The actual exchange rate of Rupiah to Dollar was down 4.29%, from 13400:1 (December 2015) fell to 14000:1 (January 2016).

5. People-to-people bond needs to be enhanced.

In Indonesia, the level of understanding by common people to the Belt and Road is quite low, and there many misunderstandings. "China Threat Theory" or neocolonialism is quite popular in Indonesia, which is shown in press reports by Indonesian media to the Belt and Road Initiative. At the beginning of 2017, commissioned by the Central Publicity Department of China, Factiva global content and business database grasped the key words of news reports in more than a dozen countries along the Belt and Road, aim to analysis their attitudes on "the Belt and Road Initiative". The result had about 56 Indonesian news, more than 900 Russian news, and more than 500 Arabic news. The number of Indonesian news is still less although most countries use Russian or Arabic to report news. This is reflected in the two issues, first, compared to the countries speak Russian and Arabic, Indonesia concerns less on the Belt and Road Initiative; second, the media of Indonesia may not definite those keywords accurately. It shows that the Indonesian media lack of knowledge of the Belt and Road Initiative, but also reflects our publicity works are insufficient and ineffective, the ways and channels need improvements.

"China Threat Theory" or neocolonialism is quite popular in Indonesia. According to data from a "Chinese Cultural Impression Survey" conducted in Indonesia, the overall impression of the interviewees toward China and Chinese culture is to be improved. Among those impressions, the impression that "China is continuing to develop" gets the highest scores, the impression that "China is innovative" and "China is rich and powerful" ranks in the middle, and the impression that "China is reliable and credible" gets the lowest scores. The survey also shows that Japan is the favorite country to Indonesian. Compared to Japan, China has rooms to improve its attractiveness to

Indonesian.

Chinese enterprises are inclined to employ Chinese workers, and some Chinese workers are not well-educated. This has caused many problems. Since the Belt and Road Initiative began its implementation, there have been many disputes over Chinese employees. For example, in order to complete the project as early as possible, Chinese enterprises tend to take thousands of Chinese workers to Indonesia. Consequently, the enterprises failed to create employment opportunities for local governments. In addition, some Chinese workers lack the necessary training of working overseas, at low level of education, they neither speak Indonesian nor English. They also lack of enough respect for the living habits and religion of the locals in daily life and work, make loud noise and gazer in public places. As a result, it is no surprise that local people have had a very negative attitude toward those Chinese enterprises and Chinese workers.

The academic community in Indonesia is the main opponent toward the idea of the Belt and Road. Most Indonesian experts have misinterpretation and bias toward the orientation and meaning of this initiative. Because the experts and scholars are generally considered to be the authority of China study in Indonesia, they have a certain power of voice and high persuasive in the people. It makes the Belt and Road Initiative not only lack solid support from public, but also the lack of intellectual support. For example, some experts believe the Belt and Road Initiative is equivalent to the "Marshall Plan", and its essence is to solve China's problem of domestic excess capacity and unemployment. Some radical Islamist newspaper even called Chinese investments in Indonesia is "Penjajahan Baru", or "Chinese economic hegemony" in English.

Countermeasures and recommendations

1. On the national level

(1) The two countries should strengthen top-level design and communications, and solve the disputes arising from overlapping waters around the Natuna Islands through peaceful negotiations.

China and Indonesia should continue to enhance high-level visits and communications to form a desirable situation of friendly interactions. China should invite Indonesian leaders to participate in various kinds of activities sponsored by China. In this way, the two countries can consolidate their political common understandings and strengthen top-level designs. The two countries should create conditions for the successful holding of the second meeting of the high-level mechanism of Sino-Indonesian human communication, the fifth meeting of China-Indonesia deputy prime ministerial level dialogue mechanism, and the second meeting of Sino-Indonesian high-level economic dialogue. The two countries should make good arrangements in the three fields of political mutual trust, trade and investment, and human communications to expand room of cooperation. The two parties should facilitate negotiations about "Action Plan on Implementation of Sino-Indonesian Comprehensive Strategic Partnership" and the signing of this plan with the aim to provide a detailed roadmap for cooperation of the two countries in relevant areas. The two countries should steadily advance the implementation of bilateral and multilateral agreements signed previously to strengthen maritime cooperation and Sino-ASEAN maritime cooperation. They should take all measures to ensure that the Belt and Road Initiative and the total plan of ASEAN Community match and complement each other.

The parties, economic departments, maritime departments, officials of local governments, and think tanks of the two countries should communicate sincerely and equally. On the one hand, China should make a comprehensive introduction to the background, orientation, purpose and action plans of the Belt and Road Initiative, and Indonesia should express its concerns about and expectations of the initiative. In this way, the two countries can communicate effectively, eliminate worries and build a friendly atmosphere of political mutual trust. On the other hand, China and Indonesia should design and refine concrete intention of cooperation and practical measures. They should, based on consideration of each other's demand, formulate detailed and feasible implementation plans, roadmaps and schedules, in order to make the common understanding of the leaders of the two countries come true.

The exclusive economic zone around the Natuna Islands overlaps with the traditional sea areas of China. In handling this dispute, the two parties should be more practical. Currently, the Belt and Road Initiative of China matches Indonesia's foreign policy which is oriented around economic development. This is beneficial in avoiding the expansion of this dispute and to solve the overlapping waters around the Natuna Islands.

(2) China should pay more attention to propaganda work, clarify basic concepts and eliminate worries and suspicions. China must eliminate worries and biases from all classes of the Indonesian society, especially from the governments and think tanks. These worries and biases toward the Belt and Road Initiative are hindering the implementation of this great initiative. Only through elimination of these worries and suspicious can China and Indonesia focus on cooperation of this initiative and realize prosperous co-building and development of the two nations.

One of the most important approaches to eliminate worries of Indonesia is to build a positive image of China. That is, the culture, education and propaganda agencies of China should pay attention in promoting a true and positive image of China among the Indonesian people, especially those original inhabitants. Another important approach is the media. First, Chinese media should change the previous discourse system. What's more, China's official media should maintain friendly communications with local media of Indonesia. The Belt and Road Initiative needs as much support and recognition as possible from the Indonesian people. Such support and recognition from the local people is of great importance to the implementation of the Belt and Road Initiative.

(3) China should initiate a campaign of public diplomacy to enhance human communications and exchanges, and to facilitate understanding and trust of the Indonesian society.

In the current global environment, public diplomacy is playing a more and more important role in the stage of diplomacy. In international relations, public diplomacy or people's diplomacy, broadly speaking, is the dissemination of propaganda to foreign public to establish a dialogue designed to inform and influence. It is practiced through a variety of instruments and methods ranging from personal contact and media interviews to the Internet and educational exchanges. Through mutual communication, public diplomacy can help people realize the imparting and recognition of policies, ideas, culture and sense of value. It can also enhance understanding and recognition of each other. Public diplomacy can make it possible for China to reach agreement and build common sense with neighboring countries. The Chinese government should review and develop its public diplomacy policy toward Indonesia, and continue to drive comprehensive human exchanges with an open and tolerant mind. While deeply conducting friendly communications in fields such as culture, tourism, science and technology, and local cooperation, China should seize opportunities to fully explore the functions of all communication channels, thus improving the mutual understanding and friendship between China and Indonesia.

(4) Indonesia should recognize the need to solve those underlying issues within the country, such as the coordination between the central government and the local governments, the continuity of polices and laws, corruption, legislation of labor force, laws on land expropriation, etc.

The above mentioned problems are very common in Indonesia. Take corruption for example. Indonesia is a country of serious corruption. According to 2016 results of Corruption Perception Index of Transparency International, Indonesia ranks 90th place out of 176 countries. Corruption is an important developmental challenge that poses economic and social costs in Indonesia. Interference in public laws and policies for the sake of personal or private gain has weakened the competitiveness of Indonesia. About one-quarter of ministries suffer from budgetary diversions in Indonesia. Households spent approximately 1% while enterprises spent at least 5% of monthly company revenue on unofficial payments. Social costs due to corruption in Indonesia include the weakening of government institutions and the rule of law.

Regarding the political, legal and institutional problems within Indonesia, the present paper make the following suggestions. Indonesia should improve the coordinating abilities of the central government with local governments. Departments within the governments should strengthen communications and support. Investment approval procedures should be simplified with the aim to strike corruption and build a good investment environment. We should realize that corruption can be eliminated in a night, and the campaign to strike corruption will endure for a long time. While striking corruption, the government should formulate more active measures to encourage officials to explore their potentials to improve the efficiency of the governments. Besides, land expropriation has become a significant obstacle for Indonesia to attract foreign investments. So, the Indonesian government should make necessary reform to the existing laws and regulations on land, clarify the ownership of land, and develop effective land expropriation procedures. This will facilitate the infrastructure construction in Indonesia and greatly speed up the economic growth of Indonesia. On the one hand, local labor agencies shall enhance the review and approve visas of Chinese workers and strike those without visas. On the other hand, local universities and colleges should cooperate with enterprises, and train sufficient Indonesian workers to improve current labor force problems.

2. On the level of enterprises

(1) Chinese enterprises should form correct understanding of the investment environment in Indonesia.

Before investing in Indonesia, Chinese companies should establish a mechanism of evaluation, insurance, exit, localization and diversification, make investment strategies according to the actual situation of Indonesian market, avoid risk and improve the return on investment. Chinese companies have invested in Indonesia in a certain scale, and there are many kinds of business association, which should be made the best use. If newcomers plan for a long term, they will get a higher return on investment.

In addition, the concept of localization should be set up. Many Chinese companies go to Indonesia with a speculative mentality, no localization concept, and mainly Chinese market-oriented. When there is quality problem after sale in Indonesia, for example, after-sales service staff will ask customers to communicate with Chinese manufacturing enterprises, which is rather counter-productive. Chinese enterprises should make full use of local resources of Indonesia, localize enterprise culture, human resources, products, brands etc, so as to promote the sound and healthy development of enterprises.

(2) Chinese enterprises should possess considerable capital capacity and risk bearing capacity, which are indispensible prerequisite to investment projects in Indonesia.

In the long run, corruption will surely be diminished. But in the short term, corruption is still very serious in Indonesia. In dealing with local governments of Indonesia, Chinese enterprises often have to pay tips and so on, which will increase the operational costs of the enterprises and reduce the efficiency. Therefore, the enterprises should be more careful when contacting with local officials, keep well evidence in case of being asked for bribes, and consider to expose it to anti-corruption commission or BPK.

To avoid the risk of deposits loss, Chinese companies should deposit money in the Indonesian branches China/industrial and commercial bank. Funds they deposit in local bank should be kept in small amounts just for daily use.

(3) Chinese enterprises should employ worker legally and optimize human resource structures.

Chinese enterprises investing in Indonesia should create employment opportunities for local people. Those Chinese enterprises who want to invest in Indonesia for a long period should pay attention to human resource training and reserve talents for the development of the enterprises. At the same time, enterprises should make good preparations for Chinese employees participating in overseas projects. Chinese enterprises are the actual performers of China's "going out" strategy. Chinese employees are the outward manifestation of China's international image and the emissary of Chinese civilization and etiquette. In order to participate in engineering projects overseas, Chinese employees should master basic communication skills and respect the religious beliefs and social customs of the Indonesian people.

In addition, Chinese companies should cooperate with local government, especially the department of labor, and sign a formal and effective labor contract with local employees, and do vocational skills and pre-service training. it will act in accordance with the labor contract if defaults.

Prospect of cooperation

Within the framework of the Belt and Road Initiative, China and Indonesia have broad room for cooperation and bright future for development, especially in the area of infrastructure construction in Indonesia. The domestic economy of Indonesia is still in the stage of fast growth, and the area of infrastructure construction is one with huge demand. Indonesia is the largest potential market for China to conduct construction contracting service in Southeast Asia. According to "2015-2019 Medium Term Construction Development Plan" of Indonesia, in the coming five years, Indonesia will construct 250 kilometers of highway, 1000 kilometers of expressway, 3258 kilometers of railway, 24 large ports, 60 ferries, 15 modern airports, 14 industrial gardens, 49 reservoirs, 33 hydraulic power stations, and build irrigation systems for one million hectares of farm land. It is expected that if the projects are completed, the infrastructure of Indonesia will be greatly improved. It is good news that China and Indonesia have made quite a few achievements in connectivity and infrastructure construction cooperation. In the coming five years, Indonesia will put the construction of highway, railway, bridges, ports, and ferries on its priority list, and the estimated investment will be up to 600 billion US dollars. China is able and willing to support the infrastructure of Indonesia. China can participate in the project contracting and investment of ports, power stations, highway, railway, airports, bridges, etc, and provide planning and designing support.

With the sustained development of bilateral relations and economic ties between China and Indonesia, the two parties face desirable opportunities in cooperation in the area of infrastructure construction. When investing in overseas projects, Chinese enterprises should adjust their operation concepts to benefit local people. We believe that in the forthcoming five to ten years, with the participation of Chinese enterprises, the infrastructure construction in Indonesia will vastly improve.

5 中国"一带一路"与英国科技合作机会

熊榆　梁嘉敏

近年来，中英合作关系不断深化，正处于黄金发展时期。作为第一个加入亚投行的欧洲国家，英国正努力争取在各个方面与中国加强合作关系，更发布了系列报告提出将"一带一路"计划与英国北方经济振兴计划相结合，实现互利共赢友好合作。英国于2017年3月29日正式启动《里斯本条约》第50项条款进入脱欧程序，这也意味着英国正式脱离欧盟单一市场，亟需找到新的替代市场和合作伙伴，而中国的地位将变得更加无可取代。本文为中英两国在"一带一路"计划合作提供了一些思路与建议，着重介绍"一带一路"与英国北方经济振兴计划的战略背景与具体实施情况、英国对一带一路计划的态度、英国参与合作的不确定性，从而详细分析中英就"一带一路"计划与英国北方经济振兴计划合作可能的具体方式与具体内容。

"一带一路"计划简介

战略背景

2008 年经济危机后，随着中国经济实力持续高速增长，周边区域大环境日趋稳定，中国已成为世界经济复苏的两大引擎之一[①]。然而，发展至今，中国的经济模式已然进入了瓶颈期亟需转型，中国的产能过剩及外汇资产过剩等问题也逐渐显露出来[②]。为了释放过剩的产能，推动资本流出，进而实现人民币的国际化，2013 年 9 月，习近平主席于哈萨克斯坦纳扎尔巴耶夫大学提出"丝绸之路经济带"跨国经济带战略构想，后又在印度尼西亚的国会演讲中提出了创建"21 世纪海上丝绸之路"的设想[③]。2015 年 3 月，国家发改委、外交部、商务部联合发布《推动共建丝绸之路经济带和 21 世纪海上丝绸之路的愿景与行动》，正式宣布"一带一路"计划进入具体实施阶段[④]。

一带一路是中国利用跨国区域经济带提出的崭新战略构想。通过一条结合历史文化及现有情况而成的现代"丝绸之路"建立中国与沿线国家的密切合作伙伴关系，构建一个行之有效的区域合作平台。这一路线计划贯通中亚、东南亚、南亚、西亚及欧洲部分区域，沿线总人口约 44 亿，经济总量约 21 万亿美元，沿经区域多为新兴经济体和发展中国家[⑤]。这意味着这一计划一旦正式投入实施，将不

---

① 苑基荣：《中国仍是全球经济的引擎（外国名家眼中的中国经济）——访印度尼赫鲁大学中国与东南亚研究中心教授狄伯杰》，《人民日报》，发布时间：2017 年 2 月 2 日，http://paper.people.com.cn/rmrb/html/2017-02/02/nw.D110000renmrb_20170202_7-03.htm。

② The challenges of China's economic transition, *BBC News*, 发布时间：2016 年 3 月 5 日，http://www.bbc.co.uk/news/av/business-35878563/the-challenges-of-chinas-economic-transition。

③ Ministry of Foreign Affairs of PRC, "President Xi Jinping Delivers Important Speech and Proposes to Build a Silk Road Economic Belt with Central Asian Countries", September 7, 2013, http://www.fmprc.gov.cn/mfa_eng/topics_665678/xjpfwzysiesgjtfhshzzfh_665686/t1076334.shtml.

④ 《推动共建丝绸之路经济带和 21 世纪海上丝绸之路的愿景与行动》，中国网，发布日期：2015 年 9 月 15 日，http://www.china.org.cn/chinese/2015-09/15/content_36591064_2.htm。

⑤ The new Silk Road, *The Economist*, September 10, 2015, http://www.economist.com/news/special-report/21663326-chinas-latest-wave-globalisers-will-enrich-their-countryand-world-new-silk-road.

仅仅解决中国过剩的产能问题、促进中国经济的转型，并进一步实现西部大开发，更可以通过一系列切实有效的建设方案形成双/多边机制国家间互利互惠的利益共同体，促进彼此经济的发展，更能为中国以及世界各国提供一个广阔的市场和投资平台①。

地域范围

丝绸之路一词最早起源于德意志帝国地理学家费迪南·冯·李希霍芬男爵的地图集，其基本走向定于两汉时期，用于指代连接亚非欧的古代商路网络。从运输方式上看，广义的丝绸之路又可主要分为陆上丝绸之路和海上丝绸之路，这也是现今"一带一路"计划中"丝绸之路经济带"与"21世纪海上丝绸之路"的由来。

"一带一路"分别通过"丝绸之路经济带"与"21世纪海上丝绸之路"两个部分实现欧亚大陆海上与陆地的全面资源整合与联通（见图5–1）。"丝绸之路经济带"作为陆上部分将从中国东部沿海出发一路向西，以中国西部作为核心区，穿过蒙古、俄罗斯、中亚及南亚的多个国家并一路延伸至西欧，建设起以物流链为主要形式的"欧亚大陆桥"，开发多条连接沿线各新兴经济体与国家的经济走廊，并进一步实现西部大开发，以新疆为核心区大力促进青海、甘肃、陕西、宁夏、重庆、四川、广西、云南以及内蒙古等地的进一步发展。

"21世纪海上丝绸之路"则是涵盖江苏、浙江、福建、广东、海南及山东6个沿海省份，以福建为核心区从海上联通欧亚非三个大陆②。

---

① 《美国退出并不意味着TPP的结束》，中证网，发布日期：2016年12月9日，http://www.cs.com.cn/xwzx/hwxx/201612/t20161209_5115366.html。

② 《推动共建丝绸之路经济带和21世纪海上丝绸之路的愿景与行动》，中国网，发布日期：2015年9月15日，http://www.china.org.cn/chinese/2015-09/15/content_36591064_2.htm。

图 5—1 "一带一路"路线示意图①

战略影响

"一带一路"的建设坚持开放合作、坚持市场运作、坚持和谐包容与互利共赢等原则，这使得"一带一路"更具独创性与优势。与同样是多边关系的自由贸易协定——跨太平洋伙伴关系协定（TPP）相比，一带一路的战略优势主要凸显在以下方面：

第一，TPP 协议是以降低关税的手段来促进各签署国的经济增长②。而"一带一路"则是通过对周边各国基础设施建设的投资、建立有效的物流链更大限度地推动贸易的方式来实现经济的增长和共赢，这种方式从根本上打破了一些新兴经济体与发展中国家的经济发展瓶颈，更能创造一个良好可持续的经济增长环境。

第二，TPP 的签署国包括美国、日本、马来西亚等 12 个国家，其中美国于2017 年 1 月 23 日正式签署有关退出 TPP 协议的文件。而"一带一路"计划秉承开放合作的原则，相关国家基于但不单单限于丝绸之路地理范围所经各国，所有国家及国际、地区组织均可参与，使得资源配置得以最大化最有效利用，更好地发

---

① Source: China presses on with new Silk Road plan, *The Daily Star*, November 9, 2014, http://www.thedailystar.net/china-presses-on-with-new-silk-road-plan-49386.

② British Institute of Turkish Affairs, "Trans-Pacific Partnership challenges emerging markets", 2015，http://www.bitaf.org/trans-pacific-partnership-challenges-emerging-markets-3/.

挥协议本身的作用①。

第三，TPP协议涵盖的原主要内容包括实施劳工与环境标准，保护知识产权等其他权益，目的是建立一个类似欧盟的新单一市场。这样的实施内容会削弱新兴经济体的竞争优势，在美国初次退出TPP协议后仍存有可能随之变动的不确定性②。而"一带一路"计划则更为实际，涵盖的内容都是实质有效的。对于新兴经济体的实质性基建扶持，轻工业产品、机械与制造业等产能的输出以及从西亚、东盟自由贸易区进口所需原材料和能源，将真正实现市场的稳定增长与健康发展③。

第四，随着美国于2017年1月23日退出TPP协议，TPP的稳定性大幅下降，其余签署国的意见也趋于不稳定。然而，从以前的经验分析，有许多专家指出，美国更可能借此重新开启新一轮TPP的谈判要求各方让步，美国是否真正退出了TPP仍是未知数。这些都增加了TPP的不稳定性，对TPP协议的期望也随之下降，更对美国的可信赖度有所损害。而中国的"一带一路"这一更加开放包容的合作机制在此时更加显露出自己的优势所在，对世界经济的影响显得愈发重要④。

"一带一路"的实施不仅对全球经济形势及相关各国产生重要影响，更能解决中国经济本身的问题。

第一，更好地促进产业结构、经济增长模式的转型。中国自改革开放以来一直采取粗放型的经济增长模式。对于现今的中国来讲，一味地引进外资、引进国外的技术和管理模式已不再能够满足中国的发展需求⑤。国务院于2015年6月发布《关于大力推进大众创业万众创新若干政策措施的意见》，出台三十条鼓励创业创

---

① 姜跃春：《中国的"一带一路"建设对世界经济的影响》，中国国际问题研究院官网，发布时间：2016年4月6日，http://www.ciis.org.cn/chinese/2016-04/06/content_8684132.htm。

② TPP: seven things worth knowing, Financial Times, 发布时间：2015年10月12日，https://www.ft.com/content/df9ce46c-6aea-11e5-8171-ba1968cf791a。

③ 《外媒：亚太15国承诺推动TPP替代协议保留TPP最核心部分》，网易新闻，发布时间：2017年3月17日，http://news.163.com/17/0317/11/CFNOJ9GG00018AOQ_all.html。

④ US leaving TPP: A great news day for China, Carrie Gracie, *BBC News*, November 22, 2016, http://www.bbc.co.uk/news/world-asia-china-38060980.

⑤ Ferguson R.J. &Dellios, R., The politics and philosophy of Chinese power: The timeless and the timely, (MD: Lexington Books, 2016), pp.112-116.

新的政策措施，大力鼓励自主创新，推进经济转型，变粗放型经济增长模式为集约型经济增长模式，传统产业逐步市场出清，产业结构正由工业主导逐步转向服务业，过剩的产能亟需寻找释放的渠道①。"一带一路"作为很好的平台，可以把国内过剩的产能有效输送出去，顺利为下一步的产业结构转型做好铺垫②。

第二，更好地促进人民币国际化。中国的外汇储备过剩。多年以来，由于经常性的贸易顺差，人民币的持续预期走高，外贸政策和汇率制度的导向效应，中国的外汇储备一直处于过剩的状态，即使最近不断缩水，中国的外汇储备仍是世界第一，占据全球外汇储备规模的30%。只有加快人民币国际化的进程，才能保证外汇储备的安全。"一带一路"计划提出之际，已先于2013年提出成立亚洲基础设施投资银行并于2015年正式建立，建设金砖国家新开发银行以及在相关各国开设人民币清算行，打破基础设施的融资瓶颈约束，筹集建设资金，并与境外货币当局签署多份本币互换协议，建立人民币清算行③。可以说，"一带一路"计划的实施，将极大地加快人民币国际化的进程，而人民币的国际化，势必成为"一带一路"基础建设的强有力支持，二者相辅相成，更能有利地规避使用第三方货币结算的风险④。

第三，更好地维护国家安全。中国的油气、矿产等能源资源对国外的依存度高，从国家安全的角度来说，当务之急是寻找到一个稳定持续的能源资源进口模式。西亚与东盟都有丰富的矿产能源，西亚更是中国最大的原油来源地⑤。通过"一带一路"的实施，中国可以与西亚新兴经济体及东盟自由贸易区形成长期稳定

---

① Mckinsey&Company, "what'next for china? ", January, 2013, http://www.mckinsey.com/global-themes/asia-pacific/whats-next-for-china.

② 《"一带一路"建设进展报告："进展和成果超出预期"》，国务院新闻办公厅官网，发布日期：2016年9月27日，http://www.scio.gov.cn/ztk/dtzt/34102/35189/35192/Document/1492411/1492411.htm。

③ 《"一带一路"战略下的金融递变》，凤凰网财经网站，发布时间：2017年10月26日，http://finance.ifeng.com/a/20171026/15747193_0.shtml。

④ 《英媒：一带一路重塑世界经济》，BBC中文网，发布时间：2016年7月1日，http://www.bbc.com/zhongwen/trad/press_review/2016/07/160701_press_review。

⑤ "一带一路"创造新兴经济体合作模式，搜狐财经，发布日期：2015年3月20日，http://business.sohu.com/20150320/n410051925.shtml。

的合作关系，通过双方优势的高度互补实现互利共赢，更能与东盟地区合作共同发展海洋经济，共同护卫海洋安全。

进展与现状

自 2013 年首次提出"一带一路"以来，中国就一直积极推进计划的具体实施进程。从 2013 年至今，"一带一路"计划已在如下方面取得了实质性的突破：

据 2016 年 6 月 30 日的统计结果显示，中国已与沿线 11 个国家签署了自贸区协定，还与 56 个沿线国家签署了双边投资协定，并发表了对接"一带一路"倡议的联合声明。

在基础建设方面，中国已在"一带一路"沿线承建 38 项大型交通基建项目，涉及 26 个国家，承包的工程项目已多达三千余项。已开始着手签署建设的运输油、电、气等重大能源项目多达 40 项，涉及 19 个沿线国家。在通信网络建设方面，中国电信企业也正在通过 TD-LTE 全球倡议组织（GTI）加快推进"一带一路"沿线国家和地区跨境项目传输系统建设，积极完善国际基础网络布局。目前已拥有 116 家运营商及 97 家设备商，30 个国家已开通共计 52 个 TD-LTE 商用网络，另有 83 个涉及 55 个国家的 TD-LTE 商用网计划正在部署中[1]。

在对外贸易方面，中国已在"一带一路"沿线 18 个国家开展建设 52 个经贸合作区，完成考核的有 13 个，累计完成投资 156 亿美元。与"一带一路"沿线国家货物贸易额为 3.1 万亿美元，占对外贸易总额的 26%；中国对"一带一路"相关国家的累计投资达 511 亿美元，占同期对外直接投资总额的 12%；与"一带一路"沿线国家新签服务外包合同金额 94.1 亿美元，同比增长 33.5%。

在筹集建设资金方面，中国已在 7 个"一带一路"沿线国家设立了人民币业务清算行，其经常项下跨境人民币结算金额超过 2.63 万亿元[2]。亚投行已于 2016

---

[1]　China's Belt and Road Initiative delivers promising initial results. *China Daily*, May 7, 2017, http://europe.chinadaily.com.cn/business/2016-12/19/content_27712045.htm.

[2]　《"一带一路"国际合作高峰论坛成果清单（全文）》，"一带一路"国际合作高峰论坛官方网站，发布时间：2017 年 5 月 16 日，http://www.beltandroadforum.org/n100/2017/0516/c24-422.html.

年 6 月 25 日批准 5.09 亿美元的贷款用于首批四个项目。金砖国家新开发银行也于
2016 年 4 月 21 日公布了总额为 8.11 亿美元的首批贷款项目。

2017 年 5 月 14 日，"一带一路"国际合作高峰论坛在北京举行，习近平主席
在开幕式上发表讲话[①]。本次合作高峰论坛是各国分享互利合作成果的国际盛会，
也是加强国际合作，对接彼此发展战略的重要合作平台。随后，国际合作高峰论
坛官方网站还发布了"一带一路"国际合作高峰论坛成果清单，总结和梳理了论
坛期间一系列合作共识、重要举措及务实成果，清单主要涵盖政策沟通、设施联
通、贸易畅通、资金融通、民心相通 5 大类，共 76 大项、270 多项具体成果[②]。英
国首相特使、财政大臣哈蒙德来华出席了"一带一路"国际合作高峰论坛，转交
了英国首相特雷莎·梅（Theresa May）致李克强总理的亲署信。他表示，英方致
力于发展英中全面战略伙伴关系，愿保持两国高层交往，进一步加强双边贸易投
资合作，密切在国际事务中的沟通协调。李克强总理也表示，中方愿同英方巩固
互信，落实好核电、金融等重点领域合作共识，打造新的合作亮点，推动中英关
系与合作迈上新台阶[③]。

在习近平主席的十九大报告中，也着力强调了"一带一路"的建设，提出要
以"一带一路"建设为重点，坚持引进来与走出去并重，创新对外投资方式与促
进国际产能合作[④]。

英国对一带一路计划的态度

英国对于"一带一路"的主流态度是有目共睹的。基于对世界经济形势的预

---

① 《习近平出席"一带一路"国际合作高峰论坛开幕式并发表主旨演讲》，"一带一路"国际合作
高峰论坛官方网站，2017 年 5 月 14 日，http://www.beltandroadforum.org/n100/2017/0514/c24-397.html。

② 《英国宣布计划加入亚洲基础设施投资银行》，英国政府官网，发布时间：2015 年 3 月 12 日，
https://www.gov.uk/government/news/uk-announces-plans-to-join-asian-infrastructure-investment-bank.zh。

③ Geoff Dyer and George Parker ,US attacks UK's "constant accommodation" with China, *Financial
Times*, 2015 年 3 月 12 日，https://www.ft.com/content/31c4880a-c8d2-11e4-bc64-00144feab7de。

④ 《习近平作十九大报告，新华网直播全文实录》，搜狐网，发布时间：2017 年 10 月 19 日，
http://www.sohu.com/a/199121450_821486。

测与挽救经济衰退的迫切心态，英国排除万难、顶着美国反对的声音成为欧美国家中首个加入亚投行的成员①，更是在多个方面抛出橄榄枝积极加强与中国的合作，并首先提出建议将中国的"一带一路"计划与自己的"北方振兴计划"相结合②，在中英合作的黄金时代更好地使两国的资源整合，寻求更多更广更深入的合作机会。而中国的回应也是十分积极的，双方至今已在各领域各层次多次交流对话，极大地促进了"一带一路"中英之间的合作进展。友好的对话、积极的发言促进了实际的合作，而实际合作的成功又促进了更深入积极的对话，创造了良好和谐的氛围③。

中英商业理事会主席兼英国上议院议员詹姆斯·萨松（James Sassoon）表示，英国对"一带一路"的贡献早已不止停留在法律与金融的层面，更是着眼于中英在第三国市场合作的长期机会，也积极地寻求制造业、农业、食品加工业、科技与教育、医疗与保健、零售与物流等一系列其他产业的合作机会④。

特蕾莎·梅在上任前曾经质疑过前英国财政大臣乔治·奥斯本（George Osborne）对于中国表现出的热忱态度。然而，随着她的正式上任以及正式脱欧的开始，中英之间的合作所能带来的利益使她的态度明显有所转变⑤。她在上任后的采访中表示，她的上任并不会影响中英之间所处的"黄金时代"。这一态度的转变已明确地在她接受的采访中多次体现出来⑥。在一次采访中，特蕾莎更是特意

---

① HM Treasury, UK announces plans to join Asian Infrastructure Investment Bank, (2015),https://www.gov.uk/government/news/uk-announces-plans-to-join-asian-infrastructure-investment-bank.

② 《英国财政大臣公布"北方经济引擎"计划超过 240 亿英镑的投资机会》，英国政府官网，发布日期：2015 年 9 月 24 日，https://www.gov.uk/government/news/chancellor-opens-book-on-more-than-24-billion-of-northern-powerhouse-investment-opportunities-in-china.zh。

③ Angus Mcneice, "UK Further Embraces Belt & Road Initiative", China *Daily*,April 14, 2017, http://usa.chinadaily.com.cn/epaper/2017-04/14/content_28930391.htm.

④ Peter Barker &Gui Tao，"Interview: China-UK cooperation on Belt and Road perfect fit: UK business leader", *Xinhua Net*, May 4, 2017, http://news.xinhuanet.com/english/2017-05/04/c_136256201.htm.

⑤ Beth Rigby, "Theresa May to visit China in bid for trade deal", *Sky New*，February 7, 2017, http://news.sky.com/story/theresa-may-to-visit-china-in-bid-for-trade-deal-10759589.

⑥ Barry Piper, "China's 'One Belt, One Road', a drive for Great Britain's businesses?", *China Daily*，February 3, 2017,http://www.chinadaily.com.cn/opinion/2017-02/03/content_28093936.htm.

指出，中国对英国的投资早已远超其他任何一个欧洲国家，并对此表示感谢①。

"一带一路"正在成为中英产业合作的新平台

随着中国对人民币国际化、鼓励自主开发、加速经济转型的迫切需要，亟需寻找长期稳定的发达国家作为合作伙伴。而英国作为中国在欧洲最大的投资目的国，近年来中英双边经贸关系迅猛加速，中英关系已进入"黄金时代"。中国对英国的青睐，一方面是因为产业需求的匹配，另一方面也是想通过英国进而打开与欧盟各国合作的渠道，由英国加入亚投行这一举动更大限度地加快人民币国际化的速度。英国脱欧无疑会对人民币国际化的进程带来一定的冲击，却也由此带来了更大的机遇，中英之间的合作仍是至关重要、不可放弃的。英国政府更是发布系列报告，全面分析讨论在"一带一路"计划中更好的中英合作方式，提出将一带一路与英国北方经济振兴计划相结合（在本章将有具体介绍），从而使得英国更好更积极地在一带一路计划实施中占有一席之位，发挥最大的主观能动性。作为联合国五个常任理事国的两个国家，更加一致地站在一起，在全球事务上成为利益共同体，为两个国家的发展、社会的稳定和人民的利益带来巨大的贡献。鉴于中英两国各自的独特优势及已有的合作形式，中英之间如能继续强化双边合作以及开展在第三国的合作机遇，将会给两国创造更大的机遇并带来更大的利益。

Northern Powerhouse：北方经济振兴计划

战略背景

"北方经济振兴计划"是乔治·奥斯本 2014 年提出的产业战略②，覆盖区域为英

---

① Theresa May talks trade at G20 summit in China, *Channel* 4 News, September 5, 2016, https://www.channel4.com/news/by/gary-gibbon/blogs/theresa-talks-trade-g20-summit-china.

② Northern powerhouse to benefit from industrial strategy proposals, *Northern Powerhouse HM Government*，January 24, 2017, http://northernpowerhouse.gov.uk/2017/01/northern-powerhouse-to-benefit-as-government-launches-industrial-strategy-proposals/.

格兰北部，其中包括东北部地区、西北部地区、约克郡及汉伯地区三大地区；覆盖曼彻斯特、利兹、纽卡斯尔、利物浦和谢菲尔德等 11 个核心重点城市，旨在利用行政体制改革、大力发展基础设施建设、增加科技创新投资等强政策手段，大力促进英格兰北部地区的经济发展，使其成为继伦敦之后的第二个经济中心。英国首相特蕾莎·梅上任后，更是发表声明将继续支持对北方地区的发展投资计划，并保证其不会受到英国脱欧所带来的可能影响[①]。

英格兰东北部地区主要包括特斯谷和达勒姆郡、诺森比亚及泰恩河畔郡两大地区；英格兰西北部地区主要包括柴郡、坎布里亚郡、大曼彻斯特郡、兰开夏郡和默西塞德郡五大地区[②]。

具体实施

北方经济振兴计划通过政府财政拨款和企业投资相结合的方式，为北部重点城市的各自优势产业建设发展提供资金支持，逐步实行权力下放，并重点改善和发展北部地区的交通，建立自伦敦后第二个经济与交通枢纽[③]。

由英国政府所有的英国商业银行与当地企业合作伙伴关系[④]（LEPs）一起建立的北方经济振兴计划投资基金（NPIF），以协助英格兰北部的初创企业。资金总额达 4 亿英镑，全部用于小额信贷，商业金融和股权融资领域[⑤]。NPIF 由欧洲区域发

---

① "Northern prosperity is national prosperity: a strategy for revitalising the UK economy", *IPPR North and the Northern Economic Futures Commission*, November 5, 2012, http://www.ippr.org/files/images/media/files/publication/2012/12/northern-prosperity_NEFC-final_Nov2012_9949.pdf?noredirect=1.

② 同上。

③ The Northern Powerhouse, Nehal Bradley-Depani, Louise Butcher & Mark Sandford, November 1, 2016, https://www.google.co.uk/url?sa=t&rct=j&q=&esrc=s&source=web&cd=1&cad=rja&uact=8&ved=0ahUKEwiX-dbenObTAhVGFMAKHeMoBV8QFggnMAA&url=http%3A%2F%2Fresearchbriefings.files.parliament.uk%2Fdocuments%2FCBP-7676%2FCBP-7676.pdf&usg=AFQjCNGjuTdKaPVXudUV4ioFrbP1hmJypg&sig2=Jr-glaYPGOiCLPwvo9nKNg.

④ Northern Powerhouse Strategy, *Northern Powerhouse HM Government*, November 5, 2016, https://www.liverpoollep.org/wp-content/uploads/2016/11/Northern-Powerhouse-Strategy-November-2016.pdf.

⑤ Launch of £400m Northern Powerhouse investment fund,UK Business Angels Association, February 22, 2017, https://www.ukbusinessangelsassociation.org.uk/news/launch-400m-northern-powerhouse-investment-fund/.

展基金（ERDF），欧洲投资银行（EIB）和英国政府资助。该基金于 2017 年 2 月 22 日在曼彻斯特由 Andrew Percy 正式启动，将与当地企业合作伙伴关系、当地会计师、基金经理和银行一起开展业务，帮助处于各个发展阶段的中小型企业及创业企业①。

在英国政府发布的北方经济振兴战略计划中提到，政府总计拨款 1500 亿英镑用于北部地区的健康医疗②，450 亿英镑用于大学教育设施的升级建设，130 亿英镑用于建设北部的铁路交通枢纽，27 亿英镑用于东北部城市间的公路建设，500 亿英镑用于建设高铁 HS2。对曼彻斯特亨利·罗伊斯新型材料研究所投资 2.35 亿英镑；对沃灵顿计算机研发中心投资 1.13 亿英镑；对曼彻斯特工厂、剧院和展览中心投资 7800 万英镑；对纽卡斯尔老龄医学研究中心投资 2000 万英镑③。逐步下放权力的第一个试点城市为曼彻斯特，它将成为除伦敦地区外第一个由直选市长管理的城市，在 2017 年 5 月进行第一次市长选举，选举后的市长将掌握数十亿英镑的公共资金，更自由地用于城市建设开发④。

据英国建造承包商协会（CECA）简报，乔治·奥斯本未来的预算公告表明，英国政府将总共投资 3 亿英镑用于升级建设北部英格兰地区的公路、铁路和港口等整个交通网络。

① £400m Northern Powerhouse Investment Fund opens for business in Leeds, *Leeds City Region Enterprise Partnership*, March 10, 2017, http://www.the-lep.com/news-and-blog/news/northern-powerhouse-investment-fund-opens-for-busi/.

② CECA Briefing: Budget 2016, *Civil Engineering Contractors Association*, March 16, 2016, http://www.ceca.co.uk/media/217688/ceca-briefing-budget-2016-16-march-2016.pdf.

③ "Northern Powerhouse Strategy", (2016), HM Government, https://www.gov.uk/government/uploads/system/uploads/attachment_data/file/571562/NPH_strategy_web.pdf.

④ Budget 2016, HM Treasury, March 16, 2016. https://www.gov.uk/government/uploads/system/uploads/attachment_data/file/508193/HMT_Budget_2016_Web_Accessible.pdf.

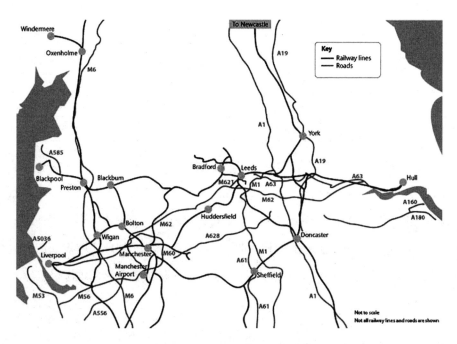

图 5-2　北部交通战略示意图[①]

北方地区企业投资项目主要包括港口、机场、铁路、海洋工程、有机能源等多个领域。据 2016 年统计，企业投资总数在汉伯地区为 11.1 亿英镑，利物浦地区 12.7 亿英镑，大曼彻斯特区 18 亿英镑，东北部地区 2.32 亿英镑，谢菲尔德地区 8 亿英镑[②]。

然而，有趣的是，一些研究指出，比起英国北方经济振兴计划所涉及的其他地区，约克郡及英国东北部地区（特斯谷和达勒姆地区、诺森比亚和泰恩河畔地区）看上去似乎是被"抛弃了"。BBC 更是做出了直观的政府投资统计分析表格，如图 5-3 所示：

[①]　Source: Government boost for Northern Powerhouse, Gov.UK, August 11, 2015, https://www.gov.uk/government/news/government-boost-for-northern-powerhouse.

[②]　《英国北部振兴计划》，中华人民共和国商务部，发布日期：2016 年 5 月 11 日，http://www.mofcom.gov.cn/article/i/ck/201605/20160501315871.shtml。

表 5-1：北方振兴计划财政支出分析①

地区	基础设施总支出额	投资项目总数	投资额/人
西北部地区	£41.4bn	88	£5,771
东北部地区	£5.9bn	27	£2,230
约克郡及汉伯地区	£9.0bn	29	£1,684

东北部地区的基础建设仍有很大的投资空间。具体而言，英国政府的高铁建设计划（HS2）将连接北部地区城市伯明翰、利兹、曼彻斯特与伦敦，而纽卡斯尔作为英国东北部地区最大的城市，至今还未有明确的高铁建设计划。此外，东北部地区的投资项目总数也远远少于西北部地区。虽然西北部地区覆盖的重点城市数量相对东北部地区更多，这一数据统计也间接反映出了东北部地区仍有巨大的可挖掘潜力②。

英国参与合作的方式

在 2015 年的习近平总书记访英中，重点提出了将中英之间的合作重点与"五通"相匹配③，即政策、道路物流、贸易、金融及人文相通④，而具体的合作领域以及合作方式主要可从如下方面开展：

在合作领域层面，主要可在基础建设、服务业、人文产业及海洋领域四个主

---

① Funding plans show Northern Powerhouse split, David Rhodes, *BBC News*, http://www.bbc.co.uk/news/uk-england-38054837.

② UK infrastructure: unlocking UK cities and commercial property, Bilfinger GVA, September 9, 2015, https://www.google.co.uk/url?sa=t&rct=j&q=&esrc=s&source=web&cd=1&cad=rja&uact=8&ved=0ahUKEwjR2qL2nObTAhVDI8AKHWhoAVIQFggjMAA&url=http%3A%2F%2Fwww.gva.co.uk%2Fresearch%2Funlocking-uk-cities-and-commercial-property%2F&usg=AFQjCNFh7LEDHWQz0LgSZ6KQnReAlEMUIA&sig2=10-gOLQwynloz8LBrj2B2g.

③ 《习近平对英国进行国事访问期间中英双方达成的成果》，中华人民共和国驻大不列颠及北爱尔兰大使馆，发布时间：2015 年 10 月 22 日，http://www.chinese-embassy.org.uk/chn/zygx/zzwl/t1308215.htm。

④ 刘晓明大使在 2016 年投资机构论坛上的主旨演讲:《把握"一带一路"机遇，开创美好未来》，中华人民共和国驻大不列颠及北爱尔兰大使馆，发布时间：2016 年 11 月 21 日，http://www.chinese-embassy.org.uk/chn/dsxx/dashijianghua/2016niandashijianghua/t1417771.htm。

要方面开展合作[①]。中英之间已签订欣克利角核电项目、高铁项目等重点合作项目协议[②]，在核能、高铁等重点基础设施领域已逐步开展合作，今后的挑战将是如何更好更有效地深化合作。

在服务业领域，英国在金融、法律、咨询等产业一直处于国际领先地位[③]，在"一带一路"的建设过程中，中国需要在沿线国家设立金融服务平台并逐步建立法律保障体系。中国使用的是民法法系，而大多数"一带一路"沿线国家采取的是和英国相通的英美法系，这就使得中国在对法律保障体系的构建方面更多地依靠英国的支持与合作。从长远来看，中英之间在这些领域的合作潜力和合作空间都是十分巨大、不容忽视的[④]。

在人文产业领域，英国的教育、影视、媒体产业都是非常丰富多元化的。中英之间如能大力促进人才交流，将会更有效地从根本上促进中国的技术自主创新。而中英在影视文化创意、媒体产业方面的合作一直处于短板，"一带一路"大力实施之际，为中英之间在这些领域的合作提供了非常好的机会。更多的人文产业合作更能促进中英两国人民对彼此的了解，从而更好地为中英之间其他领域的合作提供跳板[⑤]。

在海洋合作领域，英国在海洋科技研发、海洋经济发展、海洋能源利用及国

---

① 《中英签署多项合作协议总额400亿英镑》，BBC中文网，发布日期：2015年10月21日，http://www.bbc.com/zhongwen/simp/uk/2015/10/151021_uk_xi_visit_deals。

② Industrial strategy: UK sector analysis，Department for Business, *Innovation & Skills*，September 9, 2012, https://www.gov.uk/government/uploads/system/uploads/attachment_data/file/34607/12-1140-industrial-strategy-uk-sector-analysis.pdf.

③ UK Industry Performance Report-Based on the UK Construction Industry Key Performance Indicators, Department for Business, Innovation & Skills, 2015, https://www.glenigan.com/sites/default/files/UK_Industry_Performance_Report_2015_883.pdf.

④ One Belt One Road: a role for UK companies in developing China's new initiative - new opportunities in china and beyond, China-Britain Business Council, May 18, 2015, http://www.cbbc.org/sectors/one-belt,-one-road/.

⑤ 《今后3~5年对英重点合作项目清单》，中华人民共和国教育部，发布时间：2016年12月8日，http://www.moe.gov.cn/jyb_xwfb/moe_1946/fj_2016/201612/t20161208_291172.html。

际航运规则等方面都走在世界的前列[①]。这些领域的科技也是中国所缺乏的，而"一带一路"的一个重要方面更是建设海上丝绸之路，中英之间如能加深这些领域的合作，将大力促进海上丝绸之路的建设。中英之间的具体合作方式可通过实施项目的主要目的地分为三种主要的形式[②]。

第一，以英国为合作建设的目的地。中英高铁项目就是中国在英国开展、合作进行英国基础建设的最好例子。与此类似的还有中国企业直接进入英国参与科技创新项目落地，如科控（Cocoon Networks）已在伦敦开展建设科技孵化器，这既是欧洲单体面积最大的孵化器，也是欧洲最大的创新中心，更是欧洲首家具有中资背景的科技初创企业培育中心及科技研究转化中心。

第二，以中国为合作建设的目的地。中国要想大力发展科技创新，人才的积极交流与科技项目的落地是不可或缺的。中国可通过将英国的科技项目、大学的教育项目直接引进至国内，将极大地促进英国高等教育本土化，提升人才的整体素质。

第三，以第三国市场为目的地。英国可在基础设施、能源利用、海洋安全等领域与中国在第三方市场进行合作开发，也可以为第三方市场提供法律咨询和金融等服务。类似的案例有，英国石油和天然气公司（BP）为中石油在伊拉克的项目和中海油在印度尼西亚的项目提供咨询服务；英国年利达律师事务所（Linklaters）为巴基斯坦的煤电一体化项目融资提供法律服务等。

---

① 《中英达成数百万英镑全球研究合作》，英国政府官网，2014 年 6 月 17 日，https://www.gov.uk/government/news/uk-and-china-agree-multi-milion-pound-global-research-deals。

② 《开启面向全球的中英全面战略伙伴关系黄金时代——外交部长王毅谈习近平主席对英国进行国事访问》，中华人民共和国驻大不列颠及北爱尔兰大使馆，2015 年 10 月 24 日，http://www.chinese-embassy.org.uk/chn/zt/xifangying2015/t1308691.htm。

英国参与"一带一路"合作的不确定性

英国参与者对于中国投资能力和方式有所顾虑

"一带一路"计划作为近年来中国走出国门的最宏大的计划，涉及的国家和地区繁多，覆盖范围内的人口和市场也空前巨大，所以一些金融决策机构对于中国这样一个新兴经济体能否运营好"一带一路"项目有所质疑。

惠誉评级公司（Fitch Ratings Inc）是"三大信用评级机构"之一，另外两家是穆迪和标准普尔。惠誉评级在纽约和伦敦设有两个总部，是1975年美国证券交易委员会指定的三个国家认可的统计评级组织（NRSRO）之一。2017年初，惠誉评级公司的一份报告显示，中国在新兴市场上投资数亿美元的基础设施的计划，可能无法为中国银行带来回报，并导致新的资产质量问题。报告还显示："由于中国实施一带一路的政策性银行提供的贷款往往有着很长的还款期，与商业银行和非中国开发银行相比，它的披露普遍较差[1]。"

"一带一路"计划旨在为欠发达的欧亚大陆和非洲国家建立港口、道路和铁路，是中国率先引领全球发展和增长的第一大尝试，也引起了传统金融投资银行和评级机构的怀疑。惠誉评级在报告中表示，"一带一路"计划或正在进行的项目超过9000亿美元。这笔资金大部分可能来自中国政策性银行和大型商业银行，但是如何选择相应的投资项目是个非常有挑战性的问题。因为负责投资的中国银行并不像国际商业银行和多边贷款人那样具有数十年在全球新兴市场进行基础设施融资经验[2]，所以惠誉评级质疑中国银行能否识别有利可图的优质项目，更好地管理风险。惠誉评级还质疑"一带一路"的一些参与国有利用投资改善国内公共财政状况的投机嫌疑。

这些质疑的声音可以说正反映了英美等老牌资本主义国家投资界对于"一带

---

① Fitch warns on expected returns from One Belt, One Road, *Financial Times*, January 25, 2017, https://www.ft.com/content/c67b0c05-8f3f-3ba5-8219-e957a90646d1.

② China warned of risk to banks from One Belt, One Road initiative, *Financial Times*, January 26, 2017, https://www.ft.com/content/6076cf9a-e38e-11e6-8405-9e5580d6e5fb.

一路"的部分观点。中国虽然已经成为世界第二经济体，但是走出国门、参与国际投资和建设的机会还很少，这也导致很多国家尽管加入了"一带一路"计划，对于中国实际执行的能力还有所质疑。另外，这些传统经济强国也并不能完全理解中国带领第三世界国家协同发展、共同建设新生活的这种国际责任感，所以对中国的投资计划也颇有微词。

面对这样的质疑，中国只能以切实的案例和行动证明中国本身的决策能力以及一带一路沿线国家发展自己的决心。只有"一带一路"沿线国家经济发展、市场不断扩大、创造更多的经济价值，才能充分证明中国自身的能力和"一带一路"计划的价值。

英国对于中国影响力日益扩大有质疑声音

随着国家经济利益在国外扩张，其大规模的安全机构和军事力量可能会被拉到更大的区域作用。中国没有外国军事基地，坚决不干涉任何国家的国内政治。然而，2015 年 12 月，中国已通过《中华人民共和国反恐怖主义法》[①]，首次将中国士兵在外国土地上的驻扎合法化。这部法律的实施，将使得中国未来更加积极地参与海外军事行动，对于"一带一路"实际项目的实施也具有重大意义。

不稳定地区的项目不可避免地会考验中国在国外避免安全纠缠的政策。巴基斯坦已经派出了 1 万名士兵来保护中国的投资项目，而在阿富汗，中国投资的铜矿是由美军保护的。然而，这种保护必然是不可持续的。中国如想更好地保护"一带一路"的投资项目，最好的方式是用自己的军队给予保护力量，而这种预期也导致了一些国家对中国"一带一路"所带来的政治威胁，"中国威胁论"再一次不可避免地被提出，成为国际社会对"一带一路"背后所蕴含的意义争论的焦点。

《金融时报》更是声称，中国军方也渴望得到随着"一带一路"计划推动所带来的政治影响和财政支持。据其采访的一位美国前官员说，他被某解放军高级将

---

① 《中华人民共和国反恐怖主义法》，北大法律英文网，发布时间：2016 年 1 月 1 日，http://lawinfochina.com/display.aspx?id=20901&lib=law。

领告知,"一带一路"战略将会有一个对"安全部分"的投入①。

斯里兰卡、孟加拉国和巴基斯坦等国家的港口建设引起了一些分析人士质疑中国的最终目标。他们怀疑中国对于这些国家的港口建设是为了通过资助获得秘密的军舰海外基地,也是为了下一步建立双重海军物流设施"珍珠链"做好准备②。

在英国,关于"一带一路"计划的实施也不乏有这些质疑的声音。美国媒体的不断发难,更是让一部分发达国家疑窦重重。对宾夕法尼亚大学沃顿商学院教授、伦敦帝国理工学院财务与经济学教授、布莱文霍华德中心执行董事弗兰克林·艾伦(Franklin Allen)的采访可能是最好的例子。他在采访中声称一带一路"是一个经济举措,但中国将趁机扩张自己的军事基地。在海路及陆路,他们也将发展他们的军事能力"。③对于这些过度解读、带有偏见的声音,中国也应通过中英合作中媒体人文合作的机会,逐步消除社会偏见,更应以此为契机向其他欧美国家发声,逐步扭转对中国海上力量发展长期不利的国际政治环境。

第三方市场合作可能导致的风险

伦敦建筑情报中心的经济学家内森·海耶斯(Nathan Hayes)表示,英国可以深度挖掘"一带一路"中涉及的二级项目,通过"一带一路"沿途国家不断增长的开放市场促进跨部门的合作。但他同时也指出,这些第三方市场涉及国家大多数都是具有潜在风险因素的新兴市场,外汇波动、经济衰退以及政府活动导致的私营部门投资"挤出"等都将极大地增加英国投资的不确定性与经营风险。这将要求英国在涉及第三方市场的业务时加大项目管理的力度。因此,英国对于在第

---

① China's Great Game: Road to a new empire, *Financial Times*, October 12, 2015, https://www.ft.com/content/6e098274-587a-11e5-a28b-50226830d644.

② Jean-Marc F. Blanchard ,Probing China's Twenty-First-Century Maritime Silk Road Initiative (MSRI): An Examination of MSRI Narratives, Geopolitics, Volume 22, 2017 - Issue 2, December 10, 2016, http://www.tandfonline.com/doi/abs/10.1080/14650045.2016.1267147?src=recsys&journalCode=fgeo20&.

③ "Where will China's 'One Belt, One Road' initiative lead?", Knowledge Wharton, March 22, 2017, http://knowledge.wharton.upenn.edu/article/can-chinas-one-belt-one-road-initiative-match-the-hype/.

三方市场的合作可能并不能像预计的那样倾尽全力①。

英中商业委员会（CBBC）于2016年发布的《一带一路指南》报告中也有描述，"'一带一路'不仅是一项经济举措，也是一个主要的地缘政治的风险。"②同时指出，中英在第三方市场的合作中可能会存在由于政治或社会不稳定、区域争端而引起的法律和财务风险③。

在第三方市场的合作中，中国与英国一样，同样会受到这些风险因素的影响。正因如此，中国才更加需要像英国这样具有相关丰富经验的老牌发达国家合作。比起消极地减少合作，不如积极地去寻求一个可以合理降低风险隐患的合作方案、更高效地进行项目管理的方式，从而使得在第三方市场的合作更具可操作性与合理性。

西藏问题存在的隐患

中英之间关于西藏的争议由来已久。自十七世纪以来，英国与西藏之间一直有着千丝万缕的联系，两次侵藏战争均由英国发起，这使得西藏问题一直是中英之间合作交流的敏感之处。2013年，戴维·卡梅隆（David Cameron）就因会见达赖喇嘛而使得中英关系骤降至冰点，许多投资项目因此取消或推延④。

现今，英国政府对于西藏问题的态度是审慎的。2015年，当达赖喇嘛再次要求会见首相时，他的要求被驳回了。但是，达赖喇嘛及一些藏独分子并未放弃与

---

① UK hopes to underpin developments, ChinaDaily, April 23, 2017, http://www.chinadaily.com.cn/world/2017-04/23/content_29047329.htm.

② One Belt One Road: a role for UK companies in developing China's new initiative - new opportunities in china and beyond, China-Britain Business Council, May 18, 2015, http://www.cbbc.org/sectors/one-belt,-one-road/.

③ "The Impact of China's One Belt One Road Initiative on Developing Countries", The London School of Economics and Political Science, January 30, 2017, http://blogs.lse.ac.uk/internationaldevelopment/2017/01/30/the-impact-of-chinas-one-belt-one-road-initiative-on-developing-countries/.

④ Andrew Woodcock, "David Cameron 'must apologise' for meeting Dalai Lama to restore diplomatic relations with China", Independent, May 7, 2013, http://www.independent.co.uk/news/uk/politics/david-cameron-must-apologise-for-meeting-dalai-lama-to-restore-diplomatic-relations-with-china-8606341.html.

英国建立联系的尝试。这也使得西藏问题依然是今后中英关系的一大隐患。有些学者已经提出了"达赖喇嘛效应"来总结中国政府削减对接收或会见达赖喇嘛的国家出口政策。今后倘若藏独分子与英国有关部门取得联系,势必会影响到中英"一带一路"的合作进程。要想避免这一问题的出现,英国政府自身必须明确对西藏问题的立场,避免做出任何可能引起争议的举动。

中英合作:影响与机遇

英国脱欧的重要影响

近期,英国公投脱欧及其后续效应引起国际社会的广泛关注。英国于 2017 年 3 月 29 日正式启动《里斯本条约》第 50 项条款进入脱欧程序。脱欧程序在两年内正式完成,届时,英国将离开欧洲单一市场,这也意味着英国必须在两年内找到新的替代市场才能度过经济和政治难关。而英国的脱欧,会给全球世界经济、英国自身、欧盟与中国都分别造成不同程度的影响。

对世界经济而言,自 2008 年全球金融危机以来,全球产业结构已进入一个复苏缓慢的深度调整期,发达经济体由于沉重的债务压力、紧缩的货币环境、严重的失业问题等因素,在全球经济增长中的主导地位已经开始动摇,而英国的脱欧又使得全球经济避险情绪上升,风险偏好恶化,全球经济带来剧烈动荡。英国作为世界金融中心之一,对跨境信贷、离岸金融等方面有着深远的影响,脱欧后英国将不可避免地通过投资、贸易与金融渠道给世界经济带来冲击。

对英国自身而言,英国政府本来就缺乏基础建设的投资,欧投行今后对英国项目的贷款也将不可避免地有所减少,这将给伦敦横贯城铁(Crossrail)项目或伦敦地铁升级项目等大型基建项目带来影响。英国脱欧也意味着脱离了欧盟经济体,可以自主地与其他经济体展开贸易谈判,与此同时,英国是否能继续享受欧盟的零关税政策仍没有明确的答案。

此外,根据《金融时报》分析,欧盟提出的退出费用将可达到 1000 亿欧元。

欧盟委员会首席Brexit谈判代表米歇尔·巴尼耶（Michel Barnier）则表示，英国在2020年之前必须继续支付英国项目的未偿还养老金负债、贷款担保和支出的份额，这与英国在欧盟时所支付的费用几乎没有不同[1]。根据欧盟若干成员国的要求，农业补贴以及欧盟管理费用也被添加进英国必须支付的费用明细中。英国在失去欧盟福利的同时仍然需要付出代价，这对未来的发展可能是一个巨大的威胁。在最终结果出现前，事情依然有回旋的余地。但有一件事是肯定的，不管谈判如何，英国都要付出代价[2]。

无法忽视的另一个问题是英国脱欧对北方经济振兴计划的影响。不得不提的是，欧洲区域发展基金（ERDF）和欧洲投资银行（EIB）共同参与了北方经济振兴计划投资基金，所投联合基金达到1.45亿英镑，占全部NPIF的36.25%。而这一部分资金随着英国脱欧的实施将何去何从也是人们所关心的。

脱欧也将给中英之间的合作带来一定程度的影响。伦敦已成为世界第二大人民币结算中心，而英国更能成为中国打开欧盟市场的重要平台，加速实现人民币国际化[3]。在英国宣布脱欧之前，英国已经表明愿意支持将人民币纳入特别提款权篮子，但要符合国际货币基金组织即将进行的特别提款权审查的现行标准。英国此次脱欧，将会使人民币通过英国在欧洲推广的战略所产生的成本大大增加，也使得英国在一定程度上丧失中国在人民币国际化的推动进程中最重要战略伙伴的地位[4]。

---

[1] The multi-billion-euro exit charge that could sink Brexit talks, *The Economist*, January 11, 2017, http://www.economist.com/news/britain/21716629-bitter-argument-over-money-looms-multi-billion-euro-exit-charge-could-sink-brexit。

[2] Peter Dominiczak, Steven Swinford& Peter Foster, Britain will be handed £50bn exit bill by EU when Theresa May triggers Article 50, chief negotiator for Brussels warns, *The telegraph*, March 31, 2016, http://www.telegraph.co.uk/news/2016/12/15/britain-will-handed-50bn-exit-bill-eu-theresa-may-triggers-article/.

[3] 驻英大使刘晓明：《"一带一路"为中英合作开拓更广阔空间》，凤凰咨询，发布时间：2017年1月24日，http://news.ifeng.com/a/20170124/50622652_0.shtml。

[4] Lu Xinhong, RMB Internationalization Spreads Wings with 'Belt and Road' Strategy, China US Focus, January 8, 2015, http://www.chinausfocus.com/finance-economy/rmb-internationalization-spreads-wings-with-belt-and-road-strategy.

风险常与机会并存。英国此次脱欧，也为中国的发展带来了丰厚的机遇。一方面，英国为了消除脱欧带来的负面效应，势必要加强与其他国家的经济合作，而中英之间正处于"黄金时代"，依靠中国无疑是最简单有效的选择。而英国退出后，也会削弱欧盟的一体化。作为欧盟的主要经济体之一，英国的退出同样会给欧盟的经济造成动荡，这也从另一个角度增大了中国与欧盟间的合作机会。2017年3月下旬，中国进出口银行前主席李若国在博鳌亚洲论坛年会上接受采访时表示，英国脱欧后开启的与中国之间的贸易对话可以更好地促进两国间的关系。

英国的优势产业及合作的机会

考虑到当前两国产业结构的特点，加强中国制造业与英国高端服务业合作，同时加强英国与中国间的科技创新合作，有望成为未来若干年加强中英产业合作的重点[①]。

中国正处于经济转型期，从自身需要出发，加强制造业与服务业的合作，既能促进自身的转型，又能在"一带一路"沿线国家的建设中实现中英资源的完美整合，是不容忽视的一大方面。

在科技创新合作方面，中国虽然在一些领域取得了可喜的成果，然而对制造业的自主创新能力还很薄弱，支撑产业升级的技术储备明显不足，在技术转移的供应链方面仍有不同程度的脱节。因此，中国更应在中英合作上把科技创新的合作作为一大重点。对于可以合作的技术领域，不仅仅要关注英国的古老优势产业，如海洋技术、海洋安全等，也应关注英国自身想要加强的产业领域，更好地实现双赢[②]。

---

① "China, Britain hold security dialogue, agree to strengthen cooperation", the state council of the PRC, February 19,2017, http://english.gov.cn/news/international_exchanges/2017/02/19/content_281475572247225.htm

② 《英国国务大臣宣布已成功投入2亿英镑支持中英研究创新合作》，英国驻上海总领事馆，发布时间：2016年9月23日，https://www.gov.uk/government/world-location-news/minister-celebrates-successful-commitment-of-200m-in-uk-china-research-and-innovation-collaboration.zh。

在 2017 年 1 月最新出台的绿皮书《如何建立我们的工业战略》中①，英国政府再次
强调了英国的八大重点产业领域——清洁能源、机器人和人工智能、卫星与空间
技术、保健与医药、制造工艺及材料、生物科学与技术、量子技术、转型数字
技术（包括超级计算、高级建模及 5G 移动网络技术）。英国政府更提出计划在
2020~2021 年前增加 47 亿英镑的研发投入总额，建立新的工业战略基金用于机器
人、清洁能源与生物技术等方面，并将拨款 1 亿英镑深化对生物医药的研究，1 亿
英镑用于激励大学合作开展技术转让及相关的业务合作等。这些技术领域都是至
关重要，极富需求潜力的，而英国也有足够的知识和技能来开发新技术。因此，
在中英技术合作中，应把这些产业领域都纳入可能的合作范围，进行科技创新合
作。科技创新的合作带来的将是两国之间技术与人才的直接流动，这将大大节省
中国用于技术积累的时间，快速获取产业升级与政策调整所需经验与人才。

中英科技创新合作可能出现的难题与解决办法

在科技创新合作过程中，中英合作将不可避免地在信息、政策、人文交流以
及知识产权等方面因两国差异而出现问题。

在信息交流方面，由于信息的不对称，将有可能造成中英之间资源的无法成
功持续匹配，中国的投资找不到心仪的投资项目，难以推进可持续的合作。

在政策方面，首先，中国自身的科技项目评估体系尚未得到有效的完善，这
会直接影响到中国对英国新科技项目的引进水平。其次，中英之间仍然缺乏一个
统一的对技术引进、合作研发及资本合作的操作规范，这使得科技项目的引进实
施操作更为麻烦。第三，中英两国的技术标准不一致，这使得科技项目商业化后
的产品质量水平仍有待商榷。第四，中英两国间在政府审批、实际政策落实与执
行方面可能会缺乏效率，影响科技项目的落地速度。第五，中英两国间可能由于
政策导向性的不同而在一定程度上对中英科技的合作造成影响。此外，地方保护
主义也会使得中英之间的合作往来受到阻碍，在一定程度上影响多方利益。

---

① Building our industrial strategy, gov.uk, January, 2017, https://www.gov.uk/government/uploads/
system/uploads/attachment_data/file/586626/building-our-industrial-strategy-green-paper.pdf.

在人文交流方面，中英两国间本身就因为历史、文化、语言、社会制度等方面的根本性差异而影响双方社会的交流，更容易产生偏见[1]。这样不仅仅会影响中英之间加深推进推广合作，更可能会由于中英双方实际合作人在投资中英科技项目时出现一定程度的观点分歧，在项目评估时造成不一致并影响后续的项目监管。

在知识产权方面，由于中国有关法律尚未完善，国内尊重保护知识产权的氛围尚未成型，英国对于中国的知识产权保护一直有所质疑。这也是可能导致双方合作分歧的关键因素。

对于可能影响中英科技创新合作的四个主要方面，中英之间唯有不断加强交流合作，利用媒体手段进行社会层面的推广，同时不断完善政策规范，逐步消除可能出现的障碍。

十九大对中英科技创新合作的启示

中国共产党第十九次全国代表大会（简称党的十九大）于 2017 年 10 月 18 日至 10 月 24 日在北京召开，习近平主席于 2017 年 10 月 18 日向大会作了题为《决胜全面建成小康社会，夺取新时代中国特色社会主义伟大胜利》的报告，及时为国家未来的发展调整了方向。

在十九大的报告中，提出将加快建设创新型国家作为重点发展内容，"并将深化科技体制改革，建立以企业为主体、市场为导向、产学研深度融合的技术创新体系，加强对中小企业创新的支持，促进科技成果转化。倡导创新文化，强化知识产权创造、保护、运用。"[2]这也进一步表达了中国着手逐步消除因为知识产权保护等问题而产生的国际技术合作障碍的决心。预计在短时间内，中国的科技潜力将得到大幅释放，科技进步带来的社会发展将普遍惠及人民群众。报告中提出的"建立以企业为主体、市场为导向、产学研深度融合的技术创新体系"标志着中国

---

[1]　Martin Vander Weyer, "Theresa May's right: we need China's money, not their friendship", Spectator, August 6, 2016, https://www.spectator.co.uk/2016/08/theresa-mays-right-we-need-chinas-money-not-their-friendship/#.

[2]　《习近平出席"一带一路"国际合作高峰论坛开幕式并发表主旨演讲》，"一带一路"国际合作高峰论坛官方网站，2017 年 5 月 14 日，http://www.beltandroadforum.org/n100/2017/0514/c24-397.html。

的科研体系日趋成熟完善，让科研成果加快转化生产力。

从国家战略方向来说，创新将进一步发挥对中国经济的主导作用，这一特点在下一步的经济变革中将更加突出。国家对科技发展的规划充分考虑到国情和历史使命，领导核心对中国创新发展方向定位准确，也为中英之间的技术合作提供了强有力的保障。随着中国更加开放，对创新及国际合作领域更加重视，未来中英科技创新合作中，英国将会从如下方面获利：

1. 政策将更偏重于对绿色经济发展及高新技术领域的支持。政策导向带来更大的市场，无疑会为英国的相关技术企业及研究机构带来更大的吸引力。英国离岸可再生能源国家技术中心就提出了愿意进一步开拓中国市场，与中国相关企业及研究机构共同研发海上风电领域技术的计划。中国方面的回应也是积极而热烈的。2017年10月，英国离岸可再生能源国家技术中心的有关人员来中国进行了为期一周的访问考察，与相关企业机构及政府部门关于下一步的合作进行了深入洽谈。

2. 中国关于知识产权保护领域的政策制度将更加完善，切实保护国外先进技术的利益，这为今后英国先进技术的进驻与开展合作坚实了信心基础。在过去，中国对于专利的保护体系不够完善，这使得很多国外的技术止步不前，不敢进入国内市场。十九大报告中强调加强对知识产权的保护，这无疑是对国外企业的一大承诺，也是为中英科技合作提供的强有力的保障。

3. 政策将更加偏重于创新对外投资方式，促进国际产能合作，与此同时也保障保护外商投资的合法权益。中英之间资源、技术、优势互补，正是国际产能合作的最佳选择。新的对外投资方式必将为中国投资者"走出去"提供更好的机会与更多的选择，为英国技术优势企业与高新技术创业企业带来更多潜在的合作伙伴；保障外商投资的合法权益更能为英国企业进入中国市场开通便利渠道。

中英科技创新合作的可能的方式

第一种合作方式是政府间的直接合作。包括政府间的直接投资，合作建立联合基金会，支持相关创新研究的合作计划等。2013年12月卡梅伦首相访华时提出共建中英联合科学创新基金（牛顿基金项目）[1]，自2016年统计时起已开展了44个项目，涉及130项合作，由85家中方机构与57家英方机构共同参与。根据中英科技合作协议统计，中英两国在基础研究、卫生、农业、航空航天等领域至今已签署了20多份对口协议或备忘录[2]。中英两国政府也应将共同出台中英科技合作规范、建立切实有效的科技项目共同评估体系、建立中英知识产权保护协同机制等政策规范作为短期目标之一，"工欲善其事，必先利其器"，唯有确定一个官方标准的合作规范与合作政策，才能更好地切实有效地推进中英科技创新合作项目的实际运行。

第二种合作方式是两国的科研部门与大学之间的合作。中科院与英国帝国理工学院一直保持着紧密的合作，而英国研究理事会（RCUK）也已与中科院设立关于太阳能燃料与合成生物学两大联合研究项目。两国之间最前沿的科研部门与具有对口优势的大学直接合作，势必能更有效地鼓励更多的科研成果产出[3]。

第三种合作方式是企业与大学间的直接合作。不少研究证明，像硅谷类企业与创新结合，大学与企业合作的模式是最容易吸引创新的发展模式。中国的企业如能直接入驻与英国大学建立合作，将会打破时间地域等交流障碍，更快更好地推动科技创新商业化。科控集团已在英国东安格利亚大学建立基金用于对低碳环保问题的研究，就是很好的例子。设立PPP模式的基金，流动性与目的性更强，能更好地筛选实用前沿的技术项目，推动中英联合产出更多的商业及创新成果[4]。

第四种是中英大学之间的直接对接，这其中既包括中英大学之间的科技创新合作项目，又包括中英之间大学的人才交流项目。大学之间的科技创新合作是各国建立全球学术联系的重要手段。在2014年英中教育论坛上，罗素集团主席兼诺丁

---

[1]　Newton Fund, British Council, 2017, https://www.britishcouncil.org/education/science/newton.

[2]　《中英科技部门对口合作情况》，中华人民共和国驻大不列颠及北爱尔兰联合王国大使馆官网，发布日期：2010年4月29日，http://www.chinese-embassy.org.uk/chn/kjjl/t688734.htm。

[3]　《中英协力促进创意和科技产业发展》，英国政府官网，发布日期：2015年10月21日，https://www.gov.uk/government/news/uk-and-china-join-forces-to-boost-creative-and-technology-industries.zh。

[4]　《中英政府间科技合作简况》，中华人民共和国驻大不列颠及北爱尔兰联合王国大使馆官网，发布日期：2010年4月29日，http://www.chinese-embassy.org.uk/chn/zygx/kjjl/t422158.htm。

汉大学校长 David Greenaway 教授说："只有通过全球研究合作共同努力，才能解决大的科学、经济和社会挑战。"①中英之间大学人才交流项目的出台，既能直接影响人才技术的交流共享，又能通过中国留学生来吸引中国的投资。对留学生进行企业家精神教育的培养，往往有助于创建高水平的企业。同时，企业家也倾向于投资子女就读的城市或国家，对英国房地产的投资也有所助益。中国教育部签署《中国孔子学院总部/国家汉办与英国文化教育协会谅解备忘录（2016~2020 年）》，宣布未来 3~5 年将继续实施五年万人留学英国项目，推进人才的交流及语言教学的合作②。

第五种是中英两国孵化器、风险投资、初创企业多层次、多领域的合作。中英两国的初创企业在资本运作、技术研发方面都有很大的合作空间；而在两国孵化器平台合作的基础上，在两国政府政策支持下，风险投资则可以更加畅通无阻地在中英两国众多初创企业中参与投资。这不仅有助于发挥中英国两国孵化器、风险投资、初创企业各自的专长和优势，也会极大地促进中小企业的发展，创造更多的就业机会，推动技术创新。比如 2017 年 2 月，清华启迪创投集团一行到英国伦敦、剑桥以及纽卡斯尔进行实地考察访问，为下一步在英国北部建立创新园区、建立创业生态系统打下基础。

中英一带一路合作为全球第三方市场带来的影响和机会

2015 年 6 月底，李克强总理在访问比利时和法国期间，首次使用了"第三方市场合作"这一概念，并且同法方正式发表了《中法关于第三方市场合作的联合声明》③。

第三方市场合作，主要是指中国与有关发达国家一起开发作为第三方的发展

---

① Strengthening links with leading Chinese universities, University of Leeds Faculty of Engineering News, 2016, https://engineering.leeds.ac.uk/news/article/319/strengthening-links-with-leading-chinese-universities.

② 《今后 3~5 年对英重点合作项目清单》，中华人民共和国教育部，发布日期：2016 年 12 月 8 日，http://www.moe.gov.cn/jyb_xwfb/moe_1946/fj_2016/201612/t20161208_291172.html.

③ Ministry of Foreign Affairs of PRC, "Li Keqiang Attends the 17th China-EU Summit and Visit Belgium, Pays an Official Visit to France and Visits the Headquarters of the Organization for Economic Cooperation and Development", January 30, 2015, http://www.fmprc.gov.cn/mfa_eng/topics_665678/lkqcxds qczgomldrhwbsfblsdfgjxzsfwbfwjjhzyfzzzzb/.

中国家市场。许多文献也指出，虽然现阶段中国是全世界工业门类最齐全的国家，处于全球产业链的核心，工业化的技术水平却仍处于中等亟需提升；而发达国家拥有先进技术和装备，却由于产能不足成本过高无法有效开发第三世界市场。与此同时，大量第三世界国家苦于缺乏技术和资金，无力提升本国经济水平。在第三方市场合作中，由中国提供产能及工业产品，发达国家运用自身丰富的经验，二者共同开发第三方发展中国家的市场，促进三方经济互利共赢。英国可以以自身丰富的经验，先进的技术，以及完善的专业服务在中国提供的平台上一起合作。亚洲以外的其他地区仍存在非常大的基建需求。据联合国估计，非洲的发电量仅占全球发电总量的4%。对于非洲发电量最多的南非，目前的电力短缺依然处于非常严峻的阶段。由于设备老化、管理运营不善等问题，为南非提供95%供电的南非国有电力公司频频拉闸限电。南非种族研究所的报道称，若南非经济以3%的速度增长，那么南非在2030年的电力缺口将达18000兆瓦[①]。这也同样给中英的合作带来了丰富的机会，也能满足广大非洲地区急需的基础设施建设需求。

"一带一路"与北方振兴计划的结合

英国北方经济振兴计划：英国版的一带一路？

2015年10月习主席访问英国期间，中英双方发表《中英关于构建面向21世纪全球全面战略伙伴关系的联合宣言》[②]，提出结合"一带一路"倡议和北方经济振兴计划实现共同发展[③]。中国通过这次合作，既能满足英国北方振兴计划中对基建

---

① 《南非推进能源结构转型》，新华网，2015年3月21日，http://news.xinhuanet.com/world/ 2015-03/21/c_127604722.htm。

② "Full text: China-UK Joint Declaration on Building a Global Comprehensive Strategic Partnership for the 21st Century", *China Daily*, October 22, 2015, http://europe.chinadaily.com.cn/2015-10/22/content_22264267_3.htm.

③ Osborne hopes Xi can turn Northern Powerhouse into a UK Silk Road, *Financial Times*, October 20, 2015, https://www.ft.com/content/602a77cc-7647-11e5-933d-efcdc3c11c89.

的需求，又能在英国自身寻求技术升级的同时增强自身的科技实力，实现高效的资源优化配置，使两国经济共同持续增长。

2016 年 11 月 10 日，英国贸易投资署（UKTI）在第八届英中经济金融对话（EFD）上发布了北部振兴计划投资项目包（Northern Powerhouse Investment Portfolio，NPIP）[①]，以更好地分析中国投资者对北部地区的投资潜力项目。

表 5–2　北部振兴计划投资项目包[②]

项目名称	区域	开发类型	说明
AeroCentre	唐卡斯特	办公室，物流，工业，制造	与唐卡斯特谢菲尔德机场在下一阶段的开发工作，以创建新的办公室、物流单位和航空机库。拥有企业入驻区域，这入驻企业将受益于政府大量的税收优惠。
Future Carrington	老特拉福德	住宅零售，办公室，社区基础设施	投资大型住宅和就业发展的机会，提供超过 14000 个新工作机会，并年增加 7.2 亿英镑的总增值额。
Kampus	曼彻斯特	住宅办事处/运输署	曼彻斯特市中心总计 200 万英镑的重建计划。包括新的城市中心公寓、零售商店、酒吧、咖啡馆。
Kirkstall Forge	利兹	住宅，办公室，零售	开发一个拥有 1050 套新房屋的新社区，33 万平方英尺的办公空间，零售、休闲和社区空间。
Liverpool Waters	利物浦	住宅，办事处，酒店和零售业	项目提供土地出售，开发全方位的用途，改造城市的北部码头。也划分了企业区位置，入驻企业可以受益于政府大量的税收优惠。

---

① 《英国北方经济增长区投资机遇向中国投资者推介》，英国政府官网，发布日期：2016 年 11 月 10 日，https://www.gov.uk/government/news/northern-powerhouse-investments-showcased-to-chinese-investors.zh。

② Source: Moore, D. (2016). The Northern Powerhouse and wider opportunities for Chinese investment in UK infrastructure. http://www.lexology.com/library/detail.aspx?g=bcfe5b57-c298-4170-a1ee-4ffafb3cb369.

（续表）

项目名称	区域	开发类型	说明
MediaCityUK	索尔福德，大曼彻斯特	办公室媒体，技术零售	MediaCityUK一期投资于2011年完成，由BBC、ITV以及超过250个较小的创意和数字业务的公司组成。现在开发二期，目标为规模扩大一倍。
Pall Mall	利物浦	住宅，零售，办事处，商业	涉及与利物浦市议会合作进行重大改造项目，提供1000处新房、办公空间、零售休闲和社区设施。
Protos – Ellesmere Port	柴郡	能源工业，铁路，基础设施制造	该项目包括天然气发电、能源发电、工业发展、铁路和泊位基础设施等一系列投资机会，创造3000多个新工作岗位，首期生产总值预期达3.5亿英镑。
Sirius Minerals, Polyhalite Project	惠特比，北约克郡	矿业，运输，物流	有机会在英国建设第一个长达40年以上的钾盐矿。全年生产能力将达2000万吨，直接创造1000多个新工作岗位。
Stockport Exchange	斯托克波特	办事处，商业，休闲，零售	为Stockport Exchange提供资金，建造高品质的办公空间与零售、休闲设施和停车场的混合用地。项目赞助商是Stockport Metropolitan Borough Council，开发商是MUSE项目，价值1.45亿英镑。
Unity	唐卡斯特	住宅，办事处，商业，休闲，零售	一个主要的再建和基础设施项目，将创造3100处新房，建设交通枢纽、学校和社区。还有机会投资用于制造业的商业空间，6000个新工作岗位，一个新的电站和一个材料回收设施。
Vaux	桑德兰	住宅，办事处，商业，零售	投资1亿英镑开发提供办公室、休闲、酒店、住宅和零售空间。
Advance Manufacturing Innovation District	谢菲尔德	住宅，办事处，商业，休闲，零售	有机会投资超过2000英亩以创新为主导的金属和材料先进制造中心。该区也将新建超过4000处新房。开发商为谢菲尔德和罗瑟勒姆议会；谢菲尔德大学、谢菲尔德哈勒姆大学；Harworth房产及谢菲尔德商业园项目。项目规模估计超过10亿英镑。

中国投资者的眼光也逐渐放宽，不仅仅局限于伦敦、牛津、剑桥等老牌科技

创新集群。2016 年 12 月，清华启迪科技服务集团（简称"清华启迪"）与纽卡斯尔市政府签署合作协议，在海洋科技和生物医药领域进行全面的双向合作，以"两国双园"作为主要平台，集聚双方资源进行互补和整合，运用自有成熟的集群式创新机制在海洋科技产业及生命科技产业领域实现技术创新并转移、商业化合资并投入市场这样一个完整的产业链，大力推动两国相关产业的发展，促进经济繁荣。

北方经济振兴计划涵盖东北部地区、西北部地区、约克郡及汉伯地区三大地区，本报告将以东北部地区的重点目标城市纽卡斯尔、西北部地区重点目标城市曼彻斯特及利物浦、约克郡及汉伯地区的重点目标城市利兹为例，重点分析其在北方经济振兴计划中的地位以及中国从中可能获得的潜在合作机遇。

北方经济振兴计划 Growth Deal

Growth Deal 是英国政府针对北方振兴计划提出的一项旨在为地方政府和企业之间的伙伴关系提供资金，促进本地区经济项目受益的项目。对于 Growth Deal 项目投入的统计，从另一方面更能反映出北方经济振兴计划对于中小型企业及创业企业的扶持力度，更能直观地看出哪些地区仍存在扶持的潜力。

表 5–3　Growth Deal 发展细节[①]

Region's Local Growth Fund Award	Growth Deal One (July 2014)	Growth Deal Two (Jan 2015)	Growth Deal Three (Nov 2016)	Region's Total Fund
Cheshire and Warrington	£142.7m	£15.1m	£43.3m	£201.1m
Cumbria	£26.8m	£20.9m	£12.7m	£60.4m
Greater Manchester	£476.7m	£56.6m	£130.1m	£663.4m
Humber	£103.7m	£9.9m	£27.9m	£141.5m
Lancashire	£233.9m	£17.2m	£69.8m	£320.9m

---

① Source: Department for Communities and Local Government et al. (2017). Northern Powerhouse: Growth Deals. https://www.gov.uk/government/publications/northern-powerhouse-growth-deals.

（续表）

Region's Local Growth Fund Award	Growth Deal One (July 2014)	Growth Deal Two (Jan 2015)	Growth Deal Three (Nov 2016)	Region's Total Fund
Leeds City Region	£572.9m	£54.6m	£67.5m	£695m
Liverpool City Region	£229.3m	£31.6m	£72.0m	£332.9m
North East	£289.3m	£40.6m	£49.7m	£379.6m
Sheffield City Region	£297m	£31m	£37m	£365m
Tees Valley	£90.3m	£13.9m	£21.8m	£126m
York, North Yorkshire and East Riding	£110.1m	£12.1m	£23.7m	£145.9m

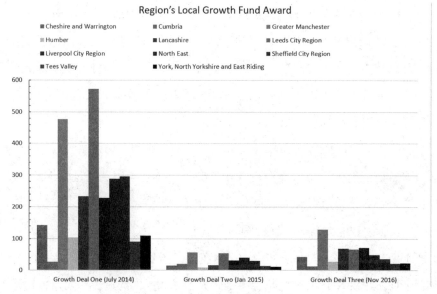

图 5-3　Growth Deal 分析[①]

令人惊讶的是，利兹是获得最多项目投入的地区[②]，而不是至今已引起许多争

---

①　Data Source: Department for Communities and Local Government et al. (2017). Northern Powerhouse: Growth Deals. https://www.gov.uk/government/publications/northern-powerhouse-growth-deals. The figure is drawn based on the data provided by authors.

②　Northern Powerhouse: Growth Deals, *Gov.UK*, January 23, 2017, https://www.gov.uk/government/publications/northern-powerhouse-growth-deals.

议的曼彻斯特（总共获得投资 6.634 亿英镑）。这是因为 Growth Deal 针对的只是地方政府与企业间的资金投入，在北方经济振兴计划的其余方面如医疗、基建等，对于曼彻斯特的投入是最多的（1.301 亿英镑）。然而，这也从另一方面反映出，利兹也许是创业精神最发达、中小型企业最活跃的城市，而其余城市仍拥有很大的投资潜力。在统计数据中，需要注意的一点是，纽卡斯尔作为英国东北部地区最大的城市，甚至没有单列统计，而是并入了英国东北部地区作为一个统计项。

纽卡斯尔的发展机遇

财政部长奥尼尔（Lord O'Neill）是 Powerhouse 和权力下放计划的主要策划人，他在 2016 年 6 月纽卡斯尔核心部门举行的科学中心（Science Central）新闻发布会上指出[1]，科学中心的大量投资使纽卡斯尔成为北方振兴计划的核心。他说："北方振兴计划是纽卡斯尔前所未有的机会。在纽卡斯尔市议会和纽卡斯尔大学的支持下，科技中心将成为一个具有里程碑意义的开发项目，将为该地区带来巨大利益。科学和教育是我们计划平衡经济并结束南北差距的核心，这个项目将成为北方地区其他城市的样本和蓝图。"

自 2012 年戈登·布朗（Gordon Brown）首相宣布纽卡斯尔是政府的科学城市之一以来，已经有数百万的投资投入在它的科技研发当中。经过多年的小活动，科学中心核心办公楼已经开通，目前正在为纽卡斯尔大学建立城市科学中心、实验室，以及国家智能数据和能源系统中心。

纽卡斯尔拥有强大的科研实力和来自英国一流院校的人才储备。纽卡斯尔大学和纽卡斯尔医院 NHS 的信托基金会是研究罕见和虚弱的遗传疾病（特别是神经肌肉疾病）方面世界级的领先中心之一。诺森比亚大学设计学院为跨国和国家制造与服务部门公司提供设计主导的创新专业知识。诺森比亚大学设计学院目前的合作伙伴包括飞利浦、联合利华等，已有超过 10 多年的研究合作。诺森比亚大学

---

[1] Graeme Whitfield, "Government Minister hails Newcastle's role in Northern Powerhouse after science investment", *Chronic Live*, January 16, 2016, http://www.chroniclelive.co.uk/business/business-news/government-minister-hails-newcastles-role-11484796.

同时专长于支持数字取证、模糊系统和机器学习以及自动化运动识别和监视的关键工业和专业应用[①]。

英国政府于 2016 年 11 月发布北部振兴计划战略,作为东北地区最大的城市,纽卡斯尔在中英战略合作中将取得新的发展机遇[②]。

(一)纽卡斯尔大学作为 N8 大学(北部八所大学之一),将积极转化科技成果,并支持初创和寻求进一步发展的企业。N8 大学(杜伦,兰卡斯特,利兹,利物浦,曼彻斯特,纽卡斯尔,谢菲尔德和约克)将在 2020 左右完全获得由北部振兴计划提供的 1 亿镑资金,主要投入在科技转化方面。N8 大学将组织一个城市改革中心网络,将研究成果转化为商业成果。

(二)政府在支持北部研究和创新的过程中,将在纽卡斯尔大力发展海上能源的研究。

(三)政府认识到文化对区域建立和地方增长的作用,将投资 500 万英镑于 2018 年在纽卡斯尔和盖茨黑德地区举办"the Great Exhibition of the North"。

(四)政府将投资 1500 万英镑给位于纽卡斯尔的国家智能数据创新中心(the National Institute for Smart Data Innovation)。

(五)纽卡斯尔通向伦敦的 A1 公路也将得到整修和升级。

项目投资方面,诺森比亚及泰恩河畔地区在科技转化、海上能源、生物医学及智能数据创新方面的研究必将有更进一步的发展和更大的飞跃。这些领域的创新更具潜力,富有很大的投资合作空间。

基础建设方面,纽卡斯尔市作为北部最大的城市,却尚未有建立直通伦敦的高铁计划,这一事实是潜在的投资机会。

---

① "Newcastle Science Central secures multi-million pound deal with L&G", Newcastle University Press Office, January 16, 2016, http://www.ncl.ac.uk/press/news/2016/06/l&gannouncement/.

② "Northern powerhouse investment opportunities", *Gov.UK*, 2016, https://www.gov.uk/government/uploads/system/uploads/attachment_data/file/595701/NPH_pitchbook_2016_Brochure_English_low_res_version.pdf.

利物浦的发展机遇

利物浦现已得到了 7200 万英镑投资用于：

（一）促进创新，提高整个地区的企业生产力。

（二）加强城市道路网络的关键路线，提供交通和无障碍改善，以支持住房和就业的增长。

（三）提高工作者的技能水平，满足雇主的技能需求，并帮助留住熟练工人在城市地区。

利物浦实行的新政策之一在于把权利下放给当地人民。利物浦也会在 2017 年直接选举出自己的市长，在未来的 30 年里，市长将控制每年价值 3000 万英镑的投资。总共 9 亿英镑将用于建设新的超级港口以激发更多的经济潜力。国际商业节、利物浦标志性文化景点，以及国家博物馆也都是利物浦下一步的发展优势[1]。

曼彻斯特郡的发展机遇

曼彻斯特郡拥有丰富的教育资源及最大的学生群体，本身就具有得天独厚的投资优势。英国政府在北方经济振兴计划中对曼彻斯特的主要投资与建设手段有[2]：

（一）3800 万英镑投资于国家石墨烯研究中心；

（二）7800 万英镑投资于工厂戏院（the Factory theatre）；

（三）30 亿英镑将用于曼彻斯特的房地产项目建设，预计在 2020~2021 年建造 4 万套房屋；

（四）升级从曼彻斯特到约克（经过利兹）的铁路线，提速后路程时间最多 15 分钟；

（五）升级 M60 和 A66 公路；

（六）对企业进行合理减税；

---

[1] "Liverpool devolution deal boosts the Northern Powerhouse", Gov.UK, November 17, 2015, https://www.gov.uk/government/news/liverpool-devolution-deal-boosts-the-northern-powerhouse.

[2] HM Government, Northern Powerhouse Strategy, (2016), https://www.liverpoollep.org/wp-content/uploads/2016/11/Northern-Powerhouse-Strategy-November-2016.pdf.

（七）对区域下放权力，并增加更多投资使城市更好地发展。N8 学校对科技成果的转化也将适用于曼彻斯特地区①。

利兹的发展机遇

利兹市被公认为英国第二大经济和人口中心，其国民经济产值占全国的前五位，就业人数达 140 万人。它也被广泛称为英国第二大金融中心，预计于 2022 年实现 55% 的经济增长并达到超过 130 亿英镑的经济产值②。作为伦敦以外最大的功能经济区，利兹的战略经济计划是 2021 年达到 52 亿英镑额外的经济产出，创造 6.2 万个额外就业岗位。为了实现这一目标，利兹的主要投资与建设手段有：

（一）超过 10 亿英镑的投资在交通、住房、城市中心；

（二）加强发展创新力度，实现更大的业务增长；

（三）超过 50 亿英镑投资于开发渠道；

（四）成为北方经济振兴计划的重点扶持城市。

利兹正在展示其巨大的经济潜力，吸引越来越多的国际企业。据调查，在 2015 年利兹获得的外国直接投资项目，与 2013 数据相比已增加到 145%，成为增长最快的一个投资热点③。

利兹在 2017 年获得 Growth Deal 第二大的资金量用于扶持中小型企业。至今，从创新技术初创公司到全球律师事务所，共有 10.9 万家公司已扎根于利兹开展自己的业务。该地区提供了八个世界一流的大学与创新的悠久传统，并通过公路、铁路、航空和高速互联网连接到英国其他地区及世界各地。利兹市地区有四个行

---

① "Devolution to the Greater Manchester Combined Authority and transition to a directly elected mayor", *Gov.UK*, November 13, 2014, https://www.gov.uk/government/publications/devolution-to-the-greater-manchester-combined-authority-and-transition-to-a-directly-elected-mayor.

② Investment and development opportunities - Leeds City Region, Leeds City Region Enterprise Partnership, 2015, http://investleedscityregion.com/system/files/uploaded_files/Development%20Brochure%20LR.pdf.

③ Leeds City Region – Investment Opportunities, Leeds City Region Enterprise Partnership, 2015, http://investleedscityregion.com/system/files/uploaded_files/Leeds%20City%20Region%20Prospectus.pdf.

业投资机会特别强劲：

1. 金融及专业服务；

2. 制造业和低碳产业；

3. 健康与创新；

4. 数字信息经济。

利兹还为投资者和中小企业提供城市企业区。企业区紧邻利兹市中心和国家高速公路网，并提供税收优惠（高达 27.5 万英镑，超过五年）等一系列扶持企业的政策。

这些主要的投资与建设手段对中国来说也是潜在的投资机会，中国完全可以参与到共同建设中来。对科技成果的加大转化将意味着科技的进步与创新，是很好的投资方向。

笔者主持了 2017 年 7 月 20 日举办的首届"一带一路"伦敦科技论坛，此论坛由科控集团和诺森比亚大学、兰卡斯特大学、东安格利亚大学、盘古智库、中国青年创业就业基金会、全英中国创业发展协会、Hitech 论坛、天下依邦以及重庆欧美同学会留英分会共同举办；由清华启迪控股集团、浙江赛创未来投资管理有限公司、英国北部华人企业家协会、安创空间、深圳市投资发展署及国家技术转移东部中心共同协办。在此论坛上，政府机构、大学、企业纷纷踊跃加入讨论，就"科技"与"创业"两个议题进行深度探讨，表现出对"一带一路"计划的合作意愿与积极响应。该论坛聚焦于科技、农业、工业、经济与互联网+五个方面，也是未来中英"一带一路"合作的发展方向。

5 "The Belt and Road" and the Opportunities It Could Bring to the UK

Xiong Yu   Liang Jiamin

In recent years, China-UK relationship has been continuously deepened and remains "Golden". As the first Europe member who joined the Asian Infrastructure Investment Bank (AIIB), Britain is trying to strengthen China-UK cooperation among all the aspects to evolve the "Golden Era". Since Britain officially triggered Article 50 on March 29, 2017, Britain must find replacement markets in order to overcome the possible economic and political barriers after the Completion of the entire process, which makes China an essential partner in the background. This report offers the discussions and suggestions in the China-UK cooperation under the implementation of two policies – The Belt and Road (B&R); Northern Powerhouse. This report also discusses the strategic background, the actual process, the uncertainties for China-UK B&R collaboration and the potential opportunities to explore the possible approaches and contents for the collaboration between two countries.

Introduction

Background

Since the 2008 economic crisis, China has become one of two major engines of global economic recovery together with US. In fact, the nation has enjoyed 30 years of growing economic strength in an increasingly stable surrounding environment. As a consequence of its rapid post-recession growth, however, China has gradually begun experiencing such problems as excess capacity and excess foreign exchange assets, which have pushed its economic model into a 'bottleneck' requiring urgent action[1]. To this end, on a September 3, 2013, visit to Kazakhstan's Nazarbayev University, President Xi Jinping proposed the building of a "Silk Road Economic Zone"[2], which could help to release excess capacity, promote capital outflow, and internationalize the RMB. In a subsequent congressional speech in Indonesia during October that same year, the president unveiled his additional plan for a "21st Century Maritime Silk Road". Hence, in March 2015, China's National Development and Reform Commission, Ministry of Foreign Affairs, and Ministry of Commerce officially announced the vision and actions for the "Joint Building of a Silk Road Economic Belt and 21st Century Maritime Silk Road" with State Council authorization[3]. For convenience, the name of this initiative is commonly shortened to The Belt and Road or B&R.

This new strategic concept of B&R, designed to leverage transnational economic

---

[1] Naomi Canton, China has shifted to domestic consumption-driven economy, growth to average at 6.5%,(2015), http://asiahouse.org/chinas-shift-export-led-domestic-consumption-driven-economy-will-see-6-5-growth/.

[2] Ministry of Foreign Affairs of the People's Republic of China (MFA),President Xi Jinping Delivers Important Speech and Proposes to Build a Silk Road Economic Belt with Central Asian Countries,(2013), http://www.fmprc.gov.cn/mfa_eng/topics_665678/xjpfwzysiesgjtfhshzzfh_665686/t1076334.shtml.

[3] "Vision and actions on jointly building Belt and Road" ,(2015),China Org CN,http://www.china.org.cn/chinese/2015-09/15/content_36591064_2.htm.

regions, is founded on both historical and cultural considerations, as well as current conditions. Aimed primarily at building an efficient regional platform for collaboration, the concept is rooted in the establishment of a modern Silk Road across a network of countries with which China will form close economic partnerships. The currently planned route passes through Central Asia, Southeast Asia, South Asia, West Asia and parts of Europe, encompassing a total population of about 4.4 billion and a total economy of about $21 trillion, mostly in emerging economies and developing countries.[①] Once implemented, B&R will not only solve the excess capacity problem, promote China's industrial transformation, and further develop its western region but will also serve as a bilateral mechanism of mutual benefits shared by the community of participating countries. The initiative will address the reciprocal interests of this community through a series of effective programs to promote economic development and provide a broader equal market and investment platform.[②]

Geographical Scope

The original Silk Road, so named by German traveler, geographer and scientist Baron von Richthofen (May 5, 1833 – October 6, 1905), was a centuries old trade route connecting East and West. China's modern silk road concept aims to achieve comprehensive and complete integration using both land and sea trade connections, embodied in B&R by the Silk Road Economic Belt and the 21st Century Maritime Silk Road. The economic belt, whose core area will be China's western part, will build a logistics chain, the Eurasian Continental Bridge, by establishing a national economic corridor of multiple connections across the emerging economies of Mongolia, Russia,

---

① The new Silk Road, *The Economist*, (2015), http://www.economist.com/news/special-report/21663326-chinas-latest-wave-globalisers-will-enrich-their-countryand-world-new-silk-road.

② "Vision and actions on jointly building Belt and Road" , China Org CN, http://www.china.org.cn/chinese/2015-09/15/content_36591064_2.htm.

Central Asia, and Southeast Asia, all the way to Western Europe. The main Chinese provinces involved will be XinJiang, QingHai, GanSu, ShanXi, NingXia, ChongQing, SiChuan, GuangXi, YunNan and NeiMengGu. The maritime route, whose core area will be FuJian with involvement by JiangSu, ZheJiang, FuJian, GuangDong, HaiNan and ShanDong[1], will connect the three continents of Europe, Asia and Africa.

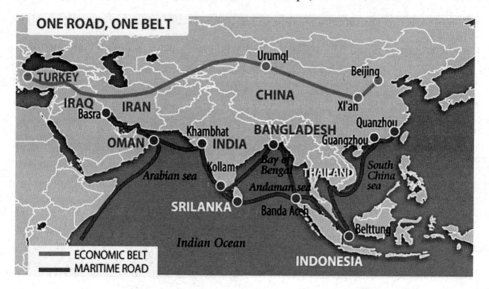

Figure 5-1　The route of B&R (The Daily Star, 2014)[2]

Strategic Implications

The principles underlying B&R are an insistence on harmonious and inclusive relationships, respect for all the different modes employed by the different participating countries and adherence to market operation practices, each of which has distinct creative advantages compared to other multilateral free trade agreements. These

---

① "Vision and actions on jointly building Belt and Road", China Org CN, http://www.china.org.cn/chinese/2015-09/15/content_36591064_2.htm.

② China presses on with new Silk Road plan,*The Daily Star*, November 9, 2014, http://www.thedailystar.net/china-presses-on-with-new-silk-road-plan-49386.

advantages are highlighted below through a comparison[①] with the Trans-Pacific Partnership (TPP):

Whereas TPP aims to enhance economic growth by reducing tariff barriers and lowering non-tariff barriers[②], B&R's goal is to create a healthy, sustainable environment by establishing an effective logistics chain through infrastructure construction.

Whereas TPP is a partnership of only 12 countries (Australia, Brunei, Canada, the U.S., Chile, Japan, Malaysia, Mexico, Vietnam, New Zealand, Peru and Singapore), with the U.S. set to leave on 23 January 2017, B&R will strive to maximize the effective use of resource allocation by encouraging the participation of all countries in (but not limited to) the geographic area of the ancient Silk Road[③].

Because the TPP focuses primarily on the implementation of labour and environmental standards, the setting up of new global trade standards, and the protection of intellectual property, plus a few features to achieve regional (Donnan, 2015), its new trade market will be similar to the EU. It will thus undermine the competitive advantage of emerging economies, most of which have not signed on to TPP. The TPP has been made even more unstable by the U.S. intention to quit it. B&R, in contrast, because it is more practical and offers substantial infrastructure support to emerging economies, will create a healthy and stable global market rather than a limited regional agreement[④].

Although many researchers have pointed to a likelihood that, based on previous experience, the U.S. may eventually negotiate to rejoin the TPP, public trust in both

---

① US withdrawal does not mean the end of TPP, *China Securities News*, December 9, 2016, http://www.cs.com.cn/xwzx/hwxx/201612/t20161209_5115366.html.

② "Trans-Pacific Partnership challenges emerging markets", (2015), British Institute of Turkish Affairs (BITAF), http://www.bitaf.org/trans-pacific-partnership-challenges-emerging-markets-3/.

③ "The Impact of China's B&R on the World Economy", (2016), China Institute of International Studies, http://www.ciis.org.cn/chinese/2016-04/06/content_8684132.htm.

④ Foreign media: Asia-Pacific 15 countries committed to promoting TPP alternative agreement to retain the core of TPP, *Netease News*, March 17, 2017, http://news.163.com/17/0317/11/CFNOJ9GG00018AOQ_all.html.

the TPP and the U.S., as well as expectations of TPP effectiveness, has declined since the U.S. decision to leave. Hence, B&R, as a stable and open mechanism, is likely to become an effective key engine to global economic growth[1].

B&R can serve as an effective platform for relieving such overcapacity and laying the groundwork for the industrial transition[2]. In particular, the initiative has the following goals:

(a) Implementing B&R will solve several of China's current economic problems, including the need, propounded by numerous economists and researchers, to transform its industrial and economic structure from the current investment-led economic growth model to a domestic consumption-driven economy and a stage of innovation-led growth[3]. China has already shown its determination to make this transition by establishing a series of policy measures to enhance self-dependent innovation capabilities and facilitate the economic transition of a shift from extensive to intensive growth (embodied in the State Council's 2015 Opinions on Several Policies and Measures for Vigorously Advancing Popular Entrepreneurship and Innovation)[4]. This transition will involve the reining in of the tendency to overcapacity in some traditional industries and reform of the industry structure from manufacturing to service.

(b) To better promote RMB internationalization. For years, a frequent trade surplus has led to excess foreign exchange reserves, leading to constant increases in RMB prices and an undue influence over foreign trade policy. Although China still occupies first place by owning 30% of the foreign exchange reserves globally, the

---

① US leaving TPP: A great news day for China, *BBC News*, November 22, 2016, http://www.bbc.co.uk/news/world-asia-china-38060980.

② State Council Information Office PRC,B&R progress report: progress and results beyond expectations,(2016), http://www.scio.gov.cn/ztk/dtzt/34102/35189/35192/Document/1492411/1492411.htm.

③ Canton, China has shifted to domestic consumption-driven economy, growth to average at 6.5%.

④ "What's next for China?" , (2012), Mckinsey&company, http://www.mckinsey.com/global-themes/asia-pacific/whats-next-for-china.

only way to ensure the safety of these reserves is to speed up the process of RMB internationalization. To this end, in 2013, Asian Infrastructure Investment Bank (AIIB) was proposed that was officially established in 2015. RMB internationalization has been further supported by BRICS' founding of the New Development Bank (NDB) and China's setting up of RMB offshore Clearing Banks[1]. Not only will B&R inevitably turn China into a net capital exporter, but its implementation will be greatly facilitated by the more open liberalization of the capital market and the hedging of exchange rate risks during the implementation process[2].

(c) To better safeguard national security. Because China relies heavily on imported resources such as oil and gas, it must search for a constant and stable importation mode. Western Asia and AESAN are rich in energy resources, with the former being China's largest provider of crude oil[3]. By implementing B&R, China can build a long-term stable partnership with AESAN and the emerging economies of West Asia, achieving a win-win situation through highly matched needs. This cooperation could also lead to better development of the marine economy and ensure safety on the seas for ASEAN countries[4].

Progress and Status

Since the B&R concept was first proposed in 2013, China has been actively promoting strategies for its actual implementation[5] and has already achieved the

---

① The Financial upgrading under the Belt and Road, iFeng Finance, October 26, 2017, http://finance. ifeng.com/a/20171026/15747193_0.shtml.

② Zhang Yansheng, Development strategy of B&R and the road for revival, (2014), http://zt.ccln.gov. cn/xxxjp/jzjd/jj3/9613.shtml.

③ "The Belt and Road" creates new cooperation mode for emerging economies, Sohu finance, March 20, 2015, http://business.sohu.com/20150320/n410051925.shtml.

④ British media: Xi Jinping's B&R strategy to reshape the world economy, *BBC Chinese*, July 1, 2016, http://www.bbc.com/zhongwen/trad/press_review/2016/07/160701_press_review.

⑤ Wang Yiwei, B&R presents seven new features,(2017), http://theory.people.com.cn/n1/2017/0327/ c40531-29172265.html.

following substantial breakthroughs:

• According to RDCY data, by June 30, 2016, China had signed a free trade agreement (FTA) with 11 countries and a bilateral investment treaty (BIT) with 56 countries and had issued joint statements about B&R.

• Under B&R, China has tendered 38 large scale transportation infrastructure projects related to partnerships with 26 countries and over 3,000 contracted projects. It has also seen more than 40 major energy projects put into operation involving 19 countries. In the area of telecommunication network construction, China Telecom has actively engaged in B&R by building its Global Information High Speed Rail, involving 116 operators and 97 equipment manufacturers, with 30 countries having opened a total of 52 TD-LTE commercial networks, and a further 83 networks deployed in 55 countries[1].

• In terms of foreign trade, under B&R, China has constructed 52 economic and trade cooperation zones in 18 countries, 13 of them assessed at $15.6 billion total investment. According to data collected since B&R implementation in June 2016, the total amount of China's goods trade with countries along the B&R routes reached $3.1 trillion, accounting for 26% of its total foreign trade. During the same period, China's total investment in B&R reached $51.1 billion, accounting for 12% of total foreign direct investment. Between June 2013 and June 2016, China also signed $9.41 billion worth of outsourcing service contracts with B&R countries, a 33.5% increase over 2013.

• As regards construction funding, as of January 2015, China has already set up RMB clearing banks in seven countries in the B&R network (hereafter, B&R countries), since when the total amount of its cross-border RMB settlement has been more than 2.63 trillion yuan (Phoenix Finance, 2015). On April 21,2016, the NDB announced a first batch of $811 million loan projects, and on June 25 the same year, AIIB approved a $509

---

① China's Belt and Road Initiative delivers promising initial results. *China Daily*, May 7, 2017, http://europe.chinadaily.com.cn/business/2016-12/19/content_27712045.htm.

million loan for four initial projects.

In his opening speech at the May 14, 2017, Belt and Road Forum for International Cooperation (BRFIC) in Beijing, Xi Jinping promoted the forum as an international event at which participating countries could share the fruits of mutually beneficial cooperation. He also described it as an important platform for strengthening international cooperation and docking with each other's development strategy[1]. After the meeting, the International Cooperation Summit published a summary of the forum results on its official web site that included a series of cooperation consensuses, important initiatives, and pragmatic outcomes[2]. Although this summary covers a total of 76 major items and 270 specific results, it classifies them into five main categories: policy communication, facilities unicom, trade flow, capital intermediation, and cultural communication. British Prime Minister's Special Envoy and Minister of Finance Hammond attended the forum and brought Premier Li Keqiang a letter signed by British Prime Minister Teresa May. Hammond said that Britain is committed to developing a comprehensive strategic partnership between itself and China, and is willing to maintain high-level exchanges between the two countries to further strengthen bilateral trade and investment cooperation and close communication and coordination in international affairs. Li Keqiang replied that China is willing to consolidate mutual trust with the British; implement cooperation on nuclear power, finance, and other key areas; create new cooperation highlights; and raise China-UK relations and cooperation to a new level[3].

---

① "Speech by Xi Jinping at the Opening Ceremony of the 'International Cooperation Summit Forum' (Full Text)" , (2017), Belt and Road Forum for International Cooperation (BRFIC), http://www.beltandroadforum.org/n100/2017/0514/c24-407.html.

② "List of results of Belt and Road Forum for International Cooperation (Full Text)" , (2017), Belt and Road Forum for International Cooperation (BRFIC), http://www.beltandroadforum.org/n100/2017/0516/c24-422.html.

③ "Li Keqiang Meets with British Prime Minister Special Envoy and Minister of Finance Hammond" , (2017), Belt and Road Forum for International Cooperation (BRFIC), http://www.beltandroadforum.org/n100/2017/0514/c24-370.html.

In the report of 19th National Congress of the Communist Party of China opened on October 18, 2017, President Xi has emphasized the importance of the Belt and Road. He says: "…We should pursue the Belt and Road Initative as a priority, give equal emphasisto 'bringing in' and 'going global'…and increase openness and cooperation in building innovation capacity."[①]

UK Public Attitudes to B&R

The prevailing attitude of the UK public to B&R is soundly positive, with the UK becoming the first major Western country to join the Asian Infrastructure Investment Bank (AIIB) on March 12, 2015[②]. The UK, therefore, faced with predictions about the world economic situation and the urgent need to recover from economic recession, has ignored U.S. attempts to keep Western countries from partnership with China because of wariness "about a trend toward constant accommodation of China, which is not the best way to engage a rising power"[③]. The UK has also been working to build and strengthen an active constant cooperation with China on a number of aspects and has proposed combining B&R with its own Northern Powerhouse project[④]. By doing so, it would be leveraging the present "golden era of relations" with China to seek deeper and profound opportunities between the two countries[⑤].

---

① The Read of 19th National Congress of the Communist Party of China, Dr. GuoLv (with the completed report in both Chinese and English version), (2017). Sohu, http://www.sohu.com/a/198922409_788233.

② HM Treasury, UK announces plans to join Asian Infrastructure Investment Bank, (2015),https://www.gov.uk/government/news/uk-announces-plans-to-join-asian-infrastructure-investment-bank.

③ US attacks UK's "constant accommodation" with China. *Financial Times*, March 12, 2015, https://www.ft.com/content/31c4880a-c8d2-11e4-bc64-00144feab7de.

④ HM Treasury,Chancellor opens book on more than £24 billion of Northern Powerhouse investment opportunities in China,(2015),https://www.gov.uk/government/news/chancellor-opens-book-on-more-than-24-billion-of-northern-powerhouse-investment-opportunities-in-china.

⑤ China's "One Belt One Road" plan greeted with caution, *Financial Times*, November 19, (2015),https://www.ft.com/content/5c022b50-78b7-11e5-933d-efcdc3c11c89.

China's response has also been positive and passionate, meaning that the dialogue at all levels in various fields has greatly promoted China-UK cooperation[1]. The success of such practical cooperation has in turn engendered a more in-depth and positive dialogue, thereby creating a healthy and stable atmosphere[2]. In fact, according to James Sassoon, chairman of the China-Britain Business Council (CBBC) and Conservative member of the House of Lords, Britain's contribution to B&R, rather than being limited to law and financial services, may well be extended into long-term cooperation in third-country markets as well as a range of other industries, including manufacturing, agriculture, food processing, technology and education, health care and retail and logistics.

Even Theresa May, who before becoming Prime Minister questioned George Osborne's enthusiasm for China, has changed her attitude significantly on assuming the premiership and embarking on Brexit and has recognized the benefits that cooperation with China could bring to the UK[3][4]. In a recent interview, for example, she asserted that the change in UK Prime Minister would not affect the 'golden age' of China-UK relations[5]. Likewise, in her other interviews, Teresa May specifically pointed out and expressed gratitude that China had invested far more in the UK than any European country[6].

---

[1]   Ministry of Commerce of the People 's Republic of China, Northern Powerhouse, (2016), http://www.mofcom.gov.cn/article/i/ck/201605/20160501315871.shtml.

[2]   Uk Further Embraces Belt & Road Initiative. *Chian Daily*, April 14, 2017, http://usa.chinadaily.com.cn/epaper/2017-04/14/content_28930391.htm.

[3]   Theresa May: UK will be "global leader in free trade", *BBC News*, September 3, 2016, http://www.bbc.co.uk/news/uk-politics-37257006

[4]   Theresa May to visit China in bid for trade deal. *Sky News*, February 8, 2017, http://news.sky.com/story/theresa-may-to-visit-china-in-bid-for-trade-deal-10759589.

[5]   China's "One Belt, One Road", a drive for Great Britain's businesses?,China Daily, February 3, 2017, http://www.chinadaily.com.cn/opinion/2017-02/03/content_28093936.htm.

[6]   Theresa May talks trade at G20 summit in *China,Channel 4 News*, September 5, 2016, https://www.channel4.com/news/by/gary-gibbon/blogs/theresa-talks-trade-g20-summit-china.

B&R as the New Platform of China–UK Industrial Cooperation

There is no doubt that China needs to find a developed country as its long-term partner to accelerate RMB internationalization, encourage self-innovation and speed up the transition of its economy. The UK, as China's largest investment destination in Europe, has already entered a golden relationship era with China through rapid economic and trade cooperation. There are two important reasons for China to show enthusiasm for this relation: the perfect match of industry demands between the two countries and China's wish to open the gate of cooperation with other European countries through its relationship with the UK. If the UK becomes a member of the AIIB, it will greatly accelerate RMB internationalization[①], which will also be affected by Brexit but partly in the form of greater opportunities.

Whatever the Brexit outcome, China-UK cooperation will remain essential and unchangeable given the series of reports already released by the British government to achieve a comprehensive analysis and discuss potential approaches to this cooperation. As two permanent members of the United Nations Security Council, the collaboration between China and the UK tends to make the two countries become a community of interests in global affairs. That will definitely make a huge contribution to the development of both countries, boost the economy and enhance a stable society. Given the unique advantages of each nation, as well as the existing forms of cooperation, China-UK cooperation will create greater opportunities and bring greater benefits by strengthening the existing bilateral cooperation and seeking out new cooperation opportunities in third countries.

---

① HM Treasury, Chancellor makes historic first visit to China's North West, (2015), https://www.gov.uk/government/news/chancellor-makes-historic-first-visit-to-chinas-north-west.

Northern Powerhouse

Strategic Background

• Northern Powerhouse is a national industrial strategy, put forward in 2014 by former Chancellor George Osborne and supported by Theresa May, which aims to boost economic growth in the North of England by promoting administrative reform and infrastructure construction and attracting investment in science and technology[1]. The overall aim is to make "a second London" of major cities in the three Northern regions covered: North East England (Northumberland, County Durham, Tyne and Wear and the Tees Valley), North West England (Cheshire, Cumbria, Greater Manchester, Lancashire and Merseyside), and Yorkshire and the Humber (most of Yorkshire, North Lincolnshire and North East Lincolnshire). Eight of the key cities in this area are already members of the Core Cities Group formed in 1995: Birmingham, Bristol, Leeds, Liverpool, Manchester, Newcastle, Nottingham, Sheffield[2].

Strategy Implementation

To fund its goal of encouraging, developing and promoting economic growth while also improving transportation, the Northern Powerhouse initiative draws on

---

[1] "Northern prosperity is national prosperity: a strategy for revitalising the UK economy", (2012), IPPR North and the Northern Economic Futures Commission (IPPR North & NEFC), http://www.ippr.org/files/images/media/files/publication/2012/12/northern-prosperity_NEFC-final_Nov2012_9949.pdf?noredirect=1.

[2] HM Government,Northern powerhouse to benefit from industrial strategy proposals, (2017), http://northernpowerhouse.gov.uk/2017/01/northern-powerhouse-to-benefit-as-government-launches-industrial-strategy-proposals/

two financial resources: government funding and private investment[1]. As regards the first, on November 23, 2016, the UK government published the Northern Powerhouse Strategy policy paper, which details the extent of government support for the project and the four major aspects this support will cover; namely, connectivity, skills, enterprise and innovation, and trade and investment. In promoting these areas, the government will engage with such local partners as local authorities, local enterprise partnerships (LEP), and local businesses[2].

To promote private investment, the UK government-owned British Business Bank, together with LEPs, has established the Northern Powerhouse Investment Fund (NPIF), which will provide up to £400m for micro, business and equity financing[3]. Officially launched in Manchester on February 22, 2017, the fund will be operated by LEPs and growth hubs, together with local accountants, fund managers and banks, with the goal of assisting SMEs at all stages of their development[4]. In addition to financing from the UK government, the fund also receives support from the European Regional Development Fund (ERDF) and the European Investment Bank (EIB), which still could not confirm how much influence Brexit would have on their funding plan.

In addition to funds for economic development, from the Northern Powerhouse

---

① Depani, B.N., Butcher, L. and Sandford, M, The Northern Powerhouse, (2016), https://www.google.co.uk/url?sa=t&rct=j&q=&esrc=s&source=web&cd=1&cad=rja&uact=8&ved=0ahUKEwiX-dbenObTAhVGFMAKHeMoBV8QFggnMAA&url=http%3A%2F%2Fresearchbriefings.files.parliament.uk%2Fdocuments%2FCBP-7676%2FCBP-7676.pdf&usg=AFQjCNGjuTdKaPVXudUV4ioFrbP1hmJypg&sig2=Jr-glaYPGOiCLPwvo9nKNg.

② HM Government,Northern Powerhouse Strategy,(2016), https://www.liverpoollep.org/wp-content/uploads/2016/11/Northern-Powerhouse-Strategy-November-2016.pdf.

③ "Launch of £400m Northern Powerhouse investment fund" , (2017), *UK Business Angels Association*, https://www.ukbusinessangelsassociation.org.uk/news/launch-400m-northern-powerhouse-investment-fund/.

④ "£400m Northern Powerhouse Investment Fund opens for business in Leeds" , (2017), Leeds City Region Enterprise Partnership, http://www.the-lep.com/news-and-blog/news/northern-powerhouse-investment-fund-opens-for-busi/.

Strategy, the British government is committed to allocating £150 billion for health care in the northern region[1] over the next four years, as well as £45 billion for upgrading university education facilities, £13 billion for building a northern rail transport hub, and £2.7 billion for constructing northeast highways between cities. It will also allot £50 billion for constructing the High Speed 2 (HS2) railway linking Birmingham (as the Northern centre) with London, the East Midlands, Leeds and Manchester. Other investments include £235 million for the Sir Henry Royce Institute for advanced materials research and innovation in Manchester; £113 million for the Warrington Computer Research and Development Centre; £78 million for the Manchester factory, theatre and exhibition centre; and £20 million for the Newcastle Aged Medical Research Centre. The first pilot city for the gradual decentralization of power will be Manchester, which will become the first city not in the London area to be managed by a directly elected mayor. The first mayoral election will be held in 2017, after which the mayor will take control of billions of pounds of public funds with great freedom to use them for city construction and development[2].

According to the briefing note made by Civil Engineering Contractors Association (CECA), George Osborne announced that the UK government will use a total of £300 million to support Northern Powerhouse through a series of proposals linked to the Transport for the North (TFN) for Northern Transport Strategy, which covers all transportation in Northern England, including highways, railways and ports[3]. Northern enterprise investment projects will thus cover harbours, airports, railways, marine

---

[1]   "CECA Briefing: Budget 2016" , (2016), Civil Engineering Contractors Association (CECA), http://www.ceca.co.uk/media/217688/ceca-briefing-budget-2016-16-march-2016.pdf.

[2]   "Northern Powerhouse Strategy" , (2016), HM Government, https://www.gov.uk/government/uploads/system/uploads/attachment_data/file/571562/NPH_strategy_web.pdf.

[3]   "Budget 2016" , (2016), HM Treasury, https://www.gov.uk/government/uploads/system/uploads/attachment_data/file/508193/HMT_Budget_2016_Web_Accessible.pdf.

engineering and organic energy, as well as myriad other fields[①].

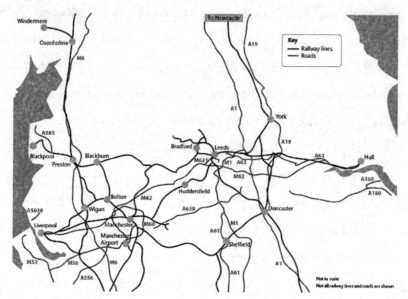

Figure 5–2　Northern Powerhouse Transportation Investment Blueprint[②]
(Department for Transport et al., 2015)

Corporations' investment projects mainly include the construction of ports, airports, railways, marine engineering and energy resources, From the investigation of 2016, corporations have invested £1.11 billion in the Humber, £1.27 billion in Liverpool, £1.8 billion in Greater Manchester, £232 million in the North East of England, and £800 million in Sheffield[③].

Interestingly, however, some researchers have argued that North East England is more likely than the other regions to be 'abandoned', prompting BBC News to make a comparative chart of the exact funding to these three major investment areas:

①　"CECA Briefing: Budget 2016", (2016), Civil Engineering Contractors Association (CECA), http://www.ceca.co.uk/media/217688/ceca-briefing-budget-2016-16-march-2016.pdf.

②　Figure source: UK gov, "Government boost for Northern Powerhouse, (2015), https://www.gov.uk/government/news/government-boost-for-northern-powerhouse.

③　*Northern Powerhouse* (2016), Ministry of Commerce of the People's Republic of China, http://www.mofcom.gov.cn/article/i/ck/201605/20160501315871.shtml.

Table 5-1　Northern Powerhouse Infrastructure spending[1]

Region	Total Infrastructure Spending	Number of Projects	Spending/person
North West	£41.4bn	88	£5771
North East	£5.9bn	27	£2230
Yorkshire and The Humber	£9.0bn	29	£1684

Obviously, there is still much room for investment in North East England's infrastructure[2], especially given that although the planned HS2 will link London, Birmingham, the East Midlands, Leeds and Manchester, there is as yet no clear plan for a high-speed railway to link Newcastle, the largest city in the north, with the other cities. The total number of investment projects in North East England is also far lower than for North West England. Hence, although North West England admittedly has a relatively higher number of key cities, the data show a huge potential for additional investment in the North East.

UK Access to B&R Participation

During President Xi's 2015 visit to the UK[3], five main B&R-related initiatives

---

① Funding plans show Northern Powerhouse split, *BBC News*, November 22, 2016, http://www.bbc.co.uk/news/uk-england-38054837.

② UK infrastructure: unlocking UK cities and commercial property, (2015), Bilfinger GVA, https://www.google.co.uk/url?sa=t&rct=j&q=&esrc=s&source=web&cd=1&cad=rja&uact=8&ved=0ahUKEwjR2qL2nObTAhVDI8AKHWhoAVIQFggjMAA&url=http%3A%2F%2Fwww.gva.co.uk%2Fresearch%2Funlocking-uk-cities-and-commercial-property%2F&usg=AFQjCNFh7LEDHWQz0LgSZ6KQnReAlEMUIA&sig2=10-gOLQwynloz8LBrj2B2g.

③ Ministry of Foreign Affairs of the People's Republic of China (MFA), Li Keqiang Attends the 17th China-EU Summit and Visit Belgium, Pays an Official Visit to France and Visits the Headquarters of the Organization for Economic Cooperation and Development, (2015), http://www.fmprc.gov.cn/mfa_eng/topics_665678/lkqcxdsqczgomldrhwbsfblsdfgjxzsfwbfwjjhzyfzzzzb/.

were proposed: policy coordination, facilities connectivity, unimpeded trade, financial integration and a people-to-people bond[1]. The specific areas and modes of possible UK-China cooperation can be broadly classified into four main types: infrastructure projects, services, cultural industries and marine industries[2].

As regards key infrastructure construction, the 2016 approval of the Hinkley Point C nuclear power station project together with China's strong will to back the UK's HS2 railway project represents a first collaborative step[3]. The challenge now is to deepen this cooperation in the most effective manner possible[4]. For example, to construct its B&R networks, China must set up financial service platforms in all participating countries and gradually establish a legal security system[5]. However, because of the UK's leading position in international financing, law, consulting and service industries[6], most B&R countries use British and U.S. common law rather than the civil law employed in China. This reality increases China's need for British support and cooperation in the establishment of the B&R legal protection system, especially given the magnitude of the

---

① "Vision and actions on jointly building Belt and Road", China Org CN ,http://www.china.org.cn/chinese/2015-09/15/content_36591064_2.htm.

② Embassy of the People's Republic of China in UK (EPRCU), Ambassador Liu Xiaoming's keynote speech at the Investment Institutional Forum in 2016: grasping the opportunity of B&R to create a better future,(2016),http://www.chinese-embassy.org.uk/chn/dsxx/dashijianghua/2016niandashijianghua/t1417771.htm.

③ China and UK signed a total of 40 billion pounds of cooperation agreements, *BBC Chinese*, October 21, 2015, http://www.bbc.com/zhongwen/simp/uk/2015/10/151021_uk_xi_visit_deals.

④ David Moore, The Northern Powerhouse and wider opportunities for Chinese investment in UK infrastructure, (2016), http://www.lexology.com/library/detail.aspx?g=bcfe5b57-c298-4170-a1ee-4ffafb3cb369.

⑤ Department for Business, Innovation & Skills (BIS), UK Industry Performance Report-Based on the UK Construction Industry Key Performance Indicators,(2015), https://www.glenigan.com/sites/default/files/UK_Industry_Performance_Report_2015_883.pdf.

⑥ Department for Business, Innovation & Skills (BIS),Industrial strategy: UK sector analysis, (2012), https://www.gov.uk/government/uploads/system/uploads/attachment_data/file/34607/12-1140-industrial-strategy-uk-sector-analysis.pdf.

potential and space for UK-China cooperation in these fields[1].

In the area of culture, given Britain's strong and diverse educational, film and television, and media industries, if China and Britain can implement talent exchange programs, it will promote Chinese innovation in these fields. In particular, B&R will provide an excellent opportunity for boosting UK-China cooperation in the film, television, and media industries, which to date has been minimal. Increased collaboration in the cultural industries could also improve mutual understanding between the Chinese and British people, which would benefit cooperation in other fields[2].

Likewise, in establishing its 21st Century Maritime Silk Road, China would benefit from the UK's world-class expertise in marine sciences and technology research and development[3]; in particular, as regards marine economic development, marine energy use and international shipping rules, all of which China lacks but urgently needs. If China and the UK can strengthen cooperation in these areas, it would greatly benefit construction of the B&R maritime connections[4].

The specific modes of cooperation between China and Britain can be divided into

① "One Belt One Road: a role for UK companies in developing china's new initiative - new opportunities in china and beyond", (2015), China-Britain Business Council, http://www.cbbc.org/sectors/one-belt,-one-road/.

② Ministry of Education of the People's Republic of China (MEPRC), List of key cooperation projects for the next 3-5 years, (2016), http://www.moe.gov.cn/jyb_xwfb/moe_1946/fj_2016/201612/t20161208_291172.html.

③ Department for Business, Innovation & Skills (BIS), UK and China agree multi-million-pound global research deals, (2014), https://www.gov.uk/government/news/uk-and-china-agree-multi-milion-pound-global-research-deals.

④ Department for International Trade, UK government ministers attend first maritime trade mission in China, (2017), https://www.gov.uk/government/news/uk-government-ministers-attend-first-maritime-trade-mission-in-china.

three major forms dependent on the different destinations of project implementation[1][2].

The first mode relates to UK-based projects such as the China-UK high-speed rail project and UK scientific and technological innovation projects in which Chinese companies are participating directly. These latter include Cocoon Networks' efforts to set up a technology incubator in London that will be the largest single incubator in the area and the largest innovation centre in Europe. This incubator will also be the first China-funded centre in Europe for nurturing scientific and technological start-up enterprises and facilitating technology transfer.

The second mode refers to China-based science and technology projects for which effective talent exchange is indispensable to successful innovation. China can enhance the overall quality of its local talent by directly importing British science and technology projects and university education projects and localizing British higher education.

The third mode concerns projects based in third-party markets in which the UK could cooperate with China on infrastructure, energy use and marine safety while also providing legal advice and financial services. For example, the British Petroleum and Natural Gas Company (BP) has provided consulting services for PetroChina's projects in Iraq and CNOOC's projects in Indonesia, while the UK law office Linklaters has offered legal services for financing China's coal-electricity integration project in Pakistan.

---

① Embassy of the People's Republic of China in UK (EPRCU), Beginning of China-UK strategic partnership for globalization – comments from Minister of Foreign Affairs Wang Yi about President Xi Jinping's state visit to Britain, (2015), http://www.chinese-embassy.org.uk/chn/zt/xifangying2015/t1308691.htm.

② Embassy of the People's Republic of China in UK (EPRCU). Achievements between China and Britain during Xi Jinping's state visit to the United Kingdom, (2015),http://www.chinese-embassy.org.uk/chn/zygx/zzwl/t1308215.htm.

Uncertainties for China-UK B&R Collaboration

Concerns about China's Investment Capabilities and Methods

As China's largest contemporary project – one involving numerous related countries, regions, populations and markets – B&R has prompted many questions about China's capability to successfully operate the project and the methods it will use to accomplish its goals. For example, a 2017 report by Fitch Ratings, one of the U.S.'s Big Three nationally recognized statistical rating organizations (NRSRO), claimed that China's plan to invest hundreds of millions of dollars in emerging markets may bring benefits for China but may create new asset quality problems. Such loan problems, however, 'may take a long time to emerge, as China's policy banks that are most heavily involved in B&R often offer very generous grace and repayment periods and disclosure is generally poor compared with commercial banks and non-Chinese development banks'[1].

The suspicions of traditional financial investment banks and rating agencies have also been raised by China's plan to build harbours, highways and railways in less developed Eurasian and African countries as the first attempt under B&R to stimulate global economic growth. Fitch Ratings, for example, has claimed that the total cost of B&R projects will exceed $900 billion, most from policy banks and large commercial banks[2]. One problem with financing is that Chinese banks, unlike experienced international commercial banks and multilateral lenders, find it difficult to identify the most beneficial, quality projects so as to better manage risk. Fitch Ratings also questioned that some counties involved in B&R have speculation suspects to use

---

[1] Fitch warns on expected returns from One Belt, One Road, *Financial Times*, January 25, 2017, https://www.ft.com/content/c67b0c05-8f3f-3ba5-8219-e957a90646d1.

[2] China warned of risk to banks from One Belt, One Road initiative, *Financial Times*, January 26, 2017, https://www.ft.com/content/6076cf9a-e38e-11e6-8405-9e5580d6e5fb.

investment to relieve and whitewash their tight domestic public financial situation[①].

These voices of doubt, however, reflect the viewpoints of historically capitalist countries, which still tend to offer China few opportunities to participate in international investment and construction despite its now being 'the world's second economic engine'. This reluctance itself creates concerns, even among B&R countries, about China's capability to actually execute projects. The traditional economic powers also fail to fully understand – and are suspicious of – China's goodwill and feeling of responsibility to assist third-world countries and emerging economies develop and succeed economically.

Faced with these questions, China's only recourse is to prove its own decision-making capacity through regional successes and efficient practical achievements under B&R. Developing countries involved in B&R should also show their own determination to develop themselves rather than relying on China's funds without long-term plans. The economic development, market expansion and increased employment that will occur in these participating nations will be direct proof of B&R's significance and China's foresight as its initiator.

Concerns about China's Growing Influence

The Counterterrorism Law of the People's Republic of China, issued and enacted on January 2016, codifies the Chinese military's right to set up bases overseas and thus enables China's more active participation in military operations abroad. This law is therefore of great significance for B&R implementation[②] in that projects in unstable areas will inevitably test China's ability to avoid overseas conflicts. In Pakistan, for

---

① China warned of risk to banks from One Belt, One Road initiative, *Financial Times*, January 26, 2017, https://www.ft.com/content/6076cf9a-e38e-11e6-8405-9e5580d6e5fb.

② "Counterterrorism Law of the People's Republic of China", (2015), *Beijing University Law Archive*, http://lawinfochina.com/display.aspx?id=20901&lib=law.

example, the government has deployed 10,000 soldiers to protect projects in which China has invested, while in Afghanistan, a China-funded copper project is protected by the U.S. military, an arrangement that will eventually become unsustainable. China's best solution for protecting B&R projects overseas, therefore, would be to send its own armed forces to furnish protection.

Nevertheless, any overseas military action by China may lead some countries to overestimate B&R's political and national security threat. As a result, the "China threat theory" has resurfaced and become the focus of debate and doubts about B&R's strategic purposes. For instance, in a Financial Times interview, a former US official suggested that the Chinese military may hope to garner political and financial support from B&R based on claims from senior generals in the People's Liberation Army that B&R would be a security investment[1].

Another B&R analysis, which examined China's 21st Century Maritime Silk Road Initiative (MSRI) as a political strategy, questioned China's ultimate goal in constructing harbours in Sri Lanka, Bangladesh, Pakistan and other countries. The analysts suspected that these harbour projects were intended to provide financing for the build-up of secret overseas warship bases and prepare for the establishment of a "string of pearls" type double-directional naval logistics line in the Indian ocean[2].

Such continued doubts in the U.S. media about China's behind the scenes motivation has led some developed countries to hesitate in their participation in B&R. In Britain also, some voices see conspiracy in B&R implementation. Franklin Allen, for example, Wharton professor and Executive Director of Imperial College's Brevan Howard Centre, argued that although B&R is 'an economic initiative...along the way

---

① China's Great Game: Road to a new empire, *Financial Times*, October 12, 2015, https://www.ft.com/content/6e098274-587a-11e5-a28b-50226830d644.

② Jean-Marc F. Blanchard, "Probing China's Twenty-First-Century Maritime Silk Road Initiative (MSRI): An Examination of MSRI Narratives," *Geopolitics*, Volume 22, Issue 2, 2017.

China will expand its military bases and so forth. On the sea routes they will develop their military capability and on the land routes, too'[1].

To counter these over-interpretations and prejudices, China should make full use of the opportunities for China-UK cooperation in the media and culture industry to dissuade the public from such biases. It would also be a good beginning for China to make its voice heard in the EU and U.S. so as to gradually improve unfavorable political attitudes towards China's development of its maritime power.

Risk for Third-party Markets

According to Nathan Hayes, economist at Timetric's Construction Intelligence Centre, Britain could promote cross-sector cooperation by participating in B&R sub-projects in the glowing markets along its routes. He also pointed out, however, that most countries along these routes are emerging markets with potential risks. Hence, foreign exchange fluctuation, recession and government activities could all lead to uncertainty and inherent danger for the UK, which should thus spend more time and effort on project management, leading possibly to less-than-estimated China-UK cooperation in third-party markets[2].

In CBBC China-Britain Belt and Road Guide 2016 report, also explained that besides being an economic initiative, B&R is also 'a major geopolitical one', meaning that China-UK cooperation in third-party markets must be carefully handled because of the gamut of risks, from legal and financial challenges to political or social instability

---

[1] "Where will China's 'One Belt, One Road' initiative lead?" , Knowledge Wharton, (2017),http:// knowledge.wharton.upenn.edu/article/can-chinas-one-belt-one-road-initiative-match-the-hype/.

[2] UK hopes to underpin developments, *China Daily*, April 23, 2017, http://www.chinadaily.com.cn/ world/2017-04/23/content_29047329.htm.

and regional disputes[①]. Although both China and the UK will face the same risks in such markets, as the less experienced partner, China will need the assistance of fully experienced developed countries like Britain. Hence, identifying a readily available framework that can reduce the potential risks of cooperation in third-party markets will be more pragmatic and rational than reducing the cooperation itself.

Hidden Danger: Tibet issue

One hidden danger for China-UK cooperation is the two nations' dispute over Tibet, a disagreement that harks back to the seventeenth century and two British invasions of that nation. This sensitive issue led to a bottoming out of China-UK relations in 2013 when prime minister David Cameron met with the 14th Dalai Lama[②], leading to the cancellation or postponement of many investment projects. The British government's current attitude towards the Tibet issue, however, is more prudent, with the Dalai Lama's 2015 request for a meeting with the Prime Minister being rejected.

Nevertheless, the Dalai Lama and Tibetan separatists have not given up on establishing contact with the British, making Tibet a hidden threat to the future of China-UK relations. Some researchers have even applied the term 'Dalai Lama effect' to the Chinese government's policy of reducing national exports to countries or regions that meet with the Dalai Lama. Hence, to avoid damaging China-UK cooperative relations through future contact with Tibetan separatists, the British government must clarify its position on the Tibet issue to prevent any possible controversial actions.

---

① One Belt One Road: a role for UK companies in developing china's new initiative - new opportunities in china and beyond, China-Britain Business Council, May 18, 2015, http://www.cbbc.org/sectors/one-belt,-one-road/.

② David Cameron "must apologise" for meeting Dalai Lama to restore diplomatic relations with China,*Independent*, May 7, 2013, http://www.independent.co.uk/news/uk/politics/david-cameron-must-apologise-for-meeting-dalai-lama-to-restore-diplomatic-relations-with-china-8606341.html.

China-UK cooperation: Influence and Opportunities

Influence of Brexit

Since Britain officially triggered Article 50 on March 29, 2017, Brexit and its follow-up effect has been a hot topic internationally. Completion of the entire process within the next two years means that Britain must find replacement markets in order to overcome economic and political barriers. Brexit will inevitably have a deep impact on the global economic structure at a time when the global industrial structure is finally enjoying a slow recovery from the 2008 economic crisis. This crisis caused such damaging problems as heavy debt pressure, tight monetary environments and serious unemployment in many developed countries, thereby changing their role on the world stage. Brexit is now adding more uncertainty, raising investor risk aversion, and shaking the global market. Britain, as one of the world's financial centers, has a far-reaching effect on cross-border credit and offshore finance, so its departure from the EU will inevitably impact the world economy through investment, trade and finance.

In particular, because the British government lacks funds for infrastructure projects, Brexit-induced reductions in future European investment bank loans to UK projects are sure to cause funding problems for the London Crossrail subway upgrade, as well as other major infrastructure projects. On the other hand, Brexit also means that the UK can start its own trade negotiations independent of other EU countries. Nevertheless, there is still no clear answer to the question of whether the UK will continue to benefit from the EU's zero tariff policy.

Britain's exit from the EU will also be very costly. Not only will the EU charge a substantial exit fee[1], perhaps as much as €100 billion[2]. But Michel Barnier, the European Commission's chief Brexit negotiator, insists that the UK must keep paying its share of outstanding pension liabilities, loan guarantees and spending on UK-based projects until 2020. These fees will differ little from those the UK would have paid if it had stayed in the EU. In addition, based on requests from several EU member states, post-Brexit farm payments and EU administration fees have been added to the list of dues. Hence, even though there is still room for negotiation, losing EU benefits while still having to pay these charges could greatly threaten future UK development, and the UK will undoubtedly have to pay some costs no matter how the negotiation goes[3].

Another issue should not be ignored is the Brexit's impact on the UK's current key project, the Northern Powerhouse, whose funding involves the NPIF partnership of the European Regional Development Fund (ERDF) and the European Investment Bank (EIB), which has been mentioned above. Joint funding from these entities now totals as much as £145 million, accounting for 36.25% of the whole NPIF. Brexit inevitably raises concerns about whether this funding will still be invested in this project.

Brexit will also affect China-UK cooperation to a certain extent because London has become the world's second largest RMB settlement center, and the UK is an important platform for China's entry into the EU market and its acceleration of RMB internationalization[4]. Before Brexit, the UK had shown willingness to support the

---

① The multi-billion-euro exit charge that could sink Brexit talks, *The Economist*, (2017), http://www. economist.com/news/britain/21716629-bitter-argument-over-money-looms-multi-billion-euro-exit-charge-could-sink-brexit.

② Brussels hoists gross Brexit "bill" to €100bn, *Financial Times*, May 2, 2017, https://www.ft.com/content/cc7eed42-2f49-11e7-9555-23ef563ecf9a.

③ Britain will be handed £50bn exit bill by EU when Theresa May triggers Article 50, chief negotiator for Brussels warns, *The Telegraph News*, December 16, 2016, http://www.telegraph.co.uk/news/2016/12/15/britain-will-handed-50bn-exit-bill-eu-theresa-may-triggers-article/.

④ Ambassador Liu Xiaoming, "B&R provides a broader space for the China-UK cooperation", *Phoenix News*, January 24, 2017, http://news.ifeng.com/a/20170124/50622652_0.shtml.

RMB's inclusion in the International Monetary Fund's (IMF) upcoming Special Drawing Rights (SDR) subject to meeting existing IMF criteria. The implementation of Brexit, however, could increase the cost of China's strategy to promote the UK's use of the RMB in the EU, thereby compounding the difficulty of employing the UK as its primary channel for RMB internationalization dialogue with the EU. The UK for its part may lose its importance as China's main strategic partner in RMB internationalization[1]. Nonetheless, in an interview at the annual meeting of Hainan Province in Bo'Ao Forum for Asia March 2017, Li Ruokuo, the former chairman of the Export-Import Bank of China, emphasized that the post Brexit trade negotiations between China and the UK could promote fruitful relationships between the two countries.

Obviously, opportunity never comes without risks – the UK must strengthen its cooperation with other countries outside the European Union, while China, by leveraging the relationship built with the UK in recent years, can serve as the powerful, solid partner. Nor is the opportunity the UK's alone; the collaboration will also bring great opportunity to China. These opportunities may well extend to greater cooperation with EU countries after Brexit weakens EU integration.

Competitive Industries in UK and Opportunities for Cooperation

Given the current industrial structures in China and the UK, the focus of their industrial cooperation in the next few years should be to strengthen collaboration between the former's manufacturing industry and the latter's high-end service industry, as well as in science and technology innovation[2]. China's current economic

---

① RMB Internationalization Spreads Wings with 'Belt and Road' Strategy, China Us Focus, June 8, 2015, http://www.chinausfocus.com/finance-economy/rmb-internationalization-spreads-wings-with-belt-and-road-strategy.

② The state council of the People's Republic of China (PRC), China, Britain hold security dialogue, agree to strengthen cooperation, (2017), http://english.gov.cn/news/international_exchanges/2017/02/19/content_281475572247225.htm.

transformation, especially, calls for better cooperation between manufacturing and service industries to accelerate industrial upgrading and realize the perfect integration of Chinese and English resources under B&R.

Although China has already achieved gratifying results in some area of scientific and technological innovation, the independent innovation capability of its manufacturing industry is still weak, research supporting industrial upgrade remains insufficient, and technology transfer supply chains are still experiencing bottlenecks. Hence, China's collaboration with the UK should focus heavily on scientific and technological innovation. In particular, to achieve a win-win situation, China should consider not only traditionally strong UK industries like marine technology and marine safety but also industries targeted by the UK's current industrial strategy[①].

According to the British government's latest green paper, 'Building Our Industrial Strategy'[②], the UK has eight key industries: clean energy, robotics and artificial intelligence, satellite and space technology, health care and pharmaceutical technology, manufacturing technology and materials, biological science and technology, quantum technology, and transformation of digital technology (including supercomputing, advanced modeling and 5G mobile network technology). The government has thus proposed plans to increase R&D investment by £4.7 billion over the 2020-2021 period; establish a new industrial strategy fund for robots, clean energy and biotechnology; and fund £100 million to strengthen biomedical research and £100 million to encourage university cooperation in technology transfer and related business cooperation. Not only are these technical areas critical and in high demand, but the UK has sufficient knowledge and skills to develop new technologies. China-UK collaboration should

---

① British Consulate General Shanghai,Minister celebrates successful commitment of £200m in UK-China research and innovation collaboration, (2016),https://www.gov.uk/government/world-location-news/minister-celebrates-successful-commitment-of-200m-in-uk-china-research-and-innovation-collaboration.

② HM Government,*Building our industrial strategy*,(2017),https://www.gov.uk/government/uploads/system/uploads/attachment_data/file/611705/building-our-industrial-strategy-green-paper.pdf.

thus include these industries in its consideration of cooperation possibilities. Science and technology innovations will induce the direct exchange of technologies, skills and knowledge between the two countries, which will accelerate China's accumulation of technology and give it quick access to the experience and talent required for industrial upgrading and policy adjustment.

Possible Issues in China—UK Collaboration in Science and Technology Innovation and Their Solutions

China-UK cooperation in scientific and technology innovation is bound to experience difficulties linked to differences in the two countries' information pools, policies, cultures and intellectual property rights. In terms of information exchange, information asymmetry is likely to lead to unmatched resources and an unsustainable matching process. That is, it will be difficult to maintain sustainable cooperation if China's investment cannot find fully matched investment projects.

As regards policy, China still lacks a complete and sufficient system for evaluating science and technology projects, which directly impacts technology transfer through investment in the UK. A simultaneous lack of agreed-upon operational norms for cooperative R&D and capital cooperation between the two countries also raises the possibility of practical problems. Likewise, the inconsistency of China and the UK's technical standards jeopardizes the quality of commercial products from scientific and technological projects. Moreover, the governments in both countries can be slow to approve and implement actual policy, which hinders the speed of development for science and technology projects. China-UK cooperation could also be affected by political differences and disputes or hindered by local protectionism that could damage the interests of both sides.

In terms of cultural communication, fundamental differences in history, culture, language and social systems make it likely that China and the UK will have prejudices against each other[①]. Such biases will not only harm the promotion of China-UK cooperation but could lead to disagreements between project executors and inconsistent ideas on evaluating and supervising projects.

Likewise, given the UK's long history of criticizing China for its failure to protect intellectual property, China's lack of relevant laws or codified social respect for copyright could also lead to disputes.

To gradually eliminate these four potential barriers to China-UK scientific and technological innovation cooperation, China and the UK should be devoted to cooperation, invest greater effort in building a positive social environment, and constantly polish policy norms.

Enlightenment of 19th National Congress of the Communist Party of China

The 19th National Congress of the Communist Party of China has been held in Beijing from October 18 to October 24, 2017. On October 18, 2017, President Xi made a speech entitled "Secure a Decisive Victory in Building a Moderately Prosperous Society in All Respects and Strive for the Great Success of Socialism with Chinese Characteristics for a New Era", which timely makes adjustment of the direction for the future development of the country. The report of 19th National Congress of the Communist Party of China also focuses about making China a country of innovators. In the report, President Xi says, "...we will further reform the management system for science and technology, and develop a market-oriented system for technological innovation in which enterprises are the main players and synergy is created through the joint efforts of enterprises, universities, and research institutes. We will support innovation by small and medium-sized enterprises and encourage the application

---

① Theresa May's right: we need China's money, not their friendship, *The Spectator*, August 6, 2016, https://www.spectator.co.uk/2016/08/theresa-mays-right-we-need-chinas-money-not-their-friendship/#.

of advances in science and technology. We will foster a culture of innovation, and strengthen the creation, protection, and application of intellectual property."[1] This further expresses the determination of China to gradually eliminate the barriers in the international technology collaboration arising from the intellectual property protection. It is expected that in a short period of time, China's scientific and technological potential will be greatly released, the social development brought about by scientific and technological progress will benefit the people. "we will further reform the management system for science and technology, and develop a market-oriented system for technological innovation in which enterprises are the main players and synergy is created through the joint efforts of enterprises, universities, and research institutes" represents that the Chinese scientific research system is becoming more and more mature and complete, pushes the productivity of technology transfer.

Innovation will further play a leading role in China's economy in the national strategies, which will be more prominent in the next economic change. The national plan for science and technology development takes full account of the current conditions China is facing. The leadership of China is accurate in positioning the orientation of China's innovation and development. It also provides a strong guarantee for the technical collaboration between China and the UK.As China becomes more open and more focused on innovation and international collaboration, the UK will benefit from the following aspects in the future:

1. The policy will focus more on pursuing green development and be supportive to high technology industries. It will lead to a larger market, and the larger market will undoubtedly become more attractive to related technology companies and research institutions in the UK. Catapult Offshore Renewable Energy (Catapult ORE),

---

[1] The Read of 19th National Congress of the Communist Party of China, Dr. GuoLv (with the completed report in both Chinese and English version), (2017), Sohu, http://www.sohu.com/a/198922409_788233.

for example, has made a proposal of getting into Chinese market and participating in the joint-research of offshore wind energy technologies together with Chinese related enterprises and research institutions. The response from China is positive and enthusiastic. Catapult ORE has made a one-week-visit to China in October 2017. During this visit, they had meetings with core enterprises in the current offshore wind energy market in China, research institutions and related government departments, discussed the next collaboration step and made some in-depth negotiations.

2. Chinese IP protection system claims to be more mature in the future, and will become more effective to protect the interests of advanced technologies. This will build up a solid foundation for advanced technologies in British to enter Chinese market and carry out cooperation. In the past, the incomplete IP protection system in China has stopped many high-technologies get into the domestic market. In the report of 19th National Congress of the Communist Party of China, the emphasis on strengthening the protection of intellectual property rights is undoubtedly a great promise to overseas enterprises and a strong guarantee for the scientific and technological cooperation between China and the UK.

3. The policy will focus more on developing new models and new forms of trade, new ways of making outbound investments and promoting international cooperation on production capacity. The policy will also guarantee all businesses registered in China treated equally. The resources, technologies and advantages in China and the UK match perfectly, it is the best choice for the international capacity cooperation. The new models and new forms of trade will offer better opportunities and more options for Chinese investors, and it will bring more potential partners for the British high-tech enterprises and high-tech start-ups. Guarantee the legitimate rights and interests of investment overseas can open a convenient channel for the UK enterprises to enter Chinese market.

Modes of China–UK Collaboration on Science and Technology

The first collaborative mode is direct cooperation between the governments, including direct investment, cooperative establishment of joint foundations, and support for innovative research cooperation programmes. For example, the UK-China Research and Innovation Partnership Fund, which is part of the UK's Newton Fund put up by David Cameron's visit in December 2013[1], has already carried out 44 projects involving 130 fellowships with 85 Chinese and 57 British organizations. Based on an agreement on China-UK scientific and technological cooperation, the two countries have signed more than 20 counterpart agreements or memoranda in multiple areas, including basic research, health, agriculture and aerospace[2]. It is thus essential that China and the UK publish a series of joint science and technology cooperation norms so that China can build an effective evaluation system for such projects and establish regulations on copyright protection across countries.

The second collaborative mode is cooperation between scientific research institutes and universities. For instance, the Chinese Academy of Sciences and British Imperial College of Technology have been working closely together for several years, and the British Research Council (RCUK) has also set up joint research projects with the Chinese Academy of Sciences on solar fuel and synthetic biology. Such direct cooperation between the most cutting-edge scientific research institutes and universities is capable of generating many new scientific achievements[3].

The third mode is direct collaboration between firms and universities, a strategy that, like the Silicon Valley mode, has been identified by research as the most attractive

---

① Newton Fund, British Council, 2017, https://www.britishcouncil.org/education/science/newton.

② Embassy of the People 's Republic of China in UK (EPRCU), *China-UK cooperation in science and technology sector*, (2010), http://www.chinese-embassy.org.uk/chn/kjjl/t688734.htm.

③ Department for Culture, Media & Sport, *UK and China join forces to boost creative and technology industries*, (2015), https://www.gov.uk/government/news/uk-and-china-join-forces-to-boost-creative-and-technology-industries.

model for boosting innovation[①]. If China's enterprises could establish branches in the UK and cooperate with UK universities, they could eliminate the original communication barriers caused by time differences and distance, leading to faster and better commercialization of scientific and technological innovation. For example, Cocoon Networks' establishment at the University of East Anglia of a fund for research on low-carbon environmental protection includes a PPP model designed to improve capital liquidity and make a clearer target for investment. Such a model can filter the most practical and innovation technology projects and generate more commercial and innovative achievements in joint China-UK projects[②].

The fourth mode is direct collaboration between Chinese and UK universities, including talent exchange programmes that not only nurture high-quality talents and benefit both countries through knowledge spill-over but also attract Chinese investment through their students. That is, whereas the cultivation of an entrepreneurial spirit in foreign students often contributes to the establishment of high-level enterprises, entrepreneurs also tend to invest in the city or country in which their children are studying, especially in the area of real estate. For example, the Chinese Ministry of Education has signed a "Memorandum of Understanding of the Confucius Institute Headquarters/National Hanban and the British Council for Culture and Education (2016-2020)", announcing that within the next three to five years, China will continue to support five years of study with the UK project to promote cooperation in language teaching and encourage talent exchange[③].

The fifth is the multi-level, multi-field cooperation between China and the UK's

---

① Stephen B.Adams, "Growing where you are planted: Exogenous firms and the seeding of Silicon Valley", *Research Policy* Volume 40, Issue 3, April 2011, pp.368–379.

② Embassy of the People's Republic of China in UK (EPRCU), *A Brief Introduction to China-UK Intergovernmental Cooperation in Science and Technology*, (2010), http://www.chinese-embassy.org.uk/chn/zygx/kjjl/t422158.htm.

③ British Council, Newton Fund, (2017), https://www.britishcouncil.org/education/science/newton.

incubators, venture capital funds, and start-ups, which latter have much space for cooperation in capital operations and technology research and development. On the platform of cooperative incubators from both countries, the support of the UK and China governments would ensure unimpeded venture capital investment in start-up enterprises in both nations. Such investment would help the Chinese and British incubators, venture capitalists, and start-ups make full use of their respective advantages and strengths and greatly promote the development of SMEs, create more jobs and promote technology innovation. For instance, in February 2017, Tus-Holdings visited London, Cambridge and Newcastle to lay the foundation for the establishment in Northern England of innovation parks and entrepreneurial ecosystems.

Effects and Opportunities for China-UK Cooperation in Third-party Markets

The concept of "third-party market cooperation" by China was first introduced by Li Keqiang, premier of the PRC's State Council, during his June 2015 visit to Belgium and France, when he formally announced the "China-France Joint Statement on Third Party Market Cooperation" with France. The term refers primarily to a pattern of China working with developed countries to expand markets in developing (i.e., third-party) countries. As widely discussed in the literature, although China currently has the most complete industrial sectors in the world and is the core of the global industrial chain, its industrialization technology is only moderately developed and needs improvement. Developed countries, in contrast, have advanced technology and equipment but lack sufficient production capacity to effectively develop the emerging markets. At the same time, a large number of developing countries lack both the technology and funds needed to enhance their economies. Hence, in its third-party market cooperation, China will take advantage of its great production capacity and provide industrial products, while developed countries will use their own rich experience to assist market development, thereby promoting tripartite economic mutual benefit and a win-win situation. The UK can cooperate with China on whichever platform the third-party country provides, making full use of its own rich experience, advanced technology and comprehensive professional services.

The infrastructure needs in regions outside Asia are also extensive, especially in Africa whose electricity generation the United Nations estimates at only 4% of global output. Even in South Africa, which has the largest generating capacity on the continent, the current electricity shortage is still at a severe stage. Due to the old equipment, poor management and other issues, ESKOM, who is the supplier of 95% power in South Africa, has to frequently switch the power limit. If South Africa's economy grows at a rate of 3%, the power gap in South Africa will reach 18000 megawatts in 2030, according to the South African Institute for racial studies[①].The urgent need to construct infrastructure in this area represents a huge opportunity for China-UK cooperation.

Coalition of the Belt and Road &Northern Powerhouse

Northern Powerhouse: a British Silk Road?

During President Xi Jinping's October 2015 visit to the UK, the two countries made the "China-UK Joint Declaration on Building a Global Comprehensive Strategic Partnership for the 21st Century"[②], which combines the nations' major strategies (Bounds, 2015) of B&R and Northern Powerhouse. This combination aims to achieve a win-win situation of economic growth and innovation by leveraging important

---

① South Africa to promote the transformation of energy structure, Xinhua, March 21, 2015, http://news.xinhuanet.com/world/2015-03/21/c_127604722.htm.

② Full text: China-UK Joint Declaration on Building a Global Comprehensive Strategic Partnership for the 21st Century, *China Daily*, October 22, 2015, http://europe.chinadaily.com.cn/2015-10/22/content_22264267_3.htm.

opportunities for bilateral cooperation[①]. Subsequently, on November 10, 2016, UK Trade & Investment (UKTI) provided a better analysis of the 13 potential investing projects for Chinese investors in the form of a Northern Powerhouse Investment Portfolio (NPIP) launched as part of the eighth UK-China Economic and Financial Dialogue (EFD). The portfolio details, outlined below, were made public on the government website and widely discussed by other organizations:

Table 5–2　Northern Powerhouse Investment Portfolio (NPIP)[②]

Project Name	Region	Development Type	Description
AeroCentre	Doncaster	Offices Logistics, Industrial, Manufacturing	Working with Doncaster Sheffield Airport in the next phase of development to create new offices, logistic units and aviation hangars. The development also has Enterprise Zone status, meaning that businesses located there can benefit from significant government tax incentives.
Future Carrington	Trafford	Residential Retail, Offices, Community infra Transport	Opportunities for investment in a large scale residential and employment development in a prime location, providing over 14,000 new jobs and contributing an additional £720m Gross Value Added (GVA, the measure of the value of goods and services produced in an area, industry or sector of an economy) per annum.
Kampus	Manchester	Residential Offices	A £200m mixed use redevelopment scheme in Manchester city centre. An exciting opportunity to create new city centre apartments and retail including bars, cafes and shops.

---

①　Osborne hopes Xi can turn Northern Powerhouse into a UK Silk Road, *Financial Times*, October 20, 2015, https://www.ft.com/content/602a77cc-7647-11e5-933d-efcdc3c11c89.

②　Source: Moore, D. (2016). The Northern Powerhouse and wider opportunities for Chinese investment in UK infrastructure, http://www.lexology.com/library/detail.aspx?g=bcfe5b57-c298-4170-a1ee-4ffafb3cb369.

(continued)

Project Name	Region	Development Type	Description
Kirkstall Forge	Leeds	Residential Offices Retail	An opportunity to develop a new neighbourhood of 1,050 new homes and 330,000 + sqft of office space, retail, leisure and community space.
Liverpool Waters	Liverpool	Residential Offices Hotels and Retail	The sale of land for a full range of developmental purposes, as part of an overall £5 billion project that will transform the city's northern docks. This development also has Enterprise Zone status, meaning that businesses located there can benefit from significant government tax incentives.
MediaCityUK	Salford, Greater Manchester	Offices Media, Technology Retail Residential	Home to the BBC, ITV and over 250 smaller creative and digital businesses, this investment will double the size of MediaCityUK, creating studio, office, residential and retail space. Phase 1 was completed in 2011 and Phase 2 has outline planning permission.
Pall Mall	Liverpool	Residential Retail Offices Commercial	A major regeneration project together with Liverpool City Council to deliver 1,000 new homes, office space and retail leisure and community facilities.
Protos – Ellesmere Port	Cheshire	Energy Industrial Rail Infra Manufacturing	A range of investment opportunities in gas fired power generation, energy generation, industrial development and rail and berth infrastructure, generating over 3,000 new jobs with the first phase producing £350m GVA.
SiriusMinerals, Polyhalite Project	WhitbyNorth Yorkshire	MiningTransport Logistics	

(continued)

Project Name	Region	Development Type	Description
Stockport Exchange	Stockport	Offices Commercial Leisure Retail	An opportunity to provide funding for Stockport Exchange, a brand new mixed-use destination combining high quality office space with retail, leisure facilities and car parking. The project sponsor is Stockport Metropolitan Borough Council, the developer is MUSE Project and the value is £145m.
Unity	Doncaster	Residential Offices Commercial Leisure Retail	A major regeneration and infrastructure project that will create 3,100 new homes, a transport interchange, school and community facilities. Also provides the opportunity to invest in commercial space for manufacturing that will create 6,000 new jobs, a new power station and a materials recycling facility.
Vaux	Sunderland	Residential Offices Commercial Retail	An opportunity to invest in a £100 million development providing offices, leisure, a hotel, residential and retail space.
Advance Manufacturing Innovation District	Sheffield	Residential Offices Commercial Leisure Retail	An opportunity to invest in a 2,000+ acre centre of excellence for innovation-led advanced manufacturing in metals and materials, around which 4,000 new homes will be built. The developers are Sheffield and Rotherham Councils; University of Sheffield; Sheffield Hallam University; Harworth Estates; Sheffield Business Park Project. The project size is estimated to be in excess of £1 billion.

The targets of Chinese investors are no longer limited to London, Oxford, Cambridge and other traditional scientific and technological innovation clusters. In December 2016, Tus-Holdings signed a cooperation agreement with Newcastle council to build collaboration in the fields of marine technology and biomedical. With its unique and mature innovation mechanism, Tus-Holdings aims to launch a complete supply chain onto the market, from technology innovation and transfer to commercialisation, with suitable investment to enhance technology development in between China and UK and the economy boost.

The next section uses UK government data to summarize the growth details of the Northern Powerhouse initiative over the three-year period from 2014 to 2016 with a focus on the opportunities in four key cities: Newcastle (North East England's largest city), Liverpool and Manchester (its two large conurbations) and Leeds (the largest settlement in Yorkshire and the Humber).

Northern Powerhouse Growth Deal

Growth Deals aim at providing funds for LEPs to promote projects benefiting the local area and economy. Because project funding is limited only to the enterprises, the related government data accurately reflect the actual effect on SMEs and entrepreneurships, which is summarized below:

Table 5–3　Details of Growth Deal [1]

Region's Local Growth Fund Award	Growth Deal One (July 2014)	Growth Deal Two (Jan 2015)	Growth Deal Three (Nov 2016)	Region's Total Fund
Cheshire and Warrington	£142.7m	£15.1m	£43.3m	£201.1m
Cumbria	£26.8m	£20.9m	£12.7m	£60.4m
Greater Manchester	£476.7m	£56.6m	£130.1m	£663.4m
Humber	£103.7m	£9.9m	£27.9m	£141.5m
Lancashire	£233.9m	£17.2m	£69.8m	£320.9m
Leeds City Region	£572.9m	£54.6m	£67.5m	£695m
Liverpool City Region	£229.3m	£31.6m	£72.0m	£332.9m

---

① Source: Department for Communities and Local Government, Northern Powerhouse: Growth Deals, (2017), https://www.gov.uk/government/publications/northern-powerhouse-growth-deals.

(continued)

Region's Local Growth Fund Award	Growth Deal One (July 2014)	Growth Deal Two (Jan 2015)	Growth Deal Three (Nov 2016)	Region's Total Fund
North East	£289.3m	£40.6m	£49.7m	£379.6m
Sheffield City Region	£297m	£31m	£37m	£365m
Tees Valley	£90.3m	£13.9m	£21.8m	£126m
York, North Yorkshire and East Riding	£110.1m	£12.1m	£23.7m	£145.9m

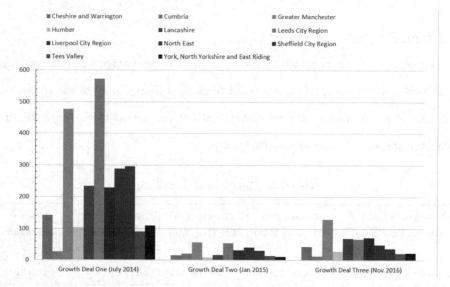

Figure 5–3   Region's local growth fund award[①]

As the above chart illustrates, the Leeds City Region rather surprisingly ranks highest with a £572.9 million growth fund (and retains first place with a total investment amount of £694.9 million) followed by Manchester with a total investment of only

---

① Data source:Department for Communities and Local Government, Northern Powerhouse: Growth Deals, (2017), https://www.gov.uk/government/publications/northern-powerhouse-growth-deals.The figure is drawn based on the data provided by authors.

£663.4 million[1]. Nonetheless, even though these figures seem to imply that Leeds City Region received the most Northern Powerhouse funding, growth deals are only part of the initiative's financing. It is in fact Manchester that benefitted from the most funding, including monies from the Northern Powerhouse Investment Fund, with investments made in transportation, health care and research.In reality, the growth deal details may reflect Leeds's position as the most enterprising city, with the most active SMEs, even though the remaining Northern England cities also have investment potential. It is also worth noting that Newcastle, North East England's largest city, is not treated statistically as a single metropolis but rather incorporated into the North East region.

Opportunities in Newcastle

According to Lord O'Neill, Commercial Secretary to the Treasury, the huge investment in Science Central has made Newcastle the core of the Northern Powerhouse, a centre with"… unprecedented opportunities for private sector investment into the Northern Powerhouse" (Newcastle University Press Office, June 2016). He also called Legal&General Capital's announcement of its collaboration with Newcastle City Council and Newcastle University "a landmark regeneration project that will bring enormous benefits to the area…fantastic news for Newcastle"[2].

Even before Legal & General Capital provided £350 million to support Newcastle's new technology and innovation cluster, the hundreds of millions already invested in science and technology R&D in the city since 2012 had prompted former Prime Minister Gordon Brown to dub it a "science city" with Science Central as its major landmark. Hence, according to Newcastle University Vice-Chancellor Chris Brink, the

---

① Department for Communities and Local Government, Northern Powerhouse: Growth Deals, (2017), https://www.gov.uk/government/publications/northern-powerhouse-growth-deals.

② Government Minister hails Newcastle's role in Northern Powerhouse after science investment, Chronicle Live, June 16, 2016, http://www.chroniclelive.co.uk/business/business-news/government-minister-hails-newcastles-role-11484796.

Legal & General Capital project not only reflects "what has been achieved so far" but is a "testament to the potential of Science Central as an exemplar of sustainable urban development" though the announcement of our three National centers – the National Centre for Ageing Science and Innovation, the National Institute for Smart Data Innovation (NISDI) and the EPSRC National Centre for Energy Systems Integration – this investment will take us a step closer to realising our vision for Science Central.[1]

Newcastle is not only strong in scientific research but benefits from a talent pool drawn from the top UK universities. For example, the University of Newcastle and the Newcastle upon Tyne Hospitals NHS Foundation Trust are among the world's leading centres for the study of rare and debilitating genetic diseases, particularly neuromuscular disorders. Likewise, the Northumbria University School of Design, which has enjoyed over 10 years of research cooperation with such companies as Philips and Unilever, provides innovative design expertise to multinational and national manufacturing and service sector. Northumbria University also specializes in supporting digital forensics, fuzzy systems and machine learning, as well as automated motion recognition and surveillance of key industrial and professional applications[2].

As North East England's largest city, Newcastle can expect the following new opportunities from China-UK cooperation[3]:

• By 2020, Northern Powerhouse will have provided all N8 Universities (Durham, Lancaster, Leeds, Liverpool, Manchester, Newcastle, Sheffield and York) with £100 million for technology transfer and the building of a network of resource centres to help commercialize research outcomes. Hence, Newcastle University, as an N8 research

---

[1] Newcastle University Press Office, Newcastle Science Central secures multi-million-pound deal with L&G, (2016),http://www.ncl.ac.uk/press/news/2016/06/l&gannouncement/.

[2] HM Government, Northern powerhouse investment opportunities, (2016), https://www.gov.uk/government/uploads/system/uploads/attachment_data/file/595701/NPH_pitchbook_2016_Brochure_English_low_res_version.pdf.

[3] Ibid.

partnership university, will be able to actively transform scientific and technological achievements, support start-ups and seek further enterprise development.

• As part of its research and innovation initiative, the government will use Newcastle as a base for marine energy research.

• The collaboration will furnish a £5 million investment in the 2018 "Great Exhibition of the North" in Newcastle Gateshead, a two-month exhibition of art, culture and design.

• It will also provide a £15 million investment in the National Institute for Smart Data Innovation and

• Upgrading of the A1 highway from Newcastle to London.

Overall, the China-UK collaboration will enable Northumbria and Tyne to make quantum leaps in research on technology transfer, marine energy, biomedicine and intelligent data, all areas in which innovation offers great investment potential. Yet despite its massive science and technology development, Newcastle still lacks a plan for developing modes of high speed travel to London, which provides yet another major opportunity for investment.

Opportunities in Liverpool

Liverpool has already received £72 million in funding to carry out the following improvements:

• Boost innovation and productivity in businesses across the city region.

• Enhance key routes of the city region's road network and improve transport and accessibility to support the growth in housing and employment sites.

• Increase skill levels, meet employers' skill needs and help retain skilled workers in the city region.

As the latest city region to climb on board Osborne's devolution revolution, Liverpool is focused on returning power from Whitehall to the local people. Hence, in 2017, Liverpool votersalsodirectly elect a mayor. The mayor will be given control over investments worth £30 million a year for the next 30 years. The total £900 million will help activate the huge economic potential of the iconic River Mersey and the new Superport, with full use of the opportunities brought by the HS2 railway[1]. The government has also emphasized boosting Liverpool's strengths in attracting major international events – for example, the city's International Festival for Business and related cultural attractions – and turning National Museums Liverpool into a sustainable business.

Opportunities in Manchester

Manchester county, with rich educational resources and the largest group of students in Northern England, has its own unique investment advantages, so Northern Powerhouse funds will be allocated as follows[2]:

• £38 million investments in Manchester's National Graphene Institute.

• £78 million investments in its Factory Theatre.

• £3 billion investments in real estate, with an estimated 40,000 houses to be built by 2020-2021.

• Funding for upgrades to the Manchester to York (via Leeds) railway line that will reduce the trip time to 15 minutes.

• Funding for upgrades to the M60 and A66 highways.

• Support for reasonable tax cuts for enterprises.

• Additional investment in city development with the goal of greater decentralization of authority over the region. Funding to strengthen the University

---

[1] HM Treasury, *Liverpool devolution deal boosts the Northern Powerhouse*, (2015), https://www.gov.uk/government/news/liverpool-devolution-deal-boosts-the-northern-powerhouse.

[2] HM Government, Northern Powerhouse Strategy, (2016), https://www.liverpoollep.org/wp-content/uploads/2016/11/Northern-Powerhouse-Strategy-November-2016.pdf.

of Manchester's collaboration on science and technology as part of its N8 Research Partnership[1].

Opportunities in Leeds

Leeds City Region is widely recognized as the UK's second largest economy and population centre, with 5% of the national economic output and 1.4 million people employed. It is also acknowledged to be the UK's second ranked financial centre, with the potential to grow 55% by 2022 to over £13 billion[2]. As the largest functional economic area outside London, one set to drive exceptional growth, Leeds City Region's strategic economic plan is to deliver £5.2 billion additional economic output and create 62,000 extra jobs by 2021. To achieve this goal, it has already secured the following:

1. Over £1 billion investment in transportation, housing and the city centre.

2. Development, skills, innovation and business growth.

3. Over £5 billion in the development pipeline.

4. A key role in the Northern Powerhouse.

Leeds City Region is thus actively demonstrating its enormous economic potential to attract growing numbers of international businesses. In fact, its 145% increase in foreign direct investment projects since 2013 makes it one of the fastest growing investment hotspots in Europe[3].

Not only has it received the second most funding in growth deals during 2017 but it

---

① "Devolution to the Greater Manchester Combined Authority and transition to a directly elected mayor", Gov.UK, November 13, 2014, https://www.gov.uk/government/publications/devolution-to-the-greater-manchester-combined-authority-and-transition-to-a-directly-elected-mayor.

② Leeds City Region Enterprise Partnership, *Investment and development opportunities - Leeds City Region*, (2015), http://investleedscityregion.com/system/files/uploaded_files/Development%20Brochure%20LR.pdf.

③ Leeds City Region Enterprise Partnership, *Leeds City Region–Investment Opportunities*, (2015), http://investleedscityregion.com/system/files/uploaded_files/Leeds%20City%20Region%20Prospectus.pdf.

has the second largest share in May's announcements of new funding. A total of 109,000 companies, from innovative technology start-ups to global law firms looking for cost-effective European headquarters, have already made Leeds City Region their base. The region also offers access to eight world-class universities with a long tradition of innovation and has convenient transportation connections to the rest of the UK, Europe and the world via road, rail, air and high-speed Internet. It enjoys particularly strong investment opportunities in four sectors:

1. Financial and professional services.

2. Manufacturing and low carbon industry.

3. Health and innovation.

4. Digital and information economy.

Leeds is also home to the Leeds City Region Enterprise Zone for investors and SMEs, located close to Leeds city centre and the national motorway network. Companies locating within the enterprise zone receive various benefits, including reduced business rates (worth up to £275,000 over a five-year period)[1].

All these investment and construction aspects offer potential investment opportunities for China, which would benefit particularly from the technology transfer that engenders science and technology innovation.

The first B&R London Science and Technology Forum was held on July 20, 2017, which is hosted by Cocoon Networks, Northumbria University, Lancaster University, University of East Anglia, Pangoal Institution and etc. Government agencies, universities, institutions and enterprises all enthusiastically joined in the discussion. The forum focuses on five aspects: science and technology, agriculture, industry, economy, the Internet plus. These five main aspects are also the future directions of China-UK collaboration.

---

[1]   Leeds City Region Enterprise Partnership. (2017b). Invest in Leeds city region. Retrieved at 7th May from http://www.the-lep.com/for-investors/invest-in-leeds-city-region/.

6 "一带一路"框架下的中白合作

许维鸿

"一带一路"作为中国经济再开放的纲领性战略，已经得到国内外越来越多的认同，位于新丝绸之路经济带核心位置的白俄罗斯更是逐渐热络起来。白俄罗斯拥有优越的自然条件和得天独厚的地理位置。然而，进入 2016 年，英国脱欧、美国孤立主义总统上台、逆全球化在欧洲大陆盛行，白俄罗斯寻找来自西方"外援"、助力实体经济发展变得愈发困难，这也就是为什么中国倡导的"一带一路"战略越来越得到白俄罗斯的积极响应。特别是在产能合作领域，中国作为全球唯一成功从计划经济向市场经济转型的大经济体，白俄罗斯产业界对中国的期待是发自内心的。

地处欧洲十字路口黄金位置的白俄罗斯

白俄罗斯是位于东欧的内陆国家，为原苏联加盟共和国，1991 年独立。与我们更为熟悉的游牧民族——俄罗斯族不同，白俄罗斯是一个传统的农耕民族，国民受教育程度高，气候的温润带来丰饶的农业物产，其细腻而高品质的饮食文化，就很容易理解为什么在独联体国家"产地白俄罗斯"就意味着更加优质的农产品。而且，白俄罗斯地处连接莫斯科和西欧的交通要道，传统繁荣的国际商业不仅带来了财富和文明，也带来了白俄罗斯更具多元包容的贵族气息。

图 6-1　白俄罗斯地理位置

正所谓"成也萧何、败也萧何"，白俄罗斯地处欧洲交通要冲的位置，不仅带来了安逸的物质生活，也让白俄罗斯成为从拿破仑到希特勒每一次欧洲霸权主义侵略俄罗斯的重要战场——首都明斯克更是在二战中基本被战火移为废墟，并从冷战后一直是欧洲各方势力明争暗斗的十字路口。

白俄罗斯的精英阶层心里明白，原有的计划经济体制尽管低效，普通百姓倒也温饱安逸；年轻一代对融入"信息全球化、工业 4.0"时代的向往，必须在夹缝中谋发展，宛若在欧美列强的监视下走钢丝，政治上稍有不慎就会重蹈前南斯拉夫、格鲁吉亚、乌克兰等东欧国家的动荡。在经济领域，俄罗斯、白俄罗斯和哈萨克斯坦三国总统于 2014 年 5 月 29 日在哈首都阿斯塔纳签署《欧亚经济联盟条约》，宣布欧亚经济联盟将于 2015 年 1 月 1 日正式启动。根据条约，俄白哈三国将在 2025 年前实现商品、服务、资本和劳动力的自由流动，终极目标是建立类似于欧盟的经济联盟，形成一个拥有 1.7 亿人口的统一市场。条约涉及能源、交通、工业、农业、关税、贸易、税收和政府采购等诸多领域，还列出了自由贸易商品清单，但其中不包含烟酒等敏感商品。该条约强化了白俄罗斯、俄罗斯和哈萨克斯坦三国的统一市场，而邻邦立陶宛虽然紧跟英美进行了市场化改革，老百姓却没有得到实惠，俄罗斯的休克疗法更是加剧了贫富差距和社会割裂。

白俄罗斯工业基础较好，机械制造业、冶金加工业、机床、电子及激光技术比较发达和先进，同时农业和畜牧业较发达，马铃薯、甜菜和亚麻等产量在独联体国家中居于前列。但由于计划经济占比依然较重，经济运行中仍存在效率偏低等问题。从 GDP 增速来看，自 2008 年金融危机后，白俄罗斯经济受到沉重打击，GDP 增速趋势性下滑，2015 年实际 GDP 开始负增长，同比增速降至 –3.89%。2016年，白俄罗斯经济继续萎缩，但降幅有所收窄，实际 GDP 同比 –2.6%。

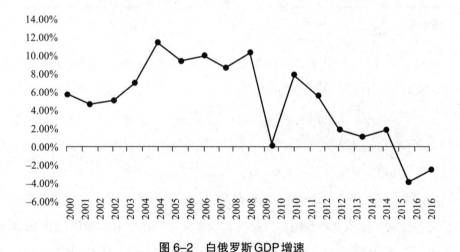

图 6-2 白俄罗斯 GDP 增速

数据来源：wind。

参考世界三大评级机构之一的穆迪（Moody's）对白俄罗斯的最新评级和展望变化，白俄罗斯经济状况由持续疲软近，几年开始显现出企稳的迹象。穆迪公司 2007 年 8 月首次覆盖白俄罗斯，此后不断调低白俄罗斯主权债务的评级，直到 2016 年 6 月时隔 9 年之后才首次发布"稳定"的展望。虽然评级依然为提示重大风险的"Caa1"级，但各项宏观经济指标显示白俄罗斯的经济状况企稳、不再恶化。

表 6-1　穆迪主权债务评级——白俄罗斯十年来首次企稳

发布日期	评级	展望
2017 年 2 月 15 日	Caa1	稳定
2016 年 6 月 17 日	Caa1	稳定
2015 年 4 月 17 日	Caa1	负面
2013 年 6 月 14 日	B3	负面
2011 年 11 月 4 日	B3	负面
2011 年 7 月 21 日	B3	负面
2011 年 3 月 29 日	B2	负面
2007 年 8 月 22 日	B1	负面

资料来源：Moody's。

白俄罗斯常年采取扩张的货币政策和财政政策刺激经济。这一政策产生的巨额赤字主要依靠外债和国际援助来填平。因此一旦国际收支账户中的投资净流入减少，经济系统就陷入瘫痪的境地。此外白俄罗斯经济高度依赖与俄罗斯的贸易，2014 年俄罗斯经济状况的恶化直接冲击了白俄罗斯的经济体系。违约风险上升之后国际融资中断的可能性不断上升，进一步加重了危机。

2016 年以来白俄罗斯经济的好转可以归结为四方面的原因：第一是随着俄罗斯经济的好转，白俄罗斯的出口恢复正常，经常项目赤字占 GDP 比例从 2014 年的 6.9% 下滑至 2015 年的 3.8%，2016 年又下滑至 3.2%。第二是俄罗斯和中国银行的贷款使得投资净流入再次回升，为白俄罗斯长期依赖外资的经济系统注入资金。第三是汇率制度改革帮助白俄罗斯实现更加有效的外汇储备管理，外汇储备逐渐企稳。第四是实行经济改革，逐步废除计划经济和物价直接管控，有效缓解了通货膨胀压力。

此外，世界银行和 IMF 对白俄罗斯未来几年 GDP 增速的预测均呈回升趋势，支持白俄罗斯经济未来将企稳向好的判断。

表 6-2　国际权威机构对白俄罗斯GDP增速的预测

	世界银行：GDP年增长率（基于2010年美元不变市场价格，%）	IMF：GDP年增长率（不变价，%）
2015	−3.89	
2016	−2.6	
2017F	−0.5	0.37
2018F	1.3	0.85
2019F	1.4	1.04
2020F		1.11

数据来源：世界银行：《全球经济展望》，IMF：《世界经济展望》。

通胀方面，白俄罗斯由于货币增速较快，通胀一直维持在较高水平，近年来通胀走势呈现"倒V"型。金融危机后白俄罗斯经济持续下滑，货币供给大幅提升，导致通胀水平显著走高，2011年和2012年CPI同比均超过50%，高通胀水平令白俄罗斯卢布大幅贬值。2012年开始货币增速快速回落，同时经济增速降至低位，需求明显减弱，这些因素导致通胀水平逐渐走低，2016年CPI同比降至11.8%，创六年来新低。

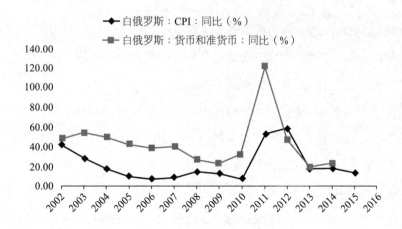

图 6-3　白俄罗斯的通货膨胀率与货币增速

数据来源：wind。

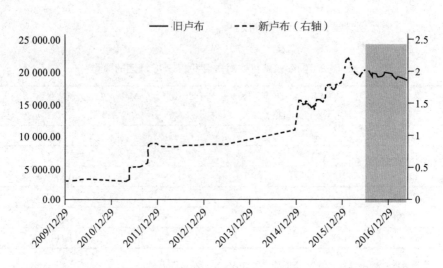

图 6-4　美元兑白俄罗斯卢布汇率走势（上升趋势显示货币兑美元贬值）

数据来源：wind。

"一带一路"框架下的中白合作

回顾中国建国后对欧洲乃至世界的经贸和外交历程，大概可以分为四个阶段：建国初期，全面谋求与苏联合作建设新中国；冷战时期，团结"第三世界"亚非拉国家寻求外交突围；改革开放初期，韬光养晦融入全球化产业链振兴经济；进入 21 世纪，以"一带一路"为代表的互联互通引领全球化新秩序。因此，新时代的白俄罗斯需要中国助力国民经济转型升级，中国也需要白俄罗斯共建全球"和平、发展"的美好未来，合作基础扎实、前景广阔！

中白之间互惠互利的合作，是中国与"一带一路"沿线国家合作的重要节点，有共性也有个性：所谓共性，就是如上文谈到的，中白合作有利于双方的市场互联互通、技术互补性共享、工业产能的转型升级。中国财富积累、人口结构、城镇化水平和经济结构的快速变化，使得新一轮的"再开放"战略需要更大的国际舞台和辐射半径：中国的高储蓄率将持续、孳生出富裕资本需要"走出去"，国内未来十年由于计划生育政策带来的新增蓝领就业人口不足；而对中国友好的白俄罗斯拥有大量具有"工匠精神"的高级技工，农村年轻人渴望国际化舞台，新增劳动力的"性价比"在欧洲出类拔萃。

而且中白合作的个性，更值得我们深入研究：一方面，白俄罗斯不同于东南亚、中东地区或者中亚五国，虽然没有石油天然气等自然资源，但是依靠丰饶的农耕和国际援助，其计划经济体制与普通百姓温饱、安逸的社会保障体系共存，改革内生性需求与民众踌躇意识共存；另一方面，白俄罗斯地处欧洲交通要冲，《欧亚经济联盟》扩宽了生存空间，普通百姓虽然工资水平不高，但是社会开放程度和国民国际化思维素质高，对欧美现代化社会的长期近距离接触甚至对抗，使得其精英阶层从骨子里依然向往冷战时期美苏争霸带来的国际政治"冲浪感"——在明斯克市郊现代化的二战纪念博物馆里，前苏联镰刀斧头的徽章依然高悬；在白俄罗斯总理办公大楼门口，列宁伟岸的雕像依然屹立，都是独联体国家绝无仅有的情怀。

无论是从中白对外开放的不同历史沿革，还是从白俄罗斯对中国独特的合作视角，中白之间基于"一带一路"框架的互联互通，都是对新一代中国外交家和商业领袖的考验。自"一带一路"倡议提出以来，中国基础设施领域的对外合作成绩斐然，但是被沿线国家更为期待的产能合作以及金融合作，则还处于萌芽状态。

在白俄罗斯首都明斯克机场附近的黄金地带——中白工业园建设从2010年习总书记奠基开始，屈指算来已经进入第八个年头，但是真正的工业企业实质性入园，则是近两三年才略有起色。除了工业园原有的建设思路不够专业，更多的还是反映了中白产能合作对双方政商两界的创新考验：白俄罗斯950万人口的本土需求，难以吸引靠规模取胜的"中国制造"国有资本；而中国民营企业对白俄罗斯僵化的计划经济体制决策效率担忧，造成中白工业园的内生性增长挑战重重。

图 6-5　中白工业园辐射图

如果把聚焦点从明斯克延展开来，白俄罗斯各州政府对中国的产能合作认识，也在变得越来越"现实"：在对首都之外其他白俄罗斯地区的实地调研中，金融服务不足成为州地方政府眼中对华招商引资的瓶颈问题——与中国的县域经济一样，中白产能合作不缺资金，而缺资本，缺少股债结合的多样化跨境直接融资服务。更有甚者，白俄罗斯很多州和城市已经与中国对口省市，特别是黑龙江省各地市建立了众多的友好城市关系，但是来访白俄罗斯的中国政商代表团基本是旅游性商务考察，真正落户投资的企业凤毛麟角，造成白俄罗斯地方政府接待工作的"审美疲劳"。

"一带一路"框架下的中白合作需要信心、耐心和恒心

"一带一路"战略的伟大，首先在于民心相通。我国改革开放之所以取得了巨大的成就，就在于中华民族务实而坚韧的民族品质。但是，由于韬光养晦时代的惯性思维，中国企业"引进来、走出去"总是刻意压抑民族自豪感，以求引进国

外资本和技术的顺利。随着中国国家实力的不断增强，无论从百姓财富积累还是高端装备制造技术含量，中国相对于"一带一路"国家的比较优势已经今非昔比，压抑已久的民族自豪感使得中国企业家，特别是年轻的80后90后对"国际被尊重"变得格外敏感，甚至会偶尔流露出对发展中国家相对落后的基础设施、市场思维和消费水平的蔑视，这显然是具有贵族情怀的白俄罗斯是无法接受的。

大到一个民族、小到一个人的自信，不应该仅仅建立在物质财富的积累上，也不应该建立在武力的征服上，而是应该希望得到他人、友邦发自内心的尊敬，这也是习总书记讲到的中华民族"文化自信"的深刻内涵。更何况中国企业利用自身资金和技术优势走出去、对外产能合作，对于中国政商两界都是新鲜事物，需要学习的东西还很多，需要从思想上避免"站在中国看世界"的惯性思维方式，力求"站在世界看中国、站在沿线国家的立场上看待一带一路"！说白了，如果中白产能具体合作项目不成熟，绝大部分中国商务考察团未必一定追求项目落地，前期调研、附带旅游无可厚非，但是应尽量多提问，并虚心倾听白俄罗斯当地的信息，不必主动宣传中国改革开放的"经验"和"成果"。

其次，中白产能合作必须有耐心。前期调研的"虚心倾听"达到知己知彼，只是中白合作的最基础层面。由于白俄罗斯固有的计划经济体制，中国企业初期更多要通过国际贸易引入白俄罗斯产品，进一步的产能合作由于没有股份制法律环境，只能通过与白俄罗斯各级政府洽谈合资渠道，针对具体项目进行新建或改造升级，商务谈判过程必然曲曲折折。

这就要求中国企业家把跨国文化功课做足，充分了解白俄罗斯本地商业特点，充分利用计划经济体制固有的政府引导特点，通过外延式产能合作谋求双赢，这对于经历过计划经济的中国企业家并不陌生。而且，"一带一路"产能合作最好是央企先行，这是中国特色对外再开放的历史使命——特别应该鼓励中航工业等非基建类的工业央企进入白俄罗斯设厂发展，并强调对项目盈利保有耐心，切勿好大喜功——没有经济效益的项目不做，中白不能双赢的项目不做，有重大政治或地缘风险的项目不做。新世纪的全球化需要"一带一路"思维，符合白俄罗斯年轻一代的诉求，时间是站在中白合作这一边的，产能合作必须尊重市场规律，不可刻意而为之。

第三，中白产能合作还需要智慧和恒心。正如前文指出的，白俄罗斯本地消费市场有限，缓慢的人口增长使得房地产等资产增值潜力有限，其真正价值所在是得天独厚的地理位置，辐射着俄罗斯和中东欧两个大市场。因此，中国企业走进白俄罗斯，很大程度上要基于对白俄罗斯和中东欧市场需求的调研，对西欧乃至英美企业和技术保持开放包容的心态，并充分利用白俄罗斯相对"高素质、低成本"的人力资源，利用白俄罗斯"讲信用、好面子"的贵族气质，用创新智慧把新丝绸之路经济带的大格局做出来。以中白工业园为例，招商引资目标企业可以不局限于中国和白俄罗斯企业，也应该把目光投向德国、法国、奥地利等国家，尽快形成规模效应。

中白产能合作的智慧还应该体现在金融领域。活跃在"一带一路"的民营企业都多多少少面临着资金缺口；国有企业虽然不差钱，但是缺乏长期风险共担的股权投资，现代金融工具的应用潜力巨大。2017年"两会"，人民币国际化和通过多层次资本市场降低企业综合融资成本，都是最热门的话题。如何借鉴"中国—俄罗斯"、"中国—哈萨克斯坦"资本互联互通尝试，利用中国A股市场对"一带一路"概念的热捧，切实为中白产能合作输送资本，靠中农工建为代表的商业银行，或者国开行等政策性金融机构显然是不行的。相反，中白工业园运营方——招商局下属的金融板块已基本实现混业经营，以及具有军工央企背景、专业进行跨境优化资源配置的中航证券，具有融资渠道和成本优势，都是最值得期待的金融创新机构。

最后需要指出的是，白俄罗斯历史上被欧洲霸权主义、意识形态集权主义反复蹂躏和掠夺，本土知识分子习惯性压抑民族自强的意愿，文学创作和绘画艺术无不体现出某种阴郁的气息。中国志在通过"一带一路"引领新世纪全球化造福民生、立意高远，与白俄罗斯的立体合作必须有恒心，敢于面对体制和文化差异带来的挫折和挑战，勇于面对自身国际化经验不足的缺点。只要我们高举和平和发展的大旗，包括白俄罗斯在内的"一带一路"沿线国家必然会跟我们走到一起，共同创造一个属于全人类的更美好未来。

6 China–Belarus Cooperation Under "The Belt and Road Initiative"

Xu Weihong

As the programmatic strategy of China's economic reopening, "The Belt and Road Initiative" has gained more and more recognition from abroad. Belarus, as it sits at the core of the New Silk Road Economy Zone, is also coming to the stage. Belarus has a good geographic location and advantageous natural conditions, but the difficulty of seeking Western assistance in developing its real economy has been constantly rising after Brexit, isolationist Trump, and the rising of anti-globalism in Europe. Consequently, Belarus has been responding positively to China's BRI. Especially in the cooperation of production capacity, Belarus industries are sincerely looking at China, as China is the only great economy that transcends from planned economy to market economy.

Belarus at Europe's crossroad

Belarus is located inland in Eastern Europe and gained independence from former

Soviet Union in 1991. Different from the Russian nomadic people that we are more familiar with, Belarus people are traditionally engaged in agriculture and generally well educated. Humid climate brings good development in agriculture and fine, exquisite dining culture, which explains why in Commonwealth of Independent States, "made in Belarus" means good quality. Moreover, Belarus is a vital connection between Moscow and western Europe. Long prosperous international trade has not only brought wealth and civilization, but also endowed Belarus with a diverse, inclusive, and noble temperament.

Figure 6–1　Belarus's geographic location

As the saying goes, fortune and misfortune comes in twins. Belarus' important geographic location not only brought calm material life, but also made Belarus an important battlefield for every European hegemonic war from Napoleon to Hitler; its capital Minsk was basically demolished in the Second World War and since the Cold War has been greatly affected by the power struggle in Europe.

Elite society in Belarus understands that the original planned economy, although inefficient, could provide comfortable life for people, but the rising aspiration for information globalization and Industrial 4.0 among young generations has demanded the country to develop in a very critical situation under the surveillance of western powers. Any slight mistakes could lead to political turmoil as already happened in Yugoslavia, Georgia, and Ukraine. In economy, presidents of Russia, Belarus, and Kazakhstan signed Eurasian Economic Union Treaty on May 29, 2014 at Kazakhstan's capital Astana and declared that the EEU will formally initiate on January 1, 2015. According to the Treaty, three countries would achieve free flow of products, services, capital, and labor before 2025. The final objective is a Economic Alliance like Europe Union and a market with 170 million people. The Treaty involves energy, transportation, industry, agriculture, tariff, trade, tax, government purchase and many other fields. It also lists free trade goods but excluding sensitive goods like tobacco and alcohol. The Treaty enhances collective market among Russia, Belarus, and Kazakhstan. However in the neighboring Lithuania, although the country underwent economic market reform after western powers, people did not receive real benefits; In Russia as well, where the Shock Therapy has increased social gaps and economic inequality.

Belarus has a good industrial foundation, especially in machinery manufacture, metallurgical processing industry, machine tool, and electric and laser technology. Its agriculture and animal husbandry are also relatively developed. Potato yield, beet yield, and flax yield has topped in the CIS. But because the planned economy still occupies a large potation of its economy, Belarus suffers from insufficiency in economic operations. The GDP report shows that Belarus suffered greatly from the economic crisis in 2008. Its GDP acceleration dropped and reached negative increase in 2015, year-on-year acceleration rate dropped to -3.89%. Belarus's economy continued to shrink in 2016, but the speed was relatively contained. Real GDP year on year rate was -2.6%.

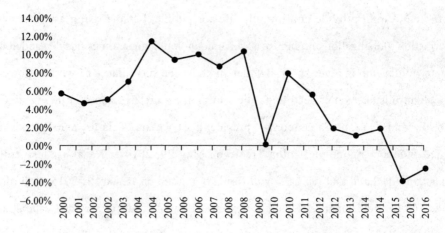

Figure 6–2　Belarus GDP Acceleration[①]

According to Moody's, one of the three largest rating agencies in the world, Belarus has showed signs of stabilization after years of economic decline. Moody's covered Belarus in August 2007 and continued to rate down Belarus's level of sovereign debt, and only published a stable prospect after June 2016. Although the rate still shows "Caa1" which means great risk, many macroeconomic parameters show that Belarus's economic condition is stabilizing.

Table 6–1　Moody's Sovereign Debt Rating — First "stabilized" In Ten Years[②]

Release Date	Rating	Outlook
2017 年 2 月 15 日	Caa1	Stable
2015 年 4 月 17 日	Caa1	Negative
2013 年 6 月 14 日	B3	Negative
2011 年 11 月 4 日	B3	Negative
2011 年 7 月 21 日	B3	Negative
2011 年 3 月 29 日	B2	Negative
2007 年 8 月 22 日	B1	Negatuve

① Source: wind.

② Source: Moody's.

For years Belarus adopted expansionist currency policy and finance policy to stimulate economy. The great economic deficit created by this policy was sustained by foreign debt and international assistance. Therefore once the invest input in these international accounts drops, Belarus' economy will paralyze. Moreover, Belarus's economy is highly dependent on trade with Russia. Russia's economy decline in 2014 directly impacted on Belarus. Possibility of suspension of international finance is rising after the risks of treaty breach increases, which creates greater crisis.

Four reasons attribute to improvement of Belarus's economy since 2016. First, as Russia's economy began to improve, Belarus's export returned to normal. Current account deficit in GDP dropped from 6.9% in 2014 to 3.8% in 2015, and 3.2% in 2016. Second, loans from Russian and Chinese banks allowed investment net input to rise again and provided capital for Belarus's economic system, which relies on foreign capital. Third, Reform in exchange rate system helped Belarus to better manage foreign capital reserve, which gradually stabilized. Fourth, economic reform in abolishing planned economy and direct control of price has effectively eased inflationary pressures.

Furthermore, predictions from World Bank and IMF on Belarus's GDP acceleration for future years show an increasing trend, which supports the judgement that Belarus is stabilizing its economy.

Table 6–2　International Agencies' Prediction on Belarus's GDP Acceleration[①]

	World Bank: GDP growth (annual, Measured in constant 2010 U.S. dollars, %)	IMF: GDP growth (annual, constant prices, %)
2015	−3.89	
2016	−2.6	
2017F	−0.5	0.37
2018F	1.3	0.85

① Source: World Bank Global Economic Prospects, IMF World Economic Outlook.

（continued）

	World Bank: GDP growth (annual, Measured in constant 2010 U.S. dollars, %)	IMF: GDP growth (annual, constant prices, %)
2019F	1.4	1.04
2020F		1.11

In regards to inflation, Belarus maintained a high level of inflation because currency increases very fast. Recently it shows a reverse-V trend. After the financial crisis, economy continued to decline and currency supply continued to rise, which significantly increased inflation. The year-on-year CPI in 2011 and 2012 all exceeded 50%. High inflation rates caused significant devaluation of Belarus Rupees. Starting from 2012, Currency increase dropped fast, economy acceleration dropped, and so as demand. These factors led to a decrease in inflation. Year-on-year CPI in 2016 dropped to 11.8%, the lowest in six years.

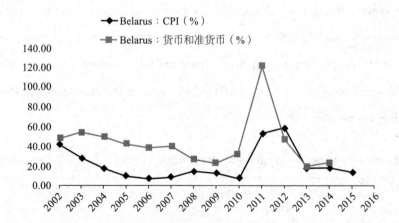

Figure 6–3　Belarus' Inflation Rate and Currency Acceleration

Source: wind.

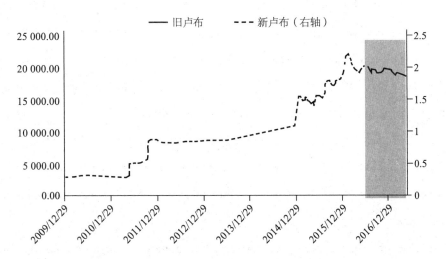

Figure 6–4　USD to BYR (increase means devaluation to USD)

Source: wind.

China-Belarus cooperation under"The Belt and Road Initiative"

Since 1949, China's economic and diplomatic development with Europe and the world can be divided into four stages: Initial stage, comprehensive cooperation with USSR to build a new China ; Cold War stage, working with "third world" (developing countries in Asia, Africa and Latin America) for diplomatic breakthrough; The beginning of reform and opening up, blend in global industry chain to vitalize economy; 21st century, global new order and connectivity under BRI. Therefore, Belarus in this new area needs China's help to transform its domestic economy, and China needs Belarus' help in constructing a global "Peace and Development" vision. There is a solid foundation and great prospect for cooperation.

China-Belarus mutually beneficial cooperation is an important point for cooperation among countries along the routes. It has commonality and differences. Commonality is the aforementioned reform and advance that could improve market connectivity, technology complementary share, and industrial production capacity. China's accumulation of wealth, fast change in population structure, urbanization, and economic structure demanded bigger international stage and radiation radius for the "reopening strategy". China's large reserve needs to export, and because of one child policy, China would face less engineer recruit in the coming ten years. Belarus has a lot of high level technicians, rural population craves for international stage, and cost performance of new labor is relatively the best in Europe.

On the other hand, the differences in China-Belarus cooperation deserve more attention. On the one hand, Belarus is different from Southeast Asia, Middle East, or Central Asia's Five Countries. Although it has no oil-gas reserve, because of good agriculture and international aid, The planned economic system coexists with the social security system for the ordinary people who have adequate food and clothing. The endogenous demand of reform coexists with the people's hesitation. On the other hand, Belarus is located in the hub of Europe. EEU expanded room for development, although people's salary level is not high, the degree of social openness and the quality of internationalization of thinking are high. Long term exposure to or confrontation with western modernized world has made the elite society nostalgic for the political disturbance in Cold War era—In Minsk Suburb WWII Memorial Museum, emblem of the Soviet Union still exists. In front of the office of its prime minister, the statue of Lenin still stands. These are the unique historical heritage of CIS countries.

No matter from the different history evolution of China/Belarus opening, or from the unique perspective of China-Belarus cooperation, for China and Belarus to achieve higher level of connectivity under BRI is a great challenge for new generation diplomats and business leaders in China. Since BRI is proposed, China has made great achievements in infrastructure, but countries along "The Belt and Road" expect more production capacity cooperation and finance cooperation, which are just at their beginning.

The Golden Belt near Minsk Airport—The Construction of China-Belarus Industrial Park has entered its 8th year since president Xi declared its opening. But the real company settlement in the zone just started one or two years ago. It may because that the construction idea of the zone is not professional enough, but more reflect the innovative challenge faced by politicians and business people from both sides in terms of production capacity cooperation. The 9.5 million domestic demand in Belarus could not attract Chinese national capital, which is used to operate on large scale. And China's domestic companies' worry about Belarus' fixed planned economy and its efficiency also created challenge for the zone to grow.

Figure 6–5　The radiation map of China-Belarus industrial park

If we expand the focus point from Minsk, state governments in Belarus are also realizing the possibility of production capacity cooperation with China. In field research in many other states in Belarus, lack of financial service has become the main problem to attracting China's investment for many state level governments. Like China's county economy, China-Belarus production capacity cooperation lacks no funding but capital. It lacks international diversity and direct finance services that combine stock and debt. Moreover, Belarus has established friendly city relationship with many Chinese provinces and cities like in Heilongjiang, but visiting groups to Belarus are more tourist-like. Only a little companies really invest and locate in Belarus, which also brings problem to local government reception works.

China-Belarus Cooperation under "The Belt and Road Initiative" needs confidence, patience and persistence

The greatness of BRI lies in people to people bond. The reason why China's reform and opening up has made great achievements is the pragmatic and tenacious national quality of China. However, due to the habitual thinking when China had to hide its capacities and bide its time, the strategy of Chinese enterprises "bring in, go out" always deliberately suppresses national pride, in order to introduce foreign capital and technology smoothly. With the growth of China's national strength, both from the perspective of people's wealth accumulation and high-end equipment manufacturing technology, China's comparative advantage to the countries alongside BRI is completely different from before. The long held sense of national pride has made Chinese entrepreneurs, especially the younger post 80's and post 90's, more sensitive to "international respect". Sometimes they even despise about the relatively backward infrastructure, market thinking and level of consumption, which is evidently unacceptable to Belarus which has aristocratic feelings.

The confidence of a nation and a person should not be based solely on the accumulation of material wealth, nor on the conquest of force, but on the genuine respect of others and friends. This is also the profound meaning of President Xi's words "culture confidence"(column 4) . What's more, for politicians and business people, it is unprecedented that Chinese enterprises use the advantage of fund and technology to go out and advance China's production capacity cooperation with foreign countries. And there is still a lot to learn. It is necessary to avoid the inertial way of thinking: "Stand in China, see the world". We need to strive to "Stand in the world, see China" and look at BRI from the position of the countries along the routes. To be honest, if specific projects of cooperation between China and Belarus in production capacity is immature, the vast majority of China's business expedition may not necessarily pursue the successful landing of projects. Preliminary research and incidental tourism are understandable. However, we should try our best to ask questions and listen attentively to local information in Belarus. We should not actively publicize the experience and achievements of China's reform and opening up.

Second, China-Belarus production capacity cooperation requires us to be patient. In the early stage of investigation, listening to each other modestly is the basis for the cooperation between China and Belarus. Because of the inherent planned economic system of Belarus, Chinese enterprises should focus more on introducing Belarus products through international trade at the beginning. As there is no legal environment for joint-stock system, the further production capacity cooperation can only be achieved through negotiations with Belarus governments at all levels and through newly building, transforming and upgrading according to specific projects. So the negotiation process must have ups and downs.

This requires Chinese entrepreneurs to do enough cross-cultural preparation to make full use of the local commercial characteristics of Belarus and the inherent characteristics of government guidance in planned economic system and seek for win-win through extensive production capacity cooperation. This is not strange to those Chinese entrepreneurs who experienced planned economy. Moreover, production capacity cooperation under "The Belt and Road Initiative" should let central enterprises go ahead of the rest, which is a historical mission of reopening with Chinese characteristics. In particular, we should encourage non construction type central industrial enterprises such as Aviation Industry Corporation of China to enter Belarus and set up factories, emphasize patience to project profitability. And avoid doing things in a big way. We should neither do those projects without economic benefits and win-win results nor those with major political or geopolitical risks. Globalization in the new century needs the idea of "The Belt and Road Initiative" and satisfies the demands of the younger generation in Belarus. There is time for cooperation between China and Belarus. Production capacity cooperation must respect the laws of the market and not do it deliberately.

Third, China-Belarus production capacity cooperation needs wisdom and persistence. As has mentioned before, the consumer market in Belarus is limited and the potential of asset appreciation such as real assets is restricted by slow population growth. Its true value lies in its advantageous geographic location which radiates to two big markets: Russia and Central and Eastern Europe. Chinese companies entering Belarus should largely rely on surveys of demand in Russia and Central and Eastern Europe, remain open and inclusive to businesses and technologies of Western Europe and even Britain and the US, make full use of Belarus's relative "high-quality, low-cost" human resources and Belarusians "good faith and good face" aristocratic temperament and build overall framework of new Silk Road Economic Belt with innovation and intelligence. Take China-Belarus industrial park for example, the goal enterprises of attracting investments should not be limited to Chinese and Belarus Enterprises. We should also turn our attention to Germany, France, Austria and other countries, so as to form a scale effect as soon as possible.

The wisdom of China-Belarus production capacity cooperation should be demonstrated in finance sector too. Private enterprises which respond actively to "The Belt and Road Initiative" are more or less facing the funding gap. Although the state-owned enterprises are affordable, they lack equity investment which can share long term risks, and the potential of modern financial instruments is enormous. During the Two Sessions held in 2017, the internationalization of the RMB and reducing the comprehensive financing cost of corporate through the multi-level capital markets, are the most popular topics. Considering how to draw lessons from "China-Russia" and "China–Kazakhstan" capital connectivity practices and make use of Chinese A-share market's enthusiastic response to BRI, so as to effectively transport capital for China-Belarus production capacity cooperation, it obviously doesn't work to rely on commercial banks represented by BC, ABC, ICBC and CCB or policy-based financial institutions such as CDB. On the contrary, the operator of China-Belarus industrial park—China Merchants Bureau's financial sector, has basically realized mixed operation. AVIC Securities, with military and central enterprises background and professional experience of cross-border optimization of resource allocation, has financing channels and cost advantages. These are the most anticipated financial innovation institutions.

Finally, As Belarus was repeatedly ravaged and plundered by European hegemonism and ideological totalitarianism, local intellectuals habitually suppress their will of national self-reliance, and their literary creation and painting art all reflect some kind of gloomy atmosphere. China is determined to lead globalization of the new century and benefit the people's livelihood through BRI. The three-dimensional cooperation with Belarus must be persistent. We must have courage to face the setbacks and challenges brought about by the system and cultural differences and the shortcomings of our own international experience. As long as we hold high the banner of "Peace and Development", the countries alongside BRI, including Belarus, will join us and create a better future for all mankind.

7 "一带一路"倡议节点国家之：意大利

吕晶华　常然

历史上，欧亚大陆通过丝绸之路联结在一起，古代的中国和罗马在两端遥遥相望。作为经济全球化的早期版本，这条贸易通道被誉为全球最重要的商贸大动脉，《马可·波罗游记》中就记载了古代丝绸之路的辉煌和两国交往的历史。如今，中国在全球化大背景之下提出了"一带一路"倡议，意大利在其中依然处于这样一种极其特殊的地位。在西欧各国中，意大利政府和企业界对于"一带一路"倡议的态度相对而言颇为积极，但在实际操作中仍存在一定的顾虑情绪。如何充分发挥中意两国在经济上的互补性，拓展更多合作领域和合作空间，关系到中意两国的长远发展，也关系到中国"一带一路"倡议在欧洲的落地。

意大利在"一带一路"倡议中的独特地位

意大利在"一带一路"倡议中所享有的特殊地位，体现在地理、经济和政治等多个层面。

从地理上看，"一带一路"由"一带"和"一路"两个部分组成，两条路线在意大利交汇，赋予了意大利极为特殊的地位。当然，更具重要意义的是中欧在"一带一路"中的合作前景及意大利在欧洲的特殊地位。

从经济角度看，欧盟需要进一步完善欧洲一体化的进程，中国则通过"一带一路"加强与区域经济及全球经济的互动。双方在区域和全球经济一体化中具有较强的共识，这是双方合作的理念前提。中欧在经济结构上也具有很强的互补性。中国在劳动密集型制造业上具有优势，欧洲在消费升级领域具有全球竞争力；中国在基础设施建设上具有领先性，欧洲在基础设施软件服务上具有优势。这是促进双方合作的核心因素。通过陆上和海上丝绸之路，中国与西欧之间的距离将大大缩短，贸易成本将大大降低。不仅中方能从中受益，对欧洲而言也是意义重大。广而言之，"一带一路"本身就是以共赢为目标的倡议，中国当然能够从中受益，但这是以相关国家共同受益为前提的。

同样重要的是，反全球化的思潮和民粹主义正在全球蔓延，并且有愈演愈烈之势。这是导致英国做出脱欧决定的原因之一，也有可能对 2017 年欧洲各国举行的一系列选举产生影响。在这种情况下，中欧这两大经济体建立更为密切的经贸关系，让更多的企业、民众从跨越国界的贸易往来中受益而不是受损，无疑有着共同抵制贸易保护主义逆潮的重要作用。

在"一带一路"倡议引领下，意大利的地缘优势可使其成为中国产品进入欧洲大陆的天然门户。国际货币基金组织 2016 年提供的数据显示，意大利是欧盟第四大国、全球经济第九大国[1]。中意建交 40 多年来，双方关系迅速提升。目前，意大利是中国在欧盟的第五大贸易伙伴，中国是意大利在亚洲的第一大贸易伙伴。2016 年，双边贸易额为 430.6 亿美元，中国对意出口 263.6 亿美元，进口 167.0 亿美元。截至 2016 年 12 月底，意在华投资项目共计 5617 个，实际使用投资 68.9 亿美元，意大利也已成为中国投资的主要目的地。[2]

---

[1] Prableen Baipai, CFA（ICFAI）, The World's Top 10 Economies, updated February 8, 2017, available at: http://www.investopedia.com/articles/investing/022415/worlds-top-10-economies.asp.

[2] 《中国同意大利的关系》，引自中华人民共和国外交部网站，http://www.fmprc.gov.cn/web/gjhdq_676201/gj_676203/oz_678770/1206_679882/sbgx_679886/，2017 年 2 月更新。

金融危机后的意大利经济面临更多挑战，仅靠欧盟内部市场很难实现全面振兴，加强与亚洲国家特别是中国的合作交流则成为其重要环节。参与"一带一路"，恰恰为中意两个文明古国共谋发展提供了机遇。

意大利各方对"一带一路"倡议的立场

意大利总统塞尔吉奥·马塔雷拉在 2017 年 2 月访华期间，表达了与中国就"一带一路"展开合作的强烈意愿。这表明，意大利政府的高层领导对于该倡议的态度愈益趋向积极。[1]意大利总理真蒂洛尼也率团参加了 5 月 14 日至 15 日在北京举行的"一带一路"国际合作高峰论坛。

由于意大利媒体对"一带一路"倡议及中意在此框架下合作可能性的报道还比较有限，很多普通民众对于该倡议的了解不多。但意大利商界的热情相当高涨，他们最有可能从相关项目中受益，因此也是最积极呼吁意大利政府积极参与其中的力量。意大利商业界人士对中国投资和并购表示欢迎，也为意政府更加积极地接受中方关于"一带一路"倡议发挥了突出作用。

2015 年，中国化工集团以 77 亿美元收购了意大利轮胎巨头"倍耐力"，充分展现了中国企业对于在意投资的浓厚兴趣。这笔交易的部分资金来源于"丝路基金"，后者在中国化工集团子公司持有股权。中国公司在意还有多项大规模投资，如国家电网公司（SGCC）从意大利存贷款公司（CDP）花费 28 亿美元收购意大利存贷款能源网公司（CDP RETI）部分股权[2]等。投资和收购额日益增多，反映了意大利商业界和商业精英对于中国的开放态度。根据美国财经媒体CNBC和博雅公关公司（Burson-Marsteller）所做的调查显示，意大利民众普遍重视商业，认

---

① Zhang Yunbi, "China, Italy Pursue Innovation", *China Daily*, February 23, 2017, available at: http://www.chinadaily.com.cn/china/2017-02/23/content_28310795.htm.

② Chu Daye , "State Grid Buys Stake in Italian Firm for $2.8b", *Global Times*, August 1, 2014, available at: http://www.globaltimes.cn/content/873704.shtml.

为商业的繁荣将对经济产生积极影响，也不反感企业对于政府产生影响。①基于这样的民意，加强双方在商业上的往来，显然将推动意大利政府更积极地参与"一带一路"。目前来看，中意的合作正在沿着这样的方向前行。

除商业界之外，意大利政府对于"一带一路"相关项目也表示了深厚的兴趣。这在一定程度上源于中意之间的良好关系。意大利不顾美国的劝阻，成为"亚投行"（AIIB）的创始成员国之一。2016 年 5 月，中国外交部长王毅在罗马与意大利总理、时任意外交部长真蒂洛尼会晤，强调应加强中国"一带一路"倡议与意国家发展战略的对接，并宣布开启多个中意合作项目，内容涵盖节能环保、农业、可持续城镇化、健康卫生和航空航天等五大重点领域。②意总统近期访华和总理出席"一带一路"峰会，进一步展示了意大利政府及领导人的积极姿态。

意大利对"一带一路"倡议在意推进的主要顾虑

当然，意大利国内对于"一带一路"倡议还有一些负面情绪，主要体现为对中国国企在海外投资与并购的顾虑。包括意大利在内的不少欧洲国家，都对外国企业收购本国企业感到担心。2014 年皮尤调查中心发布的一项调查表明，73%的意大利受访民众认为，外国企业收购本国企业是坏事。③虽然这种情绪针对的是所有收购行为，但随着中国国企大量收购意大利企业、特别是"倍耐力"等具有悠久历史、广受关注的意企时，这种反对情绪表现得更为强烈。这引发了对中国国企的不满和不信任，也因此影响到这些企业在意大利的运转。上述皮尤调查也表明，在欧洲各国中，意大利对于跨国贸易的怀疑情绪最浓，只有 13%的受访者认

---

① Alice Tidey, "Is Big Business too Influential?", CNBC, September 26, 2014, available at: http://www.cnbc.com/2014/09/26/is-big-business-too-influential.html.

② "Wang Yi Talks about China-Italy Relations", the Ministry of Foreign Affairs of the People's Republic of China, May 6, 2016, available at: http://www.fmprc.gov.cn/mfa_eng/zxxx_662805/t1361548.shtml.

③ "Faith and Skepticism about Trade", Foreign Investment, Pew Research Center, September 16, 2014, available at: http://www.pewglobal.org/2014/09/16/faith-and-skepticism-about-trade-foreign-investment/.

为与其他国家的贸易往来有助于增加就业，超过 59% 的受访者则认为这将导致就业机会减少。另外，52% 的意大利人认为，此类贸易将导致收入下降，因此对国家不利。

总体而言，包括意大利在内的欧洲国家，对于中国的投资和收购主要有三方面的顾虑：

一是投资可能导致本国重要的战略工业受中国控制。其中包括被认为对国家经济增长、全球竞争力至关重要的组织和企业，特别是高科技和技术先进企业。这种担忧导致部分欧洲国家制定了更具贸易保护色彩的政策。例如，在过去 5 年的对华贸易中一直处于顺差地位的德国，就在近期阻止了中国以 6.7 亿欧元收购"爱思强"（Aixtron）的要求。在意大利，反对全球化和要求效仿英国"脱欧"的"五星运动"正在迅速崛起。如果与这种对中国并购者的怀疑情绪相结合，加之意大利对华贸易仍存在逆差，有可能促使意大利采取类似的保护性政策。

二是公司治理和商业行为模式的差异。毋庸置疑，随着中国国企越来越多地在意大利发起收购，这些企业的领导人必然也会寻求将他们所习以为常的商业行为模式运用到意大利企业当中，从而影响甚至取代欧洲原有的架构和模式。这种方式有时会与欧洲现有的劳工法和环境保护措施相冲突，从而加剧了人们的担忧。还有一些人担心，这些意大利企业被收购后，部分业务会转移到中国国内，这会导致当地人失业。

三是对等投资不足和进入中国市场受限。在不少欧洲国家，人们普遍存在的一种看法是，虽然这些国家对中国非常开放，但中国却未保持同样的开放度，相反却给予中国国企和其他国内企业更多的优惠措施。在欧洲国家看来，中国在金融服务等重要领域依然对国外投资持限制或禁止态度，表明中国政府明显有所偏袒。不少欧洲国家一直认为中国的投资者和政治机构透明度不足，也加剧了这方面的担忧和疑虑，因此出现了对中国一些投资和并购行为的抵制。

中意在"一带一路"框架下开展的合作

总体来看，中意两国在经济结构上具有很强的互补性，在"一带一路"框架下开展经济合作的潜力巨大。对于许多中国人来说，意大利是创意时尚和高端制造的代名词。中国又是意大利纺织品及原料、家具玩具、鞋靴伞等轻工产品和皮革制品及箱包的首要来源地，是意大利机电产品的第二大进口来源地，分别占其市场份额的为 21.2%、30.1%、19.9%，16.3% 和 15.5%[①]。中国企业越来越关注可再生能源利用和环境保护问题，这对于具有丰富经验的意大利相关企业同样是巨大的发展机遇。中意已经开展的经贸合作，极具潜力的合作领域包括：

一是港口基础设施建设合作。2017 年 2 月，由中国交通建设股份有限公司领衔的中意联合公司 4C3 与意大利威尼斯港务局签订了离岸深水港口一期设计协议。威尼斯港务局主席保罗·科斯塔称，这一工程将使威尼斯港成为连接亚得里亚海各港口的重要枢纽，从而真正实现与海上丝绸之路的对接。事实上，意大利还在规划更大规模的"五港同盟"建设项目，计划在北亚得里亚港口协会管辖的五个港口（意大利的威尼斯港、的里雅斯特港、拉文纳港，斯洛文尼亚的科佩尔港和克罗地亚的里耶卡）"打造巨型多功能平台，形成离岸/在岸船泊靠泊系统"[②]。据估计，项目完成后这五个港口的集装箱容量将达 180 万至 300 万 TEU[③]。一方面，中国可以深入参与相关基础设施建设。根据目前的预算，项目总花费约为 22 亿欧元，意大利政府提供的预算仅为 3.5 亿美元，他们希望能够通过中国企业和中国政府"一带一路"相关部门募得其他所需资金[④]。另一方面，这也将使中国大型货船在地中海找到新的驻泊港湾。如能有效使用这些港

---

① 《意大利总统访华，"一带一路"加强中意经贸合作》，环球网，http://fj.china.com.cn/p/299231?page=4，2017 年 2 月 23 日。

② Nicola Casarini, OBOR and Italy: Strengthening the Southern Route of the Maritime Silk Road, *Instituto Affari Internazionali* (IAI), Rome, October 2016.

③ Ibid.

④ Ibid.

湾，相比于现在常用的汉堡港，中国货船前往欧洲的距离将缩短 3862 公里、8 天时间。①

二是中国在意"海外直接投资"（FDI）。2011 年的一项研究认为，中国在意大利的投资被称为"马可·波罗效应"。②这项研究认为，正像当年将中国的高技术带回意大利的马可·波罗一样，当今中国在意大利的"海外直接投资"主要集中于高技术领域和设计领域，通过并购大品牌和知名企业，提升其技术能力和在设计方面的水平。这样的合作显然具有双赢性质，因为中国的产业主要集中于劳动密集型产业和基建领域，可以在并购意大利企业的过程中不断完善。而在 2008 年金融危机中遭受重创的意大利，也亟需这样的投资来恢复元气。

三是教育交流。随着中意在"一带一路"倡议下经贸往来的日益密切，双方也需要在更深层面加深相互了解。事实上，确实有越来越多的意大利学生通过各类学者项目来到中国。自 2011 年以来，在意大利学习的中国留学生数量仅次于美国留学生，在所有在意外国留学生中占第二位。③单从留学生数量来看，中国年轻人对于了解意大利的热情，似乎远远高于意大利年轻人了解中国的热情。但值得注意的是，意大利有 11 家孔子学院，覆盖了多数知名大学和最主要城市④，展现了意大利对于研究中国、了解中国文化的积极姿态。

四是旅游业。意大利是中国旅游者心目中的旅游圣地之一。有旅游机构提供的数据显示，意大利在中国人海外旅游目的地中排位在前 10 名⑤。当前，意大利

---

① Nicola Casarini, OBOR and Italy: Strengthening the Southern Route of the Maritime Silk Road, *Instituto Affari Internazionali* (IAI), Rome, October 2016.

② Carlo Pietrobelli, Roberta Rabellotti and Marco Sanfilippo, "Chinese FDI strategy in Italy: The 'Marco Polo' effect", *International Journal of Technological Learning Innovation and Development*. December 2011.

③ EMN National Contact Point for Italy within the European Migration Network (EMN), "Immigration of International Students to Italy", 2012, available at: http://ec.europa.eu/home-affairs/sites/homeaffairs/files/what-we-do/networks/european_migration_network/reports/does/emn-studies/immigration-students/14a._italy_national_report_international_students_april2013_final_en.pdf.

④ Confucius Institutes in Europe, July 20, 2017, available at: http://english.hanban.org/node_10971.htm.

⑤ "China Outbound Tourism in 2016", Data source: China National Tourism Administration, June 2017, available at: https://www.travelchinaguide.com/tourism/2016statistics/outbound.htm.

正在采取提供更好的服务等措施，来吸引中国旅游者。博洛尼亚近期就与中国旅游研究院签署协定，以研究旅游者的习惯和需求，从而更好地满足他们的需要。[1]此类协定充分显示了中国旅游者对于意大利经济的重要提升作用。随着"一带一路"倡议带来的更多商机和政治合作，中国同样有可能成为意大利旅游者的重要旅游目的地。中国方面也有必要与意大利城市建立更稳固的合作关系，开启更多的直飞航线，并且培养更多的意大利语导游，以便为意大利旅游者赴华提供便利。

五是吸取意大利经验推进"中国制造2025"。自20世纪80年代以来，意大利就将"意大利制造"的标签打造成金字招牌，意味着产品是在意大利设计、生产和包装的，展示了意大利的独特地位，也是高品质的象征。通过与意大利的合作，以及在并购和投资意大利企业的过程中学习经验，中国可以更有效地推进"中国制造2025"。多年来，意大利将创新作为产业发展的支柱，其时尚、食品、家具和机械工程等行业尤其如此。"中国制造2025"也同样将创新作为驱动力，旨在借此实现产业升级。"一带一路"倡议为双方基于这一共同需求开展双赢合作提供了重要机遇。

与意开展"一带一路"合作需关注的几个问题

"一带一路"虽然是明显具有共赢特质的重要倡议，但其涉及国家多、项目多、范围广、周期长，其间必然会面临这样那样的问题，在意大利也不例外。为推动中意在"一带一路"框架下的顺畅合作，有以下几点需要关注：

第一，降低政府参与的色彩，推动"自下而上"的合作。客观而言，意大利等欧洲国家奉行的"多层治理"模式，与中国"强政府、弱社会"模式差异巨大。这也是中意"一带一路"合作中面临的最大障碍。不少人一提起与中国的经贸往

---

[1] Zhao Xinying, "Italian City Signs Agreement with Chinese Tourism Academy", March 29, 2017, available at: http://www.chinadaily.com.cn/china/2017-03-29/content_28724784.htm.

来，就自然而然地联想到政府支持、国家背景，不仅在心理层面容易产生抵触情绪，而且在实际操作中也容易与欧洲国家的法律规范相冲突。"一带一路"虽是国家最高领导人提出的倡议，但在具体落实中，还有必要考虑到欧洲的特殊性，尽量降低政府色彩和国企色彩，让更多的民营企业走在前列，强调企业、行业、城市之间的合作。

第二，降低国别属性，强调基于"欧洲一体化"理念的中欧合作。与其他"一带一路"相关国家不同，欧洲国家的一个显著特点，是在关注本国利益的同时，也强调欧洲的整体性。在中国提出"16+1合作"倡议后，欧盟出现了质疑"中国分化欧洲"的杂音，虽然未在欧洲占据主流，但依然值得关注。在合作中更多地强调与欧洲一体化相关政策相对接，如可利用"容克计划"提供的对欧投资制度性渠道，深化中欧经贸合作；在参与铁路、港口等基础设施建设时，除关注目标国需求外，也应适当考虑铁路在其他国家的延伸与贯通，港口设施在功能、容量上与邻近国家现有港口设施的差异化配置等。

第三，通过政策配套，为中、小企业对接提供便利。在欧洲国家中，意大利是除德国之外制造业基础最为雄厚的，中、小企业尤其发达，素有"中小企业王国"之称。据统计，意大利中、小企业吸纳了全国近82%的员工，在助推国民经济和解决就业方面都发挥着重要作用。在"一带一路"框架下，一方面中国众多正处于发展期的中小企业家可以到意大利学习管理经验，另一方面这些意大利传统优势企业也可以通过与中方企业的深度合作寻求更大的市场。在此方面，有必要在政策上适度放宽对外国中、小企业进入中国市场的限制，在版权和专利保护方面加大管理力度，降低这些企业的顾虑。

7 A Study of China–Italy Cooperation in BRI

Lyu Jinghua   Anurag Ram Chandran

In ancient times, Europe and Asia were connected together by the Silk Road, with Rome and China respectively serving as the two major terminals. The Silk Road was viewed as the main line of trade and business across borders at that time—an early version of economic globalization. In fact, the grand history of the Silk Road and the connection and exchanges between the two countries are well documented by Marco Polo in his Travelogue. Upholding the concept of globalization, China proposed the Belt and Road Initiative (BRI)in which Italy matters a lot. Relatively speaking, among all the countries in the Western Europe, the government and business community in Italy holds a positive stand towards BRI. Even though, it is still undeniable that there is still skepticism and doubt in carrying out relevant projects. Whether we can succeed in exploring more areas and spaces for cooperation and making full advantage of the complementarities between China and Italy, will affect not only the future development of the two countries but also the implementation of the BRI all across Europe.

Why does Italy matter in BRI?

The significance Italy enjoys in the implementation of the BRI include several aspects, including geographic, economic and political facets.

Geographically, BRI includes both the land and the maritime Silk Roads. Italy stands at the intersection of the two roads, making it uniquely special in BRI. What's more important, however, is the huge potential of the cooperation between China and Europe in the framework of BRI and Italy's special position in Europe.

From the perspective of the economy, the European Union needs to further improve the process of European integration, while China strengthens the interaction between regional economy and global economy by means of BRI. Both sides have strong consensus for regional and global economic integration, which is the core premise of cooperation between the two sides. Besides, China and Europe have mutually complementary economic structures—China has advantages in labor-intensive manufacturing industries, while Europe has global competitiveness in the field of consumption upgrades. Similarly, China has superiority in infrastructure construction, while Europe has advantages on the software services of infrastructure. This complementarity is the core factor that will promote cooperation between the two parties. Through the land and sea route, the distance between China and Western Europe will be greatly shortened, which will significantly reduce the trading costs. This not only benefits China, but also has important significance to Europe. Broadly speaking, the BRI is an initiative that aims to achieve a win-win goal. Of course, China will benefit from it—but this is based on mutual benefits and the parallel benefits for the relevant countries involved.

It is also important to note that trends of anti-globalization and populism are spreading all over the world, becoming more intense as time goes by. This is one of the primary reasons that led to the UK's decision to exit Europe, the repercussions of which, may also have an impact on the series of elections being held in several European countries this year. In this situation, if China and European economies can develop much closer economic relations, more enterprises and people can benefit from transnational trading. Undoubtedly, it will play a significant role in opposing the protectionist trends in Europe, and more broadly, throughout the world.

Italy enjoys a distinctive geopolitical advantage in being the gateway for Chinese products to find markets in Europe. Based on statistics provided by IMF's World Economic Outlook Database, October 2016, Italy is the fourth largest economy in EU and the ninth in the world[1]. In the past 47 years after the establishment of diplomatic relations between China and Italy in 1970, bilateral relations have experienced powerful acceleration. Today, Italy is China's fifth largest trade partner in Europe, while China is Italy's largest one in Asia. The annual bilateral trade volume amounts to $43.06 billion in 2016, in which China exported $26.36 billion and imported $16.70 billion. By the end of 2016, the investment projects in China initiated by Italy totaled 5617, with $6.89 billion of actual fund. [2]Italy, on the other hand, has become a main destination for Chinese investment.

It is of no doubt that Italy's economy has been facing several challenges after the occurrence of the financial crisis. As the comprehensive economic resurgence cannot be achieved solely on exchanges within the European market, it will be important for Italy to enhance cooperation with Asian countries, especially with China. BRI, therefore, will provide unprecedented opportunities for China and Italy, the two ancient civilizations, to cooperate and develop together.

---

① Prablean Baipai (ICFAI), *The World's Top 10 Economies,* updated February 8, 2017, available at: http://www.investopedia.com/articles/investing/022415/worlds-top-10-economies.asp.

② "China's Relations with Italy", in official site of Ministry of Foreign Affairs of the People's Republic of China, available at: http://www.fmprc.gov.cn/web/gjhdq_676201/gj_676203/oz_678770/1206_679882/sbgx_679886, updated in February. 2017.

How Italy reacts to BRI?

On a recent visit to China, Italian President Sergio Matarella stressed his country's desire to collaborate with China on BRI—a growing sign of the positive reception of BRI in the upper echelons of the Italian government.[①]Italian Prime Minister Paolo Gentiloni took part in the Belt and Road Forum for International Cooperation held in may, 2017.

It is important to note that not much information abounds in Italian media about BRI or the possibility of Italian and Chinese cooperation on BRI-led projects. This leads to a lot of the general public, and civilians largely being unaware of BRI. However, the business community in Italy is largely enthusiastic, as they are slated to be the biggest winners from the likely BRI-led projects, and as such, are the strongest lobbying forces in the Italian government. The business community in Italy has openly embraced the arrival of Chinese investments and takeovers, and have largely contributed to the increased positive government perception of China in Italy.

The buying of Pirelli, Italy's top tire maker, by China National Chemical Corporation (ChemChina)for US $7.7 billion is the most recent example of China's interest in Italian companies. This deal, was in fact partly funded by the Silk Road Fund, which took an equity stake in the division of ChemChina created to buy the shares. Other large investments by Chinese firms in Italy include the $2.8 billion investment in Italian energy grid unit CDP Reti by the State Grid Corporation of China (SGCC) in 2014[②]as well as other large-scale investments that have only grown in number every year. The number of increased investments and acquisitions clearly show the openness of businesses and business leaders in Italy to China. This is good, especially

---

① Zhang Yunbi, "China, Italy Pursue Innovation", *China Daily*, February 23, 2017, available at: http://www.chinadaily.com.cn/china/2017-02/23/content_28310795.htm.

② Chu Daye, "State Grid Buys Stake in Italian Firm for $2.8b", *Global Times*, August 1, 2014, available at: http://www.globaltimes.cn/content/873704.shtml.

in a country like Italy in which the majority of the people believe that strong and influential businesses have a positive impact on the economy, and are comfortable with the influence of corporations on the government—according to a survey conducted by CNBC and Burson Marsteller.[①] Thus, winning over the business community is crucial for China to steer Italian policy-making in a pro-BRI direction, and it already seems to be ahead of the curve in this task.

In addition to the business communities, it appears that the government leadership is especially supportive of embracing BRI-related projects. This is partly due to the strong relationship that Italy enjoys with China. For instance, Italy is one of the founding members of the Asian Infrastructure Investment Bank (AIIB), deciding to join after ignoring US pleas to refrain from joining. Further, after meeting in Rome in May 2016, China's Foreign Minister Wang Yi and Italy's Prime Minister Paolo Gentiloni (back then, Italy's Minister of Foreign Affairs) announced several areas of cooperation between China and Italy. These included five priority fields—energy conservation and environmental protection, agriculture, sustainable urbanization, healthcare, aviation and aerospace. There were also talks on aligning BRI with Italy's national development strategies.[②] The previously mentioned visit of Italian President Matarella and PM Gentiloni's Participation in the BRI summit is just the latest sign that the Italian government and its leaders are positively receptive to BRI-related projects in their country.

---

① Alice Tidey, "Is Big Business too Influential?", CNBC, September 26, 2014, available at:http://www.cnbc.com/2014/09/26/is-big-business-too-influential.html.

② "Wang Yi Talks about China-Italy Relations", the Ministry of Foreign Affairs of the People's Republic of China, May 6, 2016, available at: http://www.fmprc.gov.cn/mfa_eng/zxxx_662805/t1361548.shtml.

What are the main concerns about BRI in Italy?

One of the concerns often faced by China in its outbound investments and acquisitions drive is the perception of its State Owned Enterprises (SOE) abroad. In many European countries, including Italy, the general public remains apprehensive of foreign companies buying domestic companies. A Pew Research Center study in 2014 found that 73% of the Italian populace surveyed believed that foreign companies' acquisition of domestic companies is bad.[①]While this sentiment applies to all such acquisitions, it is bound to be strongest against Chinese SOEs that have recently gone on a buying spree and acquired some of the most historic and most recognizable Italian companies like Pirelli. Naturally, this creates resentment and distrust of Chinese SOEs and affects their operational capabilities in the host countries. Further, in the same survey, Italians appeared to be one of the most suspicious of trade and only 13% of those surveyed believed that trade with other countries leads to more jobs, while over 59% believed that it led to job losses. In addition, 52% Italians believed that trade reduced wages and was not beneficial to the country as a result.

Broadly speaking, European governments, including Italy, have three major concerns about Chinese investments and acquisitions in their countries:

Investments resulting in China's control of assets of key and strategic industries. These generally include organizations and companies are considered to be important for a country's economic growth and global competitiveness, especially high technology/ technologically advanced companies. This concern has led to the establishment of protectionist policies in several countries. In Germany, the country that has enjoyed

---

① "Faith and Skepticism about Trade", Foreign Investment, Pew Research Center, September 16, 2014, available at: http://www.pewglobal.org/2014/09/16/faith-and-skepticism-about-trade-foreign-investment/.

a strong trade surplus with China over the last 5 years, the government recently withdrew its approval for a €670 million takeover of Aixtron by Chinese investors.[①] In Italy, combined with the rapid rising of anti-globalist Five Star Movement that calls for following the model of Brexit, and the existing trade deficit with China, if the growing suspicion of Chinese takeovers do not subside, it will possibly institutes such protectionist policies.

Differences in corporate governance and business practices. Several of Chinese SOE takeovers in Italy have led to a major shift in governance structures and business practices, which have replaced age-old practices in Europe. The new leadership is keen on implementing the kind of business practices that they are used to, sometimes at odds with existing labor laws and environmental protection practices, which have exacerbated the concerns. There are also wide concerns if some aspects of the operation will be moved to China, thereby replacing European and Italian jobs in the process.

Lack of investment reciprocity; the limited access to Chinese markets. The general perception in some European countries is that China does not reciprocate the openness shown by the countries, and instead provide priority to Chinese SOEs and other local firms. China's prohibitions and restrictions of foreign investments in certain key sectors such as financial services, is seen by European countries as a move that tilts the playing field in China's favor. This is compounded by the fact that several European governments feel that there is a lack of transparency in the investors and political agencies in China—perceptions which further contribute to the concerns and suspicions against allowing Chinese investments and acquisitions.

---

① https://www.ft.com/content/f1b3e52e-99b0-11e6-8f9b-70e3cabccfae.

Achievements and potential areas of China-Italy cooperation in the framework of BRI

Generally speaking, China and Italy have mutually complementary economic structures. In the minds of Chinese people, Italy is almost a byword for creativity, fashion and top-level manufacturing. For Italy, China is the largest source of fabrics and its materials, furniture and toys, light industrial products, and leather goods, accounting for respectively 21.2%, 30.1%, 19.9% and 16.3% in Italian market.[1]As more and more Chinese enterprises are paying close attention to renewable energy utilization and environmental protection, Italian companies with rich experiences in these areas are also facing huge opportunities.

The ongoing economic and trade cooperation and the potential cooperation areas include:

Port infrastructure projects. In February 2017, the Chinese-Italian consortium 4C3, led by the China Communications Construction won the final design of the new Venice Offshore-Onshore Port System (VOOPS). According to Costa Paolo, president of the Venice Port Authority(VPA), the project will enable Venice to enjoy a hub position connecting Adriatic ports, so that they can connect with the Maritime Silk Road. Italy is also initiating the Five-Port Alliance program, aiming "to create an offshore/onshore docking system by building a giant multimodal platform off the shore of the city-port of Malamocco near Venice."[2] Five ports refer to the ports linked together by the North Adriatic Port Association (NAPA), including Venice, Trieste and Ravenna in

---

① "With the Arrival of Italian President in China, the Economic and Trade Cooperation between China and Italy Will Be Enhanced in the Framework of BRI". Available at: http://fj.china.com.cn/p/299231?page=4., February 23, 2017.

② Nicola Casarini, "OBOR and Italy: Strengthening the Southern Route of the Maritime Silk Road", *Instituto Affari Internazionali (IAI)*, Rome. October, 2016.

Italy, Capodistria in Slovenia, and Fiume in Croatia. This platform, when completed, is projected to have the capacity to handle between 1.8 and 3 million TEU (twenty-foot equivalent units).[①]The entire project is estimated to cost around €2.2 billion—with about $350 million already budgeted by the Italian government, and the rest expected to come in from Chinese SOEs and BRI-related money from the Chinese government.[②]It will also attract China's large cargo ships arriving in the Mediterranean Sea. The greatest advantage from the completion of these projects is that it significantly cuts the travel time, as compared to the alternative route (to Hamburg), which would take an additional 3862 km or eight additional days of navigation.[③]

Chinese FDI in Italy. Chinese investments in Italy can be termed as the "Marco-Polo effect", according to a 2011 study.[④]This study shows that just as the famous Venetian merchant traveler Marco Polo who brought back to Italy important technological and scientific discoveries from China, nowadays China' FDI in Italy is mainly in the high skills and design intensive sectors through the acquisition of big brands and other famous companies. Just like Marco Polo, China is now using the reverse strategy of acquiring and learning from Italian firms to complement its prowess in manufacturing and infrastructure. This creates an opportunity for a true win-win cooperation, where Chinese dominance in labor intensive fields and infrastructure construction and development is complimented by the technological and design knowledge learned from the acquisition of Italian firms and corporations. Especially given Italy's weak performances since the 2008 financial crisis, and some major losses

---

① Nicola Casarini, "OBOR and Italy: Strengthening the Southern Route of the Maritime Silk Road", *Instituto Affari Internazionali (IAI)*, Rome. October, 2016.

② Ibid.

③ Ibid.

④ Carlo Pietrobelli, Roberta Rabellotti and Marco Sanfilippo, "Chinese FDI strategy in Italy: The "Marco Polo effect", *International Journal of Technological Learning Innovation and Development*. December 2011.

sustained by large firms, the prospect of acquisition or investment from Chinese firms is crucial for Italy.

Education. Since China and Italy have already been on a path to increase economic and trade cooperation under the BRI, it is necessary to build understanding and trust at a deeper level. Today, more Italian students arrive to study in China through scholarships and grants, than ever. Since 2011, Chinese students have been the second largest number of foreign students studying in Italy, second only to the United States.[1]This shows the commitment of the Chinese people to learn more about and understand Italy, while the same cannot be said about the number of Italian students in China. However, it is to be noted that there are over 11 Confucius Institutes in Italy—covering most major universities and the most prominent cities.[2]This is a good start, indicating Italians' positive reception towards studying Chinese and understanding the culture and values.

Tourism. Chinese tourists largely find Italy as one of the top destinations to travel to. According to travel agencies, Italy featured as one of the top 10 destinations Chinese outbound tourists traveled to.[3]Italy is taking great measures to provide services to attract and keep up the number of Chinese tourists. Recently, the historic city of Bologna signed an agreement with the China Tourism Academy to conduct research on tourists' habits and needs in order to better cater to their requirements.[4]Such agreements and deals show the importance of Chinese tourists to Italy's economy. With greater business and political cooperation, especially from BRI, China has the potential to become an

---

[1] EMN National Contact Point for Italy within the European Migration Network (EMN) , "Immigration of International Students to Italy" , 2012, available at: http://ec.europa.eu/home-affairs/sites/homeaffairs/files/what-we-do/networks/european_migration_network/reports/does/emn-studies/immigration-students/14a._italy_national_report_international_students_april2013_final_en.pdf.

[2] Confucius Institutes in Europe, July 20, 2017, available at: http://english.hanban.org/node_10971.htm.

[3] "China Outbound Tourism in 2016" , Data source: China National Tourism Administration, June 2017, available at: https://www.travelchinaguide.com/tourism/2016statistics/outbound.htm.

[4] Zhao Xinying, "Italian City Signs Agreement with Chinese Tourism Academy" , March 29, 2017, available at: http://www.chinadaily.com.cn/china/2017-03/29/content_28724784.htm.

important travel destination for Italian tourists. As such, setting up agreements with Italian cities, direct flights, and having more Italian speaking tour guides will help establish the Italian tourist's presence in China.

Made in China 2025. Since 1980, Italy has used the Made in Italy merchandise mark to indicate that products have been planned, manufactured, and packed in Italy. For long, this has been the hallmark of Italy's uniqueness, and a major indicator of high quality products. In collaborating with Italy, and learning through acquisitions and investments in Italian firms, China can be inspired to make the 'Made in China 2025' dream a reality. For decades, Italy has relied on innovation to drive their industries, especially fashion, food, furniture, and mechanical engineering. This is the same goal that China wants to achieve—to have manufacturing driven by innovation, thereby upgrading China's industries. The BRI presents the best opportunity for a win-win cooperation, especially in this field.

Suggestions on enhancing bilateral relations in the framework of the BRI

Although it is a win-win approach, BRI, as a long-term initiative involving many countries and numerous projects, will definitely face various challenges in enhancing cooperation with related countries, including Italy. The following are some suggestions on enhancing bilateral relations within the framework of the BRI.

Promote bottom-up cooperation. It cannot be denied that China and Italy adopt different approaches to governance. While Italy and most of the other European countries adopt multi-governance, Chinese model can be described as "strong government, weak society". This is the biggest obstacle to the bilateral cooperation. It is even common that trade and business with Chinese is naturally connected with words like state-sponsored or state-backed. It can lead to not only a defensive or even antagonistic attitude, but also a violation of local laws and regulations of European countries. As an initiative proposed by China's top leader, the implementation of the BRI needs to be more adaptive to the concerns in Europe. To be concrete, the leading and major forces in business and trades with Europe should be private enterprises rather than government and state-owned enterprises; and the main cooperation should be enterprise-to-enterprise, city-to-city, and industry-to-industry ones.

Enhance China-Europe cooperation based on European Integration concept rather than cooperation with individual European countries. Different from other BRI-related countries, a distinctive character of most European countries is that they pay much attention to the integrity of Europe as well as interests of their own nations. In fact, there were speculations about China's intentions in promoting the 16+1 cooperation. Some people thought it was an act to divide European countries. Despite not mainstream in Europe, it still remains noteworthy. To address these concerns, it is important to find more docking spaces between the BRI and European Integration. For example, China can strengthen the economic cooperation with Europe via the institutional investment approach provided by the Juncker Plan. Also, in building infrastructures like railways and ports in Europe, China needs to take into consideration not only the demands of the targeted country, but also those of neighboring countries, to make sure the new infrastructures will not simply overlap with the existing ones in terms of functions and capacities.

Boost cooperation among small and medium enterprises in China and Italy by giving policy support. Italy possesses tremendous advantages in manufacturing industry, only second to Germany in Europe. With advanced small and medium enterprises, Italy is known as the kingdom of small and medium enterprises. According to some statistics, 82% of domestic employees work for small and medium companies in Italy. It is no doubt that these companies play significant roles in promoting economic development and providing jobs. In the framework of the BRI, a large number of Chinese entrepreneurs operating small and medium businesses can learn from their Italian counterparts. On the other hand, these Italian enterprises can get easier market access to China in the process of cooperating with Chinese companies. Of course, to address the concerns of foreign small and medium enterprises, it is necessary for China to relax restriction on their entering Chinese market to a certain degree, and to further improve the supervision regarding copyright and patent.

8 中巴经济走廊：现状、挑战及对策建议

李玲飞

中国－巴基斯坦经济走廊（China-Pakistan Economic Corridor, CPEC），简称中巴经济走廊，是中国和巴基斯坦两国旨在深入加强互联互通和共同发展而开展的一系列大型工程计划。中巴经济走廊北起中国新疆喀什，南至巴基斯坦俾路支省瓜达尔港，成为连接"丝绸之路经济带"与"海上丝绸之路"的枢纽，因此在"一带一路"战略部署与推进中具有非同一般的意义。2017年5月，中巴经济走廊建设已经取得多项重要进展，中巴两国政府也已展开多轮磋商，着手制定"中巴经济走廊远景规划"。值此之际，本文将对中巴经济走廊建设的现状进行归纳，就该计划即存和未来可能出现的挑战与风险予以总结和评估，并给出初步的对策建议。

中巴经济走廊的建设背景与现状

多年以来，中国与巴基斯坦的经济贸易合作，在两国之间传统友谊和共同利益基础之上得以持续稳定发展。进入21世纪之后，两国先后签署《自由贸易协定》（2006年）和《中巴自贸区服务贸易协定》（2009年），经贸合作有了更深层

次的进展。《中巴自贸区服务贸易协定》签署当年，中国成为巴基斯坦第二大贸易伙伴。

在此背景下，2013 年 5 月，李克强总理在出访巴基斯坦期间，提出了积极探索和制定中巴经济走廊远景规划的倡议。同年 7 月，巴基斯坦总理谢里夫访华。两国同意成立中国和巴基斯坦经济走廊远景规划联合合作委员会，并达成了一系列在远景规划合作框架下的早期收获项目。2014 年 2 月，巴基斯坦总统马姆努恩·侯赛因对中国进行国事访问时，中巴经济走廊远景规划联合合作委员会已经启动，综合规划、交通基础设施和能源联合工作组已经成功举行首轮会议。

2015 年 4 月，习近平主席对巴基斯坦进行国事访问时，两国同意将中巴关系提升为"全天候战略合作伙伴关系"，将中巴经济走廊提升为"一带一路"的旗舰工程。中巴经济走廊建设的规划是以走廊建设为中心，以港口、能源、基础设施建设和产业合作为重点，形成"1+4"合作布局。目前，这些项目的发展状况是：

1. 瓜达尔港

如果说中巴经济走廊是"一带一路"的旗舰工程，那么瓜达尔港就是中巴经济走廊的"明珠项目"。2013 年 2 月，中国海外港口控股有限公司（China Overseas Port Holding Company，以下简称"中国港控"）从新加坡港务集团正式接手瓜达尔港的运营权。到 2016 年 6 月底，瓜达尔港已具备基本作业能力，同年 11 月 13 日，中巴经济走廊车队顺利从喀什抵达瓜达尔，通过港口大规模出口集装箱，首次联运成功。[1]

与瓜达尔港一并移交给中国公司的还有总面积达 923 公顷的自由区，中方将首先开发其中紧邻瓜达尔港区的 25 公顷土地，这也被称为自由区的起步区。2016 年 9 月，起步区的开发建设工作正式展开，目前已经完成了约一半的工作量。起步区内的道路、水电供应、绿化等全部基础设施将在 2017 年底之前完成，其中包括一个集企业办公、政务服务、商务考察、休闲等功能于一身的一站式商务服务中心。[2]

---

[1] 王琳：《"一带一路"倡议下，瓜达尔每天都在变》，第一财经网，2017 年 5 月 8 日。
[2] 同上。

截至目前，至少有 35 家企业申请自由区营业执照，拿到营业执照的企业有 9 家，预计投资额超过 600 亿元人民币。[①]按照规划，瓜达尔自由区分为南部商贸物流区和北部加工制造区。南部依托现有码头，重点发展仓储、物流、商品展销等产业；北部为加工制造区，重点发展汽车制造及组装、家电、纺织、清真食品、医疗器械，形成具有完整产业链条的规模化产业集群。沿海岸发展旅游休闲、餐饮、水上运动以及配套生活设施。

中国港控还在瓜达尔港安装了日生产能力为 500 吨淡水的海水淡化设施，并在港口内部埋设了全套的供水和排水系统。这些淡水不仅能满足港口内施工和生活的基本用水，还可以每月定量向附近居民免费分发淡水。瓜达尔港的"早期收获"项目还包括[②]：

表 8–1　中巴合作的瓜达尔港的"早期收获"项目

	项目名称	预计投资额度	状态
1	东湾高速公路建设	1.4 亿美元	预计 2018 年建成
2	防波堤建设	1.3 亿美元	建设中
3	中巴职业技术学校	900 万美元	已建成
4	自由区及出口加工区基础设施建设	3500 万美元	建设中
5	海水处理及淡水供应设施建设	1.14 亿美元	预计 2018 年建成
6	中巴友谊医院(升级现有的医院)	1 亿美元	建设中
7	燃煤电厂	3.6 亿美元	建设中
8	瓜达尔国际机场	2.3 亿美元	运营中
9	瓜达尔港泊位通道疏浚	2700 万美元	建设中

---

① 王琳：《"一带一路"倡议下，瓜达尔每天都在变》，第一财经网，2017 年 5 月 8 日。

② http://cpec.gov.pk/gwader, http://m.yicai.com/news/5280826.html.

2. 能源

为解决巴基斯坦能源短缺问题，从提出倡议以来的近四年间，中巴经济走廊早期收获项目主要集中在能源领域，包括卡西姆港燃煤发电站、萨希瓦燃煤发电站、胡布燃煤发电站、Suki Kinari 水电站、卡洛特（Karot）水电站、旁遮普省的 Quaid-e-Azam 太阳能发电站以及位于信德省内的四个风电项目等在 2017 年内陆续投产。

卡西姆港燃煤电站项目由中国电建海外投资公司和卡塔尔 Al-Mirqad Capital 共同投资 20.85 亿美元建设，总装机容量为 1320 兆瓦，并配备海水淡化、废水处理、噪声控制、脱硫除尘等一系列环保设施。

中国的丝路基金将第一笔 16.5 亿美元的投资投在了中巴经济走廊的卡洛特水电站项目上，该项目作为中巴经济走廊优先实施的能源项目之一，采取了政府与社会资本合作（PPP）方式融资，2016 年初由三峡集团开工建设。卡洛特水电站计划 2020 年投入运营，运营期 30 年，到期后无偿转让给巴基斯坦政府。

3. 交通基础设施

按照中国驻巴基斯坦大使孙卫东的总结，走廊最具代表性的三大项目，除了瓜达尔自由区的起步区，就是白沙瓦至卡拉奇高速公路的木尔坦至苏库尔段以及喀喇昆仑公路升级改造二期工程。[①]这两个大型工程的项目总额将超过 60 亿美元。在交通基础设施领域，2016 年开工的还有瓜达尔国际机场和瓜达尔东湾高速公路两个项目，投资规模较小，约 4 亿美元。

2016 年 11 月 13 日，中巴经济走廊联合贸易车队首次试联通活动在巴基斯坦俾路支省瓜达尔港隆重举行。车队活动的结果表明，中巴经济走廊的道路已经实现初步联通，"一走廊、多通道"理念正逐步成为现实。时任巴基斯坦总理谢里夫则表示，"这标志着中巴经济走廊正从概念成为现实，掀开了本地区互联互通新的

---

① 林民旺：《五大国或将影响 2017 年南亚外交情势》，凤凰网，2017 年 3 月 24 日，http://wemedia.ifeng.com/11039344/wemedia.shtml。

一页。巴基斯坦由此成为亚洲大陆的交汇点，各国人民将共享发展繁荣。"①

中巴经济走廊特使扎法尔介绍说，由于巴基斯坦国内的能源短缺问题尚未解决，因此巴国内 1 号铁路干线的升级改造项目（将其时速从现在的 60 公里提升至 140 公里）、哈维连陆港的建设以及中巴产业园区的合作都还停留在规划和可行性研究层面，尚未开展施工。

4. 产业合作

中巴产业合作仍处在起步阶段。在工业园区建设方面，旁遮普、信德、开伯尔—普赫图赫瓦、俾路支省四省总共提出了建设 29 个产业园区的规划，另有 21 个矿业加工业园区。目前，受制于巴基斯坦国内的经济基础、能源供应以及人力资源等现实情况，这些项目还无法同时上马，最终中方从地区平衡的角度出发在每个省选了一个产业园，作为示范园区。具体的产业合作见如下项目②：

表 8-2　中巴在巴基斯坦四省的一些产业合作项目

项目名称	公司名称	阶段	进展
瓜达尔至纳瓦沙阿液化天然气端与管线项目（700 公里）	中国石油天然气管道局	即将开通	40%
海尔–鲁巴经济区（二期）	海尔电器有限公司	可行性阶段	15%
拉瓦尔品第至红其拉甫光线电缆工程	华为技术有限公司	建设中	50%
DTMB 示范项目	待定	已签署合作备忘录	5%
拉合尔橙线地铁项目	中铁—中国兵工集团	建设中	60%
加速巴基斯坦 TD-LTE 商业化项目	待定	可行性阶段	15%

---

① 《中巴经济走廊，掀开互联互通新篇章》，《人民日报》，2016 年 11 月 15 日。

② http://www.cpecinfo.com/special-economic-zones.

中巴经济走廊面临的挑战及主要问题

中巴经济走廊建设面临的主要挑战来自三个方面：国内政治和经济局势带来的投资风险，复杂地缘政治博弈带来的国际关系风险，极端主义和恐怖主义带来的安全风险。

（一）巴基斯坦国内政治经济风险

巴基斯坦国内政治和经济环境整体比较稳定，而且源于中巴之间传统友谊和战略伙伴关系，中巴经济走廊在巴基斯坦国内政府层面得到了普遍的支持。国内政治经济形势带来的主要风险在于，政党政治中的权力争夺和背后所反映出来的不同群体之间的利益矛盾，以及薄弱的经济基础和发展环境带来的投资风险。

1. 国内政治的不稳定因素：党派之争背后的地区主义与社会矛盾

巴基斯坦有 200 多个政党，派系众多。中巴经济走廊项目的规划，常常引发巴议会间各党派的争执。而这种党派之争反映出的是更深层次矛盾，背后是各个地区、族群间的利益之争。比如位于巴基斯坦东部的旁遮普省和信德省是经济较为发达的两个省份，西部的开伯尔－普赫图赫瓦省和俾路支省较为落后，急需大量基础设施建设的投入。各个省都希望来自中巴经济走廊的更多项目落户自家门口，由此出现了"东线"和"西线"之争。而且信德省是巴基斯坦最大政党人民党的大本营，与执政的穆斯林联盟（谢里夫派）旁遮普省历来不和，这种地区主义的夺利与各大党派的争权互相交织，执政的穆斯林联盟（谢里夫派）逐个说服普什图人民党、正义运动党、俾路支省的人民民族党等主要反对党，才达成一个折中方案，项目得以最后规划和落实执行。

2016 年 7 月底，参议院的数名议员联名要求谢里夫政府向民众公开中巴经济走廊项目的有关内容，附议的不仅有来自反对党的议员，也有来自执政联盟中的其他政党议员，这些议员指摘穆斯林联盟（谢里夫派）的执政根基所在地旁遮普省成为中巴经济走廊的最大受益者，而其他各省几乎什么也没有得到。2017 年 2

月以来，俾路支省民族党领导人门加尔（Sardar Akhtar Mengal）在俾路支省首府奎达组织集会反对中巴经济走廊，还对媒体称中国的投资项目"没有给俾路支省带来任何发展"，却"给旁遮普人创造了大量的就业机会"。

针对中巴经济走廊的权益争夺，还包括地方与联邦政府之争。中巴经济走廊能源领域的旗舰项目——卡西姆港燃煤电站，由中国电建海外投资公司和卡塔尔Al-Mirqad Capital共同投资20亿美元建成，是谢里夫政府为解决国内电力紧张的里程碑工程，但其土地使用权却一度陷入地方与联邦政府之争。

发电站是巴基斯坦联邦政府批准的"中巴经济走廊"项目，但其所在的信德省认为，联邦政府没有得到信德省的授权使用这块土地，信德省要求得到发电站的部分股权，或者得到与土地使用权同等的补偿。联邦政府认为根据该国宪法，联邦政府已经得到了该块土地的租用权，有权进行任何目的的开发和使用，但信德省则认为联邦政府仅有权将土地用于港口建设和海运，并无权建设发电站。

图 8-1　巴基斯坦主要政党势力

绘图：李玲飞

卡西姆港发电站的土地问题，最后通过中国政府与巴联邦政府、信德省政府以及卡西姆港发电公司等多个相关职能部门的协调努力，经过艰难的磋商和谈判，一直到 2016 年 12 月底，才得以解决。

巴基斯坦国内的政治争端，给中巴经济走廊项目规划与施工带来很大阻力，从选址到工期，都受到直接影响。而投入后的运营过程中，潜在的不确定性风险也不能低估。

此外，巴军方与民选政府之间缺乏基本信任，对巴政局长期稳定也会造成不利影响。在巴建国近 70 年的历史中，先后出现过四次军人执政，累计长达 33 年。尽管 2008 年以后，军人对政治的干涉与影响逐渐削弱，但很长一段时间内，军人干政的可能性以及由此影响经济走廊的建设的可能性并不能完全排除。

2. 经济风险

巴基斯坦经济基础薄弱、基础设施落后、电力淡水等资源匮乏、经济政策制定缓慢而混乱，是中巴经济走廊建设面临的现实问题。中方在中巴经济走廊中前期主要项目，以能源与交通等基础设施为主，以缓解能源供应不足、交通和基础设施落后造成的困难。这样的环境带来的风险主要是投资成本增加和效率低下。

以油气管线项目为例，中国海路油气运输全程基础设施已经大体齐全，但想象中的"中巴油气管线"相应基础设施则需要从头建设，东道国巴基斯坦目前连稳定的电力供给也不能保证，尚待中巴经济走廊框架下的一系列发电项目为他们化解这一难题，何况从瓜达尔到喀什需要翻越海拔五六千米的喀喇昆仑山口，这条想象中的管道需要建设功率超大的泵站，还需要为高原地区的管道提供额外的加热、保温设施，耗费的投资就更高了。因此，即使不考虑由此而增加的安保成本，"中巴油气管线"构想也注定是不经济的。

此外，在巴国内，经济问题政治化倾向严重。例如在融资方面，很多巴方人士将中巴经济走廊理解为中国为国内过剩资金和产能寻找出口途径，因此，中巴经济走廊应主要为中国投资，巴方并不需要扩大融资渠道。得到亚投行和亚洲开发银行共同投资的巴基斯坦首个高速公路项目——M4 高速公路（绍尔果德至哈内瓦尔段）也没有被巴基斯坦计划经济部列为中巴经济走廊的项目。

世界银行 2016 年 4 月发布的《南亚经济聚焦》认为，中巴经济走廊如果顺利实施，将彻底改变巴基斯坦，但是"如今该计划面临着巴国内政治经济风险"。[①] 考虑到巴基斯坦国内的政治与经济情况，世界银行的判断不能不说是一个非常现实和紧迫的预警。

（二）地缘政治的复杂性

地缘政治方面，中巴经济走廊需要面对和处理的，既有巴基斯坦与印度、阿富汗、中东等周边国家关系的因素，也有域外大国地区博弈的影响。

首先，巴印关系短期内难有实质性改善。2015 年 12 月印度总理莫迪突访巴基斯坦后，舆论均预期两国关系将有所改善，然而巴印关系却在 2016 年急转直下。2016 年 9 月 18 日，印控克什米尔地区的陆军军营乌力基地遭到恐怖主义袭击，18 名印度士兵死亡。印度指责巴基斯坦是恐袭背后的支持者，并于 9 月 29 日对巴进行"外科手术式打击"。外交上，印度还发起了"孤立"巴基斯坦的行动，主要是不参加在巴基斯坦举行的第 19 届南盟峰会。随后孟加拉、不丹、阿富汗相继作出类似表态。[②]

其次，巴阿关系受制于杜兰线问题、塔利班问题以及阿富汗对巴基斯坦在恐怖主义问题上的失望，因此暂时也难以彻底缓和。随着 2014 年 12 月 31 日北约宣布正式结束在阿战斗任务，美国从阿富汗撤军，阿国内局势动荡，由此产生的不确定性和安全风险对巴国内安全和社会稳定均构成严重挑战。[③]

此外，巴基斯坦与中东国家，特别是沙特和伊朗的关系微妙。虽然目前巴基斯坦的中东政策取得一定成效，但在中巴经济走廊问题上，地缘经济将取代地缘

[①] World Bank: South Asia Economic Focus, Spring 2016: *Fading Tailwinds*. p. 67.

[②] 林民旺：《五大国或将影响 2017 年南亚外交情势 》，凤凰网，2017 年 3 月 24 日，http://wemedia.ifeng.com/11039344/wemedia.shtml.

[③] 陈继东、丁建军：《巴基斯坦在未来阿富汗局势中的作用》，《兰州大学学报》，2015 年第 2 期，第 84 页。

政治成为影响走廊建设的主要风险因素。[①]有学者指出，印度为伊朗设计的恰巴哈尔港（Chabahar）和巴基斯坦的瓜达尔港已成为两国在全球争夺资源和影响力的较量的缩影。[②]

从域外大国在该地区的地缘政治格局来看，南亚地区越来越形成"选边站队"的"冷战"格局。首先，印美关系进一步发展，以至于印度在防务上发展为美国的"准盟友"。其次，俄罗斯与巴基斯坦开始"靠近"。就在印度发动"孤立"巴基斯坦行动时，俄与巴在9月24日举行双方首次联合军演"友谊2016"，显示了微妙的地缘政治内涵。

最复杂的问题是，在中巴经济走廊中，中国如何处理与印度的关系。我们看到，从始至今，印度对中巴经济走廊一直采取抵触、不合作甚至排斥的态度。印度不希望中国主导地区事务，已经利用且将来必然还会利用印巴之间的领土争议等话题从中阻挠，并且还会利用自身影响力拉拢其他国家提出其他倡议或项目形成竞争。印度的这种不合作态度与竞争角色也很容易被其他大国利用，形成对中国非常不利的博弈局面。

（三）极端势力和恐怖主义带来的安全风险

1. 俾路支省安全形势严峻

瓜达尔港对于中国来说，不仅是一条能源战略通道。它位于中国提出的"路带"和"海丝"的正中央，亦是中巴经济走廊的咽喉和枢纽，却处在巴基斯坦最不安宁的俾路支省腹地。首先是在巴的中方施工人员的人身安全。与2007~2009年间几乎每三天发生一起恐怖袭击的局面相比，巴基斯坦的总体安全状况已经有了明显提升，但是对于主要项目所在地——俾路支省的中资机构和中方工程人员

---

① 王旭："中巴经济走廊建设中的主要问题与对策建议"，摘自《"一带一路"跨境通道建设研究报告（2016）》，中国社会科学出版社，2016年8月。

② 驻卡拉奇总领馆经商室："伊朗高官表示不会利用恰巴哈尔港打压瓜达尔港"，2015年10月30日，http://china.huanqiu.com/News/mofcom/2015-10/7875289.html。

来说，需要时刻提防诸如"信德革命军"、"俾路支解放军"等武装组织的袭击。①

随着中方大批工程人员的到场，瓜达尔地区的安保也要升级。2004 年 5 月中国工程师在瓜达尔市区内遇袭的悲剧依然是前来瓜达尔的中国人挥之不去的阴影。俾路支省分离主义势力频繁发动的针对巴政府项目的袭击也让中国投资者心有余悸。为此，在中国政府的要求下，巴基斯坦军方划拨了 1.5 万兵力专门为中巴经济走廊项目保驾护航，其中瓜达尔港的建设和开发是护卫重点。但这种"严阵以待"的方式在投资者看来并不是能增加投资信心的加分项。这些持枪的安保力量随时出现在身边，初来乍到不熟悉情况的投资者会感到非常不适，会影响他们的投资决定。

巴基斯坦提供的安全保卫还存在着机制性的隐患。目前为走廊项目提供安保的武装力量主要由三方面构成：地方警察、武装民兵以及巴基斯坦三军武装力量。三者间严重缺乏协同调度。②

2. 极端组织"伊斯兰国"加紧渗透、暴恐势力回流

近年来，极端组织"伊斯兰国"加紧了对巴阿地区的渗透。目前，在巴基斯坦拉合尔和卡拉奇等大城市均出现了极端组织发动的小规模暴恐袭击事件。而极端组织在旁遮普省有在受过良好教育的城市青少年群体中扩散的趋势，未来旁遮普省也可能会因此面临严峻的安全挑战。

2017 年 2 月，巴基斯坦恐怖势力四天时间内连续制造六起恐袭事件，大有卷土重来之势。2 月 13 日，在旁遮普省会城市拉合尔，14 日在俾路支省首府奎塔，15 日在开普省首府白沙瓦，同日在联邦部落区，16 日在信德省一著名苏菲派清真寺，恐怖分子向国家执法部门发起攻击。"自由者党"宣称对此负责，显示其打击目标是国家机构人员和世俗媒体从业者。

此外，近期巴基斯坦旁遮普省政府发出涉恐警报，称巴参加伊拉克和叙利亚战争的极端分子正在返回巴基斯坦，为伊斯兰国在这里的活动增添力量。哪怕民选政府和军队有再好的合作，"国家（反恐）行动计划"也无望应对这一威胁。解决国

---

① 郝洲：《中国巨额投资复活瓜达尔港，还需面对五重挑战》，财经网，http://yuanchuang.caijing.com.cn/2017/0405/4256052.shtml，2017 年 4 月 5 日。

② 同上。

内恐怖主义问题的前提是，首先要解决滋养这些恐怖分子的外部环境问题。不幸的是，在与印度和阿富汗是要战争还是要和平的问题上，尚无新思维出现的迹象。

自从巴基斯坦加入到美国在阿富汗的反恐战争之后，国内安全形势的最大病灶转移到了与阿富汗边境相邻的部落区，其中又以北瓦济里斯坦（以下简称"北瓦"）最为顽固。巴军方先后于 2009 年和 2014 年在南瓦济里斯坦地区和北瓦发动了"拯救之路"和"利剑行动"的反恐军事行动，部分巴塔成员遭受打击后逃往阿富汗东部地区。[①]由于巴阿边境缺乏有效管控，两国人员可以在部分地区自由往来，因此一旦巴基斯坦反恐形势趋缓，暴恐分子有回流的可能。

对策建议

（一）正确认识、充足准备

首先，理性看待中巴经济走廊建设中出现的问题。如上文所示，巴基斯坦缺水少电的现状短期内无法改变；恐怖主义和极端主义无法快速彻底根除，是走廊项目回避不了的客观现实；巴基斯坦国内的政治斗争也是其长期以来结构性矛盾所致，与走廊建设本身无关；中巴经济走廊以交通为基础，而中巴之间的交通不可避免地经过巴控克什米尔地区，同样是地理事实，不存在中国故意为难有关国家的情况；世界上几大国势力在南亚角逐所引发的地缘政治危机，也不以中国的良好意愿为转移。所以，中巴经济走廊建设所面临的种种问题，都具有长期性、全局性、顽固性的特点，需以理性客观的心态去看待和处理。

其次，充实联委会机制，加强规划调研。我国应充分利用中巴之间的"全天候战略伙伴关系"和高度的政治互信，加强高层在协调管理方面的沟通作用，充实现有的联委会机制。与此同时，加大对重点领域和具体项目的前期调研工作，配合走廊和我国区域发展的总体规划，有步骤地落实推进。

---

① https://en.wikipedia.org/wiki/Operation_Rah-e-Nijat#cite_note-7: TIME:http://content.time.com/time/world/article/0,8599,1930909,00.html.

再次，充分认识中巴经济走廊的风险，做好应急预案。在对巴基斯坦军方、执法机构和安保人员给予充分信任与合作的基础上，也要对巴安全环境的复杂性保持清醒认识，对可能出现的各种风险和变故作出应急预案准备。

（二）坚持透明化和市场运作

首先，增加中巴经济走廊规划的透明度，加强在巴的外宣工作。既要调动巴主流媒体，也要借鉴新媒体，运用各种手段加强两国人民之间的民心交流，针对各种误解，达成增信释疑的作用。这一点可以学习日本。一个项目完成之后，当地百姓记住的是日本人怎样辛勤地工作及为他们带来的实实在在的好处。而中国人的特点是做了好事，却不善于大力传播。透明化的另一作用是增加地区互信，消除地缘政治角度的猜忌，避免出现恶性竞争和博弈。中巴经济走廊规划以及中国在巴基斯坦展开的一系列合作项目建设，实际上将为整个地区的经济、贸易发展提供合作共赢的平台，是一个分享发展红利、改善整个地区经济、政治与安全的机遇。而要使其他国家相信中国建立"命运共同体"的良好愿望并积极参与其中的办法之一，是通过中巴经济走廊这一旗舰项目在透明化的运作基础上，发挥示范效应，将中国的战略思路公开展示于世界面前。

其次，坚持市场化运作，避免经济问题政治化。虽然巴基斯坦号称我国的"巴铁"，但在项目实施过程中，还是要以市场化手段配置资源，遵守国际法及通用准则，发挥各类企业的主体作用。政府要做的是搭桥铺路等辅助性功能，尽量让"看不见的手"发挥作用，避免经济问题上纲上线，造成政治或外交纠纷。

（三）加强民间与基层交流、建立全方位的友好关系

巴基斯坦内部政治关系的复杂性，决定了在开展中巴经济走廊这样地理和时间跨度如此之大的项目时，仅仅通过与中央政府和主要党派搞好关系不能一劳永逸地解决投资环境问题。在发展与其国内主要政治派别、族群和利益集团友好关系时，应当坚持从基层入手，争取民间对投资项目和工程建设的最广泛的支持。同时，由于中巴经济走廊而出现的大规模海外投资和人员输出，也使得领事保护

工作捉襟见肘，通过与基层民众建立友好关系并由此改善投资环境，有益于降低当地资产与人员的安全风险。

具体方法可以在中巴经济走廊重点项目所在区以及与我国内陆联系密切的地区开展社会公益事业，为当地百姓在民生（饮用水、发电厂等）、医疗、教育等方面提供常态化的公共服务和社会福利，这样不仅能够增进与当地民众的友好关系，从而得以建立优良的投资环境，也能通过基层的互动，发现与创造更多的投资机会，甚至可以由此解决巴基斯坦内部地区主义所导致的争端问题。

以瓜达尔港建设为例，在项目建设过程中出现的一个主要族群和地区矛盾是工程承包商和参与建设工人之间的矛盾，建设工人主要以旁遮普省人为主，当地（俾路支省）人很难分得一杯羹。而由于巴基斯坦国内政治、经济形势限制，这种矛盾短时期内很难得以协商解决，那么我们是否可以通过其他的公益性项目或小型的基础设施建设，在当地社区开展一些福利工程，一方面既不影响正常的港口施工建设，另一方面又可以为当地民众提供就业机会，既可以缓解地区主义带来的族群矛盾冲突，又能达到增进友好关系、改善投资环境的目的。

（四）加大反恐力度、确保海外人员和财产安全

中巴经济走廊这样大的项目规划需要投入大量资金、人员，并形成规模庞大的海外资产，而巴基斯坦又是恐怖势力活动频繁的高危险区，这就要求我们必须尽全力保障海外人员的人身与财产安全。

首先，必须将该地区的反恐机制上升到国家战略高度，建立有针对性的、全面的安全防范、预警机制与应急管理机制。这就需要国家各有关部门，如外交部、国家安全委员会、国家反恐领导小组等相互协同与配合，建立完善的、跨部门的情报信息共享机制和应急反应机制。

其次，依靠与巴基斯坦及其他毗邻国家的反恐合作协调机制，提高情报共享、联合行动的能力，从而加大对该地区恐怖主义活动的打击力度。巴基斯坦及周边地区的反恐形势非常严峻，刚刚形成的中国、阿富汗、巴基斯坦和塔吉克斯坦四国军队反恐合作协调机制，是中国成为地区国家反恐合作机制中主导力量走出的

第一步。目前，我们参与和主导的协作机制，仍然坚持互不干涉原则，仍是以人员的培训、技术与情报分享、协同训练和演习等方式为主导，但也应该做好准备，当中巴经济走廊乃至"一带一路"所产生的海外资产和海外利益越来越多时，当巴基斯坦等国无法通过一己之力解决危机时，应考虑对传统的不干涉原则做出修正，在当事方同意并保证其基本权利的前提下，实施直接干预和介入。

8 China –Pakistan Economic Corridor: Current Situation, Challenges, Countermeasures and Suggestions

Li Lingfei

China- Pakistan Economic Corridor(CPEC)is a series of big engineering project that China and Pakistan develops to enhance the connectivity and common development of the two countries. CPEC, with Kashghar (in Chinese Xin Jiang Province) and the port of Gwadar (in Pakistani Baluchistan Province) at its northern and southern ends respectively, is a hub of Silk Road Economic Belt and Maritime Silk Road. So it is extraordinarily significant for the strategic deployment and promotion of Belt and Road initiative. At the moment (May 2017), the construction of CPEC has made a number of important developments. The governments of China and Pakistan have also conducted rounds of consultations to set up "long-range planning of CPEC". On this occasion, this article will conclude the current situation of the construction of CPEC, summarize and evaluate the challenges and risks that exist, and offer preliminary countermeasures and suggestions.

The Context and Current Situation of CPEC

For many years, based on traditional friendship and common interests of the two countries, the economic trade and cooperation between China and Pakistan develops sustainably and steadily. Entering the 21st century, China and Pakistan signed free trade agreements in 2006 and Agreement on Trade in Services of the Free Trade Agreement in 2009. And in the year when the latter agreement signed, China became the second biggest trade partner of Pakistan.

In this context, in May 2013, during Premier Li Keqiang's visit to Pakistan, he proposed an initiative to actively explore and formulate "long-range planning of CPEC". In July 2013, Pakistani Premier Sharif visited China. The two countries agreed to establish Pakistan-China Joint Cooperation Committee (JCC) and reached a series of early harvest projects in the framework of long-range planning and cooperation. During Pakistani President Mamnoon Hussain's state visit to China in February 2014, Pakistan-China Joint Cooperation Committee (JCC) has already launched. Integrated planning joint working group, transport infrastructure and energy joint working group has successfully held the first round of the meeting.

In April 2015, during President Xi Jinping's state visit to Pakistan, the two countries agreed to upgrade China-Pakistan relations to "all-weather strategic cooperative partnership" and enhance CPEC as the flagship project of the Belt and Road initiative. The construction of CPEC is based on corridor construction, focusing on port, energy, infrastructure construction and industrial cooperation, forming a "1+4" cooperation layout. At the moment, the developments of these projects are as follows:

1. Port of Gwadar

If we say CPEC is the flagship project of the Belt and Road Initiative, then the port of Gwadar is the "pearl project" of CPEC. In April 2013, China Overseas Port Holding Company officially took over the operational authority of Gwadar Port from PSA International Pte Ltd. By the end of June 2016, the port of Gwadar started to function with basic operational ability. On November 13, 2016, the convoy of CPEC arrived in Gwadar from Kashghar, after exporting containers massively through the port, the first time joint transportation operation was completed successfully. [①]

The free zone, which is an area of 923 hectares, was handed over to Chinese company along with the port of Gwadar. China will firstly develop the land of 25 hectares, where near the port of Gwadar. This is also called the free zone's starting area. In September 2016, the development and construction of the starting area have been officially launched, and around half of the workload has been completed. All the infrastructure projects, such as roads, water & electricity supply and afforestation, will be completed by the end of 2017, including a one-stop business service center which integrates the function of office premises, governmental service, business inspection and entertainment etc. [②]

Until now, at least 35 companies have applied for free zone business license, out of which 9 companies have got the license. It is estimated that the investment will exceed 60 billion RMB. According to the plan, Gwadar free zone will be divided into two parts: the southern part is business logistics zone and the northern one is processing zone. Relying on the existing wharf, the south focuses on warehousing, logistics, commodity exhibitions and other industries. The north, which is processing zone, focuses on the development of automotive manufacturing & assembly, home appliances, textiles, Muslim food and medical equipment, forming a large-scale industrial cluster with a complete industrial chain. Along the coast the facilities related to tourism, catering service, entertainment, water sports, and life maintenance will be developed.

---

① 王琳:《"一带一路"倡议下，瓜达尔每天都在变》，第一财经网，2017 年 5 月 8 日。

② Ibid.

China Overseas Port Holding Company also installed a desalination facility with a daily production capacity of 500 tons of fresh water and laid a full set of water supply and drainage systems. The fresh water will not only meets the basic water need for construction and life in the port, but can also be distributed to the residents nearby every month. The early harvest projects of the Gwadar port also include:

Table 8–1   The early harvest projects of the Gwadar of CPEC

	project name	Estimated amount of investment	process
1	Construction of East Bay Highway	$140 million	will be completed in 2018
2	Breakwater construction	$130 million	in construction
3	Sino Pakistan vocational and technical school	$9 million	finished
4	Construction of infrastructure in free zones and export processing zones	$35 million	in construction
5	Construction of seawater treatment and freshwater supply facilities	$114 million	will be completed in 2018
6	Sino Pakistani Friendship Hospital (upgrade of existing hospital)	$100 million	in construction
7	coal-fired power plant	$360 million	in construction
8	Gwadar International Airport	$230 million	in operation
9	berth channel dredging of Gwadar Port	$27 million	in construction

Source: http://cpec.gov.pk/gwader, http://m.yicai.com/news/5280826.html.

2.Energy

In order to solve the energy shortage in Pakistan, in the four years since the proposal was put forward, the early harvest projects of CPEC mainly concentrate on energy sector, including Port Qasim coal-fired power plant, Sahiwal coal-fired power plant, Hub coal-fired power plant, Suki Kinari Hydropower Station, Karot Hydropower Station, Quaid-e-Azam solar power station in Punjab province and four wind power projects in Sindh province, all of which will be put into operation in 2017.

Port Qasim coal-fired power plant is jointly invested by PowerChina Resources Ltd. of Power Construction Corporation of China and Qatar Al-Mirqad Capital with 2.085 billion dollars. The total installed capacity is 1320 MW, and it is equipped with a series of environmental protection facilities, such as desalination, wastewater treatment, noise control, desulfurization and dust removal.

China's Silk Road Fund invested its first capital of 1.65 billion dollars on Karot Hydropower Project of CPEC. As one of the energy projects that have been giving priorities, it is financed by the cooperation of governmental and social capital. Its construction was started by the Three Gorges group in early 2016.

3. Transportation Infrastructure

According to the summary made by Sun Weidong, Chinese ambassador to Pakistan, the three most representative major projects, besides the starting area of Gwadar free zone, are Multan to Sukkur section of Peshawar to Karachi Expressway and the second phase of the project to upgrade a transform of the Karakoram Highway. The total investment of the two major projects will exceed $6 billion. In the field of transportation infrastructure, the construction of Gwadar International Airport and Gwadar East Bay Highway is started in 2016. The investment scale is smaller, which is about 400 million dollars.

On November 13, 2016, the first connection of CPEC joint trade motorcade was grandly held in the port of Gwadar in Pakistani Baluchistan Province. The result showed that the road has been preliminarily connected with China, and the concept of "one corridor and multi channels" has gradually become a reality. Pakistani Premier Sharif said that "This marks CPEC is becoming a reality from the concept and opening a new page of interconnection in the region. Thus, Pakistan has become one of the traffic hinges of Asian continent, and the people from all countries can share this development and prosperity

The special envoy of CPEC Zafar Mahmood introduced that as domestic energy shortage in Pakistan has not been resolved, the upgrading and transformation of Pakistani Domestic No. 1 railway trunk line (boosting its speed from 60 kilometers to 140 kilometers per hour), the construction of Port Harvey and the cooperation of Sino-Pakistan industrial park are still in planning and feasibility studying level, their constructions haven't been started yet.

4.Industrial Cooperation

Sino-Pakistan industrial cooperation is still at its initial stage. As for the construction of industrial park, Punjab, Sindh, Khyber Pakhtunkhwa and Baluchistan have put forward the plan of constructing 29 industrial parks and 21 mining processing parks. At present, due to the backward reality of Pakistan's domestic economic foundation, energy supply and human resources, these projects are incapable to be launched at the same time. In the end, from the perspective of regional balance, China has chosen industrial park in each province as an exemplificative park. The following content in the table reflects specific industrial cooperation projects:

Table 8–2　Some industrial cooperation projects in Pakistan's four Province of CPEC

project name	company name	phase	process
Gwadar to Nava Shah LNG terminal and pipeline project (700 km)	China Petroleum Pipeline Bureau	will be opened	40%
Haier and Ruba Economic Zone (the second phase)	Haier Electric Appliance Co., Ltd.	Feasibility phase	15%

(continued)

project name	company name	phase	process
Rawalpindi to Khunjerab light cable engineering	Huawei Technologies Co., Ltd	in construction	50%
DTMB demonstrative project	undetermined	memorandum of cooperation has been signed	5%
Lahore Orange Line subway project	China Railway Engineering- China North Industries Group Corporation	in construction	60%
the project of accelerating the commercialization of Pakistan TD-LTE	undetermined	Feasibility phase	15 %

Challenges in CPEC

Challenges faced by China-Pakistan Economic Corridor mainly generated from three aspects, which are investment risks in domestic economy & politics, risks on international relation in complicated geopolitics, security risks in extremism and terrorism.

(I) Pakistan Domestic Economy and Politics Risks

Pakistan has a relatively stable economic and political environment. Due to China-Pakistan friendship and strategic partnership, China-Pakistan Economic Corridor has received general support from Pakistani government. Risks brought by domestic economic and political situations lie in power struggle in party politics, conflict of interest in various parties, and investment risks by weak economic infrastructure and environment.

1. Unstable Elements in Domestic Politics: Regionalism and Social Tension in Party Struggles

There are more than 200 political parties in Pakistan with many factions. Layout of CPEC projects often causes disputes among parties. These disputes reflects a deeper problem, which is the conflict of interests over regions and ethnic groups. For example, Punjab and Sindh are the two relatively developed provinces in Eastern Pakistan. Khyber Pakhtunkhwa and Balochistan in the west are relatively poor developed and urgently need infrastructure investment. Provinces all wish to invite more CPEC projects to their own places, which causes tension between "East" and "West". Sindh is also the basecamp of Pakistan People's Party, the biggest party in Pakistan which does not get along well with the governing party Pakistan Muslim League (Sharif faction) from Punjab. This regionalism and power struggle among parties require governing party Pakistan Muslim League (Sharif faction) to persuade major oppositions like National Awami Party、Pakistan Movement for Justice、Baluchistan National Awami Party, and reached a compromise, so that CPEC projects could be implemented.

At end of July, 2016 several senators in the senator jointly demanded the Sharif government to publish relevant materials in CPEC, seconded by senators from opposition parties, and other party senators from governing party league. These senators accuses Pakistan Muslim League (N) of favoring Punjab alone in CPEC. Since February 2017, the leader of Baluchistan National Party (Sardar Akhtar Mengal) has been organizing public gatherings in Quetta against CPEC, and claims to media that Chinese investment projects have brought no opportunities to Balochistan Province, but created a lot of jobs for Punjab.

Power struggle in CPEC also happens between federal and regional governments. The struggle over land-use right in Pakistan Port Qasim Power Project is an example. Port Qasim Power Project is Sharif government's milestone project to solve domestic electricity shortage. This flagship project in energy fieldwhich was founded by the joint 2 billion investment from PowerChina Resources Ltd of Power Construction Corporation of China and Qatar Al-Mirqad Capital.

The power plant was a CPEC project approved by Pakistan Federal Government, but local Sindh government believed that federal government did not acquire authorization from local government to use the land. Sindh demanded partial share in the power plant, or compensations equivalent to the land useage . Federal government believed that according to Constitution, it has already acquired a land tenure and is entitled to any development and exploitation over the land. But Sindh believed that federal government has no right to build a power plant, the government only has right for port construction and maritime transport.

This problem was solved finally in the end of December, 2016, after hard discussions and negotiations among Chinese government, Pakistan federal government, Sindh regional government, Port Qasim Energy Holding, and many relevant parties.

Disputes in Pakistan domestic politics brought great obstacles for CPEC and directly affected processes like premises selection and construction. And in the implementation process, the potential risks should not be underestimated.

Furthermore, the lack of trust between Pakistani military and elected government also brings instability to Pakistan's internal politics. In the past 70 years history of Pakistan, military governed the country for four times and amounts to 33 years in total. Although intervention from military gradually wanes away from 2008, the possibility of a military intervention and its possible effect on CPEC should not be ruled out for a long time.

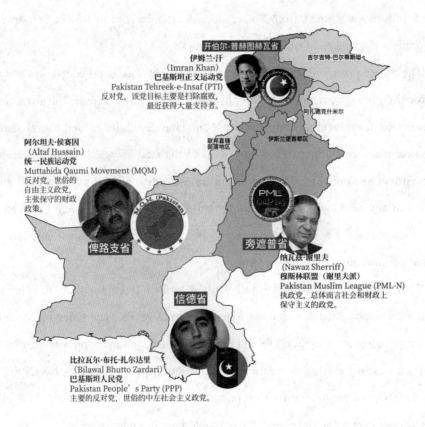

Figure 8–1　The main Parties in Pakistan

charting: Li Lingfei

2. Economic Risks

Pakistan is facing many economic problems, which are weak economic foundation, backward infrastructure construction, inefficient economic policy implementation. The initial projects of CPEC are focused on infrastructure constructions related to energy and transportation to solve the difficulties caused by energy shortage and infrastructure operation failure. The risks in this environment is an increase in investment cost and low efficiency.

Take the oil-gas pipe as an example. The whole infrastructure construction of Chinese maritime oil-gas transportation is nearly completed, but the imagined Sino-

Pakistan oil-gas pipeline infrastructure construction needs to start from zero, and the host country Pakistan could not guarantee a stable power supply. They are waiting for a series of power generation projects under CPEC framework to solve this problem. Not to mention that from Gwadar to Kashgar, they need to cross 5-6 kilometer Laci-Kunlun mountain. This imagined pipeline requires pump station with high power, and requires extra heating and insulation device in highland areas, which significantly increases the cost. Therefore, even if we do not consider the security cost, "Sino-Pakistan oil-gas pipeline" is not economic.

Moreover, in Pakistan, there is a heavy trend of politicizing economic problems. For example, in financing, many Pakistani regard CPEC as China is looking for venting approach for its domestic finance surplus. Therefore, China should be the main investor in CEPC, Pakistan need not to enlarge financing channel. Pakistan's first high speed road project M4 high speed road (from Shorkot to Khanewal), jointly invested by Asian Infrastructure Investment Bank and Asian Development Bank, was not listed as CPEC project by Ministry of Planning and Development either.

South Asia Economic Focus, issued by World Bank in April, 2016, believes that if CPEC is successfully implemented, it will bring fundamental change to Pakistan. But the project is now facing Pakistan domestic economic and political risks. Considering the domestic economic and political condition in Pakistan, the warning of World Back should be taken seriously.

(II) Complicated Geopolitics

In regards of geopolitics, CPEC is facing problem from Pakistan's relation with India, Afghanistan, Middle East and surround countries, and from big countries competition away from the region.

First, India-Pakistan relation can not be significantly improved in short terms. After India's prime minister Modi's sudden visit to Pakistan in December 2015, public believed that the relation between two countries would improve. But it went done dramatically in 2016. On September 18, 2016, military base of Uri in India controlled Kashmir was attacked by terrorists and 18 Indian soldiers died. India accused Pakistan of supporting this terrorist act and performed "surgery-strike" on Pakistan on September 29. Diplomatically, India initiated "isolating" Pakistan movement, especially by not attending the 19th SAARC Summit held in Pakistan. Later Bangladesh, Bhutan, and Afghanistan made similar voices.[1]

Second, Pakistan-Afghanistan relation was restricted by Durand Line issue, Taliban, and Afghanistan's disappointment over Pakistan in regards of terrorism. After NATO declared the end of combat mission in Afghanistan on December 31, 2014, and American's withdraw, domestic politics in Afghanistan became unstable and thus produced uncertainties and security risks that would present a grave challenge for Pakistan's domestic security and social stability.[2]

Furthermore, Pakistan has subtle relations with Middle East countries, especially with Saudi and Iran. For now Pakistan's policy to Middle East has made some achievements, but on questions of CPEC, geoeconomics would replace geopolitics and become the main risk in constructing the corridor.[3]Some scholars point out that the Chabahar port (designed by India for Iran) and Pakistan's Gwadar Port have become a miniature for the competition over global resources and influences between the two countries.[4]

---

① 林民旺：《五大国或将影响 2017 年南亚外交情势 》，凤凰网，2017 年 3 月 24 日，http://wemedia.ifeng.com/11039344/wemedia.shtml。

② 陈继东、丁建军：《巴基斯坦在未来阿富汗局势中的作用》，《兰州大学学报》2015 年第 2 期，第 84 页。

③ 王旭："中巴经济走廊建设中的主要问题与对策建议"，摘自《"一带一路"跨境通道建设研究报告（2016）》，中国社会科学出版社，2016 年 8 月。

④ 驻卡拉奇总领馆经商室："伊朗高官表示不会利用恰巴哈尔港打压瓜达尔港"，2015 年 10 月 30 日，http://china.huanqiu.com/News/mofcom/2015-10/7875289.html。

From the standpoint of big countries' geopolitical layout in the region, South Asia is leaning towards a "Cold War" situation of "choosing sides". First, India-US relation is developing further, and India is nearly becoming an ally of US on defense. Second, Russia is approaching Pakistan. When India started "isolating" Pakistan movement, Russia and Pakistan hold the first joint military exercise "Friendship 2016" on September 24, which shows a subtle geopolitical connotation.

The most complicated problem in CPEC is how China deals with India. India has long adopted an opposing and non-cooperative attitude towards CPEC. India does not want China to lead regional affairs. India has already used and will use its self influence on other countries and the territorial dispute between India and Pakistan to hinder the projects and form competition projects with other countries. India's non-cooperative attitude and competition position could be easily used by other big countries and form a disadvantage situation for China.

(Ⅲ) Security Risks from Extremism and Terrorism

1. Severe Security Situation in Balochistan Province

For China, Gwadar Port is not only a energy-strategic path. It sits at the center of China's "Belt" and "Road" and the center of CPEC, but also deep into the most restless Balochistan Province. The first concern is the security of Chinese personnel in Pakistan. Compared to 2007-2009 when there was one terrorist attack in around every three days, there has been significant improvement in general security. But to the Chinese personnel in the main project location, namely Baluchistan Province, "Sindhudesh Revolutionary Army"、"Balochistan Liberation Army" and other armed organizations present a constant threat of sudden attack.[①]

As large group of Chinese personnel are arriving, upgrade in security is needed

---

① 郝洲:《中国巨额投资复活瓜达尔港，还需面对五重挑战》，财经网，2017 年 4 月 5 日，http://yuanchuang.caijing.com.cn/2017/0405/4256052.shtml。

in Gwadar district as well. Chinese people going to Gwadar district still remembers the incident in May 2004, when Chinese engineers were attacked in the city. Attacks against government projects by separatist forces in Balochistan Province also left a dark memory on many Chinese investors. Therefore under Chinese government's demand, Pakistan military assigned 15 thousands personnels to secure CPEC projects, with heavy focus on the construction and development of Gwadar Port. But this serious gesture was not taken as optimistic signal by investors. The constant presence of armed personnels would make foreign investors very uncomfortable and would affect their decision to invest.

There is also structural worries in the security protection provided by Pakistan. Currently the armed forces providing security for Gwadar Port consists of three groups: local police, armed militia, and Pakistan military. There is a severe lack of coordination among three groups.[1]

2. Extremist Islamic State Infiltration and Terrorism Returning from Abroad

In recent years, Islamic State has tightened the infiltration to Pakistan-Afghanistan areas. There are small scale terrorist attacks in big cities like Lahore and Karachi. And extremist organizations in Punjab is likely to disseminate among teenagers with decent education. In the future, Punjab may face severe security challenge.

In February 2017, Pakistan terrorism forces produced six air strikes in four days, and looked like they would return to Pakistan with full power. Terrorist attacked law enforcement department in capital of Punjab Lahore on February 13, in Balochistan Quetta on 14, in Federally Administrated Tribal Areas on 14, and in a famous Sufism Mosque in Sindh on February 16. "Jamaat-ul-Ahrar" claimed responsibility for these incidences, and showed that the targets are government workers and secular media workers.

---

① 郝洲:《中国巨额投资复活瓜达尔港, 还需面对五重挑战》, 财经网, 2017 年 4 月 5 日, http://yuanchuang.caijing.com.cn/2017/0405/4256052.shtml。

Furthermore, Pakistan Punjab government recently issued terrorism alarm and claimed that Pakistani foreign fighters in Iraq and Syria and returning to Pakistan, as they wish to contribute to Islamic State movement in Pakistan. No matter how coordinated are the government and military, "National (Anti-Terror) Action Plan" would not successfully address this problem. The priority to domestic terrorism is the external environment that raises the terrorists. Unfortunately, there has been no new thoughts on whether India and Afghanistan prefers war or peace.

Ever since Pakistan joined US's "War On Terror" in Afghanistan, the most problematic area in domestic security has shifted to the clan areas along Afghanistan border, the most problematic being North Waziristan (hereafter NW). During the "Operation Rah-e-Nijat" and "Operation Zarb-e-Azb" counter-terrorism military operations in South Waziristan and NW, performed by Pakistan military in 2009 and 2014, many members belong to Tehrik-i-Taliban fled to Eastern Afghanistan after being hit. [1]Because there is no efficient control over the border, people could cross the border freely in some areas. Therefore, if counter-terrorism in Pakistan relaxes, terrorists may return.

Countermeasures and Suggestions

(I) Correct understanding and adequate preparation

First and foremost, we need to treat the problems in CPEC construction rationally. As have been mentioned above, Pakistan's situation of lacking water and electricity cannot be solved in a short term; terrorism and extremism are objective realities that cannot be ignored or eliminated quickly; Pakistan's domestic political struggle is caused

---

[1] https://en.wikipedia.org/wiki/Operation_Rah-e-Nijat#cite_note-7; Time:http://content.time.com/time/world/article/0,8599,1930909,00.html.

by the long term of structural contradictions and has nothing to do with the CPEC; transportation is the foundation of CPEC, and it is the geographic fact that the traffic line between China and Pakistan needs to go through the Pakistani-administered Kashmir, and China has no intention to make troubles to any relevant countries; the geopolitical crises caused by the major power of today's world cannot be solved by China's good willing. Consequently, the problems faced by CPEC construction are long-term, overall and intractable in nature. We need to view and treat these problems rationally.

Secondly, we should improve the Joint Cooperation Committee mechanism, planning, investigation and analysis. China should make full use of the the China-Pakistan all-weather strategic cooperative partnership and deep political trust, improve the role of high-level communication in coordination and management, and reinforce the current Joint Cooperation Committee mechanism. Meanwhile, we need to increase the early planning, investigation and analysis on key areas and specific projects, coordinate them with the overall plan of CPEC and China's regional development, implementing and pushing forward these areas and projects step by step.

Thirdly, we should be fully aware of the risks of the CPEC and make contingency plan in advance. On the basis of trusting and cooperating with Pakistan military, law enforcement agencies and security personnel, we also need to have clear understanding on the complexity of Pakistan's security environment and make contingency plan for the possible risks and accidents.

(II) Transparency and marketing operations

Firstly, we need to improve the transparency in planning the CPEC. The improvement of the international publicity in Pakistan not only requires the support of the mainstream media of Pakistan, but also of new media. We need to use different measures to increase the communication between our peoples, to increase mutual trust and relieve mutual distrust and misunderstandings among them. We can learn from

Japan on this point. When Japanese workers finish their projects, the local people will remember the hard work and the concrete benefits brought by these Japanese workers. However, Chinese people are always good at working, but not good at to disseminate the information. The other function of transparency is to increase the regional mutual trust and to eliminate the mutual distrust in geopolitics. That will help to prevent the vicious competition or game. The CPEC plan and other cooperative projects between China and Pakistan can actually provide the win-win platforms for the development of the regional economy and trade. They are also the opportunities for the region to share development dividends, improve regional economy, politics and security. In order to make other countries believe China's good willing of establishing the community of shared destiny, with the basis of transparent operation, we could make CPEC flagship project a model to openly present China's strategic thinking to the world.

Secondly, we should adhere to marketing operations and avoid from politicizing economic problems. There is no doubt that Pakistan is known as China's "Bhaee Pak". However, In the process of project implementation, we still need to realize market allocation of resources, obey the international law and norms and allow different kinds of enterprises to play the principal role. The government should play an auxiliary role, to pave the way and build the bridge. It should allow the "invisible hand" to play its role and avoid from politicizing the economic problems which may lead to political or diplomatic disputes.

(III) Improving people-to-people and local exchanges, establishing all-round friendship

The complexity of Pakistan's domestic political relations determines that when implementing the project of great coverage in space and time, such as the CPEC, one cannot solve the problem of investment environment once and for all by simply improving its relations with the central government or the major party. When improving its relations with the major domestic political party, ethnic groups and interest groups, one needs to start from the ground level and strive for the public support to the investment project and construction. Meanwhile, due to the large scale of overseas investments and personnel exports created by CPEC, the consular protection also becomes inadequate. By establishing good relations with the public and improving the investment environment, we could decrease the security risks faced by the local elites and personnel.

Specifically, we could improve the public welfare of the regions which are important to CPEC or have close relations with inland China. We could regularly provide public goods and services, such as water, power plants, medical services and education, to the locals. This will not only improve our relations with the local and provide better investment environment, but also create more investment opportunities through interactions on ground level. It can even help to solve the disputes caused by Pakistan regionalism.

Take the construction of the Gwadar Port for example. One of the major ethnic and regional conflict emerged during the construction is the dispute between contractors and workers. The workers are mainly Punjabis, but the local people from Balochistan Province cannot participate in the construction or gain profits. Meanwhile, limited by the domestic political and economic situation, this kind of dispute cannot be solved quickly. At that point, maybe we could improve the local public welfare by implementing public project and building infrastructures. On the one hand, this will not influence the construction of the port. On the other hand, we can provide more working opportunities for the locals. Consequently, such projects and constructions will not only relive the ethnic disputes caused by regionalism, but also achieve our goals of improving the relations with local people and investment environment.

(Ⅳ) Increasing the counter-terrorism efforts, ensuring the safety of oversees personnel and assets

The grand projects like the CPEC require a large amount of money, personnel and need to have massive oversees assets. However, Pakistan is a dangerous area which has frequent terrorism activities. This situation requires us to do our best to protect the safety of our overseas personnel and assets.

Firstly, we must raise the counter-terrorism mechanism in this region to state level. We need to make targeted and comprehensive security and early warning mechanism and emergency management mechanism. This needs the relevant departments, such as the Ministry of Foreign Affairs, the National Security Commission of the Communist Party of China and the National Leading Group on Counter-terrorism, to cooperate with each other and establish the efficient and cross-department intelligence sharing mechanism and emergency response mechanism.

Secondly, relying on our counter-terrorism cooperation and coordination mechanism with Pakistan and other neighborhoods, we can improve our intelligence sharing and joint operation abilities, and therefore improve our counter-terrorism efforts in this region. Pakistan and its neighboring regions are facing serious counter-terrorism tasks. The newly established Quadrilateral Cooperation and Coordination Mechanism in Counter-Terrorism by Afghanistan-China-Pakistan-Tajikistan Armed Forces is the first step of China in becoming the leading force of regional counter-terrorism mechanism. At present, when participating in and leading the mechanism, China still adhere to non-interference principle and treat personnel training, technology and intelligence sharing, joint training and exercise as the main measures of the mechanism. However, when CPEC and the Belt and Road Initiative are creating more and more oversees interests, and when Pakistan cannot solve the crises on its own, we should also be ready to consider changing the non-interference principle. Under the precondition of consent of the other party and the protection of its basic rights, we should launch direct interference and intervention to these countries.

后 记

此书稿的最后整理是在易鹏老师率领盘古智库代表团参加韩国济州论坛回国后。

前前后后跟随易老师出国调研好几次,这是唯一的一次领导被累病了(以往都是我们)。以前往往是经过长途飞行到达香山大本营后,易老师换个行头就直接奔赴下一个会场了。但是这次没有。这次易老师既没有唱"Country Road",也没有飙英文。那是一个高规格的午宴,有我们盘古智库的高级顾问、中联部原副部长于洪君,韩国前外交通商部长官金星焕,韩国国会外交与统一委员会主席沈载权,韩国济州特别自治道知事元喜龙,韩国总统统一外交安保特别顾问文正仁(也是我们的顾问)。紧随其后的那场论坛"中韩关系:克服分歧,重建互信"也是这些人,易老师在主旨发言以及问答环节上都是其一贯的风格——激情、新锐,再加上点湖南人的幽默。

还是有些不一样。可能是因为听众很希望听听中国的社会智库怎么看、怎么说,也可能是因为易老师的发言在韩国人看来很新鲜,所以针对他的提问很多。可是有几次,易老师都是请于部长代为回答的。论坛一结束,易老师就跟我说,"刚才差点没晕过去,我是靠着毅力硬撑下来的。"难怪!

这几年盘古智库发展很快,易老师也越来越忙。本书收录的八个国家,他基本上都率团去过。如果有那种僵持不下的会谈场面(与印度人常常会出现),他这个普通话也说不好，英文也讲不好的"弗兰人"往往三言两语就掌控了局面，把那些国际关系大咖也唬得一愣一愣的。有时候我想，易老师在"搞外交"方面这么骨骼清奇、天赋异禀，怪不得常言道，一个不好好做智库的经济学家不是一个好外交官。他自己的解释则是，"我是吃地沟油的命，操中南海的心"。

他说自己做智库全凭一股理想主义，所以常常见他像打了鸡血，一天可以见七八拨人，谈各种事项，没什么休息日的概念；也见过他谈起儿子时突然哽咽，说自己没时间陪伴……当然，光有情怀是远远不够的，盘古智库的发展靠成绩和成果说话。

这本书就是近期成果之一。它的问世除了要感谢盘古智库课题组的老师们，还要感谢中国青年出版社的两位大才皮钧社长和庄庸主编。盘古智库的助理研究员罗震、杜文睿、毕龙翔，实习生陈轲、朱浩泽对文稿的校对亦有贡献。

李玲飞
（盘古智库高级研究员
印度研究中心执行主任）
2017 年 6 月 16 日

Afterword

After Mr. Yi Peng led the Pangoal Delegation to participate in the Jeju Forum in Korea and went back to China, the final draft of this book was finished.

We followed Mr. Yi abroad for investigation several times. However, this was the only time Mr. Yi fell ill because of weariness. (Previously, it was us who usually fell ill because of the tiring journey.) Previously, despite of the long flying journey, Mr. Yi would directly hurry for the next meeting after putting on his business suit upon arrival in Xiangshan . This time, things were different. Mr. Yi did not sing Country Road, nor did he show off his English. It was a high-grade luncheon, participated by Hongjun Yu, Senior Adviser of the Pangoal Institution and the former Deputy Ministry of the International Department, Central Committee of the CPC; Kim Sung-hwan, the former Republic of Korea's Minister of Foreign Affairs and Trade; Sim Zai-quan, Chairman of the Diplomacy and Unification Committee, South Korea Congress; Won Hee-ryong, Governor of Jeju Special Self-Governing Province; and Moon Chung-in, special adviser on diplomacy and security to the President of South Korea (also our adviser). After the luncheon, those people without any stop to participant in the forum which themed on "Sino-South Korea relations: Overcoming Disagreements and Rebuilding Mutual Trust". In the keynote speech round and the Q&A round, Mr. Yi showed his passion, innovativeness and sense of humor, which is typical to Hunan people.

This time, I could clearly observe something different. Probably, the Korean audiences were eager to hear opinions and voice of a Chinese think-tank on the issue, or the speech of Mr. Yi was neoteric (innovative)to South Koreans. Against this background, Mr. Yi was bombarded with questions. More than once, Mr. Yi asked the Minister to answer for him. At the very end of this forum, Mr. Yi told me, "I nearly went faint. It was a hard time for me. I persevered with great effort." No wonder he let the Minister answer questions on his behalf.

Over the recent years, the Pangoal Institution has made great strides, and Mr. Yi has become increasingly busy. The eight countries mentioned in this book were all visited by him and the delegation. When a meeting comes to a stalemate (quite often with Indians), he who comes from Hunan Province and speaks neither good Mandarin nor English can easily turn the tables with just a few words. Even those so-called masters of international relations are often stupefied by him. Sometimes, a saying appears in my mind, "An economist not engaged in the think-tank is not a good diplomat", when I think of Mr. Yi's special gift in "handling foreign relations". However, Mr. Yi often mocks himself, saying "I am so insignificant that I cannot escape the fate of eating illegal cooking oil, but I am worried too much about national affairs, which are to be worried by leaders in Zhongnanhai, the political center of China".

Mr. Yi confesses that his dedication to the think-tank originates from idealism in his mind. Therefore, I often find him invigorated to such an extent that he holds seven to eight meetings a day, talking about everything and totally forgetting the divide between weekends and working days. I also once saw him speaking of his son, choking with sobs and feeling sorry for little time spent with him ... Of course, these feelings alone cannot explain development of the Pangoal Institution. Development of the Pangoal Institution relies on its remarkable achievements.

This book is one of the latest achievements of the Pangoal Institution. Completion of the book should be credited not only to research fellows of the Pangoal Institution Research Group, but also to two gifted scholars, Pi Jun and Zhuang Yong, Chairman and Editor in -Chief of China Youth Publishing Group. Assistant Researchers of the Pangoal Institution, Luo Zhen, Du Wenrui and Bi Longxiang and interns, Chen Ke and Zhu Haoze, are attributable to proof-reading of this book.

Li lingfei

Senior Fellow,

Executive Director of the Center for Indian Studies,

the Pangoal Institution.

June 16, 2017